D0759706

FROM CONCEPT TO CUSTOMER

FROM CONCEPT TO CUSTOMER

The Practical Guide to Integrated Product and Process Development, and Business Process Reengineering

JACK B. ReVELLE
NORMAND L. FRIGON, SR.
HARRY K. JACKSON, JR.

VAN NOSTRAND REINHOLD
I(T)P™ A Division of International Thomson Publishing Inc.

New York • Albany • Bonn • Boston • Detroit • London • Madrid • Melbourne
Mexico City • Paris • San Francisco • Singapore • Tokyo • Toronto

Copyright © 1995 by Van Nostrand Reinhold

Published by Van Nostrand Reinhold

I(T)P A division of International Thomson Publishing, Inc.
The ITP logo is a trademark under license

Printed in the United States of America

For more information, contact:

Van Nostrand Reinhold
115 Fifth Avenue
New York, NY 10003

International Thomson Publishing GmbH
Königswinterer Strasse 418
53227 Bonn
Germany

International Thomson Publishing Europe
Berkshire House 168-173
High Holborn
London WCIV 7AA
England

International Thomson Publishing Asia
221 Henderson Road #05-10
Henderson Building
Singapore 0315

Thomas Nelson Australia
102 Dodds Street
South Melbourne, 3205
Victoria, Australia

International Thomson Publishing Japan
Hirakawacho Kyowa Building, 3F
2-2-1 Hirakawacho
Chiyoda-ku, 102 Tokyo
Japan

Nelson Canada
1120 Birchmount Road
Scarborough, Ontario
Canada M1K 5G4

International Thomson Editores
Campos Eliseos 385, Piso 7
Col. Polanco
11560 Mexico D.F. Mexico

1 2 3 4 5 6 7 8 9 10   QEBFF   01 00 99 98 97 96 95

Library of Congress Cataloging-in-Publication Data

ReVelle, Jack B.
    From concept to customer : The practical guide to integrated product and process development, and business process reengineering / Jack B. ReVelle, Normand L. Frigon, Harry K. Jackson.
        p. cm.
    Includes bibliographical references and index.
    ISBN 0-442-01892-4
    1. Industrial management. 2. Product management. 3. Quality of products. 4. Consumer satisfaction. I. Frigon, Normand L. II. Jackson, Harry K. III. Title. IV. Title: Management 2000 integrated product development.
    HD30.R47 1994
    658.5'75—dc20   94-41473
                                                                CIP

CONTENTS

FOREWORD

A DELIBERATE, FACT-BASED APPROACH TO CONTINUOUS IMPROVEMENT AND PROCESS CONTROL MUST BE TAKEN TO ACHIEVE WORLD-CLASS COMPETITIVE STATUS.

A commitment to continuous improvement and process control is the hallmark of today's progressive companies. This commitment has become a way of doing business for those companies who are or who are seeking to become "world class," or the best in their industry or fields. Continuous improvement and process control, though, are not haphazardly achieved. A deliberate approach must be taken and practiced by all levels of an organization. It ideally should start at the conceptual phase of a new product or service, extend through development and production, and continue throughout the customer experience.

Fortunately, there is no shortage of techniques and tools that are available to assist in this pursuit. These have evolved over time and have been refined through usage and application. Utilized in a team problem-solving environment, they can help facilitate the understanding of an opportunity for improvement, and point the way for data-driven, corrective action. Although the techniques and tools are many (at times there seems to be a bewildering array of them), what is oftentimes lacking is a systematic approach to their use. Enter the authors.

The Management 2000 Integrated Product Development model that is discussed in the first part of this book provides the deliberate, tested approach that is needed. The discussion is richly illustrated with case studies that impart a practical understanding of the model. This is vital to the new practitioner seeking to understand the model. It is of interest also to the experienced practitioner in that it provides a sanity check for current project activity. The last part of this book is a handy compendium of data analysis tools. These tools are helpful in the application of the model, and are of interest to the new and experienced practitioner alike.

From Concept to Customer links a model for continuous improvement and process control with the technical and management tools necessary for successful implementation. It is the way of the future for all businesses.

James R. DiNitto
Vice President of Quality
ACT Manufacturing, Inc.
Hudson, Massachusetts

PREFACE

The evolution of Quality Function Deployment (QFD) in 1983 to Concurrent Engineering (CE) in 1990 to Integrated Product and Process Development (IPPD) in 1992 resulted from recognition that each preceding methodology was incomplete in its ability to deal with the full spectrum of challenges associated with the efficient and effective translation of the voice of the customer into a viable product or service in the marketplace. Included among the reasons for the evolution are missing factors for consideration, incomplete applications of existing methodology, and unsatisfactory results.

Thus, the necessity was established for creating the IPPD process as well as high-level cross-functional teams, both of which are used to help achieve organizational goals. These teams are rarely capable of independent existence, i.e., they require considerable attention and support by senior management. It has become quite clear that management's roles and responsibilities include the provision of the three "E"s: enablement, empowerment, and encouragement.

Once the critical/core processes of an organization have been created, either by carefully constructing using the various aspects of IPPD or, as has been more likely in the past, using the "by guess and by gosh" approach, each process is fair game for evaluation to determine whether or not it deserves to be reconstructed using Business Process Reengineering (BPR). Our final chapter addresses this topic.

Whenever a new way of doing things is about to be instituted, members of the affected organization will question their management regarding the expected results of the changes to the status quo. This is not unusual. In anticipation of the most obvious questions, management should be prepared to address results such as: improved market share and industry ranking; better quality, reliability, and maintainability; reduced life cycle costs and process cycle times; and greater employee, customer, and supplier satisfaction.

When the three of us came together to prepare this text, our intent was to work as a cross-functional, self-directed work team. Each of us came to the table with specific strengths as well as expertise and interests that complemented the capabilities of the others. It was in this context that we collaborated to create this text. Naturally, we went through the usual team cycle: forming, storming, norming, and performing.

The structure and composition of these IPPD teams (IPPDTs) is critical to their success. From an internal perspective, each team must have appropriate and sufficient cross-functional representation, i.e., knowledgeable personnel from engineering, manufacturing, assembly, material, quality, and other functional areas must take an active role in the team's deliberations. From an external perspective, both customers and suppliers should be invited to participate in the IPPDT meetings, as appropriate.

Every team member and all of the supporting members of an organization's staff require overall awareness training to initiate the crossover to an IPPD culture. Team members will, in addition, require specific training courses on the social and technical aspects of how to best function as an IPPD team.

The culture of an organization as it transitions from a traditional to an IPPD-oriented operational approach can seem chaotic when viewed from within. Among the broad variety of issues that must be addressed are insuring that senior management commitment and involvement are visible, both internally to all employees and externally to customers and suppliers; developing a strategic plan as well as tactical objectives and performance metrics to support the plan; and providing appropriate rewards and recognition to the teams that generate the early-on IPPD successes.

We began our joint efforts by reaching a consensus on our charter. It was composed of a mission and a vision as well as both strategic objectives and tactical goals.

Our Mission: Create a text for our customers that is easy to understand and simple to use, and which covers the dual topics of integrated product and process development (IPPD) and business process reengineering (BPR).

Our Vision: The text, *From Concept to Customer,* should be recognized by our customers as the premier text on the dual topics of IPPD and BPR, and should become a "best-seller" within the first year of its publication.

Our Strategic Objectives: Complete the writing of the book within six months and complete the publication cycle within 12 months of project initiation while making certain that quality, cost, and schedule requirements were met or bettered.

Our Tactical Goals: Complete an additional chapter every two to three weeks, including charts, tables, figures, and any other graphics needed to complement the text.

We did it. The rest is up to you, our customers, to ascertain the extent to which our efforts have met your needs. Your criticisms, suggestions, comments, and ideas for enhancing future editions are welcome at any time. In the spirit and intent of Total Quality Management (TQM) and Continuous Improvement (CI), any processes, especially ours, are forever open to review and revision.

Jack B. ReVelle, Ph.D
Orange, CA, and Tucson, AZ

Normand L. Frigon, Sr.
San Diego, CA

Harry K. Jackson, Jr.
Huntington Beach, CA

1

Introduction

> TO BE COMPETITIVE IN TODAY'S MARKETPLACE, YOUR PRODUCTS AND SERVICES MUST BE ON TARGET THE FIRST TIME, EVERY TIME.

The goal of all human endeavor is to earn a profit and to grow wealth. This is true for business, government, non-profit organizations, and our personal lives. This is an unusual concept for some, because we usually think of profit and wealth in terms of money. We need, however, to expand our definition to include other types of resources, e.g., influence, customer loyalty, credibility, and increased demand.

A government agency or non-profit organization, for example, earns a profit when it increases its efficiency and is able to provide more services with the same resources, i.e., labor, material, equipment, and money. As this efficiency grows, there is an accumulation of wealth in terms of an ability to achieve more with the same or less and to increase customer satisfaction. In our personal lives, profit and wealth may be in terms of savings, net worth, lifestyle, or credibility. In business, the profit may be measured in other terms, i.e., money or capital assets.

In all activities, customer satisfaction is the key to continuing to earn profit which enables us to grow wealth. It is not enough to sell to a customer one time; we need repeat business and word-of-mouth endorsements. Unhappy or dissatisfied customers will go to our competitors or find alternative products or services that fulfill their needs. It is true in all instances, therefore, that the customer is central to our efforts. We must provide value to the customers so that they are satisfied and want to continue to do business with us. If the customers are not satisfied, they will go to our competitors who do satisfy their expectations. In the case of government or other public or non-profit organizations, they will enact legislation, cut budgets, or otherwise limit our profit (resources).

The extent to which we meet or exceed the expectations of our customers is the measure of the quality of our products and services. These expectations are categorized as requirements, the performance model, and distinguishing characteristics. The requirements are the basic attributes that the customer demands. These are normally expressed as specifications, contractual requirements, or purchase-order requirements. These attributes may include cost, service, reliability, performance, and maintainability.

To be competitive in today's marketplace, one clearly needs to understand the customers' expectations and be capable of providing products and services on target the first time, every time. This challenge is becoming increasingly difficult. Product life cycles that included two to four years from concept to production are now two years from concept to obsolescence. Product quality is also increasing. Technology is accelerating in some areas and flattening in others. Success will, therefore, go to those who are positioned to capitalize on these changes and can react quickly to accommodate the changing forces in the marketplace.

The performance model is the entire customer experience with our product or service. This includes the tangible and intangible aspects of the customers' experience with our product or service. The performance model starts with the requirements and may add such items as availability of financing, reputation, image, ease of purchase, or billing procedures. The distinguishing characteristics are those attributes of our product or service that are assessed, by our customers, as exceeding the competitions' offerings in satisfying or delighting our customers.

It is imperative that we understand all of these elements of the customers' expectations if we are to win the competition. It is with this understanding that we are able to develop the distinguishing characteristics. After we have determined what the distinguishing characteristics are to be and developed the performance model, we are able to make the business decision to pursue the project.

Customer satisfaction applies to internal and external customers and all aspects of the customer experience, from the initial sales contact to receipt and use of the service or product. The internal customers need to work collaboratively to satisfy the external customers. This ensures that the products and services are cost effective and meet or exceed the customers' expectations. The customer experience includes all contacts with the supplier and the use of the products or services. These experiences may include financing, documentation, warranty, after-sales support, and repair.

Successful players in the marketplace understand the current business climate, implement the enterprise model as a process, implement a model for achieving long-term sustained improvement, and focus on customer satisfaction.

THE CURRENT BUSINESS CLIMATE

Companies are national, but business is international. National and political borders are transparent to nearly all aspects of business. Even in those businesses that are not directly involved in the world marketplace, the standards for products and services have been increased by the global competitive climate. Our customers simply expect more value from us due to the broadened availability of high-quality products and services and the responsiveness of our competitors. This is clearly the era of the global marketplace.

In the past, customers judged the value of a product or service on the basis of product quality and price. Today's customers have expanded the concept of value to include all elements of the total product or service experience, i.e., convenience of purchase, after-sale service, product or service characteristics, dependability, and reliability. The elements of customer value can be categorized as operational excellence, customer flexibility, and technical leadership.

Operational excellence refers to the ability to deliver, to the customers' schedules, reliable products or services at competitive prices. This also means delivering products or services that provide the characteristics desired by the customers. Customer flexibility means having the ability to address the needs of each customer or small subsegments of the market individually. This includes all aspects of customer service. Technical leadership is the ability to produce a continuous stream of state-of-the-art products or services. The standards for each of these elements of customer value are continuously being redefined as your competitors continuously improve their processes. The lowest price, highest quality, best service available from any one supplier soon becomes the benchmark for all competitors.

The future belongs, therefore, to those businesses that clearly define their customers, understand their expectations, and cost-effectively produce quality, low-cost products and services that satisfy those expectations the first time, every time. This is equally true in your local, regional, and national markets, as well as the global marketplace. In the United States, this reality has been recognized at the national level. The Malcolm Baldrige National Quality Award, established in 1987, is given to those who demonstrate that they have achieved a level of world class competition through quality management of products and services.

Since its inception, the Malcolm Baldrige National Quality Award has been awarded to five or less companies each year. The reason that so few attain it is that few understand how to develop the corporate infrastructure necessary to create and maintain the culture of a world class competitor.

THE MANAGEMENT 2000 MODEL

Most companies strive to achieve world class competitiveness by implementing various aspects of Total Quality Management, the new quality technologies, team building, customer focus programs, six sigma programs, programs to achieve the Malcolm Baldrige National Quality Award, reengineering, and international quality standards, e.g., ISO 9000. These efforts frequently start as pilot projects and proliferate in a non-systematic manner. Initial successes are not sustained, so we pursue the next "management by best seller" program or system. We need a model for achieving long-term, sustained improvement.

The model presented in Figure 1-1 is such a model. It aids in the selection, integration, and application of the appropriate tools and techniques to establish the infrastructure to achieve global competitiveness and sustain that achievement through continuous improvement. This is the Management 2000 Model described in the first book of the Van Nostrand Reinhold Management 2000 series.

The Management 2000 Model is a continuous cycle analogous to the Shewhart cycle. In Phase 1, planning is done to create the infra-

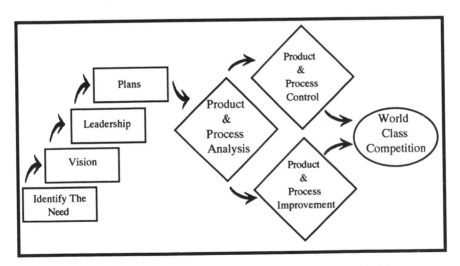

FIGURE 1-1   Management 2000 Implementation Model

structure necessary to achieve the Management 2000 culture. This is followed by deploying the plan (Phase 2). In Phase 3, you periodically assess progress and revise the plans. This action is then followed by deployment of the revised plans.

The beginning efforts in implementing the Management 2000 culture are the development of processes or systems that provide Management 2000 leadership and ensure deployment of Management 2000 plans. After the systems are defined, they are implemented. At this point, you are in a maintenance activity for the process. The implementation of the Management 2000 model establishes the infrastructure and action necessary to become a world class competitor. The Management 2000 Integrated Product and Process Development (IPPD) model enables you to win the competition. Before we discuss the IPPD model, we need to understand our organizations as business enterprises.

THE BUSINESS ENTERPRISE

Competitiveness depends on an organization's ability to provide customer satisfaction throughout the customer experience. It also means providing cost-effective products and services at a lower cost and more quickly than the competitors. Being competitive, however, is not necessarily success. An organization needs the ability to sustain the wins—that is, to thrive. Thriving is the goal; it is success.

Thriving depends on an organization's continuous ability to capitalize on the rapidly changing opportunities in the marketplace, technology, and financial and political environment. This requires that organizations develop technologies and production skills into competencies that enable the company to capitalize on changing opportunities. These are the core competencies of the enterprise. Core competencies are, therefore, the activities that enable an organization to access a wide variety of markets, are difficult for competitors to imitate, and contribute to the customer's satisfaction with the customer experience.

These core competencies require an infrastructure that focuses the business around core functions. These functions, collectively, describe the business enterprise. This business enterprise is a process with inputs. These inputs are managed and operated upon to produce the products. Figure 1-2 shows the various elements of the process and their relationships. It is a continuous process consisting of eight elements:

- ► Market-and-Customer Research and Communication
- ► Strategy Formulation
- ► Product Definition
- ► Material Management
- ► Product Operations
- ► Product Support
- ► Information-Services Network
- ► Financial Control

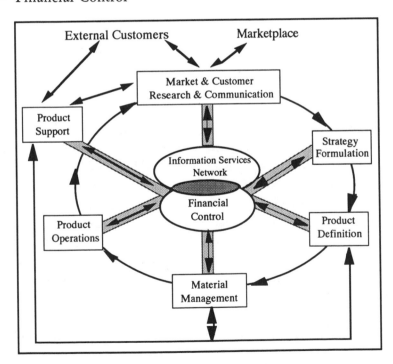

FIGURE 1-2   The Enterprise Process

There may be other activities that are required by law or for safety, hazardous material control, security, and others. Although these are required, they are enabling processes and should not be thought of as core functions.

Market-and-Customer Research and Communication

The purpose of market-and-customer research and communication is to collect data and analyze it. The results provide the needed information for effective strategic business planning. This is a two-way communication with customers and the marketplace. This element of the enterprise process enables us to:

- ► Know and understand the marketplace.
- ► Understand the needs, problems, and buying motivation of the customers.
- ► Understand the customers' requirements for a given product and service.
- ► Help customers shape their expectations.

The inputs for this activity are data from the customers and markets as well as assessments, measurements, and feedback reports from the business. The data is collected and analyzed. The resulting information is fed to the appropriate organizations of the enterprise via the information-services network. The outputs of this function include: customer requirements, customer communications, market analysis, market communications, benchmarking data, benchtrending data, and best-practices data. This information is used to develop or refine the mission, vision, goals, objectives, and strategies of the enterprise and to define the products and services that your customers need and want. The output of this element of the enterprise process is also essential for defining a strategy to reach the customers.

Strategy Formulation

The business-enterprise process starts when an entrepreneur first develops the idea for the business. After that, it is necessary to periodically review the vision, mission, and goals of the business and adjust them as circumstances require. Customer-and-market research and communication collect the data necessary to develop the strategies for conducting the business and providing the product or service offering. Strategy formulation is the development of the various strategies required to deploy the organization's vision, e.g., marketing strategy, customer-satisfaction strategy, sales strategy, and production strategy. This is the clear definition of what business you are in, what your mission is, and what your core values are.

The inputs for this function include the customer set, customer requirements, customer motivation, market analysis, benchmarking and benchtrending data, best-practices data, and the Management 2000 model. The data analysis and strategy formulation result in the concept and approach for delivering the product and service. These outputs of the strategy formulation function are expressed as:

- Vision Statements
- Mission Statements
- Policies and Guidelines
- Organization Structure
- Customer-Satisfaction Strategy
- Marketing Strategy
- Required Core Competencies
- Product and Service Strategy
- Business Strategy
- Communication Strategy

Collectively, this information provides the focus for the organization. Each element of the output is fed backward to ensure appropriate and effective market-and-customer research and communication.

It is also fed forward to ensure each function and each individual in the organization is working collaboratively and supportively to achieve the vision of the company.

Product Definition

After the business strategies are formulated, it is necessary to define the offering for the customer and design the total customer experience. This is accomplished by determining the customer requirements, determining the distinguishing characteristics, designing the customer-performance model, and defining the material and process requirements. Customer requirements are the features of the product or service that are necessary to satisfy the customer during all phases of the customer experience. Distinguishing characteristics, on the other hand, are those features that are designed so that customers will prefer your offering. These include added features and capabilities that will delight the customers. The customer performance model is the total of the tangible and intangible features that define the product or service being offered.

This element of the enterprise process involves analysis of:

- ► Vision Statements
- ► Mission Statements
- ► Customer-Satisfaction Strategy
- ► Business Strategy
- ► Marketing Strategy
- ► Required Core Competencies
- ► Policies and Guidelines
- ► Organization Structure
- ► Communication Strategy
- ► Product and Service Development Strategy
- ► Customer Requirements
- ► Customer Motivation
- ► Customer Set
- ► Market Analysis

- ► Process Metric Data
- ► Process Improvement Plans
- ► Process Maps/Flowcharts
- ► Benchmarking Data
- ► Benchtrending Data
- ► Best-Practices Data

The results of the analysis are used in the design and development of the products and services to be offered to the customers. This includes all elements of the customer experience. This function also includes the selection of materials, design of production processes, and variability-reduction activities.

Material Management

Production of the products and services requires effective and efficient management of resources. This includes all material, supplies, and equipment of the enterprise. The inputs for this function include:

- ► Vision Statements
- ► Mission Statements
- ► Customer-Satisfaction Strategy
- ► Business Strategy
- ► Marketing Strategy
- ► Required Core Competencies
- ► Policies and Guidelines
- ► Organization Structure
- ► Communication Strategy
- ► Customer-Performance Model
- ► Materials, Supplies, Equipment, and Cash

Material management includes the make/buy decisions and all aspects of the purchasing and receipt of material, supplies, and equipment necessary for the operation of the business enterprise. This includes ordering material, parts, and equipment, the receipt and distribution of these items, and cash management.

Product Operations

The purpose of product operations is to cost-effectively produce the products and services, on schedule, that meet or exceed the expectations of the customers, as defined by the customer requirements model. Product operations include all in-house activities that add value to the material to produce the product and service offered to the customer. To add value an action must: (1) do something that the customer cares about, (2) physically change a material or product, and (3) be done correctly the first time.

In addition to the material, supplies, equipment, and personnel required for production operations, the individuals in this element of the enterprise model also need to understand:

- ► Vision Statement of the Enterprise
- ► Mission Statement for the Organizations
- ► Customer-Satisfaction Strategy
- ► Policies and Guidelines
- ► Organization Structure
- ► Communication Strategy
- ► Business Strategy
- ► Marketing Strategy
- ► Required Core Competencies
- ► Customer-Performance Model
- ► Materials, Supplies, Equipment, and Personnel
- ► Capable Processes

Product operations also produce process maps, process flowcharts, process metrics, and improvement plans.

Product Support

After a product or service is provided to a customer, there are continued opportunities to service the customer. This is a troubleshooting, repair-and-replacement, data-collection, and communication activity. These product support activities are critical to customer satisfaction and provide an opportunity to collect information about customers' wants and desires. They also provide a mechanism for conveying information to the customers. This can be a critical activity in shaping customer expectations in favor of your products and services.

The inputs for this function are the same as for product operations. The outputs include post-delivery support that meets or exceeds customers' expectations, process metric data, and repair and failure data.

Information-Services Network

The success of the enterprise process is dependent on an effective information-services network. The information-services network provides data and information in a timely manner to support fact-based decision making throughout the company. The inputs are the outputs from all of the other elements of the enterprise process. These data are managed by the network and made available to each of the functions of the process in a format that meets their individual needs. This can be either as raw data or as formatted reports for analysis.

Financial Control

Positive and effective financial management is also necessary for the success of the enterprise. This is the analysis-and-budgeting function. It provides for analysis and budgeting based on the inputs of:

- Vision Statement of the Enterprise
- Mission Statements

- ► Customer-Satisfaction Strategy
- ► Business Strategy
- ► Marketing Strategy
- ► Policies and Guidelines
- ► Organization Structure
- ► Communication Strategy
- ► Budget Allocation
- ► Capital Allocation

The outputs of this element of the enterprise process are resource allocations: Personnel Requirements, Payroll, Payables, and Receivables.

The enterprise process holds for government and non-profit organizations, as well as business. The elements may be defined differently, but the principle and purpose of each element of the process are necessary for the enterprise to be successful. The first decision in this process is to pursue a segment of the market, a product, or service. This is a business decision to proceed after the appropriate data collection and analysis have been accomplished.

THE BUSINESS DECISION

The decision to develop a product or service to offer your customers is an important one. It is clearly an error to consider only the technical, engineering, and programmatic aspects of the design and development of new products and services. You must not forget that there also are business decisions to be made, and those business decisions are best made in an integrated environment with the technical and engineering elements.

When these decisions are made in isolation, the opportunity for failure is greatly increased. The engineering and technical decision makers can, based upon the voice of the customer (VOC), design and develop a product that cannot be delivered to the customer at a profit, one that cannot be financed, or one where you cannot reach the breakeven point. The business decision makers can decide upon a product or service that is not feasible from an engineering point of view or that cannot be produced or serviced. The best way to avoid these pitfalls is to integrate the project decision making process.

The project decision, therefore, must not be made in a vacuum; you must understand all aspects of the environment you are operating in. Your project decision making process needs a structured approach for answering several critical questions.

- ► **What are the aspects of your business environment?** What are the legal, competitive, financial, technical, and other aspects of your environment?
- ► **What are the market considerations?** What is the Voice of the Customer telling you? What is the market segment? What is the potential market?
- ► **What are your risks?** Can you quantify the risks involved in this project? How will you account for the potential risk on your project?
- ► **What are the costs of the project?** Can you estimate the costs? What are the cost options for different products or services?
- ► **What is your breakeven point?** Based upon the market potential and the project risks and costs, can you reach breakeven on the project? What are the potential revenue and profit?
- ► **What will be the expected effect upon some standard financial ratios?** Based upon the breakeven analysis, will the projected Return on Investment (ROI) meet your needs or standards? What will the overall effect of this project be upon the Return on Net Assets (RONA)?

Product Definition

After the decision is made to proceed to produce a specific product or service, a design team is formed. The team then starts the process of defining the product or service. This definition may be in terms of performance specifications, system specifications, design requirements, drawings, schematics, etc. The traditional method for defining products and services is a consecutive or serial approach that focuses on performance requirements.

Serial-Design Process

In the serial-design approach (Figure 1-3), the design engineers design the product, and then hand it off to manufacturing. It is then up to the manufacturing and test engineers to figure out how to build and test it. Frequently, the product-support activities are defined after the product is designed and is in production. This lack of integration and coordination is a trap that leads to unnecessary process-and-product variation. This variation inhibits competitiveness and increases operating costs.

In companies that provide a service, the subject matter experts decide what the service should be and design it according to their informed knowledge of what the customer needs. In both instances, the designers do what they think is best and use all their knowledge and talent to develop an excellent product or service. Unfortunately,

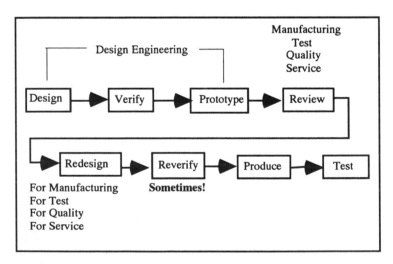

FIGURE 1-3   The Serial-Design Process

they frequently develop a product or service that is innovative, but difficult or impossible to produce without extensive redesign. The product or service design is frequently driven by technology, <u>not</u> by the customers' requirements or expectations.

The serial approach overlooks the fact that the business is an integrated enterprise. In fact, it reinforces the tendency for technical arrogance and separateness of the core functions of the business. The serial approach also fails to capitalize on opportunities for parallel activity and related cost reductions. Additionally, the costs of detecting and repairing defects at various stages of product development and integration increase greatly as you move through the design or production process, as shown in Figures 1-4 and 1-5. This information further substantiates the need for design and production of products and services that are on target the first time, every time.

Recognizing these cost relationships, companies have developed various approaches to prevent the never-ending cycle of design, redesign, and retrofit. Some have incorporated structured design reviews, formal hand-offs from design to manufacturing, and other systems to guarantee that the design is predictable. Experience has proven that these are hollow actions. They miss the point. The product-development process needs to be an integrated approach that addresses all of

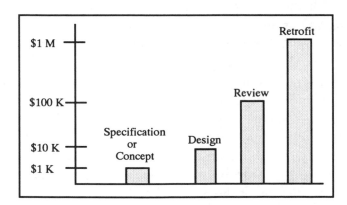

FIGURE 1-4 Cost to Detect and Repair a Defect at Various Stages of Product Development

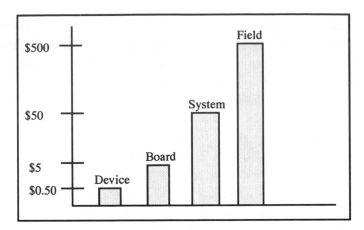

FIGURE 1-5   Cost to Detect and Repair a Defect at Various
Levels of Product Integration

the factors early in the process that impact productivity, quality, and customer satisfaction. This is the integrated product development process.

Integrated Product and Process Development

Integrated product and process development (IPPD) is the implementation of the concurrent engineering philosophy by cross-functional teams using quality-function-deployment and variability-reduction tools and techniques to optimize materials and processes. IPPD focuses on the right people using the right tools at the right time to do the right things. This approach also ensures the lowest cost and shortest cycle time for the design-and-development process itself.

Just as the implementation of the Management 2000 model develops the infrastructure for becoming a world class competitor, the Management 2000 Integrated Product and Process Development Model (Figure 1-6) provides the method for the systematic development and production of the products and services that are on target the first time, every time. In other words, it is the model for winning the competition.

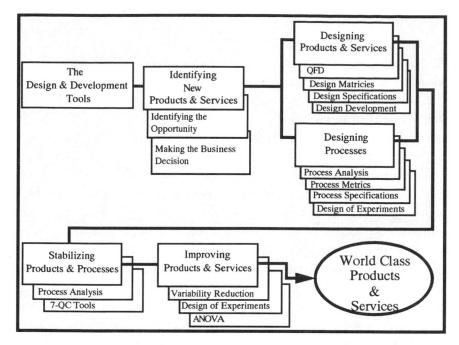

FIGURE 1-6 The Integrated Product and Process Development Model

Concurrent Engineering

Concurrent Engineering (CE) refers to a systematic approach for the integrated, simultaneous design of products and their related processes including manufacturing, test, and support. Concurrent engineering ensures that all "downstream" product considerations are moved up front. The tradeoffs for producibility, testability, and serviceability occur in real time, during the design phase, not as a result of a design review or a problem detected in the manufacturing process. The goal of CE is to optimize all critical product-and-process characteristics. It is, therefore, a critical element of the IPPD process. It is implemented by a cross-functional team. As implemented in the IPPD process, CE integrates all the requisite engineering disciplines at the beginning of the design phase.

One of the key elements of IPPD is the establishment of a team approach for the definition of the product or service. The implementation of CE in the IPPD process begins with the establishment of a cross-functional and multi-disciplinary product-development team. The development team needs to include individuals from organizations representing the key disciplines, who are able to address the full range of the customer experience. The goal of the product-development team must be a balanced design created by disciplined and controlled processes throughout the design, development, and production phases. Conflicting requirements and constraints that affect cost, performance, reliability, maintainability, and availability must be methodically resolved to maximize customer satisfaction. Decisions that alter the balance, or relationships, among these attributes must be organized so that they may be verified as the design and development progress through production.

The IPPD team has two types of members: standing members and ad hoc members. The standing members need to be individuals with technical, management, and interpersonal skills. Some situations do not have enough development work to justify assigning full-time members. It is best, however, to assign full-time members to the IPPD project, which should be limited to ten or fewer individuals. As the team plans and performs its tasks, it will identify actions that require expertise beyond the standing team members. For short-term requirements, recruit specialists as ad hoc members.

The goals of the team include:

- ► Shorter time to market
- ► Lower product-development costs
- ► Higher quality
- ► Lower manufacturing costs
- ► Reduced service cost
- ► Enhanced competitiveness
- ► Improved profit margins

To accomplish these goals, the design team needs to address at least six specific, parallel design activities:

- ► Design for performance
- ► Design for manufacturability

- ► Design for assembly
- ► Design for testability
- ► Design for serviceability
- ► Design for compliance

Because of the numerous "design for . . ." activities, they are lumped together as DFX. Each of these areas of concern addresses a set of vital design requirements and must be taken into account in the development project. Each set of requirements impacts another. It is this interrelationship that is ignored in a serial design. Concurrent Engineering ensures that the design accounts for each set of requirements, resulting in a design that satisfies the customers' requirements, optimizes the manufacturability, and satisfies the regulatory requirements.

Each design-team member needs to represent his/her discipline actively to optimize the product or service and all the associated processes throughout each of these concurrent design phases. In order for the CE philosophy to become a reality, there must be a method for ensuring that all of the design efforts are collaborative and focused on satisfying the customers' requirements. Quality Function Deployment is the method for implementing the CE philosophy.

Quality Function Deployment (QFD)

Quality Function Deployment (QFD) was developed in Japan in the 1970s. It was first applied at the Kobe Shipyard of Mitsubishi Heavy Industries Ltd. Since that time, it has become the accepted methodology for development of products and services in Japan. QFD has enabled businesses to successfully develop and introduce products in a fraction of the time required without it.

In the early 1980s, Dr. Don Clausing introduced QFD to America. Since that time, American business has shown growing interest in using QFD. The American Supplier Institute and GOAL/QPC have been the leaders in this movement. They have studied QFD, and helped businesses apply it, and they have contributed greatly to the development and innovation of QFD techniques.

QFD is a structured method that uses the 7 M&P tools to identify and prioritize customer requirements and to translate those requirements into engineering requirements for systematic deployment throughout the company at each stage of product or service development.

QFD is driven by what the customer wants, not by technology. It demands, therefore, that we clearly identify who the customers are and what they want. This knowledge drives the need for new technology, innovations, improvements, new products, or new services. This information enables the IPPD team to focus only on the characteristics that are important to the customer and to optimize the implementation of those attributes. The results are increased responsiveness to customer needs, shortened product-design time, and little or no redesign.

QFD uses the "what–how" matrix relationship demonstrated in Figure 1-7[1]. Our convention is to use *goal* to designate *what* is to be achieved and *objective* to designate *how* it is to be achieved. In a matrix, we list the goals on the vertical axis as the "Whats" and the objectives on the horizontal axis as the "Hows."

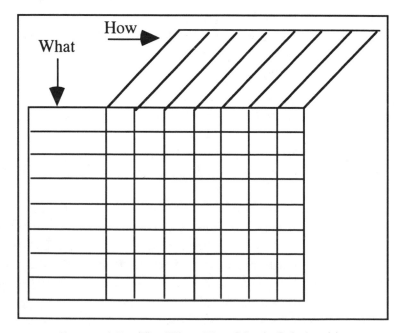

FIGURE 1-7   The What–How Matrix Relationship

The words *goal* and *objective* are often used interchangeably. The dictionary definitions for these words are, in fact, similar enough to be considered the same. In practice, however, one is used to denote *what* is to be achieved and the other *how* it is to be achieved. Confusion results when there is inconsistency in the application of the terms. It is important to establish a convention and to use it consistently.

This relationship generates a family of matrices in a matrix–waterfall fashion. This family of matrices deploys the customer performance model and related technical requirements. Figures 1-8[2] and 1-9[3] illustrate how the matrices deploy the performance model throughout the design, development, production, and support functions.

Matrix–Waterfall Concept

The matrix–waterfall method is especially powerful in developing products or services that satisfy and delight customers. It begins with the customer requirements, which are deployed in a waterfall fashion. Figure 1-8[2] illustrates this process through the design requirements and requisite engineering design to the product characteristics. Figure 1-9[3] shows how the organization deploys these product characteristics through the manufacturing and purchasing operations to the production and quality controls.

After the project is organized, we begin the Product-Planning Phase. In this phase, the customers' requirements and desires are evaluated. We use this information to develop the Requirements Planning Matrix, also known as the House of Quality. This matrix defines the product in terms of the design requirements necessary to achieve customer requirements. The elements of the matrix can be developed using a variety of tools, e.g., Tree Diagram, Affinity Diagram, PDPC, Interrelationship Digraph, Pareto Diagram, DOE, etc.

After the product is planned, we enter the Product-Design Phase. In this phase, we develop the Design Matrix and Product Characteristics Deployment Matrix. The Design Matrix identifies the engineering design activities required to achieve the product design requirements. The Product Characteristics Deployment Matrix subsequently identifies the product characteristics that satisfy the engineering

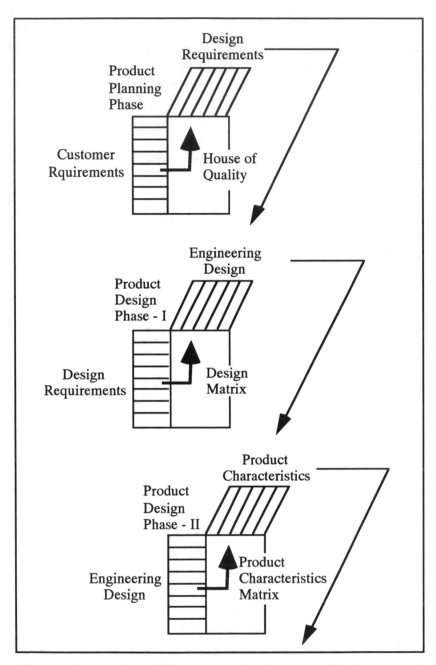

FIGURE 1-8   Deployment of Customer Requirements to Product Characteristics

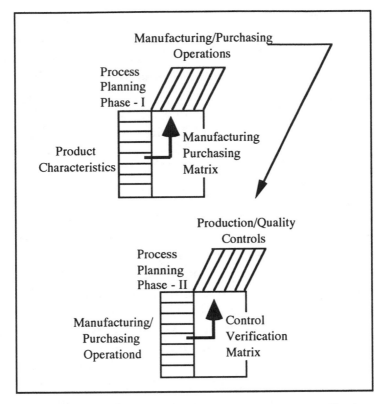

FIGURE 1-9   Deployment of Product Characteristics to Production/Quality Controls

design requirements. The product is defined at this point in terms of characteristics that satisfy the customers' requirements.

We then use the results of the Product Characteristics Deployment Matrix to develop the Manufacturing/Purchasing Matrix in the Process Planning Phase. At this point, we select the manufacturing and purchasing operations needed to achieve the product characteristics. We also develop the Control/Verification Matrix to determine the necessary production and quality controls for the selected manufacturing and purchasing operations.

The final phase is the Implementation Phase. In this phase, we are in production. As production proceeds, we implement SPC, conduct process capability studies, implement designed experiments, and achieve continuous measurable improvement. All process changes and product improvements are compared against the QFD matrices and the company's goals. If a change does not have a positive impact on satisfying customer requirements or the company's goals, it is not implemented.

QFD thus provides a methodology for ensuring that the design and production of products and services is focused on achieving customer satisfaction. At each step, it leads us to select the optimum objective to achieve a goal.

House of Quality

The House of Quality is the starting matrix for QFD. It starts as a What–How Matrix that identifies the requirements derived from the customer-performance model. This model is constructed from the market-and-customer research and communication via the information-services network. These requirements are translated into technical requirements as the "house" is constructed. The completed House of Quality is then used to start the matrix waterfall process.

The process for developing the matrix clarifies the relationships between the objectives and the goals, thus ensuring that all of the customers' requirements are addressed. The process also provides a logical basis for determining the impact of each action on the other actions. Additional features can be added to the House of Quality to provide greater understanding and to facilitate the next phases of the product-development project. This basic QFD approach is flexible and can be adapted to any given situation. Figure 1-10[4] is an example of a House of Quality.

Variability Reduction

A critical part of the IPPD process is variability reduction. This is the selection of materials and the development of processes such that the level of common causes is minimized. Reducing the variability of your process has a direct and immediate effect upon product defects, whether the products are goods, services, management, or administration. This variability reduction lessens defect rates, improves

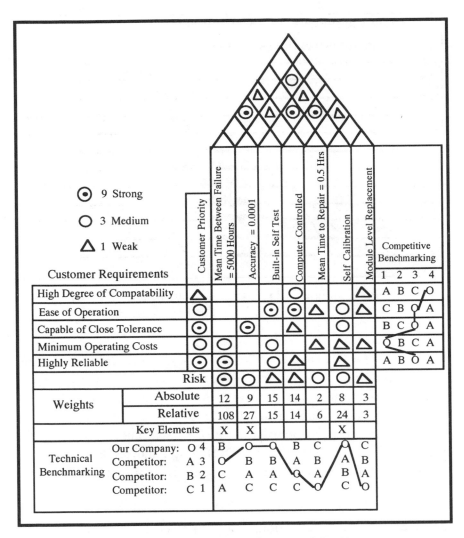

FIGURE 1-10   Example of House of Quality

yields, lowers scrap rates, reduces rework, expands market potential, and reduces warranty costs. Figure 1-11[5] demonstrates the direct relationship between process variability and product quality.

This figure demonstrates the effect of variability reduction compared to defect rates and specific world class competitors. If you have

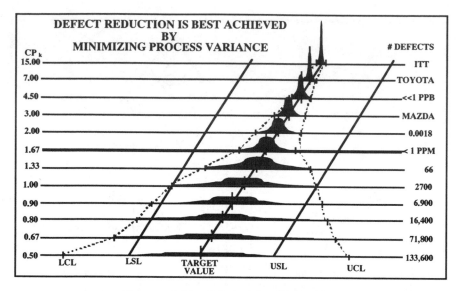

FIGURE 1-11   Minimizing Variability

achieved a process capability (C_P) of 1.00, your process is producing 2,700 failing parts per million (PPM). In today's competitive environment, the minimum acceptable process capability is actually 1.33 to compete in the global marketplace. The best world competitors today are in the parts-per-billion (PPB) class. The tools and techniques of Design of Experiments (DOE) and Analysis of Variance are key to variability reduction and achieving the required process capabilities.

DOE is one of the most powerful tools available for the design, development, characterization, and improvement of products and services. DOE is a group of techniques used to organize and evaluate experimentation to obtain the maximum data using the minimum assets. DOE is directly applicable to many types of businesses and can be effectively applied by the average business person with a little training. A "Designed Experiment" is no more than a test or trial program that has been well structured to measure the results (response variable) accurately in comparison to the inputs (treatments or input variables).

Analysis of Variance (ANOVA) is another important tool for making business and technical decisions. It tells us whether several different treatments (for example, different manufacturing processes) all have the same effect on the quality characteristics of interest. These treatments are specific values of an input (independent) variable. The variable(s) whose values are affected by these treatments are often called response variables, outcome variables, or dependent variables.

STRATEGY OF THE BOOK

The text of this book is arranged in two parts. Chapters 1 through 5 coincide with the sequence of the Integrated Product and Process Development model presented in Figure 1-6. It leads from identification of an opportunity to the business decision to proceed with a design project. This is followed by the implementation of the IPPD process.

Chapters 6 through 9 serve as the tool school part of the book. They provide a sufficiently detailed explanation of the tools and their integration to provide for the average business person to apply the model successfully. Chapter 10 presents Business Process Reengineering (BPR) and shows how the tools presented in Chapters 6–9 are used to integrate BPR with IPPD to optimize the enterprise for customer satisfaction and increased profit.

At the end of each chapter, the key points of the chapter are reviewed. The book provides a series of examples derived from a number of case studies. These case studies have been consolidated into single examples for clarity and applicability. The examples represent industrial, administrative, and managerial processes.

The book is written specifically for managers, supervisors, entrepreneurs, and business people of all levels of experience and education who are responsible for the design and development of new products and services. The book is intended as a reference handbook, to be used by the teams responsible for the design and development of products and services. It is also intended for the executives and managers who are responsible for managing IPPD projects. The book is not merely the what, but the how, to develop products and services. The structure is intended to enable the reader to follow sequentially through the chapters or to enter at whatever point is relevant to the stage of the development process in which you may be operating. The cross-referencing and indexing are designed to enable the user to refer to sections for help as required.

From Concept to Customer is all about the efficient and effective use of management and technical resources to develop products and services that meet or exceed customer expectations throughout the customer experience. It is about being customer focused and using that as a competitive advantage to win the competition as a world class competitor. This book is the companion to *Management 2000.* Where *Management 2000* provided the model for becoming a world class competitor, *From Concept to Customer* provides the tools, techniques, and the model for their integrated application to win the competition.

NOTES

[1] Jackson Jr., Harry K. & Frigon, Normand L., 1994, *Management 2000,* pp. 344. New York: Van Nostrand Reinhold.

[2] Re Velle, Jack B., 1992, *The New Quality Technology,* pp. D-20. Los Angeles: Hughes Aircraft Company.

[3] Ibid, pp. D-21.

[4] Jackson Jr., Harry K. & Frigon, Normand L., 1994, *Management 2000,* pp. 359. New York: Van Nostrand Reinhold.

[5] Ibid, pp. 369.

2

Identifying the Opportunity

TO BE COMPETITIVE IN TODAY'S MARKETPLACE,
YOU NEED TO HEED THE VOICE OF THE
CUSTOMER.

The key to business success lies in determining what the customer wants and, using this information, cost-effectively delivering products and services that satisfy and delight the customers. This determination of what the customers need or want is the first step in identifying an opportunity. The second step is identifying the potential market for the product and service. Collectively, this information is used to define the opportunity for offering products and services and then to develop a strategy and plan to reach these customers. These data about the product and service are collected from the customers and marketplace. Success, therefore, depends on listening to the voices of the customers and being responsive to their needs.

THE VOICE OF THE CUSTOMER

Products and services are usually described in terms of attributes of performance. This definition is too narrow for the world class competitor. Customers assess the quality of a product or service in terms of their reaction to an experience with the product or service. In the IPPD process, therefore, we include the entire customer experience when defining the product and service. This includes pre-sales, sales, operation, and post-sales support. The data, derived from the customers and the marketplace about our products and services, are referred to as the Voice of the Customer (VOC) in integrated product and process development.

The Voice of the Customer in the IPPD process includes the attributes of the entire customer experience that are necessary to achieve customer satisfaction. There are four types of customer satisfaction.

The first, the expecters, includes those product and service features that the customer takes for granted. These are items that customers do not ask the supplier about but which, if they are omitted, will result in extreme customer dissatisfaction. These items do not satisfy the customer if they are present, but they are significant dissatisfiers. Customers will not buy our product or service, under any circumstance, if the expected attributes are omitted or done poorly.

The second type of product and service attributes, the spoken wants, includes items that the customer will specify as wants. These are often written descriptions of a product or service. They are usually expressed as performance characteristics.

The third type of product and service features, the unspoken wants, includes characteristics that are as important to the customer experience as the second type. These are the attributes that the customer forgot to mention, did not know exactly what they were, or did not want to talk about.

The fourth type includes those characteristics that excite or "wow" the customers. These are the exciters. Customers seldom express their wants or needs about these except in vague terms. This is because the customers often have not thought about these characteristics. These are satisfiers, and never dissatisfiers, because the customers do not expect them. Figure 2-1 demonstrates the relationship of the types of product and service features and the impact on customer satisfaction.

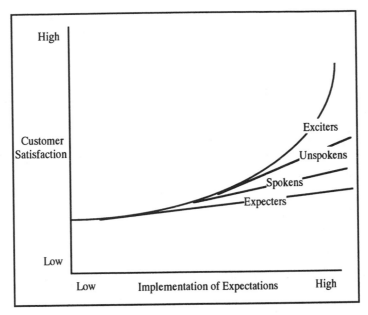

FIGURE 2-1   Customer Satisfaction Curve

As we evaluate the expectations of the customers, we need to bear in mind that an exciter today will be a specified attribute tomorrow and an expected attribute the day after. An example of this is the radio in automobiles. They have gone from an exciter, to an accessory to be ordered, to an expected item. And now customers are specifying CD players. . . .

Our challenge in the IPPD process is to ascertain the wants and needs for a new or improved product and service and then to collect the information about the four types of attributes that will motivate the customers. This information is then used to describe the product or service in terms of a requirements model, discriminating characteristics, and a performance model.

The purpose for performing the market research is to develop the data for determining the basic marketing considerations and to begin development of the Voice of the Customer Table (Figures 2-2 and 2-3). If we are to satisfy the customers' expectations, we need to understand what they expect, what their motivation is, and how to

#	Customer		Use				
		I/E*	What	When	Where	Why	How

* I/E: Internal/External

FIGURE 2-2   Voice of the Customer Table—Part I

delight them. In the IPPD process, we accomplish this by first determining what the customer requirements are. This set of requirements is sometimes called the customer requirements model. Then we determine how to excite the customer. This analysis leads to the development of the distinguishing characteristics that will be used to attract customers to your specific product or service. This information is integrated and results in the customer performance model. The performance model defines the product or service to be offered to the customer.

#	Customer Data	Customer's Expectation	Expectation Characteristic	Function	Reliability	Comments

FIGURE 2-3   Voice of the Customer Table—Part II

The Customer Requirements Model

The Customer Requirements Model is a set of expectations about a product or service that motivates customers to choose your product. These are both the attributes that they demand and desire. This expectation set typically consists of 6–10 high-level attributes. They may be specified by the customer as contractual requirements, or they may be derived from the market-and-customer research and communication.

It is important to develop the customer requirements model for internal as well as external customers. This model leads to the necessary understanding of the customers' expectations to provide the products and services that lead to continuous profitability and growth of wealth. This model leads to:

Distinguishing Characteristics

The distinguishing characteristics are those attributes of the products and services that differentiate your offering from those of your competition. This may be an enhanced, expected, or specified attribute or an attribute that no one else offers. It may be related to the delivery method, financing, or other non-functional characteristic. This includes intangibles, like image and perceptions about the product or service. These are the attributes that are targeted to give us a competitive advantage.

The Customer Performance Model

The customer performance model is the consolidation of the distinguishing characteristics and the customer requirements model. This is the total package of the customer experience. It describes each element of the customer experience in terms of the customers' expectations. This includes parametric specifications for the product and service for each phase of the customer experience.

Voice of the Customer Table

The Voice of the Customer Table (VOCT) is used to collate the data about the customers and their expectations about the customer experience. This information is then used to define the customer requirements model, determine the distinguishing characteristics, and define the customer performance model. The data are continuously refined, and the tables are updated as the IPPD project progresses. It is often convenient to divide the table into two pieces: Part I and Part II. The categories for the data may vary for a given product or service, but Figures 2-2 and 2-3 present a typical VOCT. Each entry is numbered for future reference and correlation.

Customer

This information identifies the customer for this data entry. It will be used to stratify the population of customers so that the importance of a particular response can be assessed. In addition, an entry is made to specify if the customer is an internal or external customer (I/E).

Use

In the columns for use, data about the present or intended use of the product or service and/or feature is entered. This data is critical for determining the relevance of the response and the motivation for the customers' selection of a product or service.

Customer Data

In this column, the customer's response is synthesized into a single entry. This requires the distillation of the customer's expectations from all of the input. There is an entry for each expectation.

Expectation Characteristic

This is a transformation of the customer data into statements of measurable attributes.

Function

This is what the product or service does.

Reliability

This refers to the likelihood that the product or service will provide its intended use for a specified period of time.

Comments

This column is used for additional remarks that do not fit in any of the other columns but which are important to carry forward in the IPPD project.

MARKET-AND-CUSTOMER RESEARCH
AND COMMUNICATION

Marketing is the principal activity for market-and-customer research and communication and is a discipline in itself; it is too complex to be completely covered in this text. We will provide only the basic marketing tools used for collecting the needed input from the Voice of the Customer to build the Voice of the Customer Table. Essentially, there are four elements for you to consider when performing the marketing function for a new product or service:

- ▶ **Basic Marketing Considerations:** The basic market considerations are product and service, location, promotion, and price. These are what product and service are to be offered, where they are to be offered, when they are to be offered, how they are to be offered, and how much are you going to charge for them.
- ▶ **Market Research:** Market research gathers data to determine what products and services are needed and what your customers' specifications are. It identifies the market segments, or strategic business areas, the product or service to be sold, and what distribution channels will be used. We have expanded this

activity to include the proactive aspects of market-and-customer research and communication.

► **Market Strategy:** Based upon the results of the market research, a strategy for bringing the product or service to the marketplace is formulated. This market strategy includes the marketing mix of promotion, advertising, personal selling and distribution channels.

► **Market Plan:** The market plan answers the question of how we are going to execute the market strategy based upon the market research. The plan is a road map for selling the product, just as Quality Function Deployment is a road map to the integrated design of the product. In later chapters of this book, you will see clearly how QFD fits into the marketing process and how it can be used to enhance that process.

The basic marketing considerations and the market research elements are key to the IPPD process. These are the critical components of market-and-customer research and communication in the enterprise process. The data from these activities are used by the strategy formulation function of the enterprise process to develop the market strategy and market plan elements. We will discuss basic marketing considerations and market research as they relate to the IPPD process. (The development of strategies and plans is covered in *Management 2000*.)

Basic Marketing Considerations

The goal of our market-and-customer research and communication is to understand the voice of the customer (VOC). This needs to be a two-way communication. The data collected from the customer and the marketplace are of primary importance; however, communication to the customers and the marketplace is also vital to success. This may be in the form of direct communication or may be via published works, papers, talks, and interviews. These activities allow you to help clarify and establish customer expectations and to impact the market forces. The VOC represents the needs and desires of the customers and forms the basis for the integrated product and process development of new products and services. It is the input that will be used to determine the parameters for building your product or service using Quality Function Deployment (QFD). This view of defining opportunities for the enterprise is represented by Figure 2-4.

This view places the Voice of the Customer as the target of a bull's-eye. The VOC represents the customers' expectations. Effectively answering the VOC means satisfying the customers' expectations, which leads to earning profits and growing wealth. The bull's-eye of your market strategy and market plan is surrounded by the factors that relate directly to the development of the IPPD plans—what products and services you will offer, what the pricing structure will

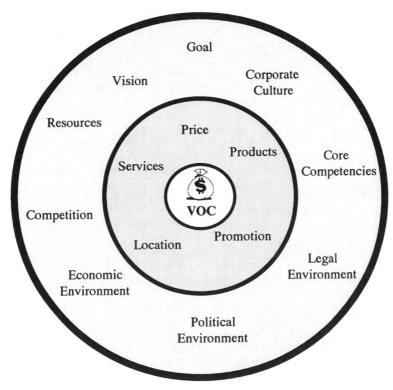

FIGURE 2-4   Management 2000 Market View

be, what promotion activities will be used, and in what geographical location you will offer your products and services. The outer ring of the target shows the environmental factors that are key for selecting, designing, and developing a product or service. They include factors that you may not control but can affect. These factors serve as enablers for your activities and must be accounted for in the determination of a potential opportunity.

Products and Services

Your products and services must be on target the first time, every time. This factor is concerned with the selection of that right product for your market that meets or exceeds the expectations of the customers. The important point here is that the product you design and develop must satisfy the customers' needs in terms of all of their expectations—cost, schedule, and performance. This satisfaction must be found throughout the entire customer experience, from sales to use and post-sales support. If you fail to meet the customers' expectations for the customer experience with your product or service, your customers will find a supplier that does meet their expectations.

Location

This factor is concerned with getting the right product and service to the target market. Timing is very important for an organization's success. A product or service is not useful to a customer if it isn't available at the right place, at the right time. Nor is a high-quality product that is priced well, that customers do not want. This holistic approach to location is critical to developing the right product or service for the target market and customers.

Promotion

This factor involves informing your customers that you have produced a product and service that are of superior quality, at a lower cost than your competitors', and that the product and service can be delivered on schedule. How are you going to sell this superior product? Personal selling, mass marketing, catalogue sales, established distribution channels—all these alternatives are possibilities for your product and service. They will be decided in the formulation of the market strategy, which is implemented by the market plan.

Price

The traditional view of price is that it is the cost of producing and delivering the product and service <u>plus</u> profit. To thrive in today's marketplace, this definition needs to change. The price of a product or service needs to be based on competition. You must consider the competition in the marketplace, customer reaction to the price, and the current practices in the market you have selected. What is a competitive price for a given product or service? How can we use the pricing structure as a competitive advantage? Profit becomes, therefore, price <u>minus</u> the cost of producing and delivering the product and service.

As well as the controllable factors mentioned above, there are a number of factors that you may not control but, in most instances, you can affect. In performing your market research and establishing a strategy and plan, you must consider all of the factors within the framework of the environment of your enterprise. Figure 2-5 demonstrates the second category of factors in the outer ring of our marketing target.

The factors in the outer ring of the target can be grouped into one of three categories: business, financial, or government. These three categories are like the three legs of a stool. They need to be properly balanced to hold the stool level, and they must be strong enough to support the intended load. This is analogous to the U.S. strategic triad (strategic bombers, intercontinental ballistic missiles, and submarines) that provided the deterrence during the Cold War. This strategic triad of business, finance, and government is essential for a nation to win the international competition. In *Management 2000,* this new strategic triad is described as:

> The government leg of the triad provides the infrastructure (education, transportation, economic policy), trade policies and tax struc-

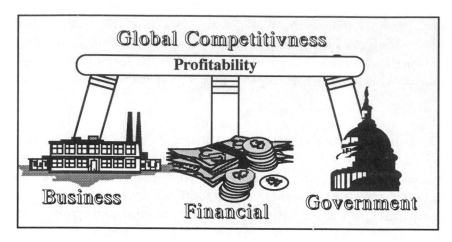

FIGURE 2-5   The New Strategic Triad

ture to create the environment in which businesses can not only compete globally, but thrive in the world marketplace. The business leg consists of companies that produce high-quality, low-cost goods and services that can compete in the world marketplace. The financial institutions leg must provide long-term investment, equity for capital formation and credit for capital purchases.[1]

When developing the IPPD project, it is essential to evaluate these factors and the impact they have on your market, customers, and the enterprise. It is the goal of the IPPD process to design products, services, and the associated processes to be robust in relationship to these elements. This means that changes in these elements have a minimal impact on your ability to satisfy your customers' expectations.

Vision

Every business begins with a vision and with the hope that what is an idea today can one day become a reality. Each company's vision is a unique, ideal image of a possible future. The vision may begin with the entrepreneur that founds the company, or it may be the product of the leadership team. In many instances, it changes over time. These changes often result from technological advances, changes in the marketplace, or changes in the economic or political climate.

The vision guides the decision about products and services to offer to the marketplace. It is the starting point for strategy formulation and guides the market-and-customer research and communication activities. The vision points the direction for the enterprise.

Goals

Goals are the long-term, intermediate, and short-term activities necessary to achieve the vision of the enterprise. These provide specific details for the guidance of the market-and-customer research and communication activities. The goals are often defined in specific measurable terms, e.g., market a new product line in 1996 and achieve 50% market share for notebook computers by 1999. As such, goals point the market research activities to specific products and services.

Corporate Culture

The corporate culture is the collection of the enterprise's mores. This includes the values as demonstrated by the way the enterprise awards and recognizes individuals and teams, the way the organization communicates, and the mechanisms used to accomplish tasks. It is how the individuals communicate and work together to achieve the vision. Although you may not attempt to change the corporate culture for a given IPPD project, it is necessary to account for the realities of the culture in deciding to pursue a given project.

Core Competencies

"Core competencies" refers to the collective learning of an organization. The core activities enable the enterprise to adapt to rapidly changing opportunities in the marketplace and continue to cost-effectively offer high-quality products on schedule. Core competencies are the abilities of a function of the enterprise that enable the enterprise to access a variety of markets, add value to the product or service offered, and are difficult for competitors to duplicate. Adding value means the customer cares about the action, the action changes the delivered product or service, and it is done correctly the first time.

The core competencies are the starting point for deciding what products and services to offer in the marketplace. If, however, the market research and communication indicates there are core competencies required for a specific product or service that you do not possess, this becomes a critical data point in the decision process.

Resources

"Resources" refers to the availability of material, equipment, trained workers, and capable processes. These issues include lead time for purchased items, as well as the availability of material and equipment. Resources directly affect the capability of the processes and the ability to produce quality products on schedule at competitive prices. Some resources you do not control, e.g., state-of-the-art technology, demographics of the workforce, and natural resources. Resources that you do not control can be accounted for in the robust design of the products, services, and processes.

Competition

What is the competition in your market? How much of the market do you possess for your products and services? What are the products and services that competitors offer, and how do they compare to your existing ones and those that you are proposing to offer? The answers to these questions will provide insight on the characteristics your products and services must possess to insure your customers choose yours over the competitions'.

Economic Environment

The availability of cash is a critical consideration for any enterprise. This includes projected cash flow, availability of credit, interest rates, and cycle times for payables and receivables. Required capital investments are also a critical element of the economic environment. There are some processes that require a large capital investment regardless of the quantity of products produced, e.g., wave solder machines for electronic circuit cards. The availability of capital equipment can greatly affect the decision about the feasibility of a specific project and the manner in which a project is implemented, i.e., what activities are purchased and which are owned.

For some products and customers, the financial environment includes down payments or progress payments. These have a significant effect on working capital by reducing the amount of cash borrowed and therefore the amount of interest paid to lenders. This information affects the decision about the ratios for return on net assets (RONA). The economic environment will therefore be a significant data point in the decision process about any project.

Political Environment

The political environment refers to the relationship of government to business. This includes trade policies and tax structures. This is the environment that will influence legislation and regulation that govern a given industry and the manner in which the individual enterprises conduct business. Generally, you will not have a direct impact on this element for a given project. Knowledge about the political environment and its impact on an enterprise's ability to offer products and services can be used to plan lobbying efforts and strategies for future marketing plans and designing robust products and services.

Legal Environment

Every organization operates under legal requirements. These include regulatory laws for safety, hazardous material, equal opportunity, workers' compensation, and environmental protection. For some enterprises, there are additional laws, such as those related to medical products, aviation products, public utilities, foreign distribution, and monopolies. Compliance with the regulations and laws associated with your specific products and services may affect costs and cycle times. It is important therefore that these be accounted for in the decision process for an IPPD project. Although you must comply with the legal environment, you can develop strategies that capitalize on the requirements.

Market Research

The entrepreneurial spirit exists at all levels of business, whether in the largest corporations or the smallest of companies. That spirit is, by nature, an optimistic one and sees opportunities everywhere. Should you pursue each and every one of these opportunities? The answer to that question can be found in market-and-customer research and communication that will bring fact-based decision making to the optimistic entrepreneur.

Frequently, attractive opportunities are close to the products and services with which you are already familiar. It makes sense to build on your strengths (core competencies) and select products and services in which you have a high degree of confidence. This, however, should not be a limiting factor. Success requires that you capitalize on your strengths as they are defined in your organizational vision, goals, and objectives and implemented through your core competencies. Market research gathers and analyzes data to provide for fact-based product-and-services decisions in several ways:

- ► **Observation Method**
- ► **Survey Method**
- ► **Research Method**

Observation Method

The observation method relies on viewing and recording the activities of potential customers. This is essentially an observation of the actions of the potential customers as it will not provide any information on the reasons, attitudes, and behavior behind the actions. Since the potential customers are not aware that they are being observed, it can be assumed that they are reacting normally.

Observation can be accomplished through personal or mechanical methods. A market observation study of the number of people entering a book store can be accomplished using an electronic recorder and compared to the number of books of a specific type that are purchased. This kind of observation can report that, of 450 people who entered a bookstore, six purchased cookbooks. If this were accomplished at a number of bookstores, we could determine the percentage (1.0% for the cookbooks) of books of any type that we can expect to sell.

This method has many lurking variables that can affect the data and lead to false conclusions. First, the correlation of the sample to the population is unknown and may be skewed. More importantly, the population sampled may not be the target population for your products and services.

Survey Method

The survey method uses three methods to collect data: mail surveys, telephone surveys, and personal interviews. Using these methods, the researcher gathers data directly from a sample of the potential customer base.

A mail questionnaire is suitable when there is a large, geographically dispersed sample to be surveyed. Mail surveys can cover a large geographical area and are inexpensive compared to the other methods. There are many disadvantages to the mail survey. First, regular customers usually respond, but others do not. This omits critical input from the database. Secondly, the typical response to a mail survey is 20–40%. Thirdly, it is difficult to ascertain the confidence in the results.

Telephone interviews are an effective compromise to the first two methods. They are flexible and can gather data quickly. Telephone interviews also allow you to cover a wide geographical area and typically have a response rate of 90–95%. An added advantage to the telephone survey is the ability of the interviewer to add individual comments from the respondents that were not in the original survey. Some of the disadvantages are that the area of coverage may be limited, it is more expensive than mail surveys, and the interviewer's individual bias may become part of the responses.

Personal interviews are the best method to apply when there is a long, complex questionnaire involved. A personal interview provides the opportunity for the researcher to obtain complete answers to questions that may not fit the yes/no or brief replies required by the other two methods. More detailed technical data can be gathered in this way. Personal interviewing is the most expensive method to gather data, but the data gathered from personal interviews is more comprehensive. This may require more data manipulation and a higher acquisition cost.

A variation of the personal interview is the focus group. This is a selected sample of customers and potential customers. They meet with a moderator in a group interview format. Focus groups provide a forum for informed discussion of ideas and opinions about products and service. They require careful selection and a trained moderator but, when properly implemented, can provide accurate information about customers' expectations and motivation.

Research

The research method uses the availability of data from such resources as the "United States Census Report," "Statistical Abstract of the United States," "The Federal Reserve Bulletin," "The Monthly Labor Review," and journals and abstracts provided by professional organizations, e.g., American Society for Quality Control, American Statistical Society, American Management Association, Institute of Industrial Engineers, etc. These resources are readily available; however, their information may be dated and may not provide all the data necessary for a new product or service decision. Therefore, this method is most often used in conjunction with one of the other market research methods.

Selection of a method is dependent upon the following criteria:

- ► **Flexibility:** Will the method allow for the collection of all the data that is required?
- ► **Length of Questionnaire:** Can the questionnaire be administered efficiently or effectively? It is doubtful that a potential client would answer a 15-page questionnaire or that a customer would submit to a two-hour interview.

▶ **Accuracy:** The selected method must provide accurate information on the product or service and not be ambiguous.

▶ **Cost:** The expense of administering the survey and analysis of the responses must be taken under consideration. Sampling plans help to control the scope of the survey and, therefore, its cost. Frequently, a company will gather more data than it needs or can cost-effectively evaluate. It is essential, therefore, that the data collection activity be carefully planned out: the type of data required, the source of the data, and how it will be analyzed and reported.

The successful enterprise does not rely on a single method, but uses a balance of market-and-customer research and communication activities to achieve the goals of the market-and-customer research and communication activity. As the strategy is implemented, the quality of the data is monitored and the methods adjusted accordingly. The customer requirements model, distinguishing characteristics, and the customer performance model are adjusted as the data is improved and expanded.

THE MARKETING PROJECT DECISION

As marketing is applied to the Management 2000 Integrated Product and Process Development, it serves three purposes. First, marketing research and communication provide a basic understanding of the marketplace and its requirements to determine if you have a viable product or service and what the potential scope of that market is. Second, marketing research and communication provides for the Voice of the Customer input that is the genesis of the integrated product and process development project. Finally, it provides for some basic information needed for a financial assessment of the project's commercial viability. There are many questions that need to be answered before an informed decision can be made about proceeding with the project:

► Is there a potential market for my new product or service? How extensive is the customer base for the product or service?

► Is my new product or service designed, or can I design it, to meet the market requirements?

► Can my new product or service be competitive in the target market?

► What is the cost of producing and delivering the product or service, and can it be priced so that a reasonable profit is earned?

This information is key input for the process of making the business decision about proceeding with the project.

KEY POINTS

The key to success lies in determining what the customer wants and, using this information, cost-effectively delivering products and services that satisfy and delight the customers.

Customers assess the quality of a product or service in terms of their reaction to an experience with the product or service.

The Voice of the Customer in the IPPD process includes the attributes of the entire customer experience that are necessary to achieve customer satisfaction.

There are four types of customer satisfaction:

► The Expecters
► The Spoken Wants
► The Unspoken Wants
► The Exciters

The purpose of performing the market research is to develop the data for determining the basic marketing considerations and to begin development of the Voice of the Customer Table.

The Customer Requirements Model is a set of expectations about a product or service that motivates customers to choose your product.

The Voice of the Customer Table (VOCT) is used to collate the data about the customers and their expectations about the customer experience. Each entry is numbered for future reference and correlation.

Marketing is the principal activity for Market-and-Customer Research and Communication. Essentially, there are four elements for you to consider when performing the marketing function for a new product or service:

- ► **Basic Marketing Considerations:** Product and Service, Location, Promotion, and Price.
- ► **Market Research:** Market research gathers data to determine what products and services are needed and what your customers' specifications are.
- ► **Market Strategy:** Based upon the results of the market research, a strategy for bringing the product or service to the marketplace is formulated.
- ► **Market Plan:** The market plan answers the question of how we are going to execute the market strategy that was based upon the market research.

The data from these activities are used by the strategy formulation function.

Basic Marketing Considerations: The goal of our market-and-customer research and communication is to understand the Voice of the Customer (VOC).

The VOC represents the customers' expectations. Effectively answering the VOC means satisfying the customers' expectations, which leads to earning profits and growing wealth.

Your products and services must be on target the first time, every time.

A product or service is not useful to a customer if it isn't available at the right place and at the right time. Nor is a high-quality product that is priced well which customers do not want.

The price of a product or service needs to be based on competition. Profit becomes, therefore, price <u>minus</u> the cost of producing and delivering the product and service.

In performing your market research and establishing a strategy and plan, you must consider all of the factors within the framework of the environment of your enterprise.

Every business begins with a vision and with the hope that what is an idea today can one day become a reality.

Each company's vision is a unique, ideal image of a possible future.

Goals are the long-term, intermediate, and short-term activities necessary to achieve the vision of the enterprise.

The corporate culture is the collection of the enterprise's mores, the values as demonstrated by the way the enterprise awards and recognizes individuals and teams, the way the organization communicates, and the mechanisms used to accomplish tasks.

Core activities enable the enterprise to adapt to rapidly changing opportunities in the marketplace and continue to cost-effectively offer high-quality products on schedule.

Resources directly affect the capability of the processes and the ability to produce quality products on schedule at competitive prices.

The availability of cash is a critical consideration for any enterprise. This includes projected cash flow, availability of credit, interest rates, and cycle times for payables and receivables.

Knowledge about the political environment, and its impact on an enterprise's ability to offer products and services, can be used to plan lobbying efforts and strategies for future marketing plans, and designing robust products and services.

Compliance with the regulations and laws associated with your specific products and services may affect costs and cycle times.

Market Research: The entrepreneurial spirit exists at all levels of business, whether in the largest corporations or the smallest of companies.

Success requires that you capitalize on your strengths as they are defined in your organizational vision, goals, and objectives and implemented through your core competencies.

Market research gathers and analyzes data to provide for fact-based product-and-services decisions in several ways:

Observation Method: The observation method relies on viewing and recording the activities of potential customers.

Survey Method: The survey method uses three methods to collect data: mail surveys, telephone surveys, and personal interviews. A mail questionnaire is suitable when there is a large, geographically dispersed sample to be surveyed. Telephone interviews also allow you to cover a wide geographical area and typically have a response rate of 90–95%.

Research: The research method uses the availability of data from other sources.

The successful enterprise does not rely on a single method, but uses a balance of market-and-customer research and communication activities to achieve the goals of the market-and-customer research and communication activity.

The Marketing Project Decision

Marketing research and communication provides a basic understanding of the marketplace and its requirements to determine if you have a viable product or service and what the potential scope of that market is.

Marketing research and communication provides for the Voice of the Customer input that is the genesis of the integrated product and process development project.

Marketing provides for some basic information needed for a financial assessment of the project's commercial viability.

This information is key input for the process of making the business decision about proceeding with the project.

EXAMPLE

Mr. Ohmar Leander and Mr. Hurbert Wiles established Leander Wiles Company Inc. (LWCI) in the early 1960s. They have grown the enterprise until it now consists of three divisions: Machine Tool Division, Electronics Division, and Production Machinery Division. They have established their management team as shown in Example Figure 2-1.

The Machine Tool Division manufactures tool and die products, the Production Machinery Division manufactures production machinery systems, and the Electronics Division designs and manufactures electronic controllers for production machinery systems.

The company management team established the company values (Example Figure 2-2) and vision (Example Figure 2-3). The company

---

LWCI MANAGEMENT TEAM

Mr. Ohmar Leander
President
LWCI

Mr. Hurbert Wiles
Vice President and General Manager,
Machine Tool Division.

Mr. Lester Hammond
General Manager
Electronics Division

Mr. Jeffrey Frank
General Manager
Production Machinery Division

Ms. Lara Hernandez
Manager
Company Safety

Mr. Frank Barret
Manager
Company Quality Operations

Ms. Linda Johnston
Manager
Company Marketing

Ms. Lucille Rowan
Manager
Company Human Resources

Ms. Rita Sanches
Company Controller

EXAMPLE FIGURE 2-1   LWCI Management Team

LWCI - We Value:

- Being ethical in all dealings with customers, suppliers, and one another.
- Practicing participative management at all levels.
- Ensuring fact based decision making.
- Practicing collaborative goal and objective setting.
- Maintaining a commitment to customer satisfaction.
- Providing a stable work environment.
- Promoting customer, supplier, and employee loyalty.
- Ensuring profitability.
- Providing a positive contribution to society.

EXAMPLE FIGURE 2-2   LWCI Company Values

management team has prepared an enterprise profile that delineates their customer set, their customers' top level requirements for LWCI products, and the LWCI core competencies (Example Figure 2-4). This data serves as the background information for LWCI business initiatives.

LWCI has identified a need to design and develop a new line of industrial production equipment. This need has surfaced due to declining sales of existing LWCI equipment, the changes in production technologies, and the increasing need of LWCI customers for greater productivity. The Production Machinery Division of LWCI

The Leander Wiles Company, Inc. will be recognized as a highly profitable enterprise producing world class quality products and services. We will focus on the design and production of manufacturing equipment. We will challenge the global marketplace, and do so while remaining committed to being a socially responsible company.

EXAMPLE FIGURE 2-3   LWCI Enterprise Vision Statement

Customer Requirements

- High-quality machinery equipment
- Tight tolerance manufacturing equipment
- High reliability
- Low-cost equipment
- Digitally controlled machinery
- High-quality tooling
- Tight tolerance tooling

Customers

- U.S. auto industry (65%)
- U.S. electronics industry (25%)
- U.S. aerospace and defense industry (10%)

Core Competencies

- Machine tool & die design
- Production of machine tools & dies
- CAM design & production
- Design & production of electronic controllers

EXAMPLE FIGURE 2-4   LWCI Enterprise Profile

has been tasked to design and develop a new line of production machinery. The new system will be designated the LWCI 1600 series.

The division established a product-development team for the LWCI 1600 series project. The team consisted of representatives from Marketing, Engineering, Product Operations, Quality, Safety, Finance, and Procurement. The team also includes a representative from the Machine and Tool Division and Electronics Division. The mission of the product-development team is to use the Management 2000 IPPD process to develop the LWCI 1600.

This team reviewed the basic market considerations and determined that the best approach to acquiring market data was the survey and research method. This method was selected because it provided the broadest coverage, providing information from existing LWCI customers and those potential customers that were not currently using LWCI equipment. Each of these market elements was approached in a different way. Existing customers were surveyed by personal interviews conducted by LWCI field service representatives. A mail questionnaire, followed up with telephone calls, was used for other manufacturers not currently using LWCI equipment. The results of the market survey are contained in Example Figure 2-5.

The result of the survey indicated that there was a potential market interested in the new series of equipment. The potential customers could be quantified and their technical requirements described for the development process. Based upon the results of the market survey, the LWCI product-development team determined that there was

---

- 216 existing customers demonstrated an interest in the new series of equipment.

- A potential new market of 476 manufacturers are interested in the new equipment.

- A competitive price for the equipment would be $35-40K.

- Approximately 50% of the potential market will be replacing their equipment in the next three years.

- The following technical concerns were cited by the potential customers:

  - Timely delivery
  - Reliability (low MTBF)
  - Documentation and training
  - System compatibility and integration
  - Safety
  - Environmental concerns for hazardous materials
  - System digitally controlled
  - Good system support (field service reps)
  - Special tooling not required

- The marketing members of the team evaluated all the data and determined that the potential sales for the LWCI 1600 is between 200 and 250 units

---

EXAMPLE FIGURE 2-5   LWCI Market Research Results

sufficient interest and market potential to continue with the development process and build a work breakdown structure (WBS) for the new product.

NOTE

[1] Jackson Jr., Harry K. & Frigon, Normand L., 1994, *Management 2000*, pp. 344. New York: Van Nostrand Reinhold.

3

The Business Decision

IDENTIFYING A VIABLE NEW PRODUCT OR
SERVICE IS THE FIRST STEP TO WORLD CLASS
COMPETITIVENESS.

One of the first decisions that must be made in
the design and development of any new product or service is the
business decision. Is your new product or service project viable from
a business perspective? That business perspective is essentially one of
marketing, finance, and benchmarking. Each of these elements is a
decision point in the process of determining if you should continue
with this project. Figure 3-1 provides the model for the business
decision.

WORK BREAKDOWN STRUCTURE

Now that you have listened to the Voice of the Customer and understand more about your potential market, we can continue the decision making process. The next step in the process is translating what
we know of the Voice of the Customer and your new product or
service into a form upon which we can make financial, technical, and

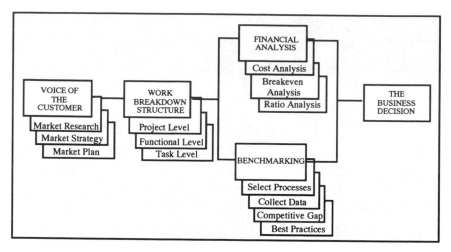

FIGURE 3-1   The Business Decision Process

benchmarking decisions. The Work Breakdown Structure (WBS) provides a framework to accomplish this. The WBS is used to estimate the costs of facilities, materials, equipment and labor. The Work Breakdown Structure is also a resource for inputs to benchmarking and the House of Quality. The WBS breaks down the overall product or service from its initial definition, taken from the VOC, into individual elements.

In this way, the tasks can be better defined on the basis of work elements and activities. The WBS provides for a better understanding of the scope of work involved in the new product or service. The WBS provides an outline that can be monitored, planned, and managed throughout the design and development process. It will also provide the basis for cost estimating and the acquisition or allocation of assets, such as facilities, equipment, materials, and personnel.

We will use the 3-level WBS described in Figure 3-2 to fully describe a design and development project. Depending on the complexity of your project, you can modify the number of levels in any WBS to coincide with your organization's needs and the scope of the design and development project.

The first level of the WBS relates to the integrated effort at the highest level and should not be related solely to any specific depart-

LEVEL	FUNCTION	DESCRIPTION
1	Project Level	Total design and development project consisting of all functional areas.
2	Functional Level	Describes the design and development requirements for each functional area of the project.
3	Task Level	Describes the individual task elements to be performed in each functional area.

FIGURE 3-2   Work Breakdown Structure Levels

ment or function. At this level, the WBS is used to describe the overall design and development project; it is the summation of all the efforts that will be required in the lower levels. Figure 3-3 demonstrates a typical Level 1 Work Breakdown Structure.

The Functional Level of the WBS provides a breakdown of the project level into homogeneous functional areas and provides the basis for assignment of project elements to specific departments or

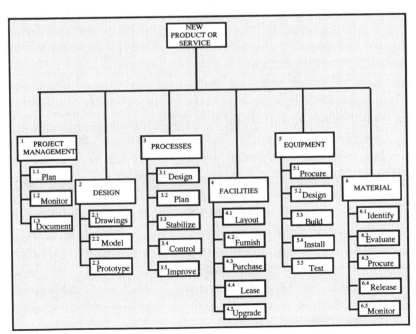

FIGURE 3-3   Typical Level 1 Work Breakdown Structure

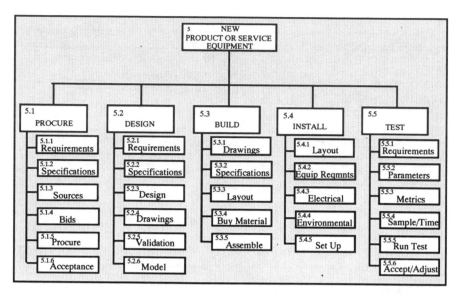

FIGURE 3-4   Typical Level 2 Work Breakdown Structure

individuals (depending on the size of your organization). Figure 3-4 demonstrates a typical Level 2 Work Breakdown Structure.

At the Task Level of the WBS, you will describe the work to be accomplished within each functional subtask of the Level 2 WBS. Be cautious when doing this; you should be describing homogeneous work elements, not minute jobs to be done by specific individuals. That would make this level of the WBS very large and unwieldy. Remember, the purpose of the WBS is to provide a basis for making financial, technical, and benchmarking decisions and as an input into Quality Function Deployment (QFD). Figure 3-5 demonstrates a typical Level 3 Work Breakdown Structure.

As indicated in each of the three Typical Work Breakdown Structures, a numbering system has been applied at each level. At the highest level, the numbering system corresponds to each functional level of the project. At the second level, these numbers are allocated down to the homogeneous work elements of the individual functional elements. In the lowest level, the numbers represent individual task elements. This same numbering system is then used in the project

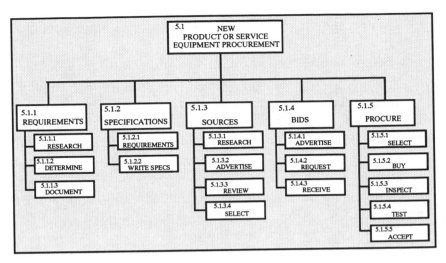

FIGURE 3-5   Typical Level 3 Work Breakdown Structure

management Gantt Chart for estimating costs and expenses. You will also see this same numbering system used in process flowcharting later in the book. This project numbering system provides an easy reference to coordinate the several elements in any management function (budgeting, milestone charts, and process analysis) and correlating these functions with the common measures of Quality, Cost, and Schedule (Q$S).

FINANCIAL DECISIONS

The financial decision to go forward with any new product or service is clearly the most critical of the business decisions. It is at this point that you will decide whether or not to proceed with your new project based upon your estimates of costs and profits. There are several questions to be answered in gathering the data to make this decision:

- ▶ What are the project development costs?
- ▶ What are fixed costs for your new product or service?

► What are the variable costs for your new product or service?

► What is the breakeven point?

► What is the expected return on the investment?

First, we need to form the basis for estimating the costs and providing the basic information to proceed with the evaluation of the financial decision. We have the basic information for this first cost element in the Work Breakdown Structure we have just completed. This provides us with a functional view of the product, to which we now add the time factors and planned expenditures. The WBS is transformed, using a Gantt Chart. As is demonstrated in Figure 3-6, the same numbering system used in the WBS is used to identify the tasks in the Gantt Chart. To this structure we then add the start and end dates for each subordinate task (milestones). This provides us with a form we can use to estimate the costs of labor, facilities,

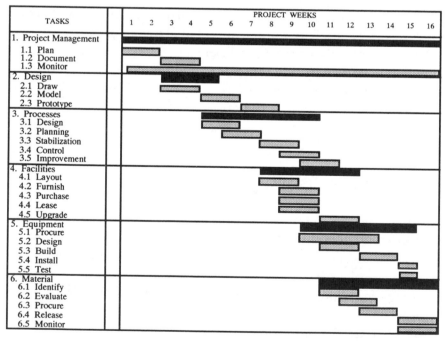

FIGURE 3-6   Gantt Chart Based Upon the WBS

equipment, and materials, as well as other cost elements as may be necessary.

In this Gantt Chart, the dark time bars represent the summary of the times required to complete the subordinate tasks. The gray lines represent individual tasks in each functional area for which individual time estimates can be made for start date and end date. In this example, the design and development process will require 16 weeks to complete. The project management functional element will continue for the complete design and development period, and subordinate tasks will start and finish during that period, ending on the 16th week. This information was accumulated from the lower level Gantt Charts that correlate with each functional area and level of the WBS.

Project Development Cost Estimate

The project cost estimate is very important since it forms the basis for all of our financial analysis. It is necessary to generate this cost estimate to determine if you have the finances available to complete the development project and to provide data to determine the other financial decision factors. The cost estimate, coupled with the project schedule (Gantt Chart), also allows you to monitor the project and to control costs and progress based upon this initial estimate. There are many methods for estimating project costs. We will use a basic method based upon the WBS and Gantt Chart. Most project management software packages provide the capability to perform this evaluation quickly and easily.

First, use the WBS and its associated Gantt Chart to obtain estimates of the scope of the project and the time and workhours required to complete the project. Use this knowledge to prepare a cost estimate based upon:

- ► The cost performance of past projects
- ► Inputs from each functional area defined in the WBS and Gantt Chart
- ► The appropriate budget for risk and contingencies

▶ A multiplier for overhead and other non-project costs
▶ The periodic (or unitized) and cumulative costs

These cost estimates can then be applied to the Gantt Chart as indicated in Figure 3-7. The costs here have been estimated based upon the weekly labor utilization with any appropriate multipliers (remember, labor costs you more than simple salary), the costs of facilities, equipment, and material. The costs for each week of the project are provided, as well as the cumulative costs.

In this cost estimate, the total development project costs are estimated to be $184,000 over a 16-week period. The project starts in Week One with a cost of $2,000 and ends on the 16th week with a

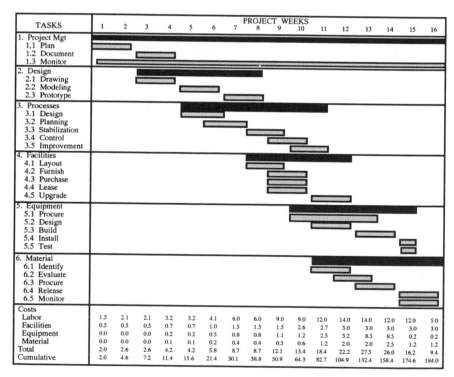

FIGURE 3-7   Development Project Cost Estimate

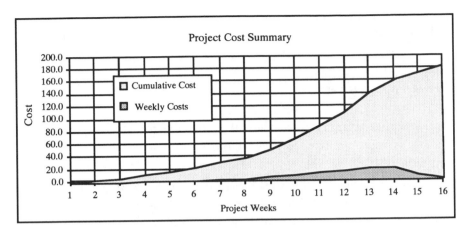

FIGURE 3-8   Landscape Graph of Project Costs

cost of $9,400. The highest costs are during the 11th through 14th weeks, peaking at $27,500 in the 13th week. This cost peak is due to the acquisition of equipment and materials during those periods. The proportion of costs over this period of time can be graphically demonstrated in Figure 3-8.

This type of graph can also be used to visualize the proportion of project cost for individual cost functions. This is demonstrated in

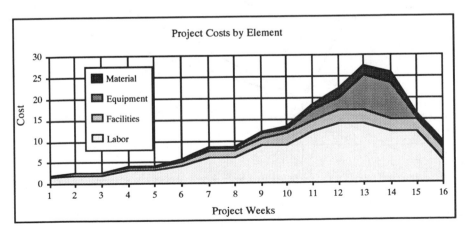

FIGURE 3-9   Project Costs by Cost Function

Figure 3-9. Notice that the most significant project costs are attributable to labor.

Breakeven Analysis

Breakeven analysis is an analytical technique for studying the relationships between fixed and variable costs and profits. Breakeven analysis is used in the financial community as a profit planning approach for selecting the optimum mix of costs and potential revenues to produce the highest profit. With this as the basis of breakeven analysis, we can easily appropriate it as a basic business decision making tool for the design and development of new products and services.

The nature of breakeven analysis is depicted in Figure 3-10, the basic breakeven chart. This chart demonstrates breakeven analysis on

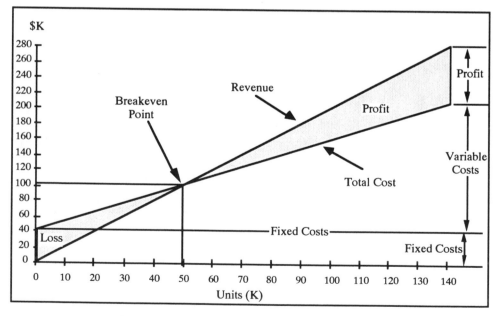

FIGURE 3-10   Basic Breakeven Analysis Chart

a unit's produced and sold basis. The number of units is shown on the horizontal axis (X-axis). Income and costs are measured on the vertical axes. The fixed costs are $40,000, represented by the horizontal line on the chart. Variable costs are estimated to be $1.20 per unit. Units are planned to be sold at $2.00 each.

Two critical factors in breakeven analysis are fixed costs and variable costs. Fixed costs are those costs that are incurred before the first item is produced. They are the basic costs of being in business that do not vary with the number of units sold or the revenue received. Variable costs are the costs of labor and materials required to produce a single product or service. Figure 3-11 provides examples of fixed and variable costs.

Breakeven analysis can be used in three distinct ways. In new product decisions to determine how large a sales volume will be needed for a product to break even; to study the effects of changes in practices, procedures, equipment, or technology on a product's prof-

FIXED COSTS	VARIABLE COSTS
Plant Expenses	Production Labor
Equipment	Production Materials
Interest	Sales Commissions
Salaries of staff	Product Delivery Costs
Salaries of executives	Product Packaging
Product Development Costs	Production Quality
Research	Shipping and Reveiving
General Office Expenses	

FIGURE 3-11   Examples of Fixed and Variable Cost

itability; and to analyze modernization and improvement programs based upon the tradeoff of fixed and variable costs. As we will use breakeven analysis for the design and development of new products and services, it will provide the following information vital to the financial decision.

- ► The breakeven point
- ► The projected profitability of the project
- ► The estimate of fixed and variable costs

In breakeven analysis, a linear relationship is generally assumed. The equation we will use to calculate the breakeven point is

$$\text{Breakeven Quantity} = \frac{\text{Fixed Cost}}{\text{Price} - \text{Variable Costs}}$$

The data we have developed to this point will provide a good example of the effective use of breakeven analysis for new product decisions. From Figure 3-8, the total development costs are $184,000. Assessing that all other fixed costs for the period of the analysis will be $66,000, the total fixed costs are $250,000. The variable cost for labor and material is assessed to be $7.50 per unit. The projected competitive sales price is $32.00 per unit (revenue). What then is the number of units that must be sold to break even?

$$Q = \frac{FC}{P - VC} \qquad Q = \frac{250,000}{32 - 7.50} \qquad Q = 10,204$$

Before this project can make any profit, 10,204 units must be sold. What, then, is the project's potential profitability? That can be demonstrated on the breakeven chart in Figure 3-12. Superimposed upon the breakeven chart is a table showing the relationships between Units Sold, Revenue, Operating Cost, and Operating Profit. These factors will be very useful when performing other kinds of financial analysis.

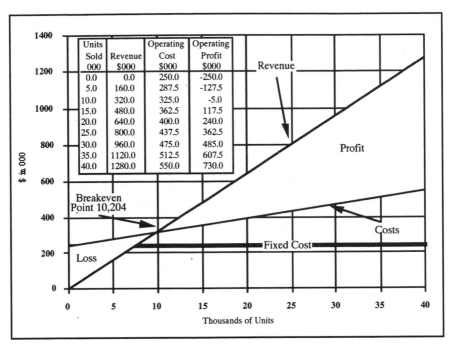

Units Sold 000	Revenue $000	Operating Cost $000	Operating Profit $000
0.0	0.0	250.0	-250.0
5.0	160.0	287.5	-127.5
10.0	320.0	325.0	-5.0
15.0	480.0	362.5	117.5
20.0	640.0	400.0	240.0
25.0	800.0	437.5	362.5
30.0	960.0	475.0	485.0
35.0	1120.0	512.5	607.5
40.0	1280.0	550.0	730.0

FIGURE 3-12   Breakeven Analysis for Units Sold

It is also useful to calculate breakeven analysis based upon value of sales, rather than units sold. This is the main method used for service industries, where units sold may not be a useful measure. The equation for Breakeven in Dollars is provided below:

$$ BEP \; \$ \; (D) = \frac{Fixed \; Costs}{1 - \dfrac{Variable \; Costs}{Revenue}} $$

Using this equation, you can then calculate your Breakeven Point in Dollars of Revenue. Assuming that during a period, a service firm's operating costs are $100,000, total sales are $800,000, and total variable costs are $600,000, applying the above equation to this data yields:

$$D = \frac{FC}{1 - \dfrac{VC}{R}} = \frac{\$100,000}{1 - \dfrac{\$600,000}{\$800,000}} = \frac{\$100,000}{.25} = \$400,000$$

In this instance, $400,000 in revenue would be required before the project would yield any profit. This method of calculating breakeven analysis is applicable to firms that provide services that cannot be readily described in the form of units sold. These are such activities as accounting, repair services, consulting, training, banking, and other activities where revenue is generated based upon services rendered, rather than units provided.

Return on Investment

Return on Investment is also known as Return on Total Assets (ROTA). This measure of profitability is based upon the "Dupont Equation." It measures the ratio of net profits to total company assets. For the purpose of the business decision in the design and development of new products and services, we will use two different ROI ratios. The first one used will be the traditional $ROI_{Company}$, which will measure the total company profitability with our new project. The second measure will allow us to evaluate the projected profitability of the new product or service. It is the $ROI_{Project}$.

$$ROI_{Company} = \frac{Net\ Profit\ After\ Taxes}{Total\ Assets}$$

$$ROI_{Project} = \frac{Net\ Profit\ After\ Taxes}{Total\ Assets}$$

The $ROI_{Company}$ utilizes factors taken from a company's income statements. This factor can then be compared to industry averages to determine a firm's comparative profitability. In the below example, a firm with $230,411 in net profits after taxes and $3,596,773 in total assets would have a $ROI_{Company}$ of 6.40%. The current industry average is 8.75%. The company therefore is not competitive in its profitability.

$$ROI_{Company} = \frac{\text{Net Profit After Taxes}}{\text{Total Assets}}$$

$$ROI_{Company} = \frac{\$230,411}{\$3,596,773} = 6.40\%$$

The $ROI_{Project}$ is taken directly from the projected values we used in determining the project's breakeven point. The BEP table in Figure 3-12 has been modified in Figure 3-13 below, to include a column for Net Profit After Taxes and Interest. This column was calculated simply by using a scaling factor on the Operating Profit column, to account for interest expense and taxes. The Resulting $ROI_{Project}$ is given below.

$$ROI_{Project} = \frac{\text{Net Profit After Taxes}}{\text{Total Assets}}$$

$$ROI_{Project} = \frac{\$379,600}{\$550,000} = 69.0\%$$

There are three questions you must answer to make the business decision for your new product or service:

- ► Will the project positively affect the company ROI?
- ► Is the Project ROI greater than the ROI from investments and projects with less or no risk (e.g., bank accounts and investments)?
- ► Does the Project ROI meet some established company standard for profitability?

Units Sold $000	Revenue $000	Operating Cost $000	Operating Profit $000	Net Profit $000
0.00	0.00	250.00	-250.00	-130.00
5.00	160.00	287.50	-127.50	-66.30
10.00	320.00	325.00	-5.00	-2.60
15.00	480.00	362.50	117.50	61.10
20.00	640.00	400.00	240.00	124.80
25.00	800.00	437.50	362.50	188.50
30.00	960.00	475.00	485.00	252.20
35.00	1120.00	512.50	607.50	315.90
40.00	1280.00	550.00	730.00	379.60

FIGURE 3-13   Calculations for Net Profits Based Upon BEP Estimates

BENCHMARKING

To this point, you have gathered a significant amount of information about your new product or service. You know what your market is and what is expected of you from the Voice of the Customer. The basic elements of your new venture are in a work breakdown structure, and you have a good estimate of the costs and profitability of the project. But there is still more information you need to make an informed business decision:

▶ What are your competitors doing?
▶ Who is the recognized best in class?
▶ What are the processes and practices of the best in class?
▶ How does your new product or service and its associated processes compare to the best in class?

To answer these questions, we will use a tool called benchmarking. Benchmarking is a systematic process for evaluating the products, services, and work processes of organizations that are recognized as representing the best practices for the purpose of comparison. You must benchmark your new product or service during the business decision phase to determine what you will need to accomplish to be competitive. As we will use benchmarking, it will encompass the benchmarking initially required for making the business decision and the continuous benchmarking needed to maintain a competitive position. There are three types of benchmarking:

► Internal Benchmarking
► Competitive Benchmarking
► Functional Benchmarking

Internal Benchmarking

Depending upon the size of your organization, processes may be performed in more than one location, department, or division. You may even be providing products and services in more than one country. In organizations such as this, the benchmarking process begins internally. The starting point for benchmarking is to determine what your best business practices are within your own organization. This does not assume that your current practices are the best in class, it is just a starting point.

The primary objective of internal benchmarking is to identify and define your current standards and to promote internal information sharing. Internal benchmarking assumes that the business practices and production processes in one part of an organization may be more effective than the work practices in another part of the company. Many organizations are able to realize immediate gains by identifying their best internal practices and applying that information to other parts of the company. This internal benchmarking knowledge is then used as a baseline for the subsequent research, using external (competitive and functional) benchmarking. Internal benchmarking also encourages employees to communicate across your internal organizational boundaries. This may be difficult at first, since some divisions and departments within a company can be very competitive.

The size of your organization will determine the efforts required for internal benchmarking. In large and diversified companies, the internal benchmarking activity may be large and complex. The internal benchmarking effort in these large organizations will follow the formal step-by-step procedure provided in this section. In smaller organizations, the internal benchmarking may be of limited scope and informal. The important points to remember in internal benchmarking are that you must collect all the information available on a product, service, or process, and that information needs to be free of organizational bias and internal competitiveness.

Competitive Benchmarking

Competitive benchmarking includes the research, identification, and description of the products, services, and processes of your direct competitors. The purpose of competitive benchmarking is to gather information that you can use to compare your new (or existing) product or service and its associated processes with your direct competitors and the best in class competitors. These two specific comparisons do not assume that your most direct competitor is the best in class. While it is your goal to always be the best in class, the strategic market segment for your new product or service may require you to start with a benchmark of only your immediate competitors. This is a market, financial, and technical consideration.

The information gathered from competitive benchmarking is used to position your new product or service within the marketplace. It will also provide information on the efforts (technical and financial) that will be required to design, develop, or improve your current processes to meet the needs of that market. This information is also valuable because the practices and procedures of your competitors affect the perception of your customers, suppliers, shareholders, and potential customers, all of whom will have a direct effect on the success of your new product or service.

You can anticipate difficulties when doing benchmarking among competitors. This in itself is not surprising. You must approach the issue of competitive benchmarking with caution and sensitivity. We all think of our competitors as "the enemy" and perfidious. Not unexpectedly, they may view you in the same way. To respond to this concern, you must accept the fundamental concept that benchmarking is different from traditional competitive analysis. You should approach those you wish to benchmark in a direct, up-front manner, with no hidden agendas. If you approach a competitor as an enemy, you will evoke the expected result. If you present your purpose and objectives in benchmarking to your competitor in a professional, honest, and forthright way, you will receive a professional, honest, and forthright reply. This will begin the benchmarking process based on respect and trust.

Your own fears and antagonistic attitudes are the greatest obstacle to partnering with your competitors in benchmarking. Do not allow these fears and attitudes to dissuade you from using this important tool. The possibilities and potential benefit from competitive benchmarking are realized when you gain experience in the process of dealing with your competitors. Contact with your competitors is only one resource you will be using for benchmarking. Some other resources are:

- ► Professional organizations
- ► Journals, periodicals and other publications
- ► Archives
- ► Benchmarking consultants

We will discuss these resources further during our step-by-step procedure for benchmarking.

Functional Benchmarking

Functional benchmarking is the identification of products, services and processes of organizations that are not your direct competitors. The objective of functional benchmarking is to identify practices of any organization that is recognized as the "best in class." Functional benchmarking is centered on the benchmarking of functional areas, such as manufacturing, engineering, management, human resources, and finance. Functional benchmarking, therefore, looks at generic activities, such as warehousing, rather than at Westinghouse's warehousing of electronic parts.

Functional benchmarking is focused on the generalized processes in any industry, rather than the specific business practices of a particular organization. Therefore, in a functional benchmarking effort, experts from your company's functional areas (engineering, production, management, support, etc.) limit their benchmarking investigation to their own areas of expertise. Functional benchmarking requires you to keep an open mind and, at times, to think in the abstract when considering the business practices of a company in another industry. You must keep in mind that you are looking for common process applications, rather than trying to critique the differences.

The Benchmarking Process

All three of these benchmarking approaches previously discussed apply directly to your new product or service. Benchmarking is also a continuous activity that is used in conjunction with an effective continuous measurable improvement (CMI) plan to keep your company competitive in the global marketplace. Now that you understand what benchmarking is, we will describe the benchmarking process in five steps.

1. Define the product, service, or process to be benchmarked
2. Form a benchmarking team
3. Identify benchmarking resources
4. Collect and analyze information
5. Take action

The benchmarking process must be well focused and defined before you start the process. Remember that benchmarking is performed for a specific product, service, or process. One of the most common failings of benchmarking is the collection of large amounts of data on many processes that are not focused on the project at hand. This strains your resources for benchmarking and complicates the analysis phase of your benchmarking. Determine who your internal customers are for benchmarking information, define their needs, and focus on acquiring the data needed to satisfy those requirements. Do not take the shotgun approach to benchmarking and collect all the data that is available from all sources. Focus on the well defined and structured needs of the functional areas of your organization that will use the benchmarking data. Now you must determine who within your organization will be the customer for benchmarking data and establish some benchmarking ground rules.

- ► Establish a clear purpose for your benchmarking efforts.
- ► Identify subjects to be benchmarked, based upon some critical need.
- ► Use measures that are as specific and as quantifiable as possible.
- ► Know and understand your own processes before proceeding.
- ► Know what companies legitimately represent the best practices.
- ► Prepare adequately for meetings with benchmarking partners.
- ► Be sure that your benchmarking target is reasonable and not too large to manage.

Step 1. Define the Product, Service, or Process to be Benchmarked

You actually started to answer this basic question when you began performing the market research for your new product or service. Market research is a valuable input to the benchmarking process. You have already received information from your potential customer and used that information to define your new product or service. Step 1 of the benchmarking process will provide three additional elements needed to successfully benchmark your product or service.

- ► Identify the product, service, or process to be benchmarked
- ► Identify your internal customer for benchmarking
- ► Identify critical process metrics (or critical success factors)

Identify the Product or Service to be Benchmarked   Using the work breakdown structure you developed earlier, break down the product or service into its contingent elements. Each of these processes that go into producing your new product or service is a candidate for benchmarking. For example, if you were to offer a new product that you were going to manufacture, some of the processes that you could consider benchmarking are:

- ► Production process
- ► Materials purchasing process
- ► Pricing process
- ► Materials management process (JIT)
- ► Quality program processes (SPC/SQC)
- ► Assembly sub-process
- ► Improvement process (DOE)
- ► Planning process (QFD)

The important point here is to break down the product or service into contingent processes to determine which of them are critical to your competitive position, then to select these processes for benchmarking. There may be several benchmarking efforts identified for an individual product or service. It is critical that you know and understand your own processes before you begin the benchmarking process and contact potential benchmarking partners. Knowing and understanding your process is also critical to identifying the critical metrics (sometimes called critical success factors) that you will use to decide what information to gather during benchmarking.

Identify Your Internal Customer for Benchmarking   This step is important because the internal customer that will use the benchmarking information must identify the specific information that is required from the benchmarking effort. Identifying the internal customers for benchmarking also identifies the benchmarking team members. Each internal functional area that requires benchmarking information should also be a member of the team and provide the needed support (time, talent, and material) to accomplish the benchmarking process.

Benchmarking should not be used as a substitute for market research, to test potential markets, or to find out what is going on in other companies. Your internal customers for benchmarking are the functional business areas that require the information to be competitive. These functional areas are directly responsible for such activities as designing, marketing, manufacturing, maintenance, budgeting, buying, billing, etc. They therefore should be looking for specific measures that they will require to make your product or service competitive.

The internal customer for your benchmarking effort should provide some very specific information on what they expect to acquire through the effort. For example, the internal customer for benchmarking information can take a broad subject, such as the need to optimize accounts receivable by improving billing cycles, and identify specific measures that are of interest for the benchmarking team, such as billing cycle time, billing voucher signature cycle, and computer software used in billing. Not only can the team member from the functional area of the company identify specific measures that are required, but they also have the technical and professional knowledge to determine the best format for the data, what measures should be used (cost, time, quality characteristic), and the specific companies or types of companies that should be included in the benchmarking effort.

Identify Critical Process Metrics (or Critical Success Factors)   In some benchmarking literature, these are also called critical success factors. We will use the critical process metric term to provide consistency with the process analysis parts of this book and to be analogous with other *Management 2000* texts. These are the measures that have a critical effect on the bottom line results of the business. Frequently, they are the same factors that are used to measure critical process elements. The same basic rule applies to this factor that applies to critical process elements, which states that they should be measures of Quality, Cost, and Schedule (Q$S).

These selected critical process metrics are the quantitative and qualitative information that you will seek to acquire during Step 3, Identify Benchmarking Resources, and collect during Step 4, Collect and Analyze Information. As you are identifying the critical process metrics for your benchmarking effort, it is important to be as specific as possible in your definitions and the metrics you select. This level of detail is important at every stage of the benchmarking process, but it is most critical at this stage because the definitions and metrics you select here will be used during the planning and throughout the benchmarking process.

Critical process metrics may occur at any level (or indenture) of a process. It is common to break these processes down into three levels of specificity. Each of these levels provides distinctly different metrics. Level 3 defines the broadest subject area for investigation, and this may be a department function or an overall production process. Level 2 is more specific than Level 1 because it is the next lower level of process and represents output that can be measured with averages and total numbers. Level 3 is the lowest level of process to be considered for benchmarking because it is at this level that we are dealing with specific processes for a specific functional area producing a good or service. Some examples of critical process metrics at each of these levels are provided in Figure 3-14.

Step 2. Form a Benchmarking Team

Now that you have identified your internal customers, you are ready to form your benchmarking team. In any organization, the stimulus for benchmarking or any other innovative activity must be supported by management. It is the management, after all, that must commission the benchmarking activity and form the team. Depending on the type of benchmarking to be accomplished, teams can be formed either cross-functionally or as natural work groups.

- ► **Internal Benchmarking Teams:** The team that is formed to accomplish internal benchmarking should be a cross-functional team representing the organization's leadership and representatives from all the processes to be benchmarked. A strong leader-

Benchmarking Process Level Level 1:	Process Metric

The Automobile Industry	Number of Automobiles
	    Manufactured
	Types of Automobiles
	    Manufacturerd
	Market Share by Units or Dollars

Human Resources Departments	Personnel Recruited Benefit Plans Budgets for Rewards and Recognition
Level 2:	
A Specific Model of Automobile	Number Produced Number of Warranty Returns Average Repairs During First 3 Years

Company Small Business Advocate	Percent of Business Awarded to
	    Small Business
	Total Value of Small Business
	    Contracts
	Number of Minority Small Business
	    Suppliers

Level 3:	
Drive Shaft Production Line	Scrap Rate Digital Control Systems Employed Process Yield
Accounts Receivable	Invoice Delay Time Receivables Outstanding Invoice Process Time Automated Systems Used Invoice Process Flow

FIGURE 3-14   Examples of Process Levels and Critical Metrics

ship presence on these teams may be necessary, to break down internal organizational barriers.

- ▶ **Competitive Benchmarking Teams:** Competitive benchmarking teams can be of both types, cross-functional and natural work teams. This is dependent upon the scope of the project and whether it is centric to a product (cross-functional) or a specific process (natural work group or cross-functional).
- ▶ **Functional Benchmarking Teams:** This form of benchmarking lends itself to a team of subject matter experts (SMEs) in the functional area (natural work team) to be benchmarked.

All team members should be trained in the benchmarking process and possess a good knowledge of benchmarking resources. The team members that are going to interface with other companies should be skilled and experienced individuals with good communications skills and capable of understanding the sensitivity and proprietary nature of the information they are gathering. Benchmarking teams are constructed in the same way that all total quality management (TQM) teams are formed and trained. There needs to be a team leader, a facilitator, and team members. The typical cross-functional benchmarking team may look something like this:

- ▶ The benchmarking project manager as the team leader
- ▶ A facilitator skilled in running effective meetings and the use of the management tools (7-MP) and technical tools (7-QC)
- ▶ One or more team members from the functional areas to be benchmarked
- ▶ Team members from supporting areas as required
  - ▶ Legal
  - ▶ Training
  - ▶ MIS
  - ▶ Clerical support
  - ▶ Senior management

Step 3. Identify Benchmarking Resources

This phase of the benchmarking process involves the identification of benchmarking partners (those companies that supply you with information), the formation of a benchmarking network, and the identification of benchmarking resources. When identifying potential benchmarking partners and resources, a direct person-to-person approach is the most successful. This personal form of dealing with your counterparts from other companies will yield dividends in improved access to information. Although personal contact with a benchmarking partner in another company will give the best and most current benchmarking information, there are other resources that are valuable. Some of these resources are trade and professional organizations, universities, research groups, government, and periodicals. Think about this information as a resource, a tool you can use to make your new product or service competitive or more competitive. In the longer term, the relationships you form during benchmarking and the resources you develop will be used as part of a continuous program to keep you competitive.

Forming Your Benchmarking Information Network   As you develop your contacts and resources for information over time, they will begin to form a working network of organizations, individuals, government and commercial activities, and others that grows into a network of resources. As you go about your benchmarking activities with these resources, you should build on their value over the long term. This network may develop over time to the point where you can locate the information you need with a high degree of effectiveness and efficiency. You should, therefore, take advantage of every opportunity to develop your benchmarking network.

A benchmarking network is a dynamic resource. Just as your benchmarking needs will change from project to project, so too will your network change. The benchmarking network will narrow the lists of contacts necessary to draw information to those that have already demonstrated a history of reliable information. This can greatly reduce the amount of time spent tracking leads, and you will not need to start every benchmarking activity from scratch. Remember that you are also an information resource to someone else in a benchmarking network, since, ideally, the relationships are reciprocal.

The purpose of establishing a benchmarking network is to provide a resource of information that works for you. While there are many other resources, we will discuss a benchmarking network which is clearly the most effective method to gather up-to-date information on processes and products. It is therefore worth the extra effort, time, and even some frustration to get your network established.

Information Resources   What are your resources for information? Information is everywhere; it is available to you from your daily business activities: as a member of many professional business organizations; as a reader of journals, periodicals and trade magazines; and from the benchmarking partners in your network. One of the challenges for you as a benchmarker is to build a list of valid benchmarking resources which is directly relevant to the product or service being benchmarked and which can be trusted to be valid. Valid resources tend to be accredited in some specific way, such as universities, government agencies, business and trade journals, professional societies, and registered or certified consultants. You should be very cautious of resources that cannot be substantiated because they possess low levels of validity.

You must have access to information for it to be useful to you. One of the difficulties in benchmarking is acquiring information from the resources you have identified. Several resources for identified best practices are listed below, and these are resources where you can acquire benchmarking information.

Winners   The organizations that have been recognized for product and service excellence are a credible and available resource for benchmarking information. In some instances, they are expected to share information as a condition of winning an award. Some of these award winning resources can be identified through:

The Malcolm Baldrige National Quality Award
United States Department of Commerce
Technology Administration

National Institute of Standards and Technology
Route 270 and Quince Orchard Rd.
Administration Building, Room A537
Gaithersburg, MD 20899

American Society for Quality Control (ASQC)
P.O. Box 3005
Milwaukee, WI 53201-3005

The Taguchi Award
American Supplier Institute, Inc.
17333 Federal Drive, Suite 220
Allen Park, MI 48101

State Quality and Productivity Awards
    Several states, such as California, Arizona, Massachusetts,
    Minnesota, New York, North Carolina, and Indiana, have
    established awards similar to the Malcolm Baldrige National
    Quality Award.

Best Manufacturing Practices Program
U.S. Department of the Navy
2101 Crystal Plaza Arcade
Suite 271
Arlington, VA 22217-5660

Professional Associations   There are many associations that represent virtually every professional discipline and many that represent specific business interests. These organizations are a valuable resource for benchmarking information. In some instances, they can provide information directly to members upon request. Their national and regional meetings, conferences, and congresses are valuable sources of information and opportunities for forming your network. Some of the more prominent of these professional organizations are:

American Society for Quality Control
P.O. Box 3005
Milwaukee, WI 53201-3005

American Management Association
135 West 50th Street
New York, NY 10020

American Statistical Association (ASA)
1429 Duke Street
Alexandria, VA 22314-3402

American Supplier Institute, Inc. (ASI)
17333 Federal Drive, Suite 220
Allen Park, MI 48101

Council for Continuous Improvement (CCI)
2107 North First Street, Suite 680
San Jose, CA 95131

GOAL/QPC
13 Branch Street
Methuen, MA 01844

Institute of Industrial Engineers (IIE)
25 Technology Park/Atlanta
Norcross, GA 30092

International Benchmarking Clearing House
American Productivity & Quality Center
123 North Oak Lane
Houston, TX 77024-7797

Consultants   This resource is especially valuable to mid-sized and small businesses that may not have the internal assets to perform benchmarking of their products and services. Consultants often specialize in providing state-of-the-art information regarding specific functional areas or industries. Reputable consultants are specializing in benchmarking services that include identification of best-in-class practices and as members of benchmarking networks. These companies can provide benchmarking services directly or, in some cases, form benchmarking associations for information exchange by its members. It would be inappropriate for us to list for-profit consultants in this text. They can be identified as part of your network through the professional organizations and their journals, periodicals, and reports.

There are many other award winners and professional organizations that may be good resources for benchmarking information and networking opportunities. They are too numerous to mention all of them here. The above list provides a starting point and indicates the types of organizations that will be useful to you. One caution here is that specificity is important. Do not assume that because a company is an award winner in one category that it is a good benchmarking resource in your area of interest. A winner of the Malcolm Baldrige National Quality Award is not necessarily the best of class for benchmarking cost accounting processes. And winners of the Taguchi Award may not be the best candidates for benchmarking the marketing process. The best resources for specific areas such as this are the applicable award winners and professional organizations.

Other Sources of Benchmarking Information   To this point, we have discussed direct resources for benchmarking best-in-class practices and processes. However, there are other useful resources that can provide information directly or help you locate best-in-class companies. The following is a partial list of these potential resources:

► **Washington Information Directory:** A guide to information resources, both federal and private. The directory provides a good overview of the names and telephone numbers of key contacts in government organizations. Published by the Congressional Quarterly and available in most libraries and from commercial sources.

► **Annual Reports:** Annual reports are usually distributed free of charge and can be obtained from the companies upon request. The U.S. Securities and Exchange Commission is responsible for maintaining files of annual reports. Contact the SEC at 1100 L Street NW, Washington, DC 20549.

► **Freedom of Information Act:** The Freedom of Information Act can be used to acquire information on any contracts organizations have with the federal government. These documents can provide useful information on organizational structure, technologies, production capabilities, and strategic direction. The information will not contain any competitive bid or financial data. Point of contact is The Freedom of Information Clearing House, Suite 700, 2000 P Street NW, P.O.Box 19367, Washington DC 20036.

- ▶ **U.S. Industrial Outlook:** A document published annually by the Department of Commerce. It contains the annual, five-year, and long-term projections for hundreds of major companies. It can be purchased from the U.S. Government Printing Office, Washington DC 20402.

- ▶ **Cooperative Research Opportunities at NIST:** This document lists the names and locations of experts in the field of standards and measures and is an excellent resource in the area of manufacturing, engineering, and computer sciences. Available from the National Institute of Standards and Technology at Route 270 and Quince Orchard Rd., Administration Building, Room A537 Gaithersburg, MD 20899

- ▶ **Consultants and Consultants Organizational Directory:** This directory lists thousands of consultants in most professional fields. It is available commercially from Gale Research.

- ▶ **Encyclopedia of Associations:** This encyclopedia contains the names and addresses of 15,000 associations and professional societies. It is available commercially from Gale Research.

- ▶ **World Guide to Trade Organizations:** The guide contains the names and locations of international trade organizations. It is available commercially from R. R. Bowker.

- ▶ **Standard Periodical Directory:** This is a thorough directory of periodicals. Available from Oxbridge Communications.

- ▶ **Business Rankings:** Thousands of businesses ranked by category, according to performance. It is available commercially from Gale Research.

- ▶ **International Trade Commission (ITC) Reports:** The ITC maintains a database of foreign companies with which U.S. companies are doing business. They also publish reports that cover many subjects and disciplines. Contact ITC at 701 E Street NW, Washington DC 20436.

Just as with award winners and professional associations, this list could fill this book. The above information is a starting point for your data gathering efforts in benchmarking.

Step 4. Collect and Analyze Information

Please, <u>please</u> do not rush to this phase of benchmarking. It is absolutely critical to successful benchmarking that, before you collect and analyze the first bit of data, you: 1) know and understand your processes; 2) have determined the critical elements of these processes; 3) have defined the data elements (critical process metrics) you need to gather; 4) have properly established your benchmarking team; and 5) have established your network of benchmarking partners and identified resources that will provide you with that information. If you have not accomplished this, **STOP** and go back to Step 1.

If you have accomplished all of the above, you are now ready to collect and analyze information. The first step in collecting data is to plan your data acquisition and management requirements. Before you make the first contact, you should have clearly documented exactly what data you need to collect, from where you are going to collect it, and how you are going to manage the data once you have acquired it. Using all of the resources that you developed during Step 3, you can now collect information on the critical process metrics. The following methods of collecting benchmarking information can be used.

Personal Contact

Site visits are the most rewarding experience of benchmarking. These personal meetings with the members of your benchmarking network allow you to acquire information firsthand on site where you can see, feel, and taste what your benchmarking partner is doing. This type of data acquisition has several advantages. First, site visits and personal interviews always yield higher quality, and more detailed, information. Second, you have the opportunity to see the work process in action. Third, personal meetings are more likely to result in long-term relationships with your benchmarking partner than other forms of contact.

Opportunities to gather information through personal contact also occur at conferences, shows, conventions, and professional society meetings. This type of meeting is also good for network building as well as collecting information. When attending these events, you should know what benchmarking contacts you wish to make and how you will derive information from them. Plan your schedule at the meeting to coincide with these requirements. Personal contact yields the best benchmarking information. However, it is time consuming and costly.

Gathering information over the telephone is also a valuable method of personal contact. The caller can contact a wide variety of potential benchmarking resources within a few minutes and with minimal expense. With some training, employees can become skilled interviewers and develop a high degree of effectiveness in their information gathering skills. Just as with other types of data collecting activities, telephone interviews must be well planned and be conducted using a specific format for the data that is desired. Telephone interviewers must be sufficiently prepared to deal with people. Telephone interviews are especially effective when large numbers of contacts will be made over a wide geographical area. The drawback in conducting telephone interviews is time, because the individuals you are calling may not be willing to spend a significant amount of time on the phone and they may be interrupted several times.

Surveys   These surveys are not unlike the market research surveys you sent to your potential customers. They have a different purpose and will be sent to a different sample of people, but the basic rules remain the same:

- Keep your survey as short as possible
- Avoid lengthy response requirements
- Provide a stamped, self-addressed envelope for response
- Identify yourself (individually) and how you can be reached
- Design your survey for easy data transfer

You should expect a low yield from these surveys. Surveys do not allow for follow-up questions or provide the quality of information that personal contact will provide.

Research This form of data acquisition takes advantage of information that is already available from archives, publications, universities, and professional societies. Most of these resources of information are readily identifiable and the information is easily accessible. The advantage of these resources is the ease with which you can collect the data and put it into a usable format for your benchmarking activity. The drawbacks may be that the data available was not collected for your specific purposes and there may be a lot of material to review to extract the data you need. You are collecting data on specific, critical process measures. These measures may not be represented in the research resources.

Consultants The use of consultants can be a valuable method of benchmarking data collection. Many consultants specialize in specific industries or functional areas. They have already established networks and resources for data collection. This may be an especially valuable method since a reputable consultant may have up-to-date information and the ability to perform analysis of that data relative to your benchmarking needs.

Analysis We finally have arrived at the point that too many benchmarkers begin with—the analysis of benchmarking information. If you have planned your benchmarking effort well, properly established your network, and thoroughly utilized your benchmarking resources, the analysis of the resulting information will fall into place readily. If you have failed to perform the preliminary steps properly, you will find yourself with a mass (or mess) of data that may not be relevant to your critical process metric and will be difficult to assemble, organize, and evaluate.

Organize your data around the objectives of your benchmarking effort and the critical process metrics that you selected. This information should be arranged to coincide with the three levels of process

FACTORS AFFECTING OVERALL PRODUCTION PROCESS YIELD					
COMPANY	MATERIAL SCRAP RATE %	MATERIAL JIT DELIVERIES %	EQUIPMENT DOWN TIME %	EMPLOYEE TRAINING LEVEL HRS	YIELD UNITS PER SHIFT
YOUR COMPANY	3.7	97	7	4	7190
COMPANY A	2.7	99	3	16	7500
COMPANY B	3.1	98	5	6	7345
COMPANY C	3.3	98	6	8	7268

FIGURE 3-15   Benchmarking Process Level 1 Analysis Matrix

indenture previously discussed. This will provide the analyst with a clear view of the performance gaps at each level and the specific practices of your benchmarking partners that are contributing to that gap. A matrix form of data table lends itself to this analysis, as indicated in Figures 3-15 for Benchmarking Level 1, 3-16 for Level 2, and 3-17 for Level 3.

FACTORS AFFECTING EQUIPMENT DOWN TIME					
COMPANY	EQUIPMENT FAILURE RATE %	MEAN TIME TO REPAIR HRS	PREVENTIVE MAINT HOURS	AVERAGE EQUIPMENT AGE YEARS	EQUIPMENT DOWN TIME %
YOUR COMPANY	3.7	1.5	7	7.5	7
COMPANY A	2.7	0.25	3	2.5	3
COMPANY B	3.1	1.5	5	6.5	5
COMPANY C	3.3	1.25	6	7	6

FIGURE 3-16   Benchmarking Process Level 2 Analysis Matrix

FACTORS AFFECTING MEAN TIME TO REPAIR (THE REPAIR PROCESS)					
COMPANY	TYPE OF EQUIPMENT	REPAIRS BY LINE WORKERS %	LEVEL OF OF LINE REPAIR	MAINT EMPLOYEE TRAINING HRS	MEAN TIME TO REPAIR HRS
YOUR COMPANY	BAKER MODEL 1985-1	0	BOARD LEVEL REPLACE	80	1.5
COMPANY A	DIGITAL MODULAR MODEL 1992	75	REMOVE REPLACE MODULE	40	0.25
COMPANY B	BAKER MODEL 1985-4	0	ASSEMBLY REPAIR ON LINE	80	1.5
COMPANY C	BAKER MODEL 1985-1	5	BOARD LEVEL REPLACE	80	1.25

FIGURE 3-17   Benchmarking Process Level 3 Analysis Matrix

Draw Conclusions   The goal of benchmarking for the design and development of new products and services is to provide a baseline for the competitive requirements of your processes. Overall benchmarking analysis provides an understanding of the activities of other organizations (best in class) to be used in the improvement of your processes. The challenge is to draw relevant conclusions that will result in recommendations to improve your competitive position. Remember, the conclusions you draw must have a value added effect upon your process (Q$S).

The conclusions you draw from the benchmarking process should clearly be analogous to your internal processes, provide insight to your strengths and weaknesses, and determine the performance gap between you and world class competitors. This evaluation will provide you with the scope of the effort that will be necessary for you to be a competitor. At this point, you may need to return to the market analysis, work breakdown structure, and financial analysis to determine the business decision impact of your benchmarking discoveries.

The conclusions that can be drawn from the above benchmarking process analysis matrices are apparent. In Figure 3-15, the production process metrics of yield are being affected by the gap in equipment down time. Figure 3-16 then demonstrates that equipment down time is affected by mean time to repair; here we also have a significant performance gap. At the lowest level, in Figure 3-17, we see that in the best-in-class organization, 75% of the repair is performed by on-line personnel and that the associated equipment is new and modular. We also see that the training required to maintain this equipment is significantly less than for the other types. This makes the conclusions clear; however, can you afford new equipment? What effect will this have on revenue given the cost of equipment, improved yield, and reduced cost of repair and training?

Step 5. Take Action

This is the least complicated and most straightforward step of benchmarking. The reason for this goes directly to Step 1; the purpose for starting a benchmarking process is the desire to be competitive and change. Benchmarking is an action oriented process that leads to change. Now it becomes a question of implementing the change.

- ► Document your findings. A well documented report summarizing your findings is an important device to insure implementation.
- ► Identify specific actions that are to be taken.
- ► Quantify the effects of these actions on your competitive position.
- ► Recycle the benchmarking process on a continuous basis.

KEY POINTS

The Work Breakdown Structure

The WBS is used to estimate the costs of facilities, materials, equipment, and labor. The work breakdown structure is also a resource for inputs to benchmarking and the House of Quality. The WBS breaks down the overall product or service from its initial definition, taken from the VOC, into individual elements. In this way, the tasks can be better defined on the basis of work elements and activities. The WBS provides for a better understanding of the scope of work involved in the new product or service. The WBS provides an outline that can be monitored, planned, and managed throughout the design and development process.

The Financial Decision: There are several questions to be answered in making the financial decision:

- ► What are the project-development costs?
- ► What are fixed costs for your new product or service?
- ► What are the variable costs for your new product or service?
- ► What is the breakeven point?
- ► What is the expected return on investment?

The Project Cost Estimate: The project cost estimate is very important; it forms the basis for all of our financial analysis. It is necessary to generate this cost estimate to determine if you have the finances available to complete the development project and to provide data to decide the other financial decision factors. The cost estimate, coupled with the project schedule (Gantt Chart), also allows you to monitor the project and to control costs and progress based upon this initial estimate. First, use the WBS and its associated Gantt Chart to obtain estimates of the scope of the project and the time and workhours it will require to complete the project. Then use this information to prepare the cost estimate.

Breakeven Analysis: Breakeven analysis is an analytical technique for studying the relationships between fixed and variable costs and profits. Breakeven analysis is used in the financial community as a profit planning approach for selecting the optimum mix of costs and potential revenues to produce the highest profit. With this as the basis of breakeven analysis, we can easily appropriate it as a basic business decision making tool for the design and development of new products and services.

ROI: Return on Investment (ROI) is also known as Return on Total Assets (ROTA). This measure of profitability is based upon the "Dupont Equation." It measures the ratio of net profits to total company assets. For the purpose of the business decision in the design and development of new products and services, we will use two different ROI ratios. The first one used will be the traditional $ROI_{Company}$, which will measure the total company profitability with our new project. The second measure will allow us to evaluate the projected profitability of the new product or service; it is the $ROI_{Project}$.

Benchmarking: Benchmarking provides you with several key factors required to compete in the marketplace.

- ► What are your competitors doing?
- ► Who is the recognized best in class?
- ► What are the processes and practices of the best in class?
- ► How does your new product or service and its associated processes compare to the best in class?

EXAMPLE

Work Breakdown Structure

Based upon the marketing research accomplished in Chapter 2, the next step for the team is to develop a work breakdown structure for the project. This work breakdown structure would provide information on the technical requirements, facilities and equipment, and the budget needs of the project. The team reviewed all options available to them for the development of the new equipment and developed the work breakdown structure in Example Figure 3-1.

The team determined that there were five elements in the first level of the WBS. These five elements were project management, design, processes, equipment, and materials. The facilities element was omitted because the existing facilities were adequate and the project could be developed off shift, requiring no new or dedicated facilities. The team then considered the functional and task level of each of the

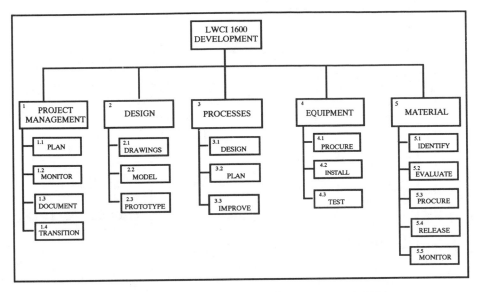

EXAMPLE FIGURE 3-1   LWCI 1600 First Level WBS

WBS elements. Examples of these lower level WBS are provided in Example Figures 3-2 and 3-3.

The team then could use these work breakdown structures to ascertain the requirements for the new product and its budget requirements. This prepared the way for the financial decision.

The Financial Decision

The development team is now ready to evaluate the project costs, breakeven point, and estimated profitability. The first step they took was to develop a Gantt Chart for the development project and use it to estimate the development costs. The resulting Gantt Chart, with the associated cost estimates, is provided in Example Figure 3-4.

Breakeven analysis is the next step in making the financial decision. In Example Figure 3-4, the LWCI team calculated the development costs for the project; when performing breakeven analysis, the fixed and variable costs of production must also be used. LWCI has

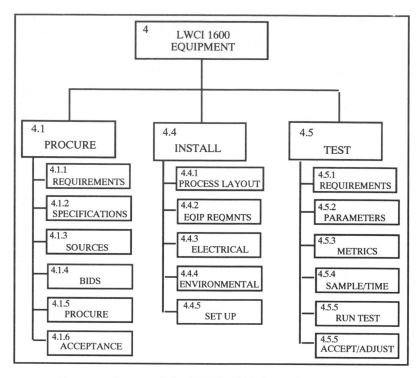

EXAMPLE FIGURE 3-2   LWCI 1600 Second Level WBS

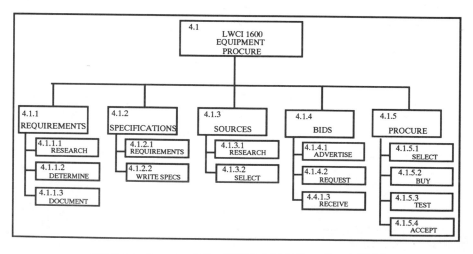

EXAMPLE FIGURE 3-3   LWCI 1600 First Level WBS

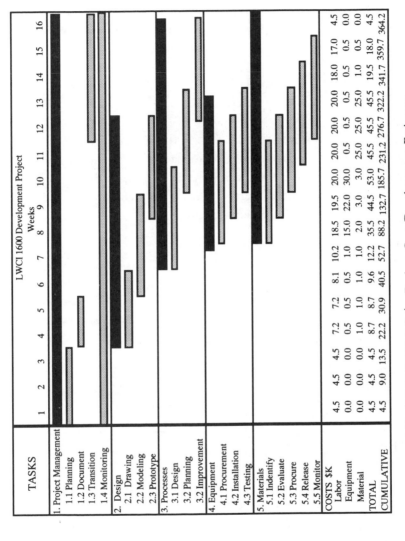

EXAMPLE FIGURE 3-4   Project Cost Development Estimate

directed the team to recoup the costs of development within three years. The team decided to calculate the breakeven point using the development costs as a part of the fixed costs. The fixed and variable costs were calculated using the spreadsheet in Example Figure 3-5.

The team then proceeded to perform breakeven analysis. They first calculated the breakeven point using a price of $37,500 for the LWCI.

$$ Q = \frac{FC}{P - VC} = \frac{667.70}{37.5 - 17.75} \qquad Q = 33.8 \approx 34 \text{ units} $$

The breakeven point for the LWCI 1600 is, therefore, 34 units. The breakeven analysis chart was then formulated in Example Figure 3-6. The associated data table is presented in Example Figure 3-7. The new product-development team was able to determine several key decision factors from the breakeven analysis:

- ► The breakeven point is 34 units
- ► The total expected sales of 250 units are greater than the breakeven point
- ► Total revenue at 250 units is expected to be $9,375,000
- ► Total operating cost at 250 units is expected to be $5,105,200
- ► Operating Profit at 250 units is expected to be $4,269,800

FIXED COSTS	$K	VARIABLE COSTS	$K
Salaries	$14.50	Production Labor	$1.75
Facilities	$146.50	Production Materials	$12.50
Materials	$60.00	Product Delivery	$1.00
Equipment	$65.00	Sales & Service	$2.50
Development	$364.20		
G&A	$17.50		
TOTAL FC	$667.70	TOTAL VC	$17.75

EXAMPLE FIGURE 3-5   LWCI 1600 Fixed and Variable Costs

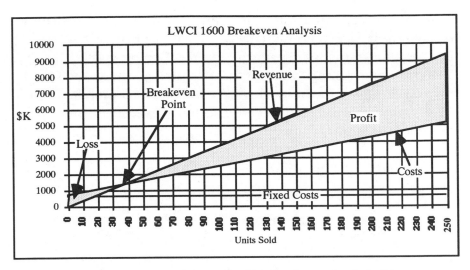

EXAMPLE FIGURE 3-6　LWCI 1600 Breakeven Analysis Chart

K Units Sold	Revenue $K	Operating Cost $K	Operating Profit $K	K Units Sold	Revenue $K	Operating Cost $K	Operating Profit $K
0	0	667.7	-667.7	130	4875	2975.2	1899.8
10	375	845.2	-470.2	140	5250	3152.7	2097.3
20	750	1022.7	-272.7	150	5625	3330.2	2294.8
30	1125	1200.2	-75.2	160	6000	3507.7	2492.3
40	1500	1377.7	122.3	170	6375	3685.2	2689.8
50	1875	1555.2	319.8	180	6750	3862.7	2887.3
60	2250	1732.7	517.3	190	7125	4040.2	3084.8
70	2625	1910.2	714.8	200	7500	4217.7	3282.3
80	3000	2087.7	912.3	210	7875	4395.2	3479.8
90	3375	2265.2	1109.8	220	8250	4572.7	3677.3
100	3750	2442.7	1307.3	230	8625	4750.2	3874.8
110	4125	2620.2	1504.8	240	9000	4927.7	4072.3
120	4500	2797.7	1702.3	250	9375	5105.2	4269.8

EXAMPLE FIGURE 3-7　LWCI 1600 Breakeven Analysis Data Table

With this information, the team is prepared to evaluate the Return of Investment for the Project ($ROI_{Project}$) and compare that figure to the overall Return on Investment for the Company ($ROI_{Company}$). Using a simple scaling factor for state, federal, and local taxes, and the cost of money (interest), the net yield from this project will be 57% of the operating profit. These calculations were performed with the following result.

$$\text{Net Profit} = \text{Operating Profit} - \text{Taxes and Interest}$$
$$\text{Net Profit} = \$4,269,800 - \$2,006,806 = \$2,262,994$$

$$ROI_{Project} = \frac{\text{Net Profit}}{\text{Total Assets}} = \frac{\$2,262,994}{\$5,105,200} = .44$$

The expected ROI for the project was then compared to the overall company ROI, the return that could be expected from risk free investments and the industry standard. The current ROI for the company is .37, and company executives have established that level as the company standard. The machine tool industry ROI is currently .32, and the yield on risk free investments is .14. From these factors, the product-development team was able to make the following determinations:

► This project will positively effect the company ROI.
► This project ROI will exceed the current company standard (.44 > .37).
► The ROI for this project exceeds the yield for risk free investments (.44 > .14).
► The ROI for this project exceeds industry standards (.44 > .32).

Benchmarking

The team then turned its attention to benchmarking. The team needed to determine several elements of information from benchmarking: the technology being used by competitors, innovative production processes, and competitive pricing. The team needed to use this information to answer some specific questions:

- ► Can the LWCI 1600 be technologically competitive?
- ► Can we build the LWCI 1600 more cost-effectively than the competition?
- ► Can we challenge the competition in price and product?

Defining the Products, Services, and Processes to be Benchmarked

Identify the Product or Process

LWCI 1600 series production equipment is a high-volume industrial production machine that is digitally controlled and can be used for production in any industry requiring cutting and shaping of sheet metal parts. Due to the nature of this piece of equipment and its high volume and size, there are only six companies worldwide that produce this type of machine. The team will benchmark the LWCI 1600 against the equipment and processes of these companies.

Resources

The team used their knowledge of the industry, the annual reports of the companies, industry periodicals, marketing information (brochures), and information from the American Society for Quality Control (ASQC), the American Supplier Institute (ASI), the Institute of Industrial Engineers (IIE), and their own field service representatives that frequently visit many different production plants frequently.

Benchmarking Customer

The primary customer for this information will be the LWCI 1600 design team. Additionally, the information can be used within the LWCI organization to improve processes and determine future equipment needs.

Critical Process Metrics

Based upon the needs of the customer as reported in the market survey, the following metrics were selected for benchmarking.

- Control technology
- Mean time between failure
- Mean time to repair
- System cost
- System yield
- System scrap rate

LWCI then formed a benchmarking team (Step 2), identified their benchmarking resources (Step 3), and collected and analyzed the resulting benchmarking data (Step 4). The team then determined that the company could take the appropriate action to be competitive in the selected marketplace with the new product.

The Business Decision

Based upon the information provided by the market survey, the work breakdown structure, the financial analysis, and the benchmarking process, the team decided this was a viable product and recommended that LWCI pursue the project.

4

Integrating Product Development

> CONCURRENT ENGINEERING IS A PHILOSOPHY
> THAT CALLS FOR PARALLEL AND INTEGRATED
> DEVELOPMENT OF PRODUCTS, SERVICES, AND
> PROCESSES.

Concurrent Engineering (CE) is the philosophy needed for developing products and services for the marketplace today and in the future. The process for implementing the CE philosophy is the Management 2000 Integrated Product and Process Development (IPPD) Process. This process uses vertical and cross-functional teamwork and the structured method of Quality Function Deployment as the implementing tools. The goal of the IPPD process is to:

► Reduce cycle time from concept to delivery
► Reduce costs for developing and producing products and services
► Minimize design changes after design release
► Improve quality of products and services, as measured by the customers

It is also the goal of the IPPD process that these improvements will create a competitive advantage by providing products and services of the highest quality, meeting all of the customers' requirements and expectations at the lowest cost. The IPPD process consists of four phases:

- ► Identifying the opportunity
- ► Making the business decision
- ► Detail design
- ► Production

In Chapter 2 we described how to identify an opportunity for a new or improved product or service. In Chapter 3 we learned how to evaluate an opportunity and make the business decision whether or not to pursue the opportunity. In this chapter we learn the details of the CE philosophy and how to build the design team to implement the IPPD process.

CONCURRENT ENGINEERING

Concurrent Engineering (CE) is "the earliest possible integrating of the overall company's knowledge, resources, and experience in design, development, marketing, manufacturing, and sales into creating successful new products, with high quality and low cost, while meeting customer expectations."[1] This is the philosophy that is implemented in the IPPD Process by Quality Function Deployment (QFD).

Experience has repeatedly proven that CE enables a manufacturer to design products and services in less than half the time of those who do not use CE. This shortens the design cycle time and gives the enterprise a distinct competitive advantage. A manufacturer using CE can support a smaller volume, a shorter lifetime, and a larger number of different products. This, in turn, enables the company to focus products on different segments of the marketplace.

The majority of the profits occurs in the early part of the product life cycle. IPPD enables you to turn over products much faster, retir-

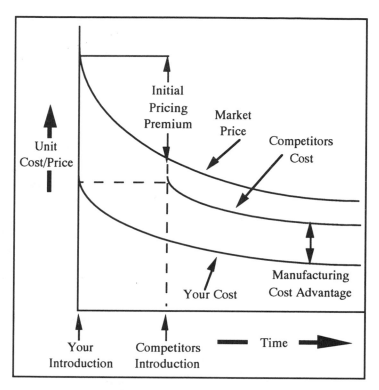

FIGURE 4-1   Cost/Price Advantage Curve

ing them at the optimum profitability. Products can be replaced by newer offerings, that are even more responsive to the customers' demands, with newer and lower cost technology.

In addition to the shorter cycle time for the product development process, CE ensures the new products meet the customers' expectations with a high level of quality and proceed competitively. There are no design errors to correct and no need to reengineer the product.

Early entrants can enjoy premium pricing and cost advantages, as indicated in Figure 4-1.[2] The early introduction of products and services also provides advantages in increased sales volume and market share (Figure 4-2).[3] This is how IPPD enables you to thrive in today's marketplace.

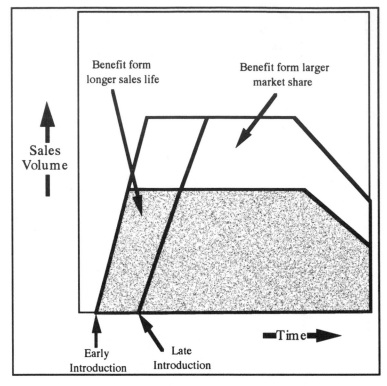

FIGURE 4-2   Benefits From Early Introduction Of Products

Elements of Concurrent Engineering

Concurrent Engineering is a systematic approach to the simultaneous and integrated design of products and processes. This includes manufacturing, testing, and after-sales support. This philosophy is a concerted effort by the enterprise. It involves teamwork, vertical and horizontal communication, commitment, culture, customer satisfaction, competitiveness, and attention to manufacturing, testing, and support issues early in the IPPD process.

There are several parallel design activities that must be accomplished during the IPPD process. Collectively, these are referred to as DFX:

► Design for Performance (DFP)
► Design for Manufacturability And Assembly (DFM/DFMA)
► Design for Testability (DFT)
► Design for Serviceability
► Design for Compliance (DFC)
► Etc.

The requirement is to recognize the need to account for the various phases of design, production, use, and post-sales support throughout the IPPD process. To provide for these requirements, they need to be defined at the beginning of the IPPD project and provided for through Quality Function Deployment.

Design for Performance

Design for performance is ensuring that the design satisfies all of the customers' expectations about the performance of the product or service. This includes human factors, reliability, maintainability, and availability.

DFP requires a detailed understanding of the customers' requirements and motivation to purchase a product or service. A product or product feature that does not perform a useful function is a useless product or feature. The customer is the only one who can assess whether a product or feature is useful. It is that assessment that initiates the decision process to purchase your product or service.

Understanding what the customer values is needed to ensure that the optimum balance is achieved among the required, spoken, unspoken, and exciter features. Functions that engineers think make a product more powerful may be viewed by customers as introducing unnecessary complexity. Additional functions, if they are the right ones, can, on the other hand, give your product or service a competitive advantage. This can be a trap, however, if the added features increase the difficulty of producing, verifying, delivering, operating, and servicing your product. This is the first of many reasons for using the IPPD process to implement CE through Quality Function Deployment. This ensures optimization of DFP collaboratively with the other design requirements.

Design for Manufacturability and Assembly

DFM and DFMA are the same thing. This is developing a design "using the minimum number of parts in the product (consistent with other tradeoffs), facilitating error free assembly, using standard components whenever possible, and fitting the product design into the process that will be used to produce it."[4] The purpose of DFM is to develop a design that is easy to build error free. This means keeping it simple. The principle of DFM is to simplify set-up and assembly operations. This shortens cycle times, reduces inventory levels, and reduces opportunities for errors.

While DFP focuses on the customer, DFM/DFMA is primarily for the benefit of the enterprise. Increased yields reduce scrap rates. Shortened cycle times improve schedules, work in process, and inventory turns and reduce manufacturing cost. The simplified assembly also provides post-sales benefits in reduced warranty and repair costs. The benefits of DFM are indirect for the customer. They may include survival for the manufacturer.

Design for Testability

The DFP and DFM efforts are not successful unless the functions and quality for the product can be verified by testing. In design for testability (DFT), automated testing, built-in test, and other techniques facilitating verification of performance are cost-effectively optimized. As in DFM, this is for the benefit of the enterprise. The customers only care about the end result, so DFT also has only indirect benefits for the customer. Improvement of testability does, however, reduce cycle times, improve confidence in verification efforts, and reduce the cost of manufacturing. DFT is, therefore, a vital strategy for thriving in the marketplace.

Design for Serviceability

DFS principles include making replaceable items accessible, replacing fuses with circuit breakers, built-in test, and strategies for lowest replaceable assemblies (LRA). The purpose of DFS is to improve the ease of calibration, adjustment, preventive maintenance, and repair. These techniques and product features are often items that increase costs of production, but which have a dramatic effect on reduced annual service costs. Some of these features are related to or are derived from the DFT and DFM initiatives.

It is essential that these principles be accounted for in the early phases of the IPPD process. The implementation of changes to improve serviceability after production is begun is very costly. And if they are required after the product is fielded, the recall or retrofit program can be financially devastating.

Design for Compliance

DFC is a big issue in the world marketplace today. There are numerous and varied regulatory agencies around the world that exercise authority over the way we do business and the products and services we offer our customers. Design for compliance is, therefore, an equally critical aspect of the design process. These are requirements that may or may not be specified by the customers. In any case, it is imperative that the IPPD team account for these requirements in the design of products, services, and processes. The team needs, therefore, members with expertise in the appropriate regulatory disciplines.

Some of the more commonly known regulatory agencies include the Federal Communications Commission (FCC), Canadian Standards Authority (CSA), Federal Aviation Administration (FAA), Environmental Protection Agency (EPA), and Federal Drug Administration (FDA). Many states, and even some municipalities, have statutes or regulations that may pertain to the products or services that you offer your customers. In addition to these, compliance with ISO 9000 is required for doing business in the European Community countries.

The issues relating to compliance quickly become complex. It is not just a matter of knowing what is required for your customers. For proper compliance, it is necessary to understand how your customers use your products. Do they incorporate your products as a sub-assembly in a product they produce, or distribute your product to third parties? These situations may require compliance with regulatory requirements that your customers have, but which you don't.

Failing to provide for compliance with the cognizant regulatory requirements may keep your products and services out of the marketplace. Compliance, after the fact, will entail added cost, e.g., extra shielding, changes in packaging material, and redesign. These engineering changes also delay entry into the market.

DFX

The elements of the design process involve DFP and DFM as well as other requirements, i.e., DFT, DFS, and DFC. There may be others on the horizon that are specific to your industry. Collectively, all of those are now referred to as DFX, and all the ones that relate to your specific situation must be accounted for in the IPPD process. The philosophy of implementing DFX from the beginning of the design process, considering all elements of the product life cycle, is concurrent engineering. The process for implementing this philosophy is the IPPD process.

The IPPD Team

The implementation of CE through the IPPD process requires a team approach. This is necessary because of the very complex and cross-functional nature of the IPPD process. The IPPD team is a synergistic group of individuals: engineers, managers, and subject matter experts (SMEs) from operations and support functions. Each member of the team needs to be committed to achieving common objectives, working together, sharing information, and producing high-quality results. Success of the IPPD team depends on each member having well defined roles and responsibilities. The team also needs clear, well defined objectives and goals for the team as a whole. In addition, the team needs a clear understanding of the completion requirements for the project, as well as metrics for measuring accomplishments of the goals and objectives.

Experience of world class companies indicates that the ideal IPPD team has the following characteristics[5]:

- There are 10 or less members.
- Members volunteer to serve on the team.
- Members serve from concept to production.
- Members are assigned full-time to the team.
- At the very least, there is representation from marketing, engineering, quality, material management, and manufacturing.
- Members are located within conversational distance of each other.

Studies and experience have repeatedly demonstrated that a successful team begins with a well established structure. This structure includes active management support and a membership with clearly defined roles. Additionally, companies find that teams are more effective if they are assisted by people with extra training in project management, group process, statistical process control, and the scientific method. The IPPD team consists of:

- Product champion
- Team leader
- Facilitator
- Team members

Product Champion

Effective teams begin with active management support. This could be a single executive, supervisor, or manager who sees the need. Or it could be a steering council that determines the need. In either case, the management responsibilities are to develop a draft mission statement for the team with preliminary goals and to assign a product champion and team leader. The product champion must work with the team leader to ensure that the resources necessary to accomplish the mission are available, and they must clear the organizational paths for action when necessary.

When a manager or supervisor establishes a team, he or she has a vested interest in the success of the team. Accordingly, the effective manager or supervisor meets with the team leader from time to time to determine how the team is progressing and to provide guidance and ensure that resources are available, as required. This relationship is analogous to a mentorship.

The product champion is one who strongly believes in the product. This is an entrepreneurial individual, external to the team, with significant influence in the company, who mentors the team. This is an individual who is responsible for ensuring that the organization, external to the team, provides timely support for the team's needs. It is critical, therefore, that the team leader have access to the product champion whenever a critical issue arises that cannot be handled by the team.

The selection of the product champion needs to be done carefully. This individual needs to understand all aspects of the enterprise, the organization of the company, the IPPD process, and have the respect of the executives. The product champion also needs to be skilled at bashing barriers and working through the culture of your company and industry.

IPPD Team Leader

The IPPD team leader manages the team. He or she calls and facilitates meetings, handles and assigns administrative tasks, orchestrates team activities, and oversees preparation of reports and presentations. It is also important to ensure that the team leader is trained in the tools and techniques of the team process.

The IPPD team leader provides leadership in the development of the product and services and in the IPPD process. This individual must have a global view of the enterprise and view the IPPD process as a business endeavor. The company must avoid selecting a team leader who views IPPD as simply a technical or marketing problem. This narrow view will have the leader focusing on the process for the sake of the process, without understanding the vision of the company and the reason you are in business—to earn a profit and grow wealth.

The effective IPPD team leader knows he or she cannot do everything alone. The leader must get others to perform what needs to be accomplished—this means teamwork. This teamwork creates a sense of ownership, and the team members will feel empowered. When people feel empowered, they are more likely to use their energies to produce extraordinary results.

The IPPD team leader needs to understand the organization of the company and how things are accomplished within the context of the environment of the company, i.e., culture, infrastructure, policies, and procedures. The effective IPPD team leader empowers others to act. He or she actively involves others in planning and gives them discretion to make their own decisions. The exemplary team leader enlists the support and assistance of all those who must live with the results and makes it possible for others to do good work. It is imperative, therefore, that the team leader understand the team building process and team dynamics.

The successful IPPD team leader will also have a vision of what the product will do for the company and what determines success. He or she must have the ability to get the best performance from the individuals on the team and will act as coach and mentor to all the members. In addition, the IPPD team leader needs to be able to quickly establish and maintain credibility with senior management, so that he or she can obtain their support and commitment of resources.

The IPPD team leader must know enough about the technical issues involved, be able to identify critical obstacles, and make accurate decisions on the technology. It is not, however, necessary that he or she be an expert in the technology being used.

The fourth skill set required for good leadership is project management. There will be a myriad of details to plan and manage throughout the IPPD process.

Clearly, the IPPD team leader should be chosen on the basis of his or her skills in these critical areas. Once the team leader is selected, he or she needs to work with the product champion to identify team members who will ensure the products and services satisfy the needs and expectations of the customers.

Facilitator

The facilitator is a specialist trained in all the total quality tools. His or her role is to work with the team leader and the team to help keep them on track, to provide training as needed, and to facilitate the application of the appropriate tools. The facilitator must possess a broad range of skills: group process, effective meetings, conflict resolution, effective communications, the total quality tools, and training. These tools are all presented in Chapters 6–9 of this book. The facilitator is only as effective as he or she is able to transfer knowledge to the team leader and members.

In the beginning of a project, the facilitator will spend a great deal of time helping the team leader prepare for meetings. The facilitator will also attend all of the meetings in the beginning phase of the project. As the team leader becomes more experienced and as a team matures, the facilitator spends less and less time assisting the team. Eventually, the facilitator's role becomes one of advisor on call. Early in the teaming process, the facilitator needs to assess the support the team leader and team will need and to ensure that he or she is able to satisfy the requirements.

IPPD Team Members

The IPPD team needs members who can address the issues from all of the disciplines that support the entire life cycle of the product. This includes marketing, engineering, quality, material management, manufacturing, and after-market support. It is possible representation from the customers and suppliers will add depth to the team. Customers and suppliers may be accessed as focus groups for information and assistance in defining requirements and production strategies.

The team members need many of the same skills as the team leader. They need vision and teaming skills. They also need strong technical skills and knowledge about their respective disciplines. The team members need to be selected based on a needs assessment for the project. This assessment should, as a minimum, identify the technologies, skill sets, and knowledge required for the design and development of the product, services, and associated processes for the project. Economy and poor selection of team leader or members will doom the project to failure. There is a limit to the effectiveness of a team if resources are inadequate or if some of the team members do not possess the required competencies.

There are two types of IPPD team members: standing team members and ad hoc team members

Standing Members: Those individuals who are a part of the team throughout the IPPD process. These members attend all of the meetings, are assigned and accept action items, complete action items, and report to the team. These are the individuals who are essential to the success of the team.

Ad Hoc Members: Those members who possess specialized skills or knowledge that the team needs to address particular issues or actions. These specialists are assigned to the team for a specific task. This may be a long-term task, short-term task, or to perform a study or provide counsel or advice to the team. Ad hoc members attend only those meetings related to their specific task.

When the team leader and product champion have selected the team members, they must recruit them. This may be as simple as contacting their management to get the selected individuals assigned to the team, or it may require more formal action. Some IPPD projects do not have enough development work to justify full-time members. Part-time members will lack concentration and commitment needed to complete the IPPD project. Other priorities will interfere and divert their attention. This will greatly affect the IPPD cycle time.

The size of the team, that is the number of team members, will vary depending on the size of your company and the complexity of the project. In a small or medium-sized company, or for a simple project, the IPPD team may be only two or three individuals. In a large company, developing a complex product, the team may be as large as ten standing members. Teams that are larger than ten members spend an inordinate amount of time in meetings and take longer to accomplish their tasks. IPPD projects that require more than ten members may charter sub-teams to address sub-elements of the IPPD project. These are ad hoc teams in support of the IPPD team.

IPPD projects are high-energy projects that require a high level of commitment and a strong sense of urgency about completing the project. It will require risk taking and extra effort beyond the normal work schedule. It does offer excitement and an opportunity to affect the future of the company. Participants in the IPPD project must, therefore, volunteer dedication to the project. It is the responsibility of the team leader to enlist the dedication and commitment of the members.

It is for these reasons that team operation is easiest if the members are volunteers. This is not realistic in most situations. Frequently, the individuals that are desired for the team are not available, or they are not motivated to volunteer. Some of the individuals that do volunteer are persons that are best not involved in the project at all. And in most situations, team members are assigned by management. It is, therefore, the challenge of the team leader and the product champion to solicit volunteers and to create an environment that will serve as a catalyst to motivate those that are assigned to the project. To this end, it is important to remember that every assignment needs to have three elements:

- ► There must be something to be gained by each member of the team. This may be monetary, experiential, or knowledge.
- ► Each team member needs to believe they are involved in an important project.
- ► There must be enjoyment in the process of achieving the goal of the IPPD project.

The extent to which any one of these elements is satisfied is dependent on the degree that the others are satisfied. But all three must be satisfied to have a successful team.

When the team members have been selected, an IPPD kick-off meeting is held. The product champion, team leader, and other appropriate company executives need to explain to the team the purpose of their project. They need to address the risks and rewards involved in accomplishing this IPPD assignment. This first meeting sets the tone for motivating the team.

TEAMING FOR IPPD

We have already identified the fundamental roles and responsibilities of the IPPD team: product champion, team leader, facilitator, and team member. Each team needs to perform certain basic team activities to be successful. In addition, it is important to understand the team phases that all teams must undergo. In this section, we will discuss: team preparation; team process; team results; team phases; and conclusion of the team. The team activities can be divided into three parts: preparation, process, and results.

Team Preparation

Each team needs to be well prepared for success. The planning stage includes:

- ► Ensuring that the mission, goals, and objectives of the team support those of the organization
- ► Selecting the right team members
- ► Training the team members
- ► Developing sound plans of action and milestones
- ► Obtaining the resources necessary for achieving the goals and objectives of the team

The individual or group that establishes the IPPD team develops the draft mission statement and preliminary goals for the team and appoints the product champion, team leader, and facilitator. The mission for the team must support the business goals of the organization. The mission statement needs to be worded such that it is related back to the vision of the organization. The IPPD project needs to be related to the core competencies of the enterprise.

The team leader meets with the product champion and the facilitator to determine the membership of the team. At this time, they review the IPPD mission statement to determine the functions affected, as well as those necessary to achieve the goals as they are understood at the time. A preliminary team membership list is developed. As appropriate, the team leader or product champion discusses the membership list with the cognizant supervisors, managers, and executives and enlists their support for the participation of the employees.

The team leader and facilitator next review the list of candidate team members, their past experience in team activities, and their training in the team process and related skills and knowledge. The team leader and facilitator use this assessment to develop a plan for training the team. Remember, all training has a half-life; if it isn't used, it decays. Training is, therefore, just-in-time training; the team should receive only the training it needs to perform the tasks at hand.

At the first meeting of the team, the members are introduced to one another and to the team process. The product champion and appropriate managers/executives discuss the purpose of the project and its importance to the company. The team then establishes ground rules regarding attendance, schedules for meetings, how assignments will be handled, and participation. After these administrative matters have been completed, the first order of business for the team is to review the mission statement and goals assigned to them. They must refine these as they understand the process.

At this time, the team takes the mission statement and goals and develops their scope. The scope for the team addresses their time frame, specifics of the project, details about the authority of the team, and the completion criteria. The mission statement, goals, and scope for the team are documented to ensure a common understanding among all of the team members.

The mission statement, goals, and scope are then used to develop the team's plan of action and milestone chart (POA&M). Next, the team determines the resources it will need to accomplish its tasks. All of these details need to be well documented, and accountability needs to be assigned for all activities. Figures 4-3 through 4-6 present some team planning sheets that can be used to document the team's plan. They cover the information that the authors have found necessary for planning any team activity. These sheets are presented as a guide, and the reader is encouraged to modify them for his or her specific situation.

The next step is for the team leader and facilitator to meet with the product champion. At this meeting, they review the team's mission statement, goals, scope, and POA&M to develop consensus. Periodically thereafter, the team leader meets with the product champion to assesses the team's progress, discuss resource requirements, and request assistance, as needed. It is recommended that the product champion meet periodically with the entire team to discuss progress, demonstrate management interest, and recognize the contributions of the team members to the success of the company.

Team Process

This is the stage where the POA&M is implemented. Each team performs according to its own POA&M, and the specific steps taken are unique for that team. In general these steps are:

- ► Record keeping
- ► Process definition
- ► Data collection and analysis
- ► Determination of courses of action
- ► Action

Team Planning Summary Sheet

Team Name:_____   Date:_____

Organization:_____   Revision:

_____   _____

1. Team Members:	2. Mission Statement:

3. Goal(s):	4. Method(s) of Measuring Success:

5. Completion Criteria:

6. Achievements:

* Attach continuation sheets if necessary.

FIGURE 4-3   Team Planning Summary Sheet (blank)

Team Planning Summary Sheet

Team Name: _____   Date: _____

Organization: _____   Revision: _____

1. Team Members:

List all team members
and their respective org.
codes. Indicate if they
are a Team Leader (L),
Facilitator (F) or
Advisor (S).

2. Mission Statement:

Provide a brief mission statement for the
team. This addresses why the team exists
and addresses the products, services
and processes to be developed.

3. Goal(s):

List the goal(s) established by this
team. If they are "TBD", indicate that
in this space and reference the
schedule , which would then
include"establishing goals" as one of
the tasks listed.

4. Method(s) of Measuring Success:

List the metrics established by this
team. If they are "TBD", indicate
that in this space and reference
the schedule, which would then
include "determining metrics" as
one of the tasks listed.

5. Completion Criteria:

List the completion criteria for each goal identified. This is where
you establish the products and/or services that must be completed
for this team to perform its mission.

6. Achievements:

List actual accomplishments, relative to each goal listed in #3
(above).

* Attach continuation sheets if necessary.

FIGURE 4-4   Team Planning Summary Sheet (annotated)

Team Activity Schedule/Milestone Chart

Team Name:_____

Date: _____
Revision: _____

TASKS	J	F	M	A	M	J	J	A	S	O	N	D

Remarks:

FIGURE 4-5   Team Activity Schedule/Milestone Chart

Record keeping is a very important administrative function. It is recommended that the team leader maintain a master file for the team. This file needs to include:

► Written mission statement, goals, and objectives
► Team planning sheets (POA&M)
► Copies of meeting agendas and minutes
► Action logs
► Copies of all presentations
► Copies of all support documentation, including data and charts

This information is used for reviewing the progress of the team, developing presentations about the project, retracing steps, educating others about the project, and reviewing decisions. Each member

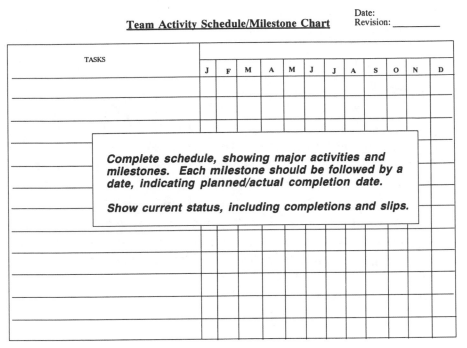

Team Activity Schedule/Milestone Chart   Date:
                                                Revision: _____

TASKS	J	F	M	A	M	J	J	A	S	O	N	D

Complete schedule, showing major activities and milestones. Each milestone should be followed by a date, indicating planned/actual completion date.

Show current status, including completions and slips.

Remarks:

FIGURE 4-6   Team Activity Schedule/Milestone Chart (Annotated)

represents a different discipline and thus will have a unique perspective about the data requirements. At the first meeting of the team, it is advisable to discuss this record keeping to develop consensus about what is needed and who will maintain it. Designate a team member as a permanent scribe to take minutes, publish meeting agendas, and keep action logs.

Regardless of the type of team or its mission, the implementation of a team POA&M begins with a process definition—a statement that defines and describes the process assigned to the team. For the IPPD team it is necessary to provide a detailed explanation of the enterprise process (Figure 1-2) and the IPPD model (Figure 1-6).

After the IPPD team understands the enterprise process and IPPD model, the team determines what information it needs to refine its

POA&M and to accomplish its goals. At this point, the team is taking direct action to achieve its goals.

Team Results

There is a tendency to focus exclusively on the results of team activity by measuring the return on investment to justify the investment in resources. This focus is a fatal pitfall in the IPPD process. It is important to measure results, to report them and to celebrate them, as appropriate. Results are what keep us motivated and reassured that our investments in time and money are worthwhile. The IPPD team, however, needs metrics for its project that are specific for the project at hand. These metrics need to address the long-term vision of the enterprise and the relationship the IPPD project has to the vision. These IPPD metrics need to be indicators of the progress and success of the team. Candidate metrics include:

- ► Progress against milestones
- ► Time from start of design to production
- ► Quantity of engineering changes following design release
- ► Number of parts versus similar assemblies
- ► Quality of product as measured against customers' requirements and expectations
- ► Hours expended versus similar projects
- ► Manufacturing cycle time versus similar products
- ► How the IPPD project contributes to the vision of the enterprise

Team Phases[6]

There are four stages, or phases, that each team passes through as it matures. The time it takes to get through each phase varies from team to team, as does the intensity of each phase. It is important to understand these stages of team development to guide your expectations for the teams.

Team Forming Phase

In the beginning of the team's life, the members are learning what is the acceptable group behavior. They are getting acquainted and struggling with the transition to their new roles. It is also common for members to test the leadership of the team leader and facilitator. There may be some excitement and optimism about the team, but there is also some uncertainty and cautiousness among some of the members.

During this stage, there is little progress toward the team's goals, but this is a normal and necessary phase for the team to go through.

Team Storming Phase

This is a difficult stage to work through. At this point in the team's life, often there is impatience at the lack of progress. There is arguing, defensiveness, and competition among members or groups of members of the team. There is, however, good news in this phase. The team members are beginning to understand one another and beginning to think of themselves as a team.

Team Norming Phase

In this phase, the conflict has been reduced and the members accept the team norms. They are working together and starting to make significant progress toward the team goals.

Team Performing Phase

In this phase, the team members are a cohesive unit, working in concert. They understand the team process and accept and appreciate individual differences. They are performing as a team.

Each time you change the structure or alter the membership of the team, however slight, you start over in Phase 1 and repeat all the other phases. The duration of the phases will be shortened, and the intensity will be lessened, but it will still occur again!

The following forms are provided in Figures 4-3[7], 4-4[8], 4-5[9], and 4-6[10] to assist you in your team building efforts. These blank forms are also provided as tear-out sheets in the workbook.

- ► Team Planning Summary Sheet
- ► Team Activity Schedule/Milestone Chart

Project Completion

The IPPD team is a means to an end, not an end in itself. It is established to contribute to the accomplishment of the business goals of the organization through the development of new products, services, and processes. In this capacity, the team is focused on a business process that is designed to earn a profit and enable the company to grow wealth. The IPPD project, therefore, has a finite life span. At the point in the process that the completion criteria have been accomplished, it is time to end the project. This is a difficult decision for the team.

The effective IPPD team has been involved in a high-energy fast-paced activity. There will be many synergistic and heuristic experiences along the way. Consequently, the team members will have given little thought to the conclusion of the project. The project will have become their purpose, and now, with the conclusion in sight, their purpose is disappearing. This can be a very traumatic and disturbing experience for the team members.

It is recommended that the company management begin planning follow-on activities and opportunities for the team members at least 60 days prior to project completion. This needs to include discussions with each member on the various options and their individual desires. This will lessen the shock at the end of the project and enable the team members to make the transition from the IPPD team to their new assignments.

It is also important to plan for recognizing the results of the team. This cheerleading is honoring the team members and sharing with them the taste of success. When you honor a team, focus on the key values that its members embodied in their efforts. Give them public and visible recognition. The message is: high-risk IPPD projects are in the best interest of the enterprise and will be rewarded.

When considering the future plans for the team members, remember that they will possess a new set of skills and knowledge. Capitalizing on these new competencies will benefit the company, provide additional job satisfaction for the team members, and encourage others to seek assignments on IPPD teams.

KEY POINTS

The goal of the IPPD process is to:

- ► Reduce cycle time from concept to delivery
- ► Reduce costs for developing and producing products and services
- ► Minimize design changes after design release
- ► Improve quality of products and services, as measured by the customers

Concurrent Engineering is "the earliest possible integrating of the overall company's knowledge, resources, and experience in design, development, marketing, manufacturing, and sales into creating successful new products, with high quality and low cost, while meeting customer expectations."[11]

There are several parallel design activities that must be accomplished during the IPPD process. Collectively, these are referred to as DFX:

Design for Performance: Design for performance is ensuring that the design satisfies all of the customers' expectations about the performance of the product or service.

Design for Manufacturability and Assembly: The purpose of DFM/DFMA is to develop and implement a design that is easy to build, error free.

Design for Testability: Design for testability facilitates verification of performance.

Design for Serviceability: DFS improves the ease of calibration, adjustment, preventive maintenance, and repair.

Design for Compliance: Failing to provide for compliance with the cognizant regulatory requirements may keep your products and services out of the marketplace.

The IPPD team is a synergistic group of individuals: engineers, managers, and subject matter experts (SMEs) from operations and support functions.

Success of the IPPD team depends on well defined roles and responsibilities.

The IPPD team consists of a product champion, team leader, facilitator, and team members.

The **product champion** is one who strongly believes in the product. This is an entrepreneurial individual who mentors the team. The product champion works with the team leader to ensure resources necessary to accomplish the mission are available.

The IPPD **team leader** provides leadership in the development of the product and services and in the IPPD process. This individual must have a global view of the enterprise and view the IPPD process as a business endeavor.

The **facilitator** is a specialist trained and experienced in all the total quality tools. His or her role is to work with the team leader and the team to help keep them on track, to provide training as needed, and to facilitate the application of the appropriate tools.

The IPPD team needs **members** who can address the issues from all of the disciplines that support the entire life cycle of the product.

There are two types of IPPD team members: **standing members** and **ad hoc members.**

IPPD teams should limit membership to a maximum of 10 members.

IPPD projects are high-energy projects that require a high level of commitment and a strong sense of urgency about completing the project.

Each IPPD team needs to be well prepared for success. The planning stage includes:

- ▶ Ensuring that the mission, goals, and objectives of the team support those of the organization
- ▶ Selecting the right team members

► Training the team members
► Developing sound plans of action and milestones
► Obtaining the resources necessary for achieving the goals and objectives of the team

IPPD metrics need to be indicators of the progress and success of the team.

The team phases are the predictable stages each team goes through during its life: forming, storming, norming, and performing.

During **forming,** the members learn the acceptable group behavior, get acquainted, and struggle with the transition to their new roles.

During **storming,** there is arguing, defensiveness, and competition among members or groups of members of the team. The team members are beginning to understand one another and beginning to think of themselves as a team.

In the **norming** phase, conflict has been reduced and members accept the team norms.

In the **performing** phase, team members are a cohesive unit, working in concert.

Each time you change the structure or membership of the team, you start over in Phase 1 and work through each phase again.

The IPPD project has a finite life span. At the point in the process that the completion criteria have been accomplished, it is time to end the project.

It is recommended that the company management begin planning follow-on activities and opportunities for the team members at least 60 days prior to project completion.

It is important to plan for recognizing the results of the team.

EXAMPLE

The LWCI management team has identified a need to design and develop a new series of industrial production equipment. This need has surfaced due to declining sales of existing LWCI equipment, the changes in production technologies, and the increasing need of

LWCI customers for greater productivity. The Production Machinery Division of LWCI has been tasked to design and develop a new series of production machinery. The new system will be designated the LWCI 1600 series.

The division established an IPPD team for the LWCI 1600 series project. The product champion is Mr. Jeffrey Frank, general manager, production machinery division. The team consisted of individuals representing marketing, engineering, product operations, quality, safety, finance, and material management. The team also includes a representative from the machine and tool division and electronics division. The LWCI 1600 IPPD team is listed in Example Figure 4-1.

The first meeting of the LWCI 1600 IPPD team was conducted by the team leader and facilitator. At that meeting Mr. Leander, Mr. Wiles, and Mr. Frank were present to express their hopes for the team and to ensure them of their support for this project. They stressed that the LWCI 1600 held an important position in their strategy for LWCI. They also stressed the urgency for the project.

The LWCI 1600 needed to be introduced into the market within 12 months. This schedule was driven by the premier position that they held by virtue of a recent technological breakthrough. There was fear that they would lose that advantage if they took longer than 12 months. This fear was based on information received from customers who had been approached by a competitor indicating that they were working on an idea similar to LWCI.

The IPPD team was given a preliminary Team Planning Summary Sheet for their project (Example Figure 4-2). The product champion indicated that the team was to review the sheet and use it as the basis for establishing their mission, goals, and objectives. Mr. Frank asked the team to be prepared to discuss these with him the following week.

Mr. Frank and Ms. Clausen were especially interested in establishing metrics for measuring the success of the project, so that they could capitalize on the experience of this project to improve future IPPD projects. The first task for the team was to 1) review and revise the mission statement, 2) review the goals and revise them to ensure they are collaborative and supportive of the mission and company vision, 3) review and revise the completion criteria to ensure they are

Product Champion: Mr. Jeffrey Frank, General Manager
                     Production Machinery Division

Team Leader: Ms. Jennifer Clausen, Engineer
                     Production Machinery Division

Facilitator: Mr. Normand Frigon

Team Members: Ms. Linda Johnston (Company Marketing)

                     Mr. Joe Dyer (Product Operations,
                     Production Machinery Division)

                     Mr. Chip Mathews (Quality Operations,
                     Production Machinery Division)

                     Mr. Mark Johnson (Company Safety)

                     Mr. David Jackson (Company Finance)

                     Ms. Judy Christensen
                     (Company Material Management)

                     Mr. George Johnson
                     (Engineer, Machine and Tool Division)

                     Ms. Christine Ward (Engineer, Electronics Division)

EXAMPLE FIGURE 4-1   LWCI 1600 IPPD Team

inclusive and appropriate for the LWCI 1600 IPPD project, and 4) review the team membership to determine that the needed skills and knowledge were represented.

The IPPD team used a Team Activity Milestone Chart to begin the project's planning (Example Figure 4-3). The first step was to identify the top-level tasks and then determine the timing to achieve the 12-month project milestone. The team decided to use a tree diagram and a Process Decision Program Chart (PDPC) to complete the

Team Planning Summary Sheet	
Team Name: LWCI 1600 IPD Team	Date: April 21, 1994 Revision:

1. Team Members:	2. Mission Statement:
Ms. Jennifer Clausen (Team Leader) Ms. Linda Johnston Mr. Joe Dyer Mr. Chip Mathews Mr. Mark Johnson Mr. David Jackson Ms. Judy Christensen Mr. George Johnson Ms. Christine Ward Mr. Norm Frigon (Facilitator) Mr. Jeffrey Frank (Product Champion)	• Develop the LWCI 1600 production machinery system. • Ensure customer satisfaction throughout the customer experience and use that as a strategy to ensure competitive advantage.

3. Goal(s):	4. Method(s) of Measuring Success:
• First LWCI 1600 in 12 months • Distinguishing Characteristics • LWCI Performance Model • LWCI 1600 Design	• Performance to milestones • Development Cycle Time • Number of parts/sub-assy • Production Cost

5. Completion Criteria:

• Customer Requirements • Distinguishing Characteristics • LWCI Performance Model • LWCI 1600 Design	• Production Strategy • Material Management Strategy • LWCI 1600 Support Strategy • LWCI Marketing Strategy

6. Achievements:

EXAMPLE FIGURE 4-2   Initial LWCI 1600 IPPD Team Planning Summary Sheet

Team Activity Schedule/Milestone Chart	Date 29 April 1994								Revision:		
	1994									1995	
Tasks	A	M	J	J	A	S	O	N	D	J	F	M
1. Finalize Mission, Goals & Objectives												
2. Est Customer Requirements												
3. Est. Distinguishing Characteristics												
4. Define Customer Performance Model												
5. Preliminary Design												
6. Detailed design												
7. Make - Buy Strategy												
8. Est. Production Plan												
9. Production Test Strategy												
10. Production First Article												
11. Est. Support Strategy												
12. Begin Production												

EXAMPLE FIGURE 4-3   LWCI 1600 IPPD Milestone Planning Sheet

milestone chart begun in the first meeting. These would be reviewed with the product champion to solicit help in procuring resources and establishing priorities.

Each task identified in the milestone chart would then be examined, and the actions necessary to achieve each would be further planned. At this point, there could be a requirement for assistance from ad hoc teams. The IPPD team served as a steering council to establish the necessary ad hoc teams.

NOTES

[1] Shina, Sammy G. *Concurrent Engineering and Design for Manufacture of Electronics Products, pp. 1, New York, NY: Van Nostrand Reinhold, 1991.*

[2] Smith, Preston G., and Reinertsen, Donald G. *Developing Products In Half The Time, pp 5. New York, NY: Van Nostrand Reinhold, 1991.*

[3] Ibid, pp 4.

[4] Turino, Jon. *Managing Concurrent Engineering, pp 6. New York, NY: Van Nostrand Reinhold, 1992.*

5   Smith, Preston G., and Reinertsen, Donald G. *Developing Products In Half The Time, pp 111. New York, NY: Van Nostrand Reinhold, 1991.*

6   Jackson Jr., Harry K. and Frigon, Normand L. *Management 2000, The Practical Guide to World Class Competition, pp 82-83, New York, NY: Van Nostrand Reinhold, 1994.*

7   Ibid, pp 84

8   Ibid, pp 85

9   Ibid, pp 86

10 Ibid, pp 87

11 Shina, Sammy G. *Concurrent Engineering and Design for Manufacture of Electronics Products, pp. 1, New York, NY: Van Nostrand Reinhold, 1991.*

5

Answering the Voice of the Customer

> ANSWERING THE VOICE OF THE CUSTOMER IS
> THE DIRECT LINE TO THRIVING IN THE
> MARKETPLACE.

The IPPD Process uses Quality Function Deployment (QFD) and Voice of the Customer to implement the Concurrent Engineering philosophy. In this way, QFD provides the method for listening to the voice of the customer and answering it. QFD was first applied at the Kobe Shipyard of Mitsubishi Heavy Industries Ltd. in Japan in the 1970s. Since that time, it has become the accepted methodology for development of products and services in Japan. Isuzu, Matsushita, Komatsu, NEC Micon, and Toyota are some of the Japanese companies that are using QFD to successfully develop and introduce products in a fraction of the time required without it. QFD has in fact improved their competitiveness by enhancing their ability to answer the voice of the customer.

In the early 1980s, Dr. Don Clausing introduced QFD to Xerox and the U.S. automotive industry. Since that time, American business has shown growing interest in using QFD. John McHugh and Larry Sullivan, of the American Supplier Institute, and Bob King, of GOAL/QPC, have been leaders in this movement. GOAL/QPC published Bob King's book, *Better Designs in Half the Time*, in 1987. This book presented a detailed model for Quality Function Deployment that has become the basis for all implementation initiatives.

Since 1987, members of ASI and GOAL/QPC have studied QFD and helped many businesses implement QFD. This has contributed greatly to the development and innovation of QFD techniques in the United States. As a result of their efforts, many practitioners claim that using QFD enabled them to reduce the product development cycle time by as much as 75% with equally impressive improvement in measured customer satisfaction. The authors have personally seen improvements of this magnitude in American industries, service companies, and government agencies.

The message is clear. If you are not using Quality Function Deployment, and do not intend to use it on your next project, you will not survive in the marketplace of the future.

DEFINING QUALITY FUNCTION DEPLOYMENT

Quality Function Deployment has been called many things: Matrix Product Planning, Decision Matrix, Customer Driven Engineering, and others. Quality Function Deployment, or QFD, is still the most appropriate name. QFD is a focused method for listening to the customers and optimizing designs, materials, and processes to ensure the customers' expectations are satisfied.

In QFD, quality is a measure of the customers' satisfaction with a product or service. QFD is a structured method that uses the 7 M&P tools to quickly and effectively identify and prioritize customers' expectations. In the IPPD process, these requirements come from the customers, directly and indirectly, through research about the customers' needs, requirements, and motivation. It also includes information about the marketplace and the current and projected state of technology. This data is analyzed and turned into information to be used in the design and development of products, services, and processes. In Chapter 2, we saw how this information is translated by the

Voice of the Customer Table (Figures 2-2 and 2-3) to create the Customer Requirements Model, which is the statement of the functions and characteristics that motivate customers to buy products and services.

The IPPD process then determines product and service characteristics that will provide a competitive advantage. These are called Distinguishing Characteristics. These are the functions and characteristics that you are going to design to motivate customers to buy your products and services over the competition. Some call these breakthroughs. These are the applications of new concepts, new technology, improved reliability, cost reductions, and other innovations that will give a distinct advantage over the competition in satisfying and delighting the customers.

Armed with the Customer Requirements Model and the Distinguishing Characteristics, the IPPD team develops the Customer-Performance Model. This is the total package being offered to the customers. This top level requirements set is the offering about which the business decision is made. It is the performance model that is given to the IPPD team for implementation.

The IPPD team uses QFD to further refine the performance model and translate these requirements into engineering requirements for systematic deployment throughout the company at each stage of product, service, and process development and improvement. The implementation of QFD by the Integrated Product Development multi-functional team thereby deploys the Voice of the Customer throughout the various functional areas of research and development, engineering, sales/marketing, purchasing, quality operations, manufacturing, packaging, and after-market support.

MATRIX RELATIONSHIPS

The basic tool used in QFD is the matrix. The other 7 M&P tools are used either to develop the inputs for a matrix or to take the output of a matrix and develop further information or insight for a set of data. The "what–how" matrix relationship, demonstrated in Figure 5-1, is

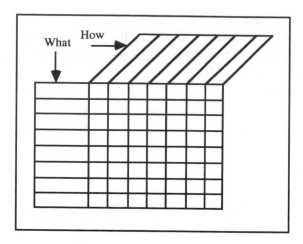

FIGURE 5-1   What–How Matrix Relationship

the characteristic that gives the power to this tool. This relationship generates a family of matrices in a matrix-waterfall fashion. This family of matrices deploys the customer requirements, and related technical requirements, throughout all related design and manufacturing processes for the development of a product or service.

In the IPPD process, we use *goal* to designate *what* is to be achieved and *objective* to designate *how* it is to be achieved. In a matrix, we list the goals on the vertical axis as the "Whats" and the objectives on the horizontal axis as the "Hows." In this way, we can take each level objective and cascade it down to further define the details for achieving the goal. This is referred to as a waterfall of matrices.

Each matrix shows the relationship between what we want to do and how it can be accomplished. This starts with top-level goals, entered on the vertical axis. The next step is to determine what actions need to be accomplished to achieve the goals. These are entered across the top, or horizontal, axis.

A simple example is illustrated in Figure 5-2. In this case, our goal is to make a profit. An objective might be to sell a product for more than it costs to manufacture. But then the question is raised: "How do we sell a product for more than it costs to produce?" This question contains a goal; that is, what we want to accomplish. We use

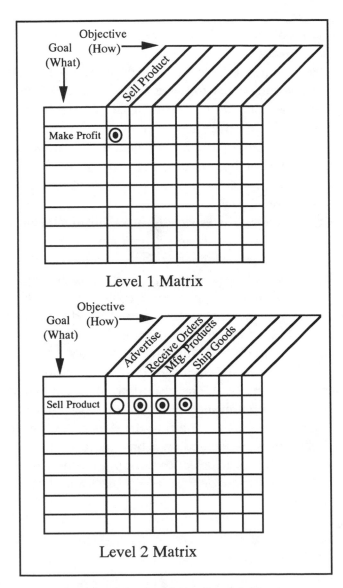

FIGURE 5-2   Level 1 to Level 2 Matrix
Deployment

successive levels of goals and objectives until we get to an action that can be taken directly.

In this illustration, the Level 1 goal is to make a profit. One of the Level 1 objectives, necessary to make a profit, is to sell the product. This objective translates into a Level 2 goal: sell the product. There are several Level 2 objectives necessary to sell the product. Each of these can, in turn, be used as a Level 3 goal to determine the Level 3 objectives. In this fashion, we can start with a top-level goal and waterfall down the objectives until we have sufficient detailed action to achieve the Level 1 goal.

This waterfall method is especially powerful in developing products or services that will satisfy and delight customers. It begins with the customer-performance model which is deployed in this waterfall fashion. Figure 5-3[1] illustrates this process, through the design requirements and requisite engineering design, to the product characteristics. Figure 5-4[2] shows how the organization deploys these product characteristics, through the manufacturing and purchasing operations, to the production and quality controls.

This method ensures the optimum design is developed to satisfy the customers' expectations. The organization then implements the design, using the optimum materials, and processes. QFD thus provides a methodology for ensuring that the design and production of products and services are focused on achieving customer satisfaction. At each step, it leads us to select the optimum objective to achieve a goal.

FIVE PHASES OF QFD

There are five phases in Quality Function Deployment: Organizing, Product Planning, Product Design, Process Planning, and Implementation. The appropriate tools or processes (7 M&P Tools, Failure Modes and Effect Analysis, Design of Experiments, SPC, SQC, Information-Services Network, etc.) are used in each phase to ensure the

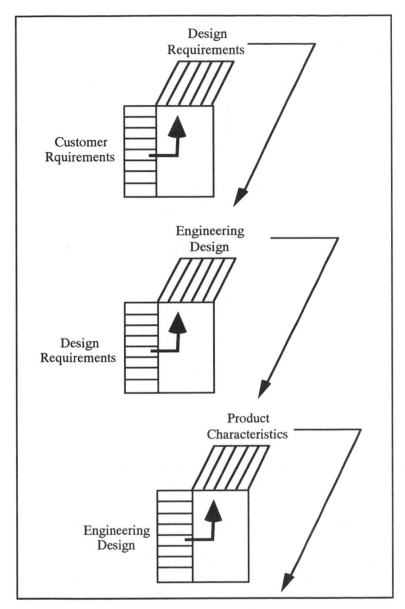

FIGURE 5-3 Deployment of Customer Requirements to Product Characteristics

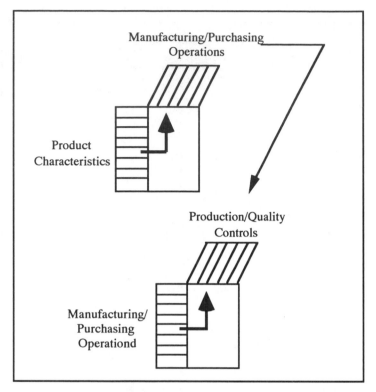

FIGURE 5-4   Deployment of Product Characteristics to Production/Quality Controls

systematic deployment of the customers' expectations throughout the design, manufacture, and service of the product.

The Requirements Matrix, which is also referred to as the House of Quality, is the starting point for the QFD method. We deploy each matrix or activity from this starting point. This basic QFD approach is flexible and can be adapted to any given situation. The complexity of the project will drive the level of detail at each phase, as well as the selection of tools and techniques. A simple task might require only one or two matrices and a few task sheets. A complex project (e.g., developing complex machinery such as the LWCI 1600) might require a complete set of matrices, supplementary investigations, and designed experiments.

It is important, therefore, to plan the QFD project carefully and to tailor each application to your specific organization, product, and processes. We need to step through each phase and to make a conscious decision about its applicability. This means evaluating the required action for each phase, determining the most appropriate tools to be used, and deciding when to truncate the application of a tool. A facilitator skilled in the application of the improvement tools can greatly assist the design project.

In the organizing phase, the opportunity has been identified and the business decision is made whether to proceed or not. If the decision is to proceed with the project, an IPPD team is chartered. The IPPD team then begins the detailed planning stage of the project.

In the product planning phase, the customer-performance model is evaluated. We use this information to develop the Requirements Matrix, also known as the House of Quality. This matrix defines the product in terms of the design requirements necessary to achieve customers' expectations. The inputs for the matrix can be developed using a variety of tools, e.g., Tree Diagram, Affinity Diagram, PDPC, Interrelationship Digraph, Pareto Diagrams, DOE, etc. After the product is planned, we enter the Product Design Phase. In this phase, we develop the Design Matrix and Product Characteristics Deployment Matrix. The Design Matrix identifies the engineering design activities required to achieve the product design requirements. The Product Characteristics Deployment Matrix subsequently identifies the product characteristics that satisfy the engineering design requirements. The product is defined at this point in terms of characteristics that satisfy the customers' requirements.

We then use the results of the Product Characteristics Deployment Matrix to develop the Manufacturing/Purchasing Matrix in the Process Planning Phase. At this point, we select the manufacturing and purchasing operations needed to achieve the product characteristics. We also develop the Control/Verficiation Matrix to determine the necessary production and quality controls for the selected manufacturing and purchasing operations.

The final phase is the Implementation Phase. In this phase, we are in production. As production proceeds, we implement SPC, conduct process capability studies, implement designed experiments, and achieve continuous measurable improvement. These activities are also referred to as variability reduction. This is where we make the design and processes robust. This means that the design, selection of materials, and the processes are such that there is little variation in quality, in spite of diverse or changing environmental conditions.

HOUSE OF QUALITY

The House of Quality is the starting matrix for QFD. It starts as a What–How Matrix that identifies the customer-performance model. These customer requirements are translated into technical requirements as the "house" is constructed. The completed House of Quality is then used to start the matrix waterfall. This is how the requirements are deployed throughout all phases and aspects of the design and manufacturing processes.

The process for developing the matrix clarifies the relationships between the objectives and the goals. This ensures that all of the customers' requirements are addressed. The process also provides a logical basis for determining the impact of each action on the other actions. Optional additions can be added to the House of Quality to provide greater understanding and to facilitate the next phases of the product development project. The construction of the House of Quality is a five-step process:

1. Establishing Customer Requirements
2. Determining Design Requirements
3. Developing the Relationship Matrix
4. Developing the Interaction Matrix
5. Establishing priorities for the Design Requirements

Step 1. Establishing Customer Requirements

The initial step in the development of the House of Quality is to establish the customer requirements. This is sometimes referred to as listening to the voice of the customer. The step involves defining what the customer needs, wants, and desires, in his own terms. This is the customer-performance model that is created from the Voice of the Customer Table. As the IPPD team progresses, it needs to constantly review this as new information or developments resulting from its efforts.

The customer-performance model requirements are entered on the vertical axis of the matrix. This can be a simple listing of requirements, or it may have two (or more) columns as secondary and tertiary requirements. In addition, enter the importance that the customers place on each feature on the matrix in the priority column. The importance is expressed as greatest, average, or least, depicted by a double circle, single circle, and triangle, respectively. Figure 5-5 illustrates these initial steps in developing the House of Quality and how the symbols are used for the customer importance rating.

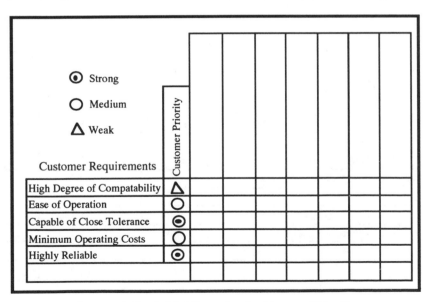

FIGURE 5-5   Initial Steps in the House of Quality

Step 2. Determining Design Requirements

The design requirements, sometimes referred to as the technical re-quirements, or the Voice of the Engineer, are the objective technical measurements that predict to what degree each customer require-ment will be met. These establish how the customer requirements are met at the top level. They are global requirements and performance parameters. There needs to be at least one design requirement for each customer requirement.

The design requirements are developed in a manner similar to that used for the customer requirements. In this case, however, the source of the data is most likely the project team or other individuals within the company. The initial data may result from brainstorming. Affin-ity diagrams are helpful in organizing the data and giving it order. Tree diagrams are helpful for expanding and clarifying the informa-tion. After determining the design requirements, enter them on the horizontal axis of the House of Quality. Figure 5-6 illustrates this step.

	Customer Priority	Mean Time Between Failure = 5000 Hours	Accuracy = 0.0001	Built-in Self Test	Computer Controlled	Mean Time to Repair = 0.5 Hrs	Self Calibration	Module Level Replacement
⊙ Strong								
○ Medium								
△ Weak								
Customer Requirements								
High Degree of Compatability	△							
Ease of Operation	○							
Capable of Close Tolerance	⊙							
Minimum Operating Costs	○							
Highly Reliable	⊙							

FIGURE 5-6   Step Two in the House of Quality

Step 3. Developing the Relationship Matrix

This is the body of the House of Quality. It visually displays the relationships between the customer requirements and the design requirements. The symbols quickly reveal patterns and identify weak points in the design requirements. Careful completion of the relationship matrix yields dividends in the form of reduced engineering changes later in the product's life cycle.

Identify the relationships by asking the question: "How well does this design requirement predict customer satisfaction for each requirement?" Do this for every intersecting point in the body of the matrix. It may seem to be a tedious exercise, but it is extremely important that the entire team participate in order to develop a common understanding and ownership.

The matrix uses our standard symbology: a double circle for a strong relationship, single circle for medium, triangle for weak, and blank for none. Although we will assign numerical values to these symbols later in the process, it is important to use the symbols. They provide a quick visual indication of patterns and quickly reveal holes in our planning. Figure 5-7 illustrates how the Relationship Matrix is developed.

Step 4. Developing the Interaction Matrix

The Interaction Matrix, also known as the Correlation Matrix, is the "roof" on the House of Quality. This matrix is similar to the J-F Interrelationship Matrix from the 7 M&P tools. It is established to determine the technical interrelationships among the design requirements (Hows). This information is valuable as the basis for decisions regarding technical tradeoffs.

We construct the roof by evaluating the interactions among the Hows and placing the appropriate symbol at each intersection point. This symbol reveals the impact of a change in a given characteristic. It answers the question: "Does this characteristic have an effect on

Customer Requirements	Customer Priority	Mean Time Between Failure = 5000 Hours	Accuracy = 0.0001	Built-in Self Test	Computer Controlled	Mean Time to Repair = 0.5 Hrs	Self Calibration	Module Level Replacement
High Degree of Compatability	△				○			△
Ease of Operation	○			◉	◉	△	○	△
Capable of Close Tolerance	◉		◉		△		○	
Minimum Operating Costs	○	○		○		△	△	△
Highly Reliable	◉	◉		○	△		△	

Legend: ◉ Strong   ○ Medium   △ Weak

FIGURE 5-7   Step Three in the House of Quality

another characteristic?" Repeat this question for each combination. Figure 5-8 illustrates how this matrix is developed.

The symbology in our example works if there is a positive relationship. This is not always the situation. Frequently, the interaction will be positive for some and negative for others. There is an alternative symbology which is more appropriate if this is the circumstance. This symbology is presented in Figure 5-8A.

Step 5. Establishing Priorities for the Design Requirements

Establishing the priorities for the design requirements is necessary to identify the key elements. This understanding is valuable for making decisions about tradeoffs, determining where to focus resources, and refining the design concept. It involves four steps: determining the

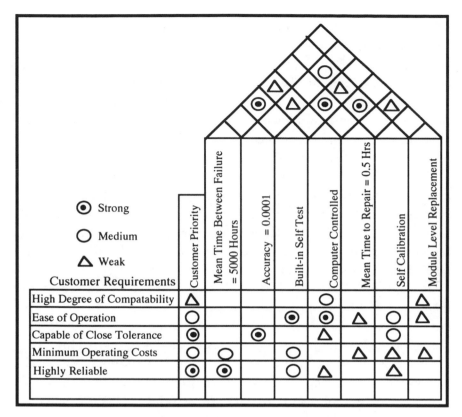

FIGURE 5-8   Adding the Roof to the House of Quality (Interaction Matrix)

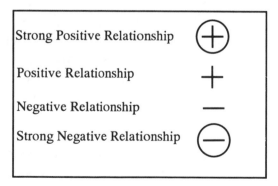

FIGURE 5-8A   Alternative Legend for Interaction Matrix

risk, calculating the absolute weight, calculating the relative weight, and identifying the key elements.

To determine the risk for each design requirement, the team needs to assess the degree of difficulty associated with each requirement. The team needs to consider cost, technical difficulty, and the relationship to the other requirements. The team assigns a risk factor of greatest, average, or least to each requirement, using the same symbols as in the other parts of the matrix.

We calculate the absolute weights for each design requirement by assigning the associated values to the symbols in the appropriate column and adding them. Then enter the total in the associated cell for the absolute weight. Calculate the relative weight by multiplying the absolute weight by the value for the associated risk. Place the result in the associated cell for the relative weight.

The absolute and relative weights can be entered as raw scores, or the scores can be ranked and the corresponding ranks entered. In either instance, the results of these calculations provide three key pieces of data. The first is the risk associated with each How. The second is a ranking of the Hows according to the impact that each has on the overall achievement of the customer requirements, based on the interaction of each How with all the Whats. This is a valuable insight, as a given design requirement sometimes has an effect on several customer requirements.

The third piece of data, relative weights, ranks the design requirements in terms of their relationship to all the customer requirements but also factors in the risk associated with each requirement. The combination of these two rankings gives a powerful insight into the importance of each design requirement. The key elements can now be determined from a comparison of the absolute and relative weights.

Figure 5-9 illustrates how the weighting is calculated and the key elements are identified. This step completes the construction of the basic House of Quality. This Requirements Matrix is the first matrix in the implementation of Quality Function Deployment and serves as the source for the follow-on Design Matrix.

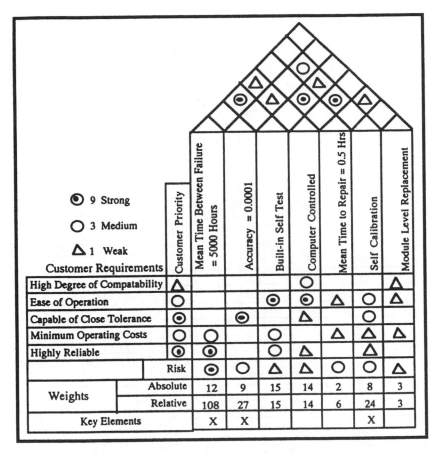

FIGURE 5-9   Identifying Key Elements

TECHNICAL BENCHMARKING

Technical benchmarking means determining how well the competition is fulfilling the customers' requirements in terms of the design requirements. We express this evaluation in terms of a score, which is plotted on the horizontal axis. Some score the design requirements on a scale of 1 to 4, with 4 being the best. This method results in a plot across the bottom of the House of Quality. Figure 5-10 illustrates how these features are entered on the House of Quality.

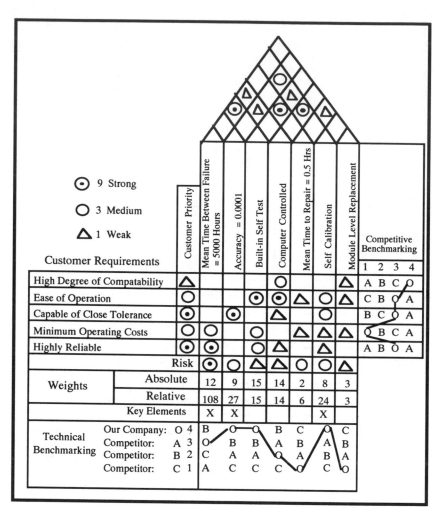

FIGURE 5-10   Benchmarking

Target Values

It is necessary to establish target values for each of the design requirements. This action establishes concrete goals for the design engineers
and further defines the customer requirements. These values need
to be measurable and can be developed from historical records, designed experiments, or analysis of what the competition is doing.

Once the team agrees on the target values, they are entered on the horizontal axis, below the row identifying the key elements.

Competitive Benchmarking

A block is added on the right side of the House of Quality to reflect how well you and the competition are satisfying the customer requirements that are identified on the vertical axis on the left side of the matrix. As in the case of the technical benchmarking, this evaluation is scored and plotted as a graph.

Comparing the results of the technical and competitive benchmarking data should show a consistency. If your product scores high in the competitive comparison, it should also score high on the technical comparison. Inconsistencies are flags that there may be a problem with a design requirement.

We can add more columns to the right side of the matrix for including other information, such as level of effort, cost, or priorities for the customer requirements. The possibilities are unlimited and should be driven by your imagination and capacity for innovation.

This completes the House of Quality. This serves as the starting point for the deployment of requirements as depicted in Figures 5-3 and 5-4. This information will be given to each of the appropriate organizations and ad hoc teams developing the product and services. The IPPD team will then manage the development of the other matrices to ensure the complete and effective design and development of the customer offering.

MATRIX OF MATRICES

Bob King, in *Better Designs in Half the Time,* published by GOAL/ QPC, describes the "matrix of matrices" approach for QFD. This is an innovation of the QFD process. It is derived by looking at the matrix concept across the broad spectrum of the design process. The result is a set of 30 matrices that can be modified or rearranged to fit the specific design goal. In this manner, the QFD process can be adapted to the complexity of the design task. Experience indicates that the initial application of QFD needs to be limited to the basic approach described above. This experience will enable the team to apply QFD to a complex design task and to use the powerful Matrix of Matrices (Figure 5-11).

Figure 5-11 presents the Matrix of Matrices. The House of Quality is the A-1 Matrix. It is the starting point for all IPPD projects.

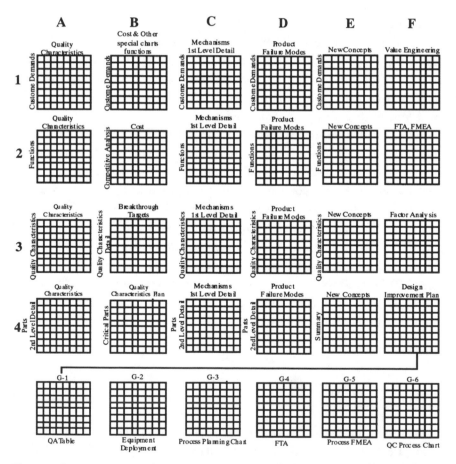

FIGURE 5-11   Matrix of Matrices (reprinted with permission from GOAL/QPC)

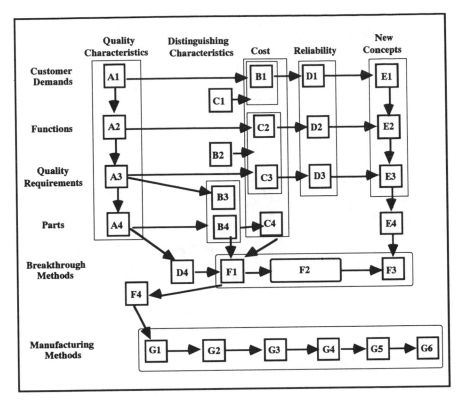

Purpose To Be Achieved	Charts To Use
Analyze Customer Demands	A1, B1, D1, E1
Critique Functions	A2, C2, D2, E2
Set Quality Characteristics	A1,A2, A3, A4, B3, B4, C3, D3, E3
Identify Critical Parts	A4, B4, C4, E4
Set Breakthrough Targets	C1, B2, B3, B4
Set Cost Targets	B1, C2, C3, C4
Set Reliability Targets	D1, D2, D3, D4
Select New Concepts	E1, E2, E3, E4
Identify Breakthrough Methods	D4, F1, F2, F3
Identify Manufacturing Methods	G1, G2, G3, G4, G5, G6

FIGURE 5-12   Matrix Relationships

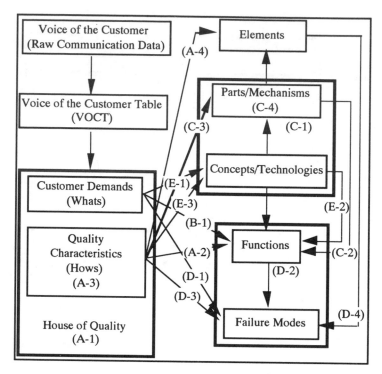

FIGURE 5-13   Matrix Process Flow

Selecting the matrix to follow the A-1 matrix is dependent upon the purpose of the project and its scope. Figure 5-12[3] presents the flow of the matrices and suggested matrices for a variety of purposes. Some of the matrices are used to develop finer detail for achieving a stated purpose. Others are charts that reveal insight about the interaction and interrelationships of sets of requirements or data.

One of the authors has developed a flow of matrices for using the matrix of matrices. This flow starts with the A-1 matrix and leads you to use the appropriate matrices to develop your specific IPPD project. It also provides an understanding of the relationships between sets of data in the IPPD process. In this way this flow is very useful for organizing the QFD activity, providing a check to ensure that the appropriate activities are performed and providing a corporate knowledge for the IPPD project. Figure 5-13[4] presents the matrix flow and Figure 5-14 is an example to show how the information is flowed.

KEY POINTS

QFD provides the method for listening to the voice of the customer and answering it. If you are not using Quality Function Development, and do not intend to use it on your next project, you will not survive in the marketplace of the future.

Quality is a measure of the customers' satisfaction with a product or service. QFD is a structured method that uses the 7 M&P tools to identify and prioritize customers' expectations. In the IPPD process, these customer requirements come directly and indirectly, through research about the customers' needs, requirements, and motivation.

Distinguishing Characteristics are the functions and characteristics that you are going to design to motivate customers to buy your products and services over the competition.

The Customer-Performance Model is the total package being offered the customers. It is the performance model that is given to the IPPD team for implementation.

The IPPD team uses QFD to further refine the performance model and translate these requirements into engineering requirements for systematic deployment throughout the company at each stage of product, service, and process development and improvement. The implementation of QFD by the Integrated Product Development multi-functional team thereby deploys the voice of the customer throughout the various functional areas of research and development, engineering, sales/marketing, purchasing, quality operations, manufacturing, packaging, and after-market support.

The basic tool used in QFD is the matrix. A family of matrices in a matrix-waterfall fashion deploys the customer requirements, and related technical requirements, throughout all related design and manufacturing processes for the development of a product or service.

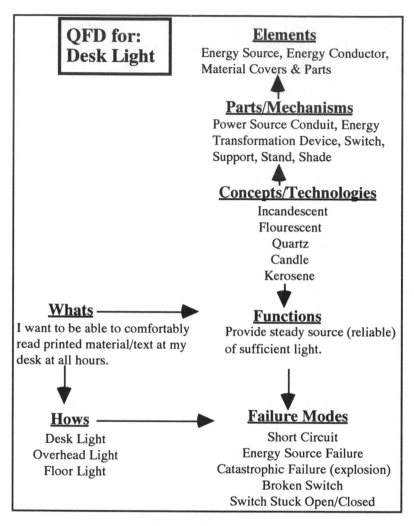

FIGURE 5-14   Sample Matrix Process Flow

The waterfall method is powerful in developing products or services that will satisfy and delight customers. It begins with the customer-performance model which is deployed in this waterfall fashion. This method ensures the optimum design is developed to satisfy the customers' expectations. The organization then implements the design, using the optimum materials, and processes. QFD thus provides a methodology for ensuring that the design and production of products and services are focused on achieving customer satisfaction.

There are five phases in Quality Function Deployment: Organizing, Product Planning, Product Design, Process Planning, and Implementation. The appropriate tools or processes (7 M&P Tools, Failure Modes and Effect Analysis, Design of Experiments, SPC, SQC, Information-Services Network, etc.) are used in each phase to ensure the systematic deployment of the customers' expectations throughout the design, manufacture, and service of the product.

In the organizing phase, the opportunity has been identified and the business decision is made whether to proceed or not. The IPPD team then begins the detailed planning stage of the project.

In the product planning phase, the customer-performance model is evaluated. We use this information to develop the Requirements Matrix, also known as the House of Quality. This matrix defines the product in terms of the design requirements necessary to achieve customers' expectations. After the product is planned, we enter the Product Design Phase. In this phase, we develop the Design Matrix and Product Characteristics Deployment Matrix. The Design Matrix identifies the engineering design activities required to achieve the product design requirements. The Product Characteristics Deployment Matrix subsequently identifies the product characteristics that satisfy the engineering design requirements. The product is defined at this point in terms of characteristics that satisfy the customers' requirements.

We then use the results of the Product Characteristics Deployment Matrix to develop the Manufacturing/Purchasing Matrix in the Process Planning Phase. At this point, we select the manufacturing and purchasing operations needed to achieve the product characteristics. We also develop the Control/Verification Matrix to determine the necessary production and quality controls for the selected manufacturing and purchasing operations.

The final phase is the Implementation Phase. In this phase, we are in production. We implement SPC, conduct process capability studies, implement designed experiments, and achieve continuous measurable improvement. These activities are also referred to as variability reduction. This is where we make the design and processes robust. This means that the design, selection of materials, and the processes are such that there is little variation in quality, in spite of diverse or changing environmental conditions.

EXAMPLE

The IPPD team for the LWCI 1600 project used Quality Function Deployment. They began with the customer-performance model. The 7 M&P tools were used extensively to collect and analyze these requirements. The information used to develop the Requirements Matrix included the customers' priority for each.

The customers' requirements, from the customer-performance model, and their priorities were entered on the left vertical axis of an A-1 Requirements Matrix (Example Figure 5-1). Next, the team identified the technical characteristics that the LWCI 1600 needed to satisfy the customers' requirements. These were entered on the top horizontal axis of the matrix.

The team added the "roof," the risk row, and the weighting factors. The team decided that they would not use the technical comparison or the competitive comparison on the matrix. They elected, instead, to use the Matrix Data Analysis Charts they had previously developed.

The team completed the matrix using the standard symbology: triangle for weak, open circle for medium, and concentric circles for strong. They evaluated each intersection in the body of the matrix for the relationship and put the appropriate symbol in the box. They then evaluated the risk for each of the technical characteristics, in terms of financial, resource, or technical risk or difficulty. Again, they used the standard set of symbols to represent high, medium, or low risk.

The weight for each technical characteristic was first determined as an absolute value and then as a relative value. The team calculated the absolute value by assigning a value of 9 for strong, 3 for medium,

Customer Requirements	Customer Priority	Industry Std. Software System	Std. LWCI Interface	Self-Test	Digital Control	Mean-Time-Between Failure: 5,000 Hrs.	Mean-Time-To Repair <0.5 Hrs.	Modular Design	Accurate Op., Maint., & Cal. Manuals	Customer Support Network	Customer Training Program	No Hazmat in process	Minimum Safety Precautions Req'd for Operation, Maintenance, & Calibration	Variability Reduction Program	Accuracy 0.0001 inch	Footprint: <20 sq. ft.	Synchronous Manufacturing
High Degree of Compatibility	●	●	●			△		○		△	△			△			
Easy to Operate	○	○	○	●	●		○	●	●				○				
Good Pre & Post Sales Support	○	△	△							●	●		△				
High Degree of Safety	●			△	△							●	●	△	△		
Capable of Close Tolerance Work	●		△		○										●		
Compact System	△		△	△	○			●								●	
Low Cost & On Time	○			△	○	○	△	△						●			●
Good Support Documentation	△	△					△		●	△	○		△	△			

Technical Requirements →

EXAMPLE FIGURE 5-1   Requirements Matrix

1 for weak, and 0 for none. The score was calculated by adding the individual scores in each column. The total was put in the corresponding absolute weight cell. The team calculated the relative weight, by multiplying the absolute weight by the risk score, and placed the result in the corresponding relative weight cell.

The team decided to use actual scores instead of rankings. They felt this would give them an insight as to the magnitude of the differences between scores, which would be important to them in selecting the key characteristics. The key characteristics they identified were:

- ► Footprint < 20 square feet
- ► Minimum safety precautions required for operation, maintenance, and calibration
- ► Customer training program
- ► Variability Reduction Program
- ► Mean Time to Repair < 0.5 hours
- ► Accurate Operating, Maintenance, and Calibration Manuals

These key elements then became focal points for the LWCI 1600 Development Team. The team did not abandon the remaining characteristics; rather, the key elements became areas of special concern. They were judged as important and more difficult to accomplish than the other characteristics. Therefore, these key elements warranted special consideration to ensure that they were accomplished.

Next, the roof of the House of Quality was completed. As discussed earlier in the chapter, this is a correlation matrix that demonstrates the interactions of the technical characteristics. A review of the Example Figure 5-2 reveals this correlation. As shown, the Variability Reduction Program affects Mean Time Between Failures, accuracy of the system, accuracy of the manuals, Mean Time to Repair, synchronous manufacturing, and the compactness of the system.

The technical characteristics were used to develop the Design Matrix, which identifies the Engineering Design requirements for the technical characteristics. The team used the Engineering Design requirements to identify the Product Characteristics in the Product

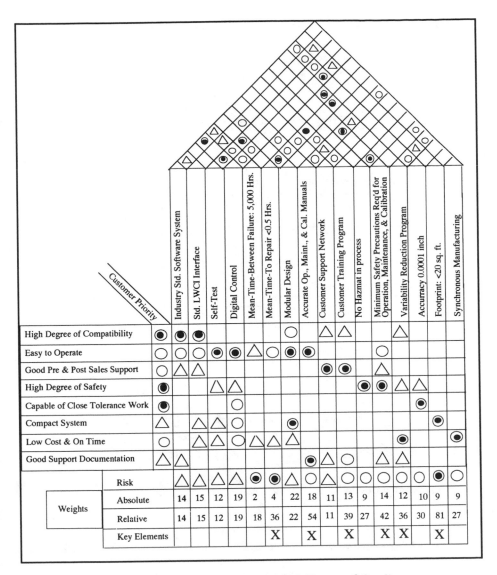

EXAMPLE FIGURE 5-2   LWCI 1600 House of Quality

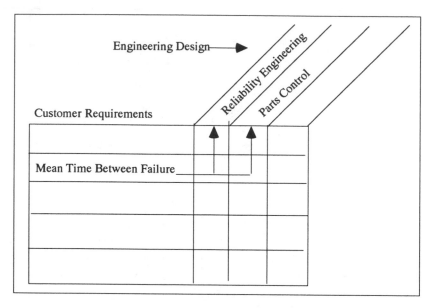

EXAMPLE FIGURE 5-3   Design Matrix

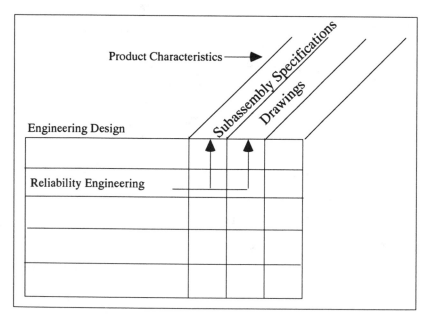

EXAMPLE FIGURE 5-4   Product Characteristics Matrix

Characteristics Matrix. They used the Product Characteristics, in the Manufacturing/Purchasing Matrix, to define the Manufacturing and Purchasing operations needed to achieve the product characteristics. The Manufacturing and Purchasing operations were entered in the Control/Verification Matrix to determine the Production and Quality Controls needed to accomplish the Manufacturing and/or Purchasing operations. Example Figures 5-3 through 5-6 follow one technical characteristic, MTBF (5,000 hours), through this process.

At each step of the QFD implementation, the team used the 7 M&P tools, and a variety of statistical tools and techniques, to develop and define the elements of the matrix. They also used these tools to execute the details of the LWCI 1600 development plan. The procedures used by the team included an extensive application of statistical process control and designed experiments.

The application of QFD provided the method for ensuring an integrated, concurrently engineered development of the LWCI 1600. In addition, the team identified numerous process improvements. In

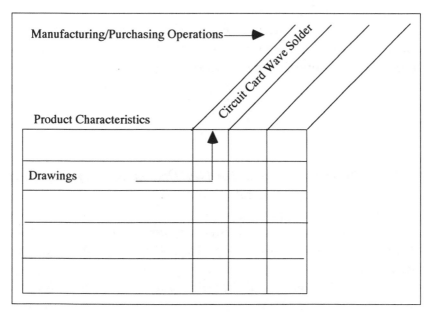

EXAMPLE FIGURE 5-5   Manufacturing/Purchasing Matrix

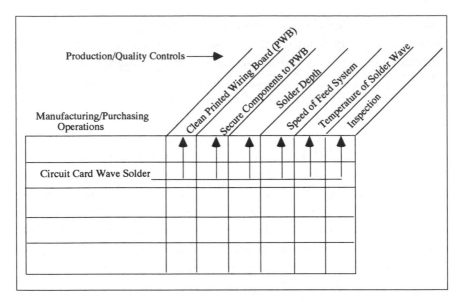

EXAMPLE FIGURE 5-6   Control/Verification Matrix

each instance, an improvement was compared against the QFD matrices before implementation. If an improvement did not have a positive impact on achieving customer satisfaction, or on achieving the goals of the company, the team dropped it.

NOTES

[1] ReVelle, Dr. Jack B., 1992, *The New Quality Technology,* pp. D-20. Los Angeles: Hughes Aircraft Company.

[2] Ibid, pp. D-21.

[3] Shina, Sammy G., 1991, *Concurrent Engineering and Design for Manufacture of Electronics Products,* pp. 154. New York: Van Nostrand Reinhold.

[4] Moran, John W. and Jack B. ReVelle, 1994, *The Executive's Handbook on Quality Function Deployment,* pp. 76. Windham, NH: Markon, Inc.

6

Analyzing Communication Data

> THE 7 M&P TOOLS PROVIDE AN EFFICIENT AND
> EFFECTIVE METHOD FOR ANALYZING LANGUAGE,
> DATA ANALYSIS, RELIABLE PRIORITY SETTING, AND
> CONTINGENCY PLANNING.

In statistical process control (SPC) and statistical quality control (SQC), the emphasis is on the collection, analysis, and interpretation of numerical data. In these activities, we count or measure things. We use the relationships of numbers and the characteristics of mathematical distributions to turn the data into information for decision making. In business planning processes, however, we must deal with large amounts of communication data, such as ideas, opinions, perceptions, or desires. The usual statistical methods do not work in the analysis of communication data.

GOAL/QPC and the American Supplier Institute (ASI) began studying and teaching the Seven New QC Tools in 1983. Since that time, many others have refined the tools and contributed to their understanding. Most, like GOAL/QPC and ASI, now refer to these tools as the Seven Management and Planning Tools (7 M&P Tools).

The 7 M&P Tools are:

1. Affinity Diagram
2. Interrelationship Digraph
3. Tree Diagram
4. Matrix Diagram
5. Process Decision Program Chart
6. Arrow Diagram
7. Matrix Data Analysis Chart

These tools are flexible in their application, and the output from one can be the input for another. In this manner, we are able to leverage their power, thus increasing their value in all planning activities. The first two tools listed are for general planning, whereas the third, fourth, and seventh tools are for intermediate planning. The fifth and sixth tools are for detailed planning. When we integrate the application of the tools in a manner that is appropriate for the task at hand, the result is efficient, effective distillation of communication data, rapid analysis of language data, reliable priority setting, and effective contingency planning.

The Matrix Data Analysis Chart seldom is used and has been replaced with the Prioritization Matrix.

DATA COLLECTION FOR THE 7 M&P TOOLS

The application of the 7 M&P Tools begins with the collection of communication data. This is the first step in all planning. As stated earlier, the term "communication data" refers to ideas, opinions, perceptions, desires, and issues. These include requirements established by the leaders of the company, customer requirements and expectations, and ideas generated by the work team itself. The data are usually collected through brainstorming, focus groups, or surveys. Brainstorming is effective when the number of individuals who possess the desired information is small. In this instance, every individual is involved in the data collection process.

There are several methods for brainstorming: multi-voting, nominal group technique, free association, and variations of all these. The recommended method for brainstorming is free association. A question is posed to the team, and each member is free to present his or her response. The question can relate to a problem, a desired result, a goal, or an objective. The ideas are not evaluated during the brainstorming. All discussion focuses on clarification and drawing out of additional ideas. Each idea or response is written on a single Post-it™ note.

If the topic is controversial, or the team members appear reluctant to offer ideas or if one or two individuals dominate the discussion, we recommend the "round-robin" method. This is a variation of the nominal group technique (NGT). During round-robin brainstorming, each individual has a turn to respond. No one may respond out of turn, nor is anyone allowed to criticize or evaluate an input. A member may, however, choose to pass. The round-robin continues until the generation of ideas is exhausted.

Surveys are appropriate when the population possessing the desired information is large. In this case, it is not practical to query every individual, so we select a sample of the population for the survey. Surveys use a set of structured questions to elicit responses from the sample. We analyze these responses to determine trends or to answer questions about a given or potential situation. Although surveys can be either written or oral, the results need to be documented in writing in preparation for further action.

AFFINITY DIAGRAM

Purpose

The planning process begins with the collection of a large set of data regarding ideas, opinions, perceptions, desires, and issues. Initially, the relationships among these data elements will not be clear, although there may be a sense of where the team wants to go. The first task, then, is to distill the data into key ideas or common themes. The Affinity Diagram is an effective tool for achieving this result. It organizes communication data into groupings and determines the key ideas or common themes. The results can then be used for further analysis in the planning process.

Process

The development of an Affinity Diagram is a three-step process. This is a creative task, requiring analysis of ideas, association of common thoughts, and determination of patterns from large amounts of data. An individual can develop the Affinity Diagram, but because it is a creative process, a team is more effective. The three steps for developing an Affinity Diagram are:

1. Group data
2. Select grouping titles
3. Refine groupings

Step 1. Group Data

Begin by collating the ideas, opinions, perceptions, desires, or issues as individual data elements. Write each one on an individual piece of paper, such as a Post-it™ note. These then are arranged on a flat surface such as a wall, white board, or window. The objective is to cluster the ideas together in logical associations. Some people like to write tentative titles and cluster the ideas under them. We do not recommend this because it can stifle creativity. Instead, let the associations and patterns drive the title.

During this step, it is important that every member of the team participate. Begin by placing the data elements on the flat surface without regard to association. Then, suggest that the team arrange the notes in logical patterns. The team does this together, without discussion or evaluation of the choices. Each person is encouraged to move the Post-it™ notes around at will. This may seem chaotic,

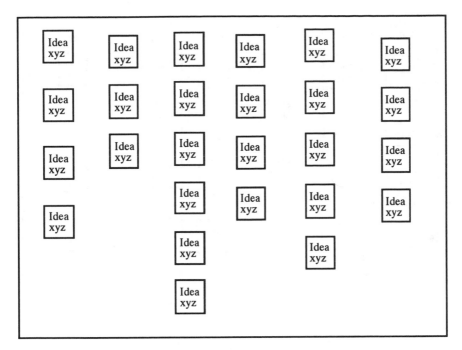

FIGURE 6-1   Associate Ideas

but set a time limit (e.g., 15 minutes) and encourage participation, and soon, order and agreement will come out of the chaos (Figure 6-1).

Step 2. Select Grouping Titles

The next step is to decide on a title for each grouping. The title needs to represent an action that reflects the main idea or theme of the grouping. The titles, therefore, need to be complete thoughts, stated as actions.

In some instances, determining the title requires a compromise among the ideas in the grouping. Keep in mind that at this point in developing the Affinity Diagram, the title is important because it defines the action to be taken (Figure 6-2). Avoid evaluating the ideas in the groupings at this point in the process. The next step will further clarify the issues and the titles.

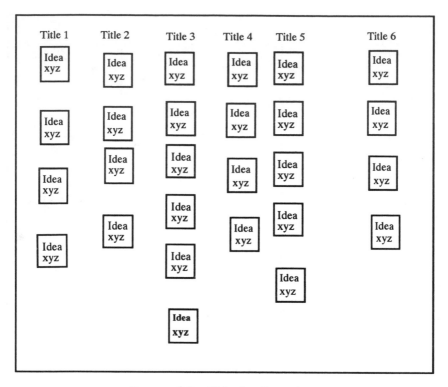

FIGURE 6-2   Title the Groupings

Step 3. Refine Groupings

After the groupings have appropriate titles, it is time to review each item under each title to see if it still fits or if it should be included under a different title. At the same time, review the titles to ascertain if any of the groupings can be consolidated. The resulting Affinity Diagram (Figure 6-3) will bring order to the original collection of apparently unrelated ideas. The full impact of what you have achieved using this tool will only become apparent when you see your ideas logically grouped into issues meaningful to you.

The Affinity Diagram is a very powerful tool for dealing with communication data. It quickly and effectively distills the data into logical patterns that reveal common themes and associations. It is

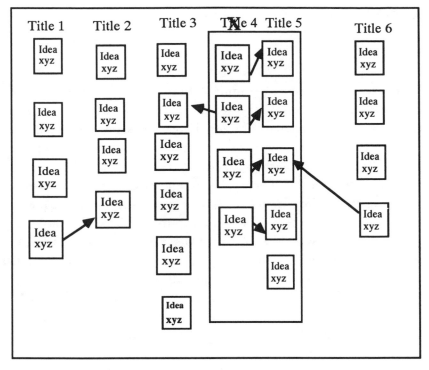

FIGURE 6-3   Refine Groupings

also effective in dealing with old issues when new creative thinking is desired. Some practitioners argue against using the Affinity Diagram when the situation is simple and requires quick results.

In our experience, the time and energy expended in developing an Affinity Diagram is amply rewarded by the resulting insights and consensus, regardless of the complexity of the situation or the quantity of data.

Application of the Affinity Diagram can extend from simple personal planning to the most complex industrial problems. A single individual or a team can use the Affinity Diagram as the starting point for planning. The results of this analysis can become the input for the Interrelationship Digraph, Tree Diagram, or Arrow Diagram.

INTERRELATIONSHIP DIGRAPH

Purpose

The relationships among communication data elements are not linear, and they are often multi-directional. In other words, an idea or issue can affect more than one other idea or issue, and the magnitudes of these effects can vary. Additionally, the relationships are often hidden or not clearly understood.

The Interrelationship Digraph is an effective tool for understanding the relationships among ideas and for mapping the sequential connections among them. The usual inputs for the Interrelationship Digraph are the results of an Affinity Diagram. The Interrelationship Digraph can, however, be used to analyze a set of actions or ideas generated without first developing an Affinity Diagram.

We use the information developed from the Interrelationship Digraph to establish priorities and to determine optimum sequencing of actions. Frequently, teams develop an Affinity Diagram, skip the Interrelationship Digraph, and go on to use another tool to develop their plan. This is a big mistake. The Interrelationship Digraph always provides an important understanding about the data you are analyzing.

There are three methods for accomplishing the Interrelationship Digraph. The original method is called the Arrow Method. GOAL/QPC teaches an alternate method referred to as the Matrix Method. There is a third method that we prefer. We call this the J-F Matrix Method. This is a cross between the Matrix Method and the Prioritization Matrix.

Arrow Method

With the Arrow Method, lay out the issues using a flat surface on which you can write (such as a white board). You can write them on the white board, attach cards or notes on the white board, or simply write them on a piece of paper. The Arrow Method consists of four steps:

1. Determine causal relationships
2. Draw directional arrows
3. Sum arrows in and out
4. Set priorities for the issues

Step 1. Determine Causal Relationships

The first step in preparing an Interrelationship Digraph is to determine the causal relationships among the issues. Take each issue, in turn, and ask the question: "Does this issue cause or influence any other issue?" Ask the same question for every issue until all combinations have been examined.

This process works well if the question is the same each time and if you move in one direction at a time, e.g., from Issue A to B, from A to C, etc. If you change the wording of the question or consider the relationships in a bi-directional manner, you will confound the issues and possibly miss a combination.

Step 2. Draw Directional Arrows

Draw an arrow from each issue to any issue it affects or causes (Figure 6-4). If issues have arrows going in both directions between them (a two-way arrow), determine which issue has the greater causal relationship, and eliminate the other arrow.

One variation is to weight the causal relationship as strong or weak. Use a solid line arrow to indicate a strong causal relationship and dashed line arrow to indicate a weak causal relationship.

Step 3. Sum Arrows In and Out

After exploring all possible combinations, sum the arrows in and out for each issue (Figure 6-5). Record the results clearly next to each issue, indicating if the total is "in" (I) or "out" (O).

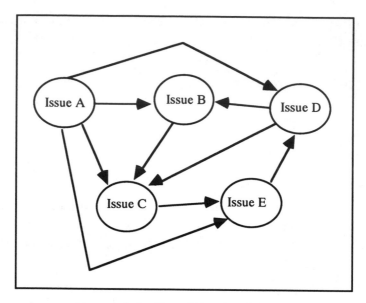

FIGURE 6-4   Draw Directional Arrows

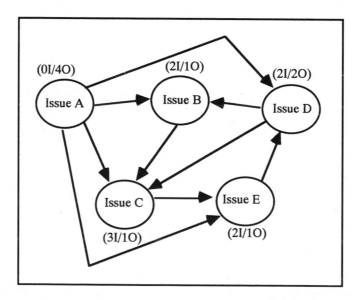

FIGURE 6-5   Sum Arrows In and Out

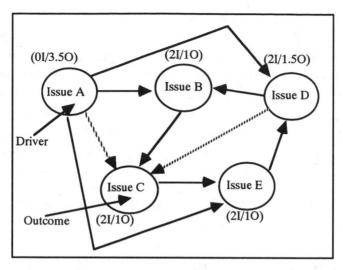

FIGURE 6-6   Strong and Weak Relationships

If you choose to discriminate between strong and weak causal relationships, give a half-point value to a dash line arrow and a whole point to a solid line arrow (Figure 6-6).

Step 4. Set Priorities for the Issues

Review the results of Step 3. The issues with the largest sum totals for arrows out have the greatest impact on the other issues. These are typically the "critical few" issues. If we solve these problems, implement these actions, or provide these services, we will have the greatest influence on the problem, goal, or customer requirement. The totals are also an indication of the expected return on our investment in time, energy, and money for addressing a given issue.

The issues with the greatest number of arrows in are the ones affected by the greatest number of other issues. These are highly dependent on the accomplishment of the other actions or issues. These may, in fact, be bottlenecks or other critical issues to be analyzed. In our example above, Issue A clearly has the greatest impact on all the other issues. Issue C is clearly the most dependent issue and might be a bottleneck for the process, problem, or goal under evaluation.

GOAL/QPC-Style Matrix Method[1]

The arrow method, as demonstrated, is easy to construct. Our example used only five issues, and the digraph is easy to understand. For
those situations with more than five issues however, the arrow method
rapidly becomes very complex and virtually impossible to follow.
GOAL/QPC teaches a simpler matrix method for developing the
Interrelationship Digraph that makes it possible to deal with a large
number of issues and ensures the methodical evaluation of each
relationship. It is presented in their book *Memory Jogger Plus* + [TM] and
is presented as an alternative to the arrow method. The matrix
method consists of five steps:

1. Develop L matrix of issues
2. Determine causal relationships
3. Draw directional arrows
4. Sum arrows in and out
5. Set priority for the issues

Step 1. Develop L Matrix of Issues

The first step in the matrix method is to develop an L matrix of the
issues. This is a matrix with two axes. For this digraph, enter each
issue on both the horizontal axis and the vertical axis. There is a
column for the sum of the arrows in, one for the sum of the arrows
out, and one for the combined total of arrows in and out (Figure 6-7).

Step 2. Determine Causal Relationships

The second step in developing the matrix is to determine the causal
relationships among the issues. Take each issue on the vertical axis
and compare it to each of the other issues on the horizontal axis. As
in the Arrow Method, ask the question: "Does this issue cause or
influence the issue on the horizontal axis?" (Or, "Does Issue A cause
or influence Issue B?")

The question needs to be worded the same way each time. Changing the wording of the question confounds the issues. Unlike the

	A	B	C	D	E	IN	OUT	TOTAL
Issue A								
Issue B								
Issue C								
Issue D								
Issue E								

FIGURE 6-7   L Matrix

Arrow Method however, you compare the issues in both directions each time and mark the direction accordingly.

Step 3. Draw Directional Arrows

Draw an arrow from each issue toward the issue it affects or causes. If a pair of issues has arrows going in both directions, determine which issue has the greater causal relationship, and eliminate the other arrow.

Step 4. Sum Arrows In and Out

After exploring all possible combinations, sum the arrows in and out for each issue. Place the totals in the respective columns. Then sum the total arrows in and out, and place that total in the last column (Figure 6-8).

Step 5. Set Priorities for the Issues

Review the results of Step 4. As in the arrow method, the issues having the largest sum totals for arrows out have the greatest impact

	A	B	C	D	E	IN	OUT	TOTAL
Issue A		↑	↑	↑	↑	0	4	4
Issue B	←		↑	←		2	1	3
Issue C	←	←		←	↑	3	1	4
Issue D	←	↑	↑		←	2	2	4
Issue E	←		←	↑		2	1	3

FIGURE 6-8   Completed Matrix

on the other issues. These are the "critical few" issues. Solving these problems, implementing these actions, or providing these services will have the greatest influence on the problem, goal, or customer requirement. The issues with the largest total of arrows out are the issues that have the greatest impact on achieving your desired results.

Management 2000 Matrix Method

The arrow method and the GOAL/QPC-style matrix method are both effective methods for developing the Interrelationship Digraph to understand the relationships and sequential connections among ideas. Experience teaches that the application of the 7 M&P tools leads to new applications and new ways of using them. The frustration of applying the arrow method in very large, complex situations also led us to develop a new matrix method for preparing the Interrelationship Digraph. To differentiate it from the GOAL/QPC-style matrix method, we call this method the J-F Matrix Method.

The J-F Matrix Method is a cross between the GOAL/QPC-style matrix method and the GOAL/QPC Prioritization Matrix. It is similar to the GOAL/QPC-style matrix method, but the symbols are different, and the interrelationships are summed along both axes. The J-F matrix method consists of five steps:

1. Develop L Matrix of issues
2. Determine causal relationships
3. Mark the causal relationships
4. Sum the interrelationships
5. Set priorities for the issues

Step 1. Develop L Matrix of Issues

The first step in developing the Interrelationship Digraph using the J-F matrix method is to develop an L matrix of the issues. Enter each issue on the horizontal and vertical axes. Add a total column and a total row to the matrix, as shown in Figure 6-9.

Depend➤	A	B	C	D	E	Total
Issue A						
Issue B						
Issue C						
Issue D						
Issue E						
Total						

FIGURE 6-9   L Matrix of Issues

Step 2. Determine Causal Relationships

The second step in developing the matrix is to determine the causal relationships between each pair of issues. Take each issue on the vertical axis and compare it to each of the other issues on the horizontal axis. For this method, the question is: "Does the horizontal issue depend on or is it caused by the vertical issue?"

As in the other two methods, the question needs to be worded the same way each time. This method is like the arrow method, comparing the issues in only one direction at a time.

Step 3. Mark the Causal Relationships

For this method, we evaluate the extent of each causal or dependency relationship: strong, medium, weak, or none. The symbols used are the same as those used for Quality Function Deployment (Figure 6-10). Figure 6-11 is an example of a matrix with symbols added.

Step 4. Sum the Interrelationships

After determining all the relationships, score them in both the vertical and horizontal axes. Place the totals in the appropriate column or row. As in Quality Function Deployment, the weights for the associated symbols are as shown in Figure 6-12. Figure 6-13 shows the matrix with the scores added.

Step 5. Set Priorities for the Issues

Review the results of Step 4. As in the Arrow Method, the issues having the largest sum totals for arrows out have the greatest impact on the other issues. In this matrix, this corresponds to the row totals

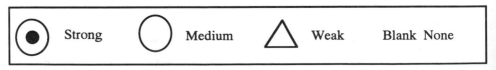

FIGURE 6-10   Symbols for Causal Relationships

Issues	A	B	C	D	E	Dep. Total
A	▓					
B	◉	▓		◉		
C	△	◉	▓	△		
D	◉			▓	○	
E	◉		◉		▓	
Ind. Total						

FIGURE 6-11   L Matrix of Issues with Causal Relationships

at the bottom of the matrix. These are the "critical few" issues. Solving these problems, implementing these actions, or providing these services will have the greatest influence on the problem, goal, or customer requirement.

The totals in the column on the right side of the matrix reflect the issues that are affected by the other issues. In this case, the highest total indicates an issue is most affected by the other issues. It is, therefore, the most dependent.

In Figure 6-13, Issue A has the highest independence score: 28. The next highest score is 10. Issue A, therefore, clearly warrants the highest priority of attention. Addressing this issue will have the greatest impact because of the extent that the other issues depend on it. It is also of interest that Issue A has the lowest dependence score. It is not affected by any of the other issues. Conversely, Issues B and E

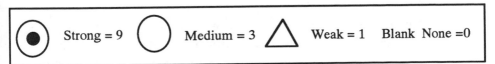

FIGURE 6-12   Weights for Symbols

Issues	A	B	C	D	E	Dep. Total
A						0
B	◉			◉		18
C	△	◉		△		11
D	◉				○	12
E	◉		◉			18
Ind. Total	28	9	9	10	3	59

FIGURE 6-13   L Matrix of Issues With Scores

are tied for the highest dependence score: 18. These issues are affected the most by the other issues under evaluation.

You can use the insight provided by this evaluation to prioritize
actions or to determine the issues necessary for further planning. It is
always valuable to perform this step even if all of the issues are to be
acted on. The resulting understanding is always of value.

TREE DIAGRAMS

Purpose

The Tree Diagram has many uses. It is a systematic tool for determining all of the tasks necessary to accomplish a goal. It can be used for
determining key factors causing a problem or to develop an action
plan for a single event or a process. You can also use the Tree
Diagram to decide on the priority for action.

Process

The Tree Diagram begins with the definition of a goal, task, or problem that we need to break into finite sub-elements. This definition is a statement of purpose, a problem statement, or some other fact. You can develop the statement from a previously developed Affinity Diagram, Interrelationship Digraph, or from a new Affinity Diagram, a new Interrelationship Digraph, brainstorming, or some other means. This definition statement becomes the focal point for generating possible tasks, causes, or issues.

The development of the Tree Diagram is a logical task. It begins with a top-level statement, proceeding in a logical, step-by-step manner to lower and lower levels of detail. As each level is defined, these new statements become the focal point for further development. This process continues until you are satisfied with the level of information you have developed. Each level can also be provided by new or previously developed Affinity Diagrams, Interrelationship Digraphs, or brainstorming.

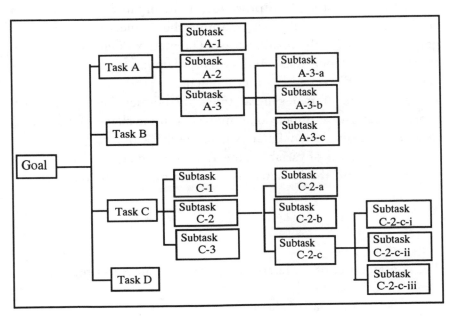

FIGURE 6-14   Tree Diagram

The example in Figure 6-14 illustrates how a goal has been broken into four key tasks. Each task has been further broken into subtasks, and each of these has been examined for further definition. For this illustration, Subtasks A-3 and C-2 have been broken down into further detail. Subtask C-2-c has been also broken into further detail.

The Tree Diagram uses linear logic to go from a broad statement to successive levels of detail. It is useful, therefore, when a task or problem is complex and when it is important to identify all key elements or subtasks.

MATRIX DIAGRAM

Purpose

The Matrix Diagram is a tool for organizing language data (ideas, opinions, perceptions, desires, and issues) so that they can be compared to one another. The procedure is to organize the data on a vertical and a horizontal axis, examine the connecting points, and graphically display the relationships. The matrix diagram reveals the relationships among ideas and visually demonstrates the influence each element has on every other element.

Matrices are of two general types: two-dimensional and three-dimensional. A two-dimensional matrix is in the shape of an L, T, Y, or X. A three-dimensional matrix is in the shape of a C. The L matrix is used for two sets of variables, the T, Y, and C matrices for three sets of variables, and the X matrix is used for four sets of variables.

Process

The construction of a Matrix Diagram is a four-step process:

1. Select the matrix elements
2. Select the matrix format

3. Complete the matrix headings
4. Determine relationships or responsibilities

Step 1. Select the Matrix Elements

The matrix elements fall into categories, which are sets of data. You can derive these elements from a new or previously developed brainstorming, Affinity Diagram, Interrelationship Digraph, or Tree Diagram.

Step 2. Select the Matrix Format

As stated above, the matrix format depends on the number of sets of data to be analyzed. The most common formats are the two-dimensional L and T matrices (Figure 6-15).

Step 3. Complete the Matrix Headings

After the language data is collected, sorted, divided into sets, and the matrix format is selected, fill in the headings of the matrix.

Step 4. Determine Relationships or Responsibilities

Examine each of the interconnecting nodes in the matrix and determine if there is a relationship. As in the J-F Matrix Method for

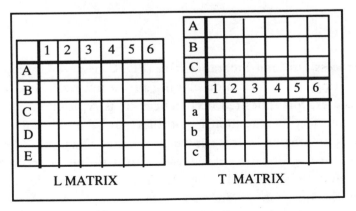

FIGURE 6-15   L and T Matrices

Issues	1	2	3	4	5	Total
A						0
B	◉			◉		18
C	△	◉		△		11
D	◉				○	12
E	◉		◉			18
Total	28	9	9	10	3	59

FIGURE 6-16   Completed L Matrix

developing an Interrelationship Digraph, evaluate the relationships and mark the matrix accordingly (Figure 6-16). At this point, sum the rows and columns and interpret the matrix.

PROCESS DECISION PROGRAM CHART (PDPC)

Purpose

The Process Decision Program Chart (PDPC) is a tool that assists in anticipating events and in developing preventive measures, or countermeasures, for undesired occurrences. It is typically used when a task is unique, the situation is complex, and the price of potential failure is unacceptable. It is similar to the Tree Diagram. It leads you through the identification of the tasks and paths necessary to achieve a goal and its associated subgoals. The PDPC then leads you to answer the questions "What could go wrong?" and "What unexpected events could occur?" Next, the PDPC leads you in developing countermeasures. The PDPC provides effective contingency planning by mapping out all conceivable events and leading the development of appropriate countermeasures.

Process

The process for developing the Process Decision Program Chart (PDPC) is less structured than any other of the 7 M&P tools discussed so far. The goal is to list and evaluate all possible subtasks or actions using the graphical method presented below, an outline, or some other construct that you might develop. These steps listed, therefore, are intended only as guidelines:

1. Construct a Tree Diagram
2. Answer key questions "What can go wrong?" and "What unexpected events could occur?"
3. Develop countermeasures

Step 1. Construct a Tree Diagram

As originally developed, the PDPC is a graphic chart. It begins with the development of a Tree Diagram of the process or activity under evaluation. For the PDPC, we prefer to orient the Tree Diagram vertically instead of horizontally (Figure 6-17). This convention is not a rigid requirement, but it does seem to provide a logical direction for the flow of activities when developing contingencies.

Step 2. Answer Key Questions

At each branch of the Tree Diagram, two questions are asked:

- ► "What can go wrong at this point?"
- ► "What unexpected events could occur?

The answers to the first question are documented on the chart. The alternate paths are added to the chart as well (Figure 6-18).

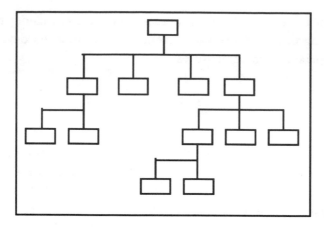

FIGURE 6-17   Vertical Tree Diagram as Basis
for PDPC

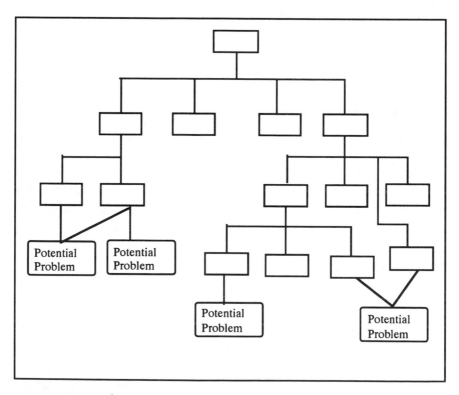

FIGURE 6-18   Potential Problems are Marked on the PDPC

Step 3. Develop Countermeasures

Countermeasures are developed for each action that could go wrong. The development of the countermeasures may involve the application of one or a combination of the following tools:

- ► Brainstorming
- ► Affinity Diagram
- ► Interrelationship Digraph
- ► Tree Diagram

Annotate each countermeasure below the potential problems. Repeat the process until all branches or paths are exhausted. Then,

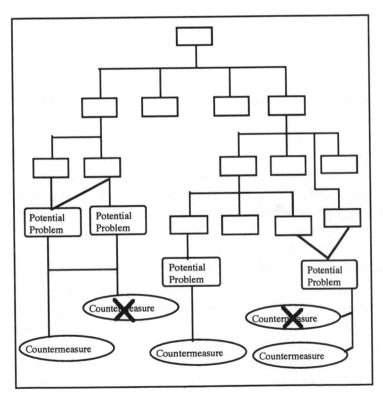

FIGURE 6-19   Countermeasures are Marked on the PDPC

evaluate each countermeasure for feasibility, cost impact, quality impact, and schedule impact. This evaluation will enable you to make an informed decision when selecting the countermeasures to implement. As you evaluate the countermeasures, mark them to indicate if they are to be implemented or not (Figure 6-19).

The PDPC is an efficient tool for evaluating a process or activity. It maps the conceivable activities (or actions) and contingencies in a methodical manner. The PDPC is especially powerful when used in conjunction with the other 7 M&P tools.

ARROW DIAGRAM

Purpose

The Arrow Diagram is derivative of the Critical Path Method (CPM) and Program Evaluation and Review Technique (PERT) developed in the United States in the 1950s. It is a tool for determining the optimum time for accomplishing a task and for graphically displaying the activity flow. This tool is most effective when the subtasks for an activity are well known and there is a high degree of confidence in that knowledge. Each subtask is plotted in sequence. The time to accomplish each task is indicated and used to determine the earliest time that a given subtask can begin.

An Arrow Diagram (Figure 6-20) clearly indicates which subtasks can be done in parallel and which subtasks must be done sequentially. In this manner, the optimum activity flow can be determined, and the minimum time to complete the entire task can be calculated. The Arrow Diagram can include the earliest and the latest start time for any given subtask. The Arrow Diagram aids in planning and in evaluating progress against the plan.

If the subtasks are not well known and understood, this is a very frustrating activity. In that case, the PDPC is a better tool for graphically displaying a task or project.

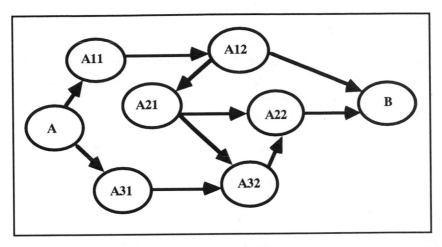

FIGURE 6-20   Arrow Diagram

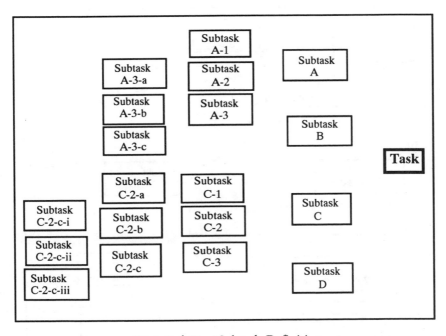

FIGURE 6-21   Subtask Definition

Process

The process for developing the Arrow Diagram is similar to that for developing the PDPC. It begins with defining all the subtasks or actions and determining their sequence. Each subtask is evaluated and the Arrow Diagram is drawn.

1. Define the subtasks for the activity
2. Evaluate each subtask
3. Construct the Arrow Diagram

Step 1. Define the Subtasks for the Activity

We begin by defining all the required subtasks. List each activity on a separate Post-it™ note and number them for easy reference. Begin to

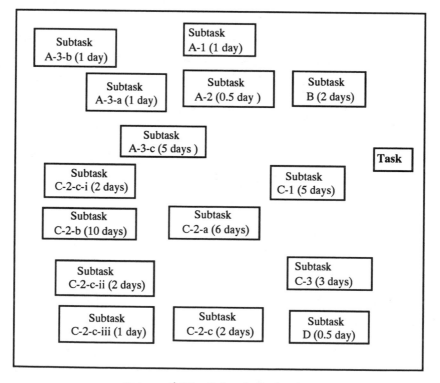

FIGURE 6-22   Subtask Evaluation

arrange the tasks on a flat surface in the required time sequence. Do this using the horizontal axis. The result is similar to the Tree Diagram, but the subtasks are arranged from right to left instead of from left to right (Figure 6-21).

Step 2. Evaluate Each Subtask

Evaluate the sequence of the subtasks, and modify the arrangement of the Post-it™ notes at this time. Carefully note those activities that can be performed in parallel with others. Mark the subtasks with the time duration. At this stage, higher level subtask titles can be eliminated. These are subtask titles that are not actual actions themselves, but are accomplished by lower subtasks. Our goal is to leave only those subtasks on the diagram that are actual actions to be accomplished (Figure 6-22).

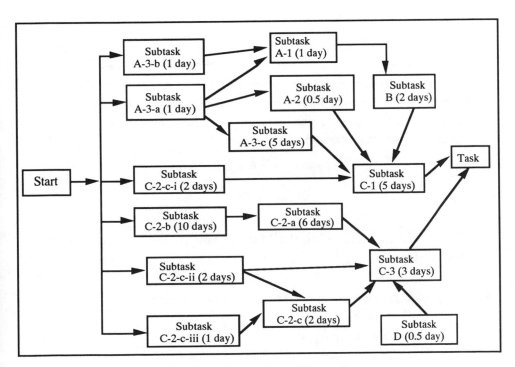

FIGURE 6-23   Arrow Diagram

Step 3. Construct the Arrow Diagram

Finalize the arrangement of the subtasks, and draw the appropriate arrows between the actions showing the flow of activity (Figure 6-23).

In the example in Figure 6-23, there are several sets of subtasks that are performed in parallel.

Mapping these subtasks in the Arrow Diagram reveals the optimum sequencing. The evaluation of the subtasks enables us to calculate that the task will take a maximum of 19 days of elapsed time to complete.

MATRIX DATA ANALYSIS CHART

Purpose

The Matrix Data Analysis Chart is used primarily in market research for the development and planning of new products or services. It is a tool for graphically presenting a comparison of products or services. In this way, one is able to evaluate a market segment and determine the relationships among products, services, or companies, based on representative characteristics.

Process

The process for developing the Matrix Data Analysis Chart consists of four steps:

1. Determine the representative characteristics
2. Collect data
3. Calculate comparisons
4. Graphically display the results

Step 1. Determine the Representative Characteristics

The first step in developing a Matrix Data Analysis Chart is to determine the representative characteristics to be compared. These are the key parameters that are used to evaluate a product, service, or process. Some of these parameters are easily defined and measured, such as concentricity, hardness, footprint, or weight. Others are more obscure and difficult to measure, for example, gentleness, flavor, or ease of use. In all cases, however, the parameters need to be representative of ways in which one would determine excellence for a product, service, or process.

Step 2. Collect Data

After determining the representative characteristics, collect data about the competing products, services, or processes.

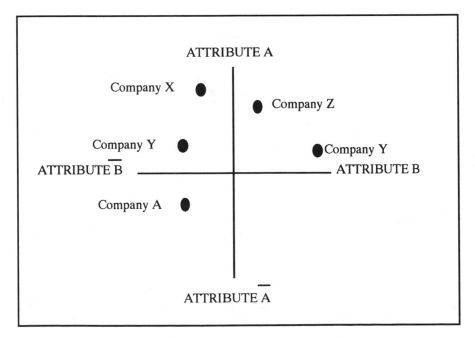

FIGURE 6-24   Matrix Data Analysis Chart

Step 3. Calculate Comparisons

Calculate the comparisons for the products, services, or processes under evaluation.

Step 4. Graphically Display the Results

Display the results of Step 3 on a four-quadrant chart, as in Figure 6-24. In this chart, you are able to compare how you perform against the competition with regard to two parameters. In this specific case, Company X is doing well in achieving Attribute A, but not as well as Company Y in achieving Attribute B.

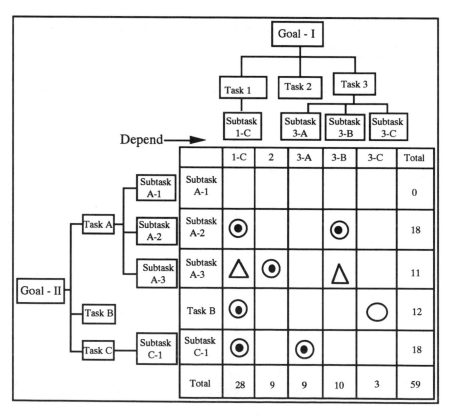

FIGURE 6-25   Prioritization Matrix

PRIORITIZATION MATRIX

The Prioritization Matrix is not one of the original 7 M&P tools. It is an innovation based on the Tree Diagram and the L-Shaped Matrix, and it is powerful enough to warrant discussion as a new 7 M&P tool.

The Prioritization Matrix is effective for sifting through a set of key issues or criteria to focus priority of action. It begins with a broad set of data, and uses Tree Diagrams to organize the information. The results of the Tree Diagrams are used to develop an L-shaped matrix. The matrix is evaluated as in the J-F Interrelationship Digraph. Figure 6-25 demonstrates the Prioritization Matrix.

KEY POINTS

The 7 M&P Tools provide an efficient and effective method for analyzing language data. The output from one tool can be the input for another. In this manner, we are able to leverage their power.

The application of the 7 M&P tools begins with the collection of language data through brainstorming, focus groups, or surveys.

The Affinity Diagram quickly and effectively distills language data into logical patterns that reveal common themes and associations.

The relationships among the data elements are not linear and are oftentimes multi-directional. The Interrelationship Digraph is an effective tool for understanding the relationships among ideas and for mapping their sequential connections. The input for the Interrelationship Digraph can be the result of an Affinity Diagram.

The information developed from the Interrelationship Digraph is useful in establishing priorities and determining optimum sequencing of action.

The Tree Diagram is a systematic tool for determining all the tasks necessary to accomplish a goal. It can be used for determining key factors causing a problem and for developing an action plan.

The Tree Diagram uses linear logic to go from a broad statement to successive levels of detail. It is useful, therefore, when a task or problem is complex and when it is important to identify all key elements or subtasks.

The Matrix Diagram is used to organize language data (ideas, opinions, perceptions, desires, and issues) so that they can be compared to one another. The matrix diagram reveals the relationships among ideas and visually demonstrates the influence each element has on every other element.

The Process Decision Program Chart (PDPC) is a tool that assists in anticipating events and developing preventive measures, or countermeasures, for undesired occurrences. It is used when a task is unique, the situation is complex, and the price of potential failure is unacceptable.

The Arrow Diagram is a tool for determining the optimum time for accomplishing a task and for displaying the activity flow. This tool is best used when the subtasks for an activity are well known and there is a high degree of confidence in the knowledge about the subtasks.

The Matrix Data Analysis Chart is used primarily in market research for the development and planning of new products or services. It is a tool for graphically presenting a comparison of products or services.

The Prioritization Matrix is effective for sifting through a set of key issues or criteria to focus priority of actions.

EXAMPLE

The Production Machinery Division of LWCI has embarked on a project to develop a new production machinery system. The new system will be designated the LWCI 1600. There will be a variety of models in the LWCI 1600 series. Each of the models will include features that are designed to address the particular requirements of a customer.

This new series of equipment will be the first product developed by the Production Machinery Division since LWCI established its vision:

> Leander Wiles Company Inc. will be a highly profitable enterprise producing world class quality products and services. We are focused on the design and production of manufacturing equipment. We will challenge the global marketplace and do so while remaining committed to being a socially and civically responsible company.

The division's steering council established a product-development team for the LWCI 1600 project. The product-development team consisted of representatives from marketing, engineering, product operations, quality, safety, finance, and procurement. The team also included a representative from the machine and tool division and electronics division. The mission of the product-development team was to use the Management 2000 model to develop the LWCI 1600.

The team's first step was to perform a customer survey. This was done in two parts: a personal interview with customers of LWCI products and a survey of companies that currently do not use LWCI products, but are potential customers. The goal of the survey was to collect information about customer requirements and expectations for use in the design and development of the LWCI 1600.

The team analyzed results of the survey. The analysis yielded a list of customer requirements, desires, and expectations to be used in the development of the LWCI 1600 (Example Figure 6-1). The team developed an Affinity Diagram for this data and then developed an Interrelationship Digraph from the Affinity Diagram. These are presented in Example Figures 6-2 and 6-3.

The message from the "voice of the customers" is that they want and expect:

> a compact system that is low in cost, easy to use, and capable of highly accurate work.

- Low cost
- Accurate schedule commitments
- Timely response to requests for information
- Reliability of systems
- Low Mean Time Between Failures (MTBF)
- Low Mean Time To Repair (MTTR)
- Easy to use
- Good availability of training on system use
- Good availability of training on system maintenance
- Competent, knowledgeable salespeople/order takers
- Upward compatible system
- Downward compatible system
- Easy to program
- Easy to incorporate modifications
- Good availability of upgrades
- Meet commitments for quality, cost & schedule
- Help line
- Good product documentation
- Accurate product documentation
- Product documentation easy to follow
- Setup instructions easy to understand
- Clear operating instructions
- Level of documentation appropriate for skill level of operators, maintenance personnel, etc.
- Minimum special test equipment required for maintenance
- Easy to calibrate
- Calibration cycle better than average for the industry
- Small equipment footprint
- Equipment safe to use
- Equipment requires a minimum of hazardous material to operate
- Equipment generates a minimum of hazardous material
- Special tools not required for setup or operation
- System digitally controlled
- High tolerance system

EXAMPLE FIGURE 6-1   Survey Results

High Degree of Compatibility
- Upward compatible system
- Downward Compatible System

Good Pre & Post Sales Support
- Availability of training in system use
- Availability of training on system maintenance
- Timely response to requests for information
- Competent, knowledgeable sales people
- Help line

High Degree of Safety to Personnel and Environment
- Equipment safe to use
- Equipment requires a minimum of hazardous material to operate
- Generates a minimum of hazardous material

Good Support Documentation
- Product Documentation
- Accurate Documentation
- Easy to Follow
- Set up instructions easy to understand
- Clear operating instructions
- Level of documentation appropriate for skill level of operators and maintenance personnel

Ease of Operation & Maintenance
- Easy to calibrate
- Calibration cycle better than or equal to current industry standard
- Special tools not required for setup or operation
- Easy to program
- Easy to modify
- Availability of upgrades
- System Reliability
- Low Mean Time Between Failure (MTBF)
- Minimum special test equipment required
- System digitally controlled
- Easy to use.

High Tolerance System
- High tolerance system

Compact System
- Small equipment footprint

Low Cost, On Time Delivery
- Low Cost
- Accurate schedule commitments
- Meet commitments for quality, cost & schedule.

EXAMPLE FIGURE 6-2   Affinity Diagram of Survey Results

Affinity Diagram "Headers"	A	B	C	D	E	F	G	H	Dep. Total
A. High Degree of Compatibility						◯			3
B. Ease of Operation and Maintenance	△		◯		◯	◉			16
C. Good Pre and Post Sales Support						◉			9
D. High Tolerance System		△				△			2
E. High Degree of Safety	◯	△				◯			7
F. Good Support Documentation									0
G. Compact System									0
H. Low Cost, On Time delivery	△		◉						10
Ind. Total	2	4	13	0	3	25	0	0	47

EXAMPLE FIGURE 6-3   Interrelationships Digraph

This result was not a surprise to the team, but what was surprising was how customers defined those characteristics and their interrelationships. It was especially significant that support documentation and pre- and post-sales support are vital for satisfying the customers. In the past, these factors were not considered important. The analysis of the survey data clearly stated otherwise.

The team developed a Tree Diagram for each of the broad characteristics of the customers' requirements. These diagrams ensure that the team understands the specific details for these characteristics. Example Figure 6-4 is the initial Tree Diagram that was developed for "Ease of Operation & Maintenance."

The design team decided that a critical target for the LWCI 1600 system was low-cost but high-tolerance accuracy. They evaluated their competitors' systems on that basis. They compared the results with the target they set for the LWCI 1600 system using a Matrix Data Analysis Chart. The team chose the industry-average cost and average-tolerance accuracy as the 0,0 point. Each competitor's system was mapped in relation to the 0,0 point (Example Figure 6-5).

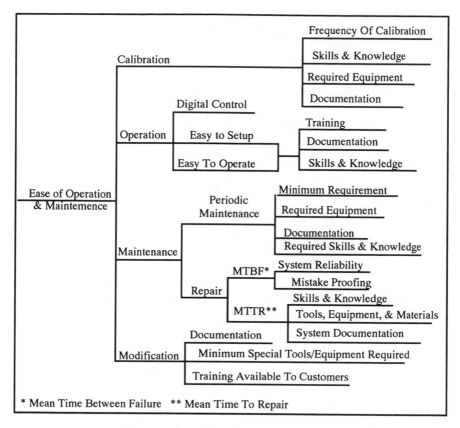

EXAMPLE FIGURE 6-4   Tree Diagram

The team concluded that the new system would provide an advantage over the competition. The LWCI 1600 would not be the cheapest in terms of acquisition cost, but it would be superior in accuracy for the cost. It would, therefore, provide superior value for the customers. The team's challenge is to meet the target for cost and accuracy and to implement the other customer requirements as determined by the survey and subsequent analysis.

As the team members explored the requirements for customer support services, they discovered that LWCI had a history of errors in customer orders. Initially, the team believed that the errors resulted

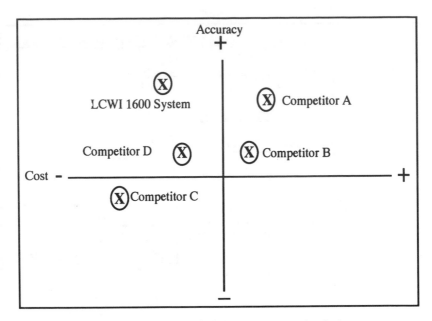

EXAMPLE FIGURE 6-5   Matrix Data Analysis

from the customers having incorrectly completed the ordering documents. The team used a PDPC to evaluate the ordering process
(Example Figure 6-6).

The Process Decision Program Chart for the Customer Orders
Process was very revealing. When the team asked what could go
wrong at each of the legs of the process, they were forced to face
possibilities that were under their control (Example Figure 6-6). The
team decided to implement several of the countermeasures they identified in the PDPC.

The LWCI 1600 development team realized that meeting delivery
schedules was important to their customers. They also realized it was
a vital element in making a profit. The team decided, therefore, to
predict the cycle time based on past performance and knowledge
about the technology for producing the LWCI 1600 systems. These
predictions would then be used to develop process flows to meet the
target cycle time. They used an Arrow Diagram to assist in the
prediction of the production cycle time (Example Figure 6-7).

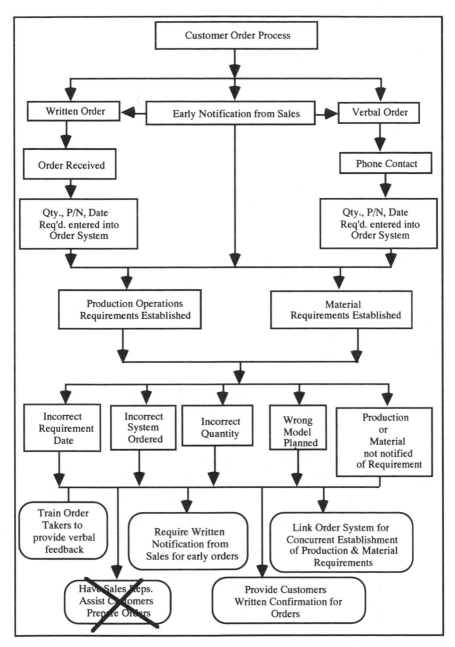

EXAMPLE FIGURE 6-6   Process Program Decision Chart

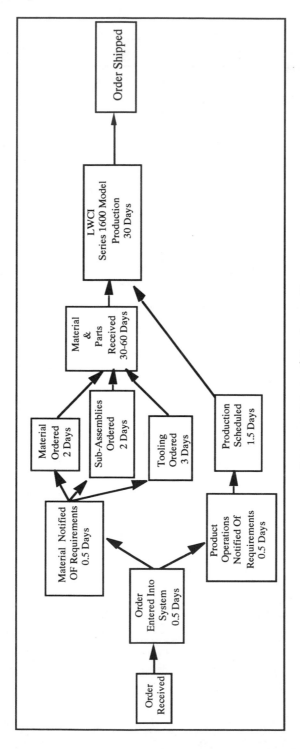

EXAMPLE FIGURE 6-7   Arrow Chart

The Arrow Diagram showed that a system could take from 64 to 94 days from receipt of an order until it was ready for packaging and shipping. This information will be used to develop work flows, establish ordering strategies, and establish warehouse requirements.

NOTE

[1] Adapted from *Memory Jogger Plus +* ^{TM} by Michael Brassard. Boston: GOAL/QPC, 1989.

CHAPTER 7

Building and Controlling Processes

> KNOWING, UNDERSTANDING, AND CONTROLLING
> YOUR PROCESSES IS CRITICAL TO A SUCCESSFUL
> ENTERPRISE.

To become world class competitors, your businesses must capitalize on the measurable factors of quality, cost, and schedule (Q$S). These <u>controllable</u> factors are the cutting edge of world class competition. Designing and developing processes that can optimize each of these factors is pivotal to the success of your new product or service.

To understand the impact of these factors, you must first have the ability to describe, quantify, and analyze them as part of a process. The first step in optimizing and controlling these factors is to develop the process and perform a process analysis. The properly completed process analysis provides the basis to implement a wide range of technical resources to accomplish the goal of becoming a world class competitor.

The Nature of Processes

Business activities can be viewed as processes that are a systematic, repetitive series of actions to develop or produce products or services. Optimization of your new product or service results directly from the proper development, management, and control of these processes. There are three types of processes: industrial, administrative, and managerial. Each of these processes is equally critical to the success of your enterprise.

Figure 7-1 demonstrates that all three have the same basic characteristics: input > > > > process > > > > output. These recursive characteristics enable us to apply the six phases of process analysis (Figure 7-2) to any of these processes. We can also apply the 7 M&P tools and the 7 QC tools to establish, control, and improve processes.

A process is a transformation of inputs, such as people, materials, equipment, methods, and environment, into finished products, through a series of value-added work activities. We will use the six phases of process analysis, presented in Figure 7-2, to provide a structured method of identifying and describing the elements of this transformation. The detailed understanding provided by a formal process analysis is a required precursor for the use of any technical resources. We must first understand a process, its elements, work

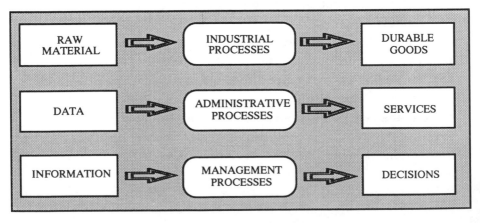

FIGURE 7-1   Three Types of Processes

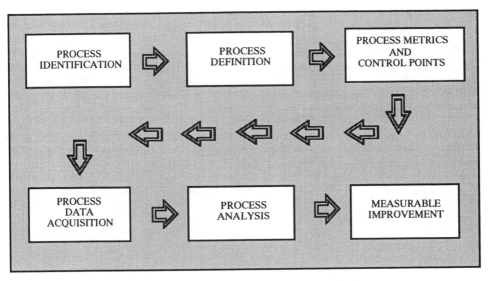

FIGURE 7-2   Six Phases of Process Analysis

activities, and measurable parameters before applying any other technical tool. Once we have performed a process analysis, we can then use the other technical tools to quantify, control, and improve the process. The Management 2000 philosophy stresses continuous measurable improvement in quality, cost, and schedule. A key factor in applying this philosophy is understanding the processes that affect these factors and their direct relationship to customer satisfaction.

When designing and developing your process, you must consider the way that operations are planned, people are organized, and how work moves through your organization when you view it as a process. Figure 7-3 demonstrates the way some processes work when they have not been designed to consider these facts. This is the old cliche, of "throwing work over the wall" to the next element in the process, without regard to the process efficiency, effectiveness, or its overall effect on the enterprise. The under-the-wall feedback in the figure represents the hidden process, where changes to the design, work practices, and problem solving occur in the back channel. Hoshin Planning and QFD have organized the design-and-development process of your product or service specifically to avoid this problem.

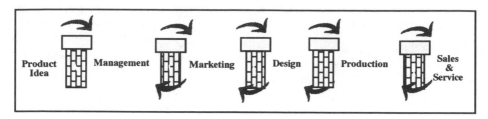

FIGURE 7-3   Bad Process Design

You must ensure that the processes you implement do not sub-optimize each process element and therefore fail to optimize your overall process.

You can clearly see the ineffectiveness of having process engineers design work processes, industrial engineers design layout, design engineers design products, and managers design the organization of people as separate functions. Each of these activities will sub-optimize the processes and provide a much less effective and efficient overall process for your new product or service. You must design and develop your process as a cross-functional team to insure the optimization of people, processes, and resources.

From the Management 2000 perspective, there are clearly good processes and bad processes. The good processes work like a well oiled machine, producing products and services nearly effortlessly. Bad processes are centric to the need of individual process elements, organizational structure, and individuals to sub-optimize. These processes are ineffective and inefficient, requiring a lot of effort and time to force out products and services. Processes with clearly defined fiefdoms will never be efficient processes. A properly designed process will enforce the requirement to be cross-functional and promote communication, cooperation, and coordination. A properly designed process will also follow your Hoshin Planning for the product in your organization and the QFD to ensure that the voice of the customer is fully implemented in the new product or service.

Another key element in understanding the nature of processes is distinguishing among the three types of processes: industrial, administrative, and management. All of these types of processes make up the overall process for every product and service.

Industrial Processes

Industrial processes come to mind immediately when we think of process analysis. These are the processes that produce things. The inputs to industrial processes are raw materials. These raw materials can be in the form of basic materials, such as iron ore, steel, and coal; subassemblies, such as computer boards and engine parts; or equipment for rework or repair, such as engines or automobiles that require overhaul or aircraft requiring upgrade and modification. Industrial processes lend themselves most easily to the technical resources for process improvement. As indicated in Figure 7-4, the output from one industrial process can be the raw material of another industrial process. Processes such as repairing, rebuilding, or upgrading things are also industrial processes. In those cases, the items to be repaired, rebuilt, or upgraded, together with the new parts, rework kits, or upgrades, are the raw materials of the process.

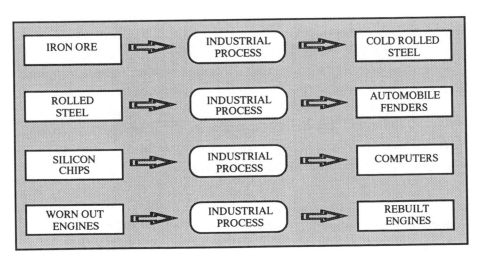

FIGURE 7-4   Industrial Processes

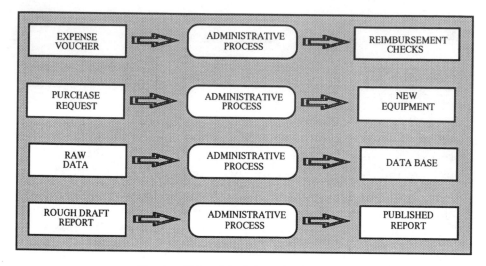

FIGURE 7-5   Administrative Processes

Administrative Processes

Administrative processes are the processes that frustrate customers (internal and external) most frequently. Administrative processes produce the paper, data, and information that other processes use. They also produce products used directly by the customers, such as tax returns, paychecks, reports, and data. Figure 7-5 displays examples of administrative processes. These processes include some of the most complex and bureaucratic challenges in the pursuit of world class competitiveness. The streamlining of administrative processes affects all other processes in an organization. Special attention must be paid to the dilatory effect of inefficient and ineffective administrative processes on personnel morale, the team spirit, management processes, and industrial processes.

Management Processes

Management processes are the structured means by which businesses and individuals make key decisions. It is very important that we

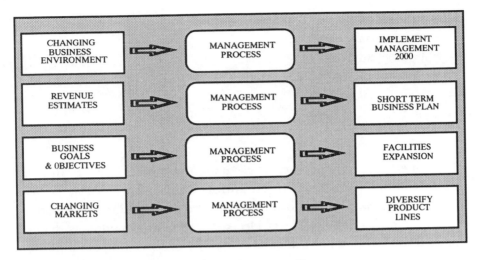

FIGURE 7-6   Management Processes

clearly understand that management is the process of using data to make decisions. This process is your decision support system. That process works best when properly accomplished in organizations with a Management 2000 infrastructure. This structured, quantifiable approach to decision making insures fact-based decisions. These fact-based decisions are supported by quantifiable data derived from the application of the management and technical tools. Figure 7-6 illustrates the nature of management processes.

In today's business environment, administrative and managerial processes contribute significantly to cost and can have the greatest effect on your new product or service schedules.

PROCESS DESIGN AND DEVELOPMENT

Process Design and Development follows the six phases of process analysis demonstrated in Figure 7-2. These phases are:

► Process identification
► Process definition

- ► Process metrics and control points
- ► Process data acquisition
- ► Process analysis
- ► Measurable improvement

Process Identification

To properly identify a process, we must determine what its initial input will be, its work activities, and its output. The starting point for this is the work breakdown structure we developed in the chapter entitled "Making the Business Decision." The process flow is developed from that basis. We must also identify process ownership of the overall process. To implement process control, we must also select those activities that are critical to the process as control points.

Many processes cross organizational boundaries. Therefore, in addition to identifying critical processes, it is equally important to understand who is in charge of each process. The person who has the responsibility to manage the process, irrespective of organizational boundaries, is the process owner. He or she must also have the means to effect changes and improve the process. In some instances, the person directly responsible for the activities that constitute the process is not in a position to detect the quality of the process product. In such cases, process management teams (project teams or continuous improvement teams) should include individuals who can best influence and effect resolution of process issues, as well as the persons responsible for the process activity.

The following two steps, and their associated actions, provide a structured method for determining process identification and the associated process ownership.

1. Process documentation
2. Process ownership

Step 1. Process Documentation

Process Specifications   These are documents, such as the Work Breakdown Structure and QFD for the product or service, that will provide the customer specifications for the process output; any other documentation provided by the customer; standard product specifications; and industry standards. What are the internal specifications for the product? Is specific equipment required? How do these specifications relate to input and output requirements? Are there any specifications for input to the process?

Process Procedures   What are the process procedures for the product or service? Who is responsible for the process documentation? Where was it written and by whom? Is specific equipment required for the process?

Process Control and Quality Control Requirements   Are these requirements part of the overall QA manual? Where were these requirements obtained? Who is responsible for these requirements and the overall QA program for this product? How are these requirements related to the customer requirements and satisfaction?

Process Input Requirements   What material or information is required as input to produce the product or service? Who are the suppliers? What are all the elements of the required input? How do they affect the output?

Process Output Requirements   Who is the customer or customers? What are the output requirements, by type, volume, quality, and schedule? How do the output requirements affect the input requirements?

Step 2. Process Ownership

Direct Responsibility   Determine what specific individual or unit of the organization will have direct responsibility for this process and its product.

Direct Contact   Determine who has the most direct contact with the process. Who is the individual(s) performing the work activities?

What individuals or elements of the organization are responsible for the activities?

Authority   Determine who has the ability and/or the authority to change the process. In identifying the process, we have determined several key factors:

- ► What kind of process it is—industrial, administrative, or management
- ► Where the process begins and ends
- ► The input and output requirements
- ► Information contained in all process documentation
- ► Ownership of the process

Now that we understand the basic parameters of the process, the next step is process definition. We will look into the internal workings of the process in great detail.

Process Definition

After identifying a process, we need to develop a method for describing it so that we can understand the process, all its elements, and what and how to measure the process. A very effective technique is to prepare a process flowchart. The process flowchart should be simple, with the minimum number of steps necessary to identify the key activities at different levels of indenture.

Process Flowcharts

The best method to provide a structured description of the process as a system is the process flowchart. This flowchart traces the product through all steps and stages. It depicts how the streams of products (or services or materials) move, disperse, and converge during all processing stages. Such a process flowchart makes it easier for all concerned to understand the process to be developed and to identify the process elements to be evaluated. Figure 7-7 is an example of such a flowchart for one element of a manufacturing process.

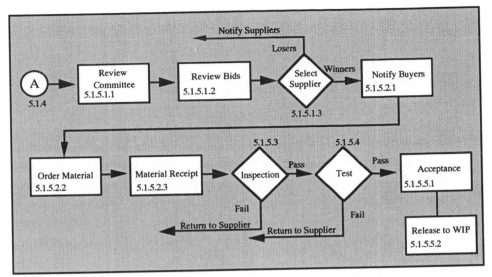

FIGURE 7-7   Procurement Process Flowchart for WBS Element 5.1.5

Note the numbering system on the process flowchart; it is the same numbering system as is found on the Work Breakdown Structure, the project Gantt chart, and the cost estimate. This is not a coincidence. The flow chart was developed from the Work Breakdown Structure, as were the Gantt chart and the cost estimate. This provides a clear audit trail from the inception of the project and allows for a detailed evaluation of the process, based upon the relationship between the process flow at every level and the Gantt chart schedule and cost estimate. This is a very efficient tool to use when evaluating your processes and to provide fact-based information to support the management decision process.

Flowcharts are drawn at various levels in the process. Each level of system complexity adds an analytical burden in the amount and type of data taken at the various points in the process. Remember that the purpose of the flowchart is to describe the process properly, so that it can be quantified and analyzed. There are several steps in performing flowcharting that will provide the necessary understanding to quantify and analyze the process. These steps are discussed fully in the following sections.

Flowcharts can become large and complex. Flowcharts that are too large or detailed cannot be clearly understood or evaluated. Very large, complex processes should be broken down into manageable sub-processes.

Flowchart Symbols

A wide variety of flowchart symbols are available. Many are symbols specifically for electronic flowcharting, mechanical process flowcharting, and computer program flowcharts, among others. Attempting to incorporate these symbols into process analysis can be very complex and confusing, and it is also unnecessary. In performing flowcharting for process analysis, we will use only six symbols, as shown in Figure 7-8 below.

Process Direction Arrow   The process direction arrow shows the direction of the process flow. This arrow points to the next step in the process. The process flowchart in Figure 7-7 uses these arrows to demonstrate how the two processes flow from their start points, converge at system integration, and flow to the process completion at the stop point.

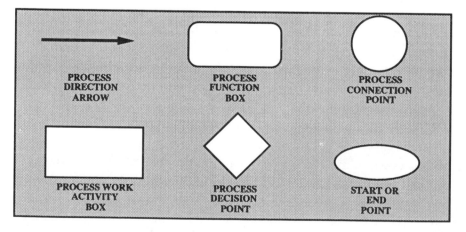

FIGURE 7-8   Flowchart Symbols

Process Function Box   This symbol represents a process function that contains more than one work activity that can be flowcharted separately. A brief description of the function is written in the box. This box is used to represent process functions, such as system integration, finishing, fault isolation, rework, and repair. Each of these process functions has more than one work activity associated with it. There are no process function boxes in Figure 7-7.

Process Connection Point   This circle will have a letter (A,B) within the circle. It is used when large complex flowcharts cover more than one page and is used to indicate where the process begins on the following page. In Figure 7-7, this symbol demonstrates that the process is continued from another page leading to motor integration.

Process Work Activity Box   This symbol represents a single work activity within the process flow. A brief description of the work activity is written in the box. Some of the single work activities represented in Figure 7-7 are Select Supplier, Order Material, Material Receipt, and others.

Process Decision Point   This is a process function or work activity that is a decision point. It has two or more process direction arrows, depending on the decision being made. The diamond contains a brief description of the process decision point. In Figure 7-7, this symbol is used to identify the receipt inspection decision points with the associated pass/fail arrows coming from the diamond. The symbol is also used to describe the decision point of dynamic test, with a "fail" arrow leading to the fault isolation rework/repair functional box and the "pass" arrow continuing the process to the inventory work activity box.

Start and End Points   This symbol signifies the start or stop points of a process. As indicated on the flowchart in Figure 7-7, there can be more than one start point for a complex process that includes the output of two or more converging processes. The number of start points depends on the manner in which you define the start of the process. Most processes have only one start point. The stop point is usually where the production of the product or service is complete.

The following steps provide a structured method to complete this phase and provide the basis for completing the flowcharts. In Steps 1–4, you develop lists of information that are used in Step 5 to create the flowchart.

1. Define the internal elements and boundaries of the process.
2. Identify the outputs and customers of the process.
3. Identify inputs and suppliers of the process.
4. Identify each work activity and sub-process and the process flow.
5. Document the process flow.

Step 1. Define Process Internal Elements and Boundaries

Within the overall process, what are the elements of the process? Are these elements themselves processes, each with several work activities? Define the element or work activity that begins and ends each process element. List the sub-processes or elements of the overall process.

Step 2. Identify Process Element Outputs and Customers

List all the products and services produced by the process elements. List all internal and external customers of the process.

Step 3. Identify Process Element Inputs and Suppliers

List all inputs the process receives. List all the suppliers, internal and external.

Step 4. Identify Each Work Activity and Sub-Process and Process Flow

For each input listed, define the work activity it feeds. For each work activity, define what outputs it produces. For each work activity output, define what process element it feeds. Determine who (specifically) performs each work activity.

Step 5. Document Process Flow

Using the techniques described earlier, chart the process flow. Start at the initial element receiving process input. Diagram the flow of each process element and its associated work activity through the process. End at the process output that produces the final product or service associated with the process.

Sequentially number each process element. These numbers will be for future referencing. For each element, develop backup details to include functional description, element criticality, ownership, performance measures, inputs, outputs, and other relevant information. In describing the process, we have looked closely at what is actually occurring:

- ► What are the several elements of the process?
- ► What are the inputs and outputs of these elements?
- ► What are the work activities involved with the process?

We have also flowcharted the process at lower levels. The next question in this logical sequence is: "How do I measure this process?"

Process Metrics and Control Points

After identifying and defining the process, the process team must establish the metrics for the control, analysis, and improvement of the process. Each metric must be concise and measurable, stressing one theme, such as process control, cost, improvement of quality, or schedule. Process metrics must be realistic, rational measures directly related to the process, the product, customer requirements, and the goal you have established for taking a measurement at this point in the process. The selection of control points and associated metrics will have a significant effect upon your process and product. The selection of metrics is not based upon what happens to be easily measurable, what has been traditionally measured in the past, what data is readily available, or what a consultant has indicated should be measured.

The metrics must then be established, documented, and clearly understood by all of the team members before the next step can be taken successfully. Some questions that help clarify metrics relate to the purpose for which they will be used:

- ► Is our goal to reduce defects?
- ► Is our goal to improve our process or activity?
- ► Is our goal to establish statistical process control (SPC)?
- ► Is our goal to establish statistical quality control (SQC)?
- ► Is our goal to reduce the queue?
- ► Is our goal to improve the throughput?
- ► Is our goal to improve our timeliness?
- ► Is our goal to reduce the cost?

Once the goals and objectives for the process analysis have been clearly and concisely written and agreed upon, the required control points and metrics can be established.

Metrics are the measurements necessary to monitor the process and to determine if it is satisfying the requirements. These measurements should be established based on customer requirements stated in the QFD. In selecting control points, remember that they must be tied to results of critical operations and that they are at process decision points. The measures of process Q$S are of prime concern when measuring processes. We will next describe the step-by-step procedure to determine process metrics and control points.

Performing Process Measurement

The following five steps and their actions provide a structured method for determining the process metrics and critical process elements.

1. Review process output requirements
2. Review process input requirements

3. Review all process elements
4. Define the measures of the process elements
5. Evaluate measures and control points

Steps 1 and 2 collect data to be analyzed in Step 3. The information derived from the analysis is used to make decisions in Step 4. In Step 5, we begin measuring the process.

Step 1. Review Process Output Requirements   Determine how process output requirements can be effectively measured. Can they be measured by:

- ► Number of output units produced?
- ► Number of output units rejected at final inspection?
- ► Cost per output unit?
- ► Average warranty cost per output unit?
- ► Output units rejected by customers, internal and external?

Step 2. Review Process Input Requirements   Determine how process input requirements can be effectively measured. A few commonly used measures are:

- ► Number and type of inputs (raw material) received by the initial process element
- ► Number, type, and source of input units rejected at receipt
- ► Cost per input unit

Step 3. Review All Process Elements   Determine what value-added is derived from each work activity. Determine effective measures for each process element and its associated work activity.

- ► Measure the cost of the element
- ► Measure the process time of the element
- ► Measure the scrap rate produced by the element
- ► Measure the quality of material produced by the element
- ► Measure the timeliness and throughput of the element

Step 4. Define Measures of Critical Process Elements   The measures selected for the process inputs, outputs, and each critical process element should relate to the goals and objectives for the process analysis. Determine the measure of each critical element and control point by its direct relationship to the goals and objectives of the process Quality, Cost, and Schedule (Q$S).

Step 5. Evaluate Measures and Control Points   Evaluate the selection of measures and control points based upon the types of analysis that will be performed. Remember that you are attempting to establish process control or improve quality, cost, or schedule (Q$S). These measures can then be used to determine what the critical points in the process are. How those points can be measured and controlled for continuous measurable improvement is described next in Process Data Acquisition and Analysis.

Process Data Acquisition

After we have identified the process critical measures and control points, we must then collect data, from existing processes or from pilot processes, to facilitate the analysis of these points. To determine if the process is meeting customer needs and expectations requires measurable data. These data are also essential to determine if the process is in control and to ensure the success of improvement efforts. The following three steps and the associated actions describe the procedure to perform data acquisition:

1. Determine data media.
2. Specify the scope of the data acquisition requirement.
3. Gather data from the critical elements/control points.

Step 1. Determine Data Media
Based upon the information obtained or learned during the selection of metrics and control points, define the data that can be obtained

from automated media. Define the data that must be manually acquired. Determine what the most efficient and effective method for data acquisition is.

Step 2. Specify Scope of Data Acquisition Requirement

Define the size of the data storage requirement. Will it be survey data, sampling data, or process control data already available in automated systems? Can the data be effectively acquired, stored, and analyzed? Define how the data will be retrieved and used. Will we use automated analysis programs? Will multiple access be required? Do we need this data on a network?

Step 3. Gather Data from Critical Elements/ Control Points

Determine if the data will be surveyed or sampled. Gather the data from each critical element and control point. Now that the method and scope of data acquisition and retrieval have been determined, we are ready to analyze the process. The next phase, Process Analysis, describes a structured approach to this effort.

Process Analysis

Many processes have evolved over time in response to specific needs. They have been incrementally changed by additions or procedural modifications. The results, in some cases, are complex processes that do not fit the current needs of the organization and your new product or service. There are several steps in the analysis of your new process. These steps involve using all of the technical and management resources (tools) available to you.

It is imperative that our activities be consistent with the stated objective for the specific process. Therefore, after prioritizing opportunities, you must base decisions for action on their impact upon quality, cost, and schedule. The following three steps and associated actions will aid in completing this phase of process analysis:

1. Analyze data using statistical techniques.
2. Compare performance and requirements.
3. Perform further analysis of selected elements.

Step 1. Analyze Data Using Statistical Techniques

Build a table that provides basic measures, using the metrics developed previously. Using this table, apply the appropriate descriptive statistical techniques.

Step 2. Compare Performance and Requirements

Establish control charts to monitor ongoing performance. Compare data acquired to process output requirements. Identify any difference between the analyzed process performance and requirements. Document all analysis findings.

Step 3. Perform Further Analysis of Selected Elements

Identify the critical problem elements or work activities, and tie those problems directly to key metrics. Expand the quantitative analysis to include engineering and technical team members. Review process problem elements to determine:

- Error sources
- Bottlenecks
- The need to clarify internal customer and supplier requirements and relationships
- The absence of adequate controls
- Process redundancies and other inefficiencies

Gather additional qualitative data as required to further investigate and validate process performance. This will lead directly to the ability to implement the last element of the six phase process development and analysis process; that is, Continuous Measurable Improvement (CMI).

PROCESS CONTROL CHARTS

Control charts provide a graphic depiction of the quantifiable characteristics of process, process element, or work activity. Control charts display the plotted values of the process and indicate if the process is approaching an established limit. In everyday business applications, control charts have five uses:

- ► Determine if a process is trending.
- ► Determine if a process is in control.
- ► Achieve statistical process control.
- ► Reduce process variability.
- ► Forecast process resource requirements.

The use of control charts focuses on the prevention of defects, rather than their detection and rejection. In business, government, and industry, economy and efficiency are always best served by prevention. It costs much more to produce an unsatisfactory product or service than it does to produce a satisfactory one. There are many costs associated with producing unsatisfactory goods and services. These costs are in labor, materials, facilities, and the loss of customers. The cost of producing a proper product can be reduced. significantly by the application of statistical process control charts.

Common Cause Variation and Special Cause Variation

Control chart analysis determines whether the inherent process variability and the process average are at stable levels; that one or both are out of statistical control (not stable); or that appropriate action needs to be taken. Another purpose of using control charts is to distinguish between the inherent, random variability of a process and the variability attributed to an assignable cause. The sources of the random variability are often referred to as common causes. These are the sources that cannot be changed readily, without significant restructuring of the process. Special cause variability, by contrast, is subject to correction within the process under process control.

To use process control measurement data effectively, it is important to understand the concept of variation. No two products or process characteristics are exactly alike, because many processes contain many sources of variability. The differences among products may be large, or they may be almost immeasurably small, but they are always present. Some sources of variation in the process can cause immediate differences in the product, such as a change in suppliers or the accuracy of an individual's work. Other sources of variation, such as tool wear, environmental changes, or increased administrative control, tend to cause changes in the product or service only over a longer period of time.

Common Cause Variability	Special Cause Variability
This source of random variation is always present in any process. It is that part of the variability inherent in the process itself. The cause of this variation can be corrected only by a management decision to change the basic process.	This variation can be controlled at the process level. Special causes are indicated by points on the control chart that are beyond the control limit or by a persistent trend approaching the control limit.

To control and improve a process, we must trace the total variation back to its sources. Again, the sources are common cause and special cause variation. Common causes are the many sources of variation that always exist within a process that is in a state of statistical control. Special causes (often called assignable causes) are any factors causing variation that cannot be adequately explained by any single distribution of the process output, as would be the case if the process were in statistical control. Unless all the special causes of variation are identified and corrected, they will continue to affect the process output in unpredictable ways.

The factors that cause the most variability in the process are the main factors found on cause-and-effect analysis charts: people, machines, methodology, materials, measurement, and environment.

Control Chart Types

Just as there are two types of data, continuous and discrete, there are two types of control charts: variable charts for use with continuous data and attribute charts for use with discrete data. Each type of control chart can be used with specific types of data. Figure 7-9 provides a brief overview of the types of control charts and their applications.

VARIABLE CHARTS	ATTRIBUTE CHARTS
$\overline{X}$ and R charts: To observe changes in the mean and range (variation) of a process. $\overline{X}$ and S charts: For the average and standard deviation of a variable. $\overline{X}$ and s^2 charts: For the average and variance of a variable.	**p chart:** For the fraction of attributes nonconforming or defective in a sample of varying size. **np charts:** For the number of attributes nonconforming or defective in a sample of constant size. **c charts:** For the number of attributes nonconforming or defective in a single item within a subgroup, lot, or sample area of constant size. **u charts:** For the number of attributes nonconforming or defective in a single item within a subgroup, lot, or sample area of varying size.

FIGURE 7-9   Types of Control Charts and Applications

Variable Charts

Control charts for variables are powerful tools that we can use when measurements from a process are variable. Examples of variable data are the diameter of a bearing, electrical output, or the torque on a fastener.

As shown in Figure 7-9, $\overline{X}$ and R charts are used to measure and control processes whose characteristics are continuous variables, such as weight, length, resistance, time, or volume.

Attribute Charts

Although control charts are most often thought of in terms of variables, there are also versions for attributes. Attribute data have only two values (conforming/nonconforming, pass/fail, go/no-go, present/absent), but they can still be counted, recorded, and analyzed. Some examples are: the presence of a required label, the installation of all required fasteners, the presence of solder drips, or the continuity of an electrical circuit. We also use attribute charts for characteristics that are measurable, if the results are recorded in a simple yes/no fashion, such as the conformance of a shaft diameter when measured on a go/no-go gauge or the acceptability of threshold margins to a visual or gauge check.

It is possible to use control charts for operations in which attributes are the basis for inspection, in a manner similar to that for variables but with certain differences. If we deal with the fraction rejected out of a sample, the type of control chart used is called a p chart. If we deal with the actual number rejected, the control chart is called an np chart. If articles can have more than one nonconformity, and all are counted for subgroups of fixed size, the control chart is called a c chart. Finally, if the number of nonconformities per unit is the quantity of interest, the control chart is called a u chart.

The p and np charts are used to measure and control processes displaying attribute characteristics in a sample. W use p charts when the number of failures is expressed as a fraction or np charts when the failures are expressed as a quantity. The c and u charts are used to measure the number or proportion of defects in a single item. The c control chart is applied when the sample size or area is fixed and the u chart when the sample size or area is not fixed.

The power of control charts (Shewhart technique) lies in their ability to determine if the cause of variation is a special cause that can be affected at the process level or a common cause that requires a change at the management level. The information from the control chart can then be used to direct the efforts of the engineers, technicians, and managers to achieve preventive or corrective action.

The use of statistical control charts is aimed at studying specific ongoing processes in order to keep them in satisfactory control. By contrast, downstream inspection aims to identify defects. In other words, control charts focus on prevention of defects, rather than detection and rejection. It seems reasonable, and it has been confirmed in practice, that economy and efficiency are better served by prevention rather than by detection.

Control Chart Components

All control charts have certain features in common (Figure 7-10). Each control chart has a centerline, statistical control limits, and the calculated attribute or variable data. Only control charts for individual measurements contain specification limits.

The centerline is a solid (unbroken) line that represents the mean or arithmetic average of the measurements or counts. On X-bar charts this line is also referred to as the X double-bar line ($\bar{\bar{X}}$). There are two statistical control limits, the upper control limit for values greater than the mean and the lower control limit for values less than the mean.

Specification limits are used when specific parametric requirements exist for a process, product, or operation. These limits usually apply to the data and are the pass/fail criteria for the operation. They differ from statistical control limits in that they are prescribed for a process, rather than resulting from the measurement of the process.

The data elements of control charts vary somewhat among variable and attribute control charts. We will discuss specific examples as a part of the discussion on each of the control charts.

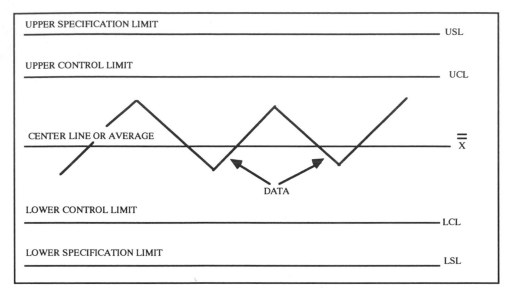

FIGURE 7-10   Control Chart Elements

Control Chart Interpretation

There are many possibilities for interpreting various kinds of patterns and shifts on control charts. If properly interpreted, a control chart can tell us much more than simply whether the process is in or out of control. Experience and training can lead to much greater skill in extracting clues regarding process behavior, such as that shown in Figure 7-11. Statistical guidance is invaluable, but an intimate knowledge of the process being studied is vital in bringing about improvements.

A control chart can tell us when to look for trouble, but it cannot by itself tell us where to look or what cause will be found. Actually, in many cases, one of the greatest benefits from a control chart is that it tells when to leave a process alone. Sometimes, the variability is increased unnecessarily when an operator keeps trying to make small corrections, rather than letting the natural range of variability stabilize. The following paragraphs describe some of the ways the underlying distribution patterns can behave or misbehave.

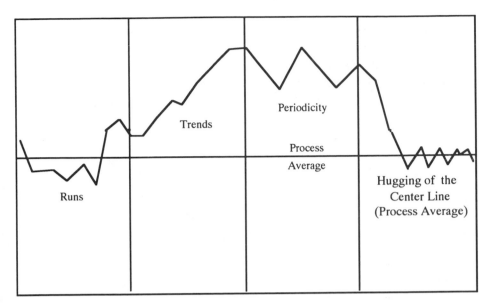

FIGURE 7-11   Control Chart Interpretation

Runs   When several successive points line up on one side of the central line, this pattern is called a run. The number of points in that run is called the length of the run. As a rule of thumb, if the run has a length of seven points, there is an abnormality in the process. Figure 7-11 demonstrates an example of a run.

Trends   If there is a continued rise or fall in a series of points, this pattern is called a trend. In general, if seven consecutive points continue to rise or fall, there is an abnormality. Often, the points go beyond one of the control limits before reaching seven. Figure 7-11 demonstrates an example of a trend.

Periodicity Points   Points that show the same pattern of change (rise or fall) over equal intervals denote periodicity. Figure 7-11 demonstrates an example of periodicity.

Hugging of the Centerline (or Control Limit)   Points on the control chart that are close to the central line or to one or both of the control limits are said to hug the line. Often, in this situation, a different type of data or data from different factors have been mixed into the subgroup. In such cases, it is necessary to change the subgrouping, reassemble the data, and redraw the control chart. To decide whether or not there is hugging of the centerline, draw two lines on the control chart, one between the centerline and the UCL and the other between the centerline and the LCL. If most of the points are between these two lines, there is an abnormality. To see whether there is hugging of one of the control limits, draw a line two-thirds of the distance from the centerline to each of the control lines. There is abnormality if two out of three points, three out of four points, or four out of ten points lie within one or both of the outer one-third zones. The abnormalities should be evaluated for their cause(s) and corrective action taken.

Out-of-Control   An abnormality is likely to exist when data points exceed either the upper or lower control limits. Figure 7-12 illustrates this occurrence.

In-Control   No obvious abnormalities appear in the control chart. Figure 7-13 demonstrates this desirable process state.

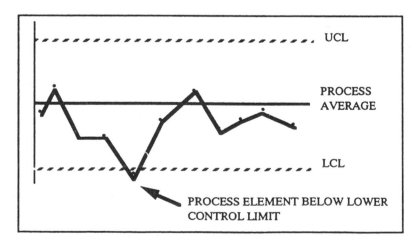

FIGURE 7-12   Control Chart Out of Control

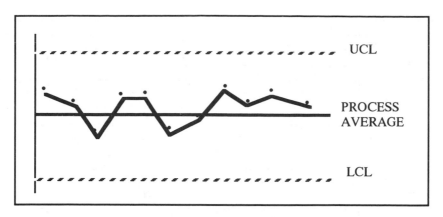

FIGURE 7-13   Process in Control

$\overline{\text{X}}$ **and R Control Chart**   The $\overline{\text{X}}$ and R Control Chart (Figure 7-14) is used when the critical process measurement is a variable. These measurements can be mechanical (diameter, length, width), electronic (resistance, RF output), or related to time (process time, on time, waiting time). The $\overline{\text{X}}$ and R variables control chart is used to describe process data in terms of their variation (item-to-item variability) and the process average (location). $\overline{\text{X}}$ is the average value in each group and is a measure of location. R is the range of values within each group and is a measure of variability. UCL_x and LCL_x represent the limits for the process averages; UCL_R and LCL_R are the control limits for the ranges.

Each subgroup should typically consist of five or more consecutive actions representing only a single process factor. The measured actions within a subgroup should all be produced in a very short time interval. Sample sizes must remain constant for all subgroups when using $\overline{\text{X}}$ and R Control Charts. Twenty-five subgroups are required to establish an $\overline{\text{X}}$ and R Control Chart. Compute the mean and range of each subgroup in Figure 7-14. The letter $\underline{n}$ represents the number of observations within each subgroup.

The mean of each subgroup (sometimes called the average) is the element of the chart; it is the summation of the readings in each cell of the subgroup divided by the number of cells. In Figure 7-14, the

Subgroup		1	2	3	4	5	6	7	8	9	10	11	12	13
Sample Measurements	1	8	9	9	7	9	7	6	9	12	6	9	8	9
	2	9	6	8	12	11	8	12	11	7	8	10	10	8
	3	8	6	8	7	9	10	7	10	7	8	9	9	8
	4	7	7	10	8	10	8	6	8	9	9	11	10	10
	5	8	8	9	8	9	9	8	10	8	8	11	11	8
Total		40	36	44	42	48	42	39	48	43	39	50	48	43
Average		8	7.2	8.8	8.4	9.6	8.4	7.8	9.6	8.6	7.8	10	9.6	8.6
Range		2	3	2	5	2	3	6	3	5	3	2	3	2

Subgroup		14	15	16	17	18	19	20	21	22	23	24	25	26
Sample Measurements	1	8	8	9	8	11	8	7	8	9	7	6	9	7
	2	10	10	8	7	7	7	8	7	11	8	8	10	8
	3	9	9	8	7	8	7	8	10	9	10	8	9	10
	4	10	10	10	10	9	8	9	8	10	8	9	11	8
	5	11	11	8	8	9	7	9	11	9	9	8	11	9
Total		48	48	43	40	44	37	41	44	48	42	39	50	42
Average		9.6	9.6	8.6	8	8.8	7.4	8.2	8.8	9.6	8.4	7.8	10	8.4
Range		3	3	2	3	4	1	2	4	2	3	3	2	3

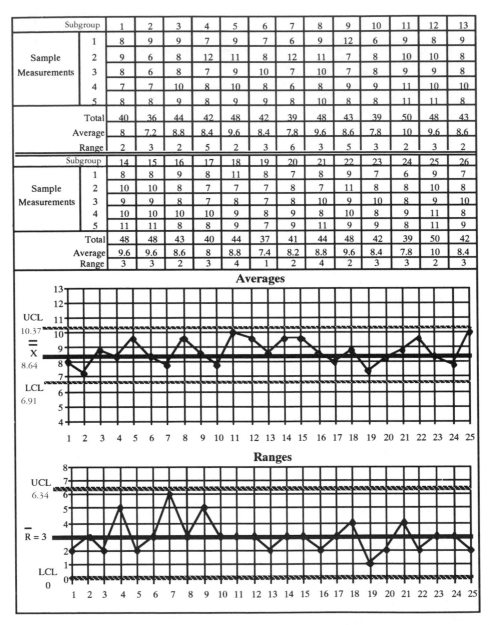

FIGURE 7-14 $\overline{X}$ and R Chart

mean ($\overline{X}$) and the range (R) are calculated as follows, using the first subgroup as an example:

$$\text{Mean} = \overline{X} = \frac{X_1 + X_2 + X_3 + \cdots + X_i}{n}$$

$$\text{Mean} = \overline{X} = \frac{8 + 9 + 8 + 7 + 8}{5} = \frac{40}{5} = 8$$

where:

X_i = The individual reading from each cell in the subgroup

n = The number of cells in the subgroup

$\overline{X}$ = The average of the individual readings in the subgroup

The range is determined by subtracting the lowest reading in the subgroup from the highest reading in the subgroup. The equation for calculating R is:

$$\text{Range} = X_{Max} - X_{Min}$$

$$\text{Range} = R = 9 - 7 = 2$$

where:

X = The individual reading from each cell in the subgroup

R = The range between the highest reading in a subgroup and the lowest reading in the same subgroup

To calculate the centerline ($\overline{\overline{X}}$) of the control chart, use the summation of the averages from each subgroup and the number of subgroups as the n factor as indicated below:

$$\overline{\overline{X}} = \frac{\overline{X}_1 + \overline{X}_2 + \overline{X}_3 + \cdots + \overline{X}_i}{n} = 8.64$$

Calculating the upper and lower control limits for $\overline{X}$ and for range is accomplished using the equations below, the $\overline{R}$ calculated as the average of R, and the factor (for subgroup size five) selected from the table for Control Chart Factors in the statistical tables appendix.

$$UCL_{\overline{X}} = \overline{\overline{X}} + (UCL_{\overline{X}} \text{ Factor})(\overline{R}) = (8.64) + (0.577)(3) = 10.37$$

$$LCL_{\overline{X}} = \overline{\overline{X}} - (LCL_{\overline{X}} \text{ Factor})(\overline{R}) = (8.64) - (0.577)(3) = 6.91$$

$$UCL_R = (UCL_R \text{ Factor})(\overline{R}) = (2.114)(3) = 6.34$$

$$LCL_R = (LCL_R \text{ Factor})(\overline{R}) = (0)(3) = 0$$

p Control Chart   The p control chart in **Figure 7-15** is applied to quality characteristics that are attribute data (pass/fail, present/absent). This chart provides the capability to evaluate processes when we can take consecutive samples with the same sample size.

This chart is used to control processes by evaluating the percentage rejected as nonconforming to some specific requirement or specifica-

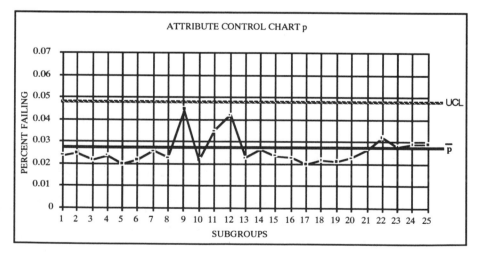

FIGURE 7-15   Completed p Control Chart

tion. It is applied to quality characteristics or to processes that produce variables data (such as measured dimensions) with pass/fail criteria. The chart has its best application in measuring inspection results during a process.

Since this chart has a shape and characteristics of the binomial distribution which is different from the normal distribution, the methods of calculating control limits look different. However, we still use the same concept of placing the control limits ± 3s on each side of the centerline. The subgroup sizes must be sufficient to determine moderate shifts in performance. A sample of 50 or more actions must be taken for each subgroup to enable the process operator/analyst/manager to interpret the chart for trends and patterns and to identify a process that is not in control. The p control chart provides the capability to analyze subgroups of differing sample sizes; however, it is recommended that sample sizes do not vary by more than 25%.

To compute the percent failing, we need the following data: the number of items inspected or tested (n) and the number of failing items (d). Calculate the proportion failing as follows:

$$p = \frac{d}{n}$$

Record all data and the computed percent failing on a data table, as indicated in Figure 7-16.

Calculate the process average ($\bar{p}$) and the average subgroup size (n) using the following equations and the data from Figure 7-16:

$$\bar{p} = \frac{\Sigma d}{\Sigma n} = \frac{\text{Total Defective}}{\text{Total Inspected}} = \frac{317}{11740} = .027$$

$$\bar{n} = \frac{\Sigma n}{\Sigma k} = \frac{\text{Total Inspected}}{\text{Number of Subgroups}} = \frac{11740}{25} = 470$$

The process control limits are the process average plus and minus the 3s allowance for common cause variation inherent in any process. The limits determine the parameters within which the process is in statistical control. When $\bar{p}$ is low and/or n is small, the lower control limit can turn out to be a negative number. In these cases, the lower control limit is treated as being zero. The p control chart upper and lower control limits are calculated as follows:

Attribute Data Table

Part No:		Operation		Chart Type		Chart No:	
Stock No:		Dept:		Sample Size:		Frequency:	
		Metric:		Specification:			

Subgroup	1	2	3	4	5	6	7	8	9	10	11	12	13
Date/Time	1-Jun	4-Jun	5-Jun	6-Jun	7-Jun	10-Jun	11-Jun	12-Jun	13-Jun	14-Jun	16-Jun	17-Jun	18-Jun
n	450	475	450	500	450	450	500	425	500	450	450	500	460
d	11	14	10	12	9	10	13	11	23	10	17	21	11
%	0.024	0.029	0.022	0.024	0.020	0.022	0.026	0.026	0.046	0.022	0.038	0.042	0.024

Subgroup	14	15	16	17	18	19	20	21	22	23	24	25	26
Date/Time	19-Jun	20-Jun	22-Jun	23-Jun	24-Jun	25-Jun	26-Jun	29-Jun	30-Jun	1-Jul	2-Jul	3-Jul	
n	475	500	465	450	500	480	475	450	500	460	450	475	
d	13	12	11	9	11	10	11	12	16	13	13	14	
%	0.027	0.024	0.024	0.020	0.022	0.021	0.023	0.027	0.032	0.028	0.029	0.029	

FIGURE 7-16   p Chart Data Table

$$\mathrm{UCL_p} = \overline{p} + 3\sqrt{\overline{p}(1 - \overline{p})}/\sqrt{n}$$
$$= .027 + 3\sqrt{.027(1 - .027)}/\sqrt{470} = .049$$
$$\mathrm{LCL_p} = \overline{p} - 3\sqrt{\overline{p}(1 - \overline{p})}/\sqrt{n}$$
$$= .027 - 3\sqrt{.027(1 - .027)}/\sqrt{470} \approx 0$$

np Control Chart We use the np control chart, Figure 7-17, when the actual number of items failing is a better indicator of the process than the percent failing. One essential requirement for this use of the np chart is that the sample sizes for the subgroups must all be the same. (This is a limitation that does not apply to the use of p charts.)

The np chart is used to control processes by evaluating the number failing to conform to some specific requirement or specification. It is applied to quality characteristics or to processes that produce variable data, such as measured dimensions, when measured to a pass/fail criteria. The chart has its best application in measuring discrepancies for an inspection lot, such as during the receipt of material.

The calculations used for np charts are based on the binomial distribution. The centerline is the average number of rejects per subgroup, denoted by $n\overline{p}$. After dividing this value by n, the number of items per subgroup, we get the value to use for $\overline{p}$ in the control limit formulas.

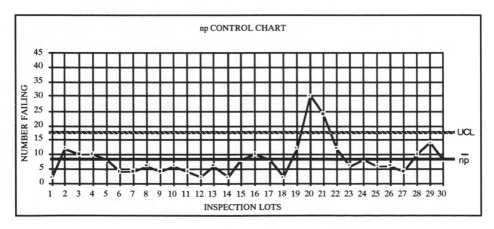

FIGURE 7-17 Completed np Control Chart

The lot sampling frequency (how often sample data is acquired) must be correlated with receipt, production, or inspection periods. It is necessary to understand the relationship between the frequency and the production run. For effective control of process performance, the data acquisition increment or period should be long enough to capture likely sources of variation. The sample size for each subgroup must be sufficient and contain 25 or more subgroups during the production run. The selection of this number of subgroups will provide the manager or analyst with information needed to determine if the process is in control and if the cause of being out of control is special or random.

Record all data and determine number failing on a standard data table, as indicated in Figure 7-18.

Calculate and draw the process average as indicated below:

$$\text{Process Average} = n\bar{p} = \frac{\Sigma d}{\Sigma k} = \frac{\text{Total Defective}}{\text{Number of Subgroups}}$$

$$\text{Process Average} = n\bar{p} = \frac{248}{30} = 8.27$$

The process control limits are the process average plus and minus the three standard deviation allowance for common cause variation inherent in any process. The limits determine the parameters within which the process is in statistical control. When $\bar{p}$ is low and/or n is small, the lower control limit may be a negative number. In these cases, the lower control limit is zero, because the lower control limit of the number failing cannot be less than zero. Therefore, we will compute only the upper control limit for all np charts.

$$\text{UCL for np Charts} = n\bar{p} + 3\sqrt{n\bar{p}\left(1 - \frac{n\bar{p}}{n}\right)}$$

Using the data from Figure 7-18 and the process average calculated in the previous step, we can calculate the upper control limit.

Attribute Data Table

Part No:	Eng Assy	Operation	A.T.	Chart Type	np	Chart No:	1
Stock No:	B765	Dept:	Mfg	Sample Size:	200-Lot	Frequency:	Lot
		Metric:	P/F Insp	Specification:	ANSI-771		

Subgroup	1	2	3	4	5	6	7	8	9	10	11	12	13	14	15
Date/Time	1-Jun			6-Jun			11-Jun			14-Jun			18-Jun		18-Jun
n	200	200	200	200	200	200	200	200	200	200	200	200	200	200	200
d	2	12	10	10	8	4	4	6	4	6	4	2	6	2	8

Subgroup	16	17	18	19	20	21	22	23	24	25	26	27	28	29	30
Date/Time	22-Jun			23-Jun			29-Jun			2-Jul					
n	200	200	200	200	200	200	200	200	200	200	200	200	200	200	200
d	10	8	2	12	30	24	12	6	8	6	6	4	10	14	8

FIGURE 7-18 np Chart Data Table

$$\text{UCL for np Charts} = 8.27 + 3\sqrt{8.27\left(1 - \frac{8.27}{200}\right)} = 16.7$$

c Control Chart   The c control chart, Figure 7-19, is used when the number of attributes nonconforming or defective is a single item within a subgroup, lot, or sample area of constant size. The method of calculation used for c control charts is based on the Poisson distribution. The center line is an average number denoted by $\bar{c}$.

The lot sampling frequency (how often data are acquired) must be correlated with receipt, production. or inspection periods. It is necessary to understand the relationship between the frequency and the production periods (work shifts, machine runs, reporting cycles). For effective control of process performance, the data acquisition increment (or period) should be long enough to capture likely sources of variation. The sample size from each subgroup must be sufficient, and there must be 25 or more subgroups. The selection of this number of subgroups will provide the manager or analyst with information to determine if the process is in control and if the cause of being out of control is assignable or random.

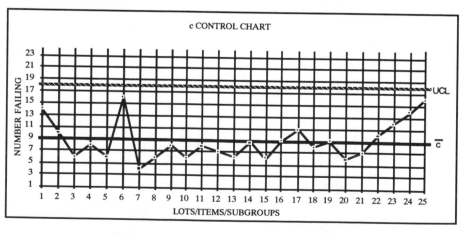

FIGURE 7-19   Completed c Control Chart

Record all data and determine the number failing on a standard data table, as indicated in Figure 7-20.

The process average is calculated from the data in Figure 7-20 and applied to the control chart as follows:

$$\text{Process Average} = \bar{c} = \frac{\Sigma c}{\Sigma k} = \frac{\text{Total Defective in All Subgroups}}{\text{Number of Subgroups}}$$

$$\text{Process Average} = \bar{c} = \frac{\Sigma c}{\Sigma k} = \frac{222}{25} = 8.88$$

The process control limits are the process average plus and minus the three standard deviation allowance for common cause variation inherent in any process. The limits determine the parameters within which the process is in statistical control. When $\bar{c}$ is low or k is small, the lower control limit may be a negative number. In these cases, the lower control limit is zero, because the number failing cannot be less than zero. Therefore, we will compute only the upper control limit for c chart.

$$\text{Upper Control Limit} = \text{UCL}_c = \bar{c} + 3\sqrt{\bar{c}}$$

$$\text{Upper Control Limit} = \text{UCL}_c = 8.88 + 3\sqrt{8.88} = 17.82$$

u Control Chart   The u control chart in Figure 7-21 is used to measure the percent not conforming (failing) in an inspection subgroup, and we are concerned with the variation between groups. This chart does not require a constant sample or lot size. It is applied in two specific process control situations: (1) Where there is a continuous flow of product, and the failures can be expressed as a ratio to total product, and (2) where failures of different types can be found in a single inspection procedure.

In a u chart, the sample size is flexible. The u chart, dealing with the proportion of defects in a sample or subgroup, is easy to construct. First, find the average number of defects per subgroup (u). Next, calculate the process average ($\bar{u}$) and use it for the centerline on the control chart. Plot the process data and compute the control limits.

Attribute Data Table

Part No:	Comp Tube	Operation	Prod, in-process	Chart Type	c	Chart No:	1
Stock No:	71B2	Dept:	Mfg	Sample Size:	10	Frequency:	Daily
		Metric:	Holes/Part	Specification:	ANSI-631		

Subgroup	1	2	3	4	5	6	7	8	9	10	11	12	13	14	15
Date/Time	3-Jun	4-Jun	5-Jun	6-Jun	7-Jun	8-Jun	9-Jun	10-Jun	11-Jun	12-Jun	13-Jun	14-Jun	15-Jun	16-Jun	17-Jun
n	10	10	10	10	10	10	10	10	10	10	10	10	10	10	10
c	14	10	6	8	6	16	4	6	8	6	8	7	6	9	6

Subgroup	16	17	18	19	20	21	22	23	24	25	26	27	28	29	30
Date/Time	18-Jun	19-Jun	20-Jun	21-Jun	22-Jun	23-Jun	24-Jun	25-Jun	26-Jun	27-Jun					
n	10	10	10	10	10	10	10	10	10	10					
c	9	11	8	9	6	7	10	12	14	16					

FIGURE 7-20   c Control Chart Data Table

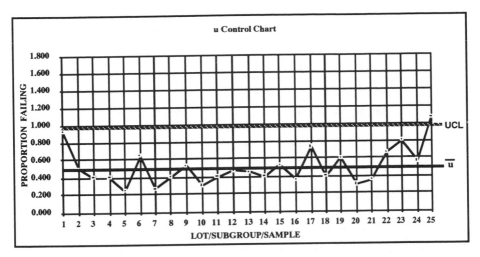

FIGURE 7-21   Completed u Control Chart

The best use of u control charts is to ascertain the variation in quality of a characteristic or piece. Record all data and determine the number failing on a standard data table, as indicated in Figure 7-22.

To compute the percent failing we need the following data: the number of items inspected or tested (n) and the number of failing items (d). Calculate the percent failing as follows.

Calculate the process control limits for the u control chart as the process average plus and minus three standard deviations (3s) to allow for common cause variation inherent in any process. These limits determine the parameters within which the process is in statistical control. When $\bar{u}$ is low or n is small, the lower control limit can be a negative number. In these cases, the lower control limit is set at zero, essentially no lower limit. The u control chart upper and lower control limits are calculated as follows:

$$\text{Control Limits for u Chart:} \quad \begin{aligned} UCL_u &= \bar{u} + 3\sqrt{\bar{u}}/\sqrt{n} \\ LCL_u &= \bar{u} - 3\sqrt{\bar{u}}/\sqrt{n} \end{aligned}$$

$$\text{where } \bar{u} = \frac{\Sigma d}{\Sigma n} = \frac{\text{Total Defective}}{\text{Total Inspected}}$$

$$= \frac{224}{455} = 0.492$$

$$\text{and } \bar{n} = \frac{\Sigma n}{\Sigma k} = \frac{\text{Total Inspected}}{\text{Number of Subgroups}}$$

$$= \frac{455}{25} = 18.2$$

$$\text{UCL}_u = 0.492 + 3\sqrt{0.492}/\sqrt{18.2} = 0.985$$

$$\text{LCL}_u = 0.492 - 3\sqrt{0.492}/\sqrt{18.2} \approx 0$$

PROCESS CAPABILITY

The basic statistical application in process control is to establish stability in the process and maintain that state of control over an extended period. It is equally important to adjust the process to the point where virtually all of the product meets specifications. The latter situation relates to process capability analysis.

Once we have established stability, it follows that we must adjust the process to a level where the output will conform to specifications. A state of control usually exists when process control charts do not show points out of control or forming unacceptable patterns or shifts over an interval of 25 subgroups. Once this control is established, we can analyze process capability to determine conformance to specifications. The primary function of a process control system is to provide statistical signals when special causes of variation are present and to enable appropriate action to eliminate those causes and prevent their reappearance.

We measure capability as the proportion of output that is within product specification tolerances. Since a process in statistical control can be described by a predictable distribution, we can express capability in terms of this distribution and evaluate the proportion of out-of-specification parts realistically. If this variation is excessive, actions are required to reduce the variation from common causes to make the process capable of consistently meeting customer requirements as indicated by the Upper and Lower Specification Limits (USL and LSL). Figure 7-23 demonstrates the relationship between process control chart limits (UCL and LCL), specification requirements, and process capability.

Attribute Data Table

Part No:	B-77 ENG	Operation		ACCEPTANCE	Chart Type	U		Chart No:	3
Stock No:	GM-B77-1	Dept:		RECEIVING	Sample Size:	15% LOT		Frequency:	LOT
		Metric:		P/P+F	Specification:	INT 386/HP			

Subgroup	1	2	3	4	5	6	7	8	9	10	11	12	13	14	15
Date/Time	3-Jun	4-Jun	5-Jun	6-Jun	7-Jun	8-Jun	9-Jun	10-Jun	11-Jun	12-Jun	13-Jun	14-Jun	15-Jun	16-Jun	17-Jun
n	15	20	15	20	25	25	15	15	15	20	20	15	20	15	15
d	14	10	6	8	6	16	4	6	8	6	8	7	9	6	8
u	0.933	0.500	0.400	0.400	0.240	0.640	0.267	0.400	0.533	0.300	0.400	0.467	0.450	0.400	0.533

Subgroup	16	17	18	19	20	21	22	23	24	25	26	27	28	29	30
Date/Time	18-Jun	19-Jun	20-Jun	21-Jun	22-Jun	23-Jun	24-Jun	25-Jun	26-Jun	27-Jun					
n	25	15	20	15	20	20	15	15	25	15					
d	9	11	8	9	6	7	10	12	14	16					
u	0.360	0.733	0.400	0.600	0.300	0.350	0.667	0.800	0.560	1.067					

FIGURE 7-22 u Control Chart Data Table

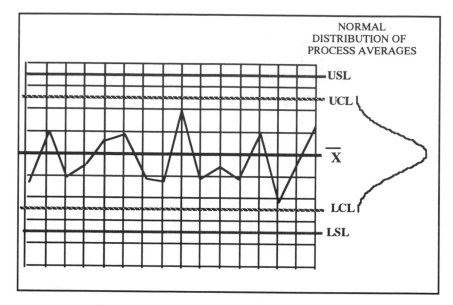

FIGURE 7-23   Process Capability and Control Chart Relationship

Cp Index

The most commonly used process status indices are Cp and Cpk. Cp, which stands for capability of process, is the ratio of design tolerance to 6 sigma (σ). The 6σ in the Cp formula comes from the fact that, in a normal distribution, 99.73% of the parts will be within a 6σ (± 3s) spread when only random variation (common cause) is occurring. The Cp for the data presented in Figure 7-24 is therefore:

$$Cp = \frac{Tolerance}{6\sigma} = \frac{USL - LSL}{UCL - LCL} = \frac{5.0 - 1.0}{3.5 - 0.5} = \frac{4.0}{3.0} = 1.33$$

As you can see from the Cp formula, values for Cp can range from near zero to very large positive numbers. When Cp is less than one, the process is said to be not-capable. The larger the number, the better the Cp index is. A Cp index of 2.00 is what it takes to be a world class competitor.

Cpk Index

While Cp is only a measure of capability, Cpk is a measure of performance. That is, the formula for Cpk takes into account both the

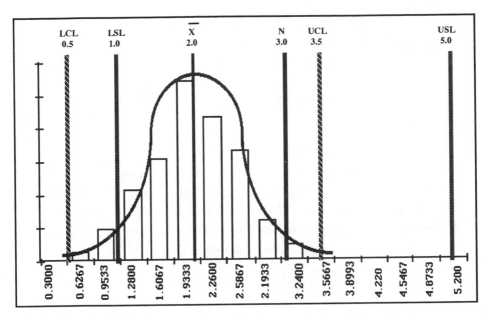

FIGURE 7-24   Cp and Cpk Relationships

spread of the distribution and the location of the distribution with respect to the upper and lower specification limits (USL and LSL). We choose the lesser of the two values calculated as the Cpk index. Using this value, we learn how capable our process is on the worst side of the distribution. Using the example in Figure 7-24, we calculate the value for Cpk:

$$\text{Cpk (USL)} = \frac{\text{USL} - \text{Mean}}{3\sigma} = \frac{5.0 - 2.0}{1.5} = 2.0$$

$$\text{Cpk (LSL)} = \frac{\text{Mean} - \text{LSL}}{3\sigma} = \frac{2.0 - 1.0}{1.5} = 0.67$$

$$\text{Cpk} = \text{minimum [Cpk(USL), Cpk(LSL)]}$$
$$= \min [2.0, 0.67]$$
$$= 0.67$$

The greater the value of Cpk, the better. A Cpk value of greater than one means that the 6σ ($\pm3s$) spread of the data occurs substantially within the specification limits. A Cpk between 0 and 1 means that part of the 6σ spread falls outside the specification limits. A negative Cpk indicates that 50% or more of the data is outside the specification limits.

KEY POINTS

Before any system can be quantified, analyzed, and subjected to continuous measurable improvement, the system must first be effectively described. The method for providing a structured description of the system is the process flowchart. There are six phases to performing process analysis, as seen in Figure 7-25.

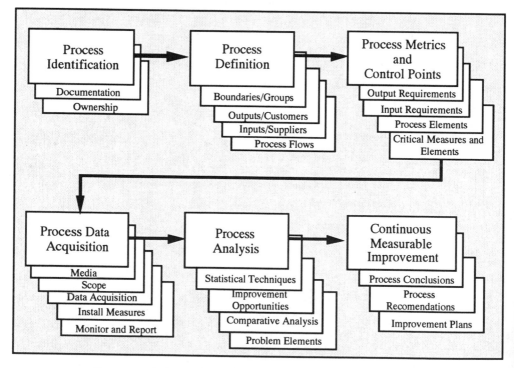

FIGURE 7-25   Key Points—Six Phases of Process Analysis

Process Identification

Each of us can identify dozens of important activities that are performed in our organizations. To implement continuous measurable improvement, however, we must select those activities that are critical to the mission of the organization and, therefore, achieving the company's vision.

The identification process requires that we understand more than the name of the process, so that we can make an informed decision about which processes to manage. It is essential to collect preliminary information about a candidate process, inputs, outputs, who "owns" the process, etc.

Process Definition

We need to describe it so that we can understand what metrics need to be measured and how to measure them. This is where we add depth to the information gathered in identifying the process. This is where we develop the process flowchart.

Process Metrics and Control Points

The process analysis team must define the goals and objectives for the analysis and improvement of the process. Each goal must be concise, stressing one theme, such as cost reduction, improvement of quality, enhancement of efficiency and effectiveness, or improving timeliness and throughput. With this goal established, the team can determine what metrics are required to measure the process and its performance relative to the goal. They can also determine where in the process flow the measurements can be taken.

Process Data Acquisition

After determining the process' critical measures and control points, we must collect data to facilitate the analysis of these points. These are also essential to determine if the process is in control and to ensure the success of improvement efforts.

Process Analysis

Process analysis is the systematic examination of the process to identify opportunities for improvement, develop cause-and-effect analysis, and prioritize corrective actions.

Continuous Measurable Improvement

The culmination of the process analysis is the phase where conclusions are drawn from the data analysis, recommendations are developed, and plans of action are established. The plans also need to include actions to institutionalize the improvements. It is important to develop milestone charts and status sheets, and then to score and report the execution of the plan.

EXAMPLE

At this phase in the design and development process for the LWCI 1600, it is necessary to design the processes that will produce the equipment. Each of the WBS elements in Example Figure 7-1 will require a process. We will focus on the development of the procurement process WBS element 4.1.

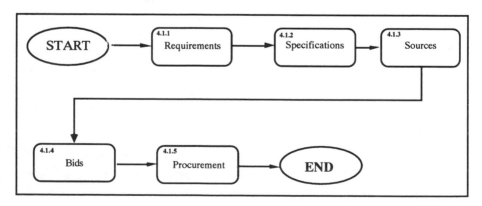

EXAMPLE FIGURE 7-1   LWCI 1600 Procurement Process

LWCI established the team to perform the design, development and analysis of the procurement process. The team consisted of members from the operating division that would be producing the LWCI 1600, as well as a member from the company controller's staff, and the head of the company procurement section. The team used the six phase process analysis to accomplish the evaluation.

Process Identification

The first phase of the six step process analysis is to properly identify the process we desire to study by determining its inputs, work activities, and outputs at the highest functional level. Here the team needed to determine when the procurement process began and when it was completed (start and stop). The two steps for process identification are to: 1) acquire and review all process documentation, and 2) determine the process ownership.

Step 1. Acquire and Review All Process Documentation

Process Specifications and Procedures   First, the team reviewed the procurement process as it is currently established in the company. The requirements for specifying materials were very well defined. The team decided that the specifications for the LWCI 1600 would be extracted from the QFD for the equipment.

Process Input Requirements   Then the team determined that the input to the procurement process would be the standard LWCI procurement request form for raw materials and equipment. This form, originated by the production division, should initiate the procurement process.

Process Output Requirements   The output of the procurement process was the raw materials, parts, assemblies and components required for the assembly process.

Step 2. Determine Process Ownership

Who has Direct Responsibility?   The manager of the procurement section had the direct responsibility for the procurement process from the time he or she received a procurement request through delivery of the requested material.

Who Has Direct Contact?   Several individuals had direct contact with the procurement process:

▶ Division managers or their staffs prepared the appropriate form.
▶ The form was processed by the procurement section.
▶ The form was approved by the controller.
▶ The buyer assigned to the procurement executed the request.

Who Has the Authority?   Clearly, there was only one individual with overall authority to change the process—Mr. Leander. All other employees, supervisors, and managers had no direct authority over the procurement process.

Process Definition

The next phase is definition. They first looked at the upper level flow from a functional point of view. The resulting flow chart was very rough and displayed only the higher level process functions and did not provide any work activities. The flow chart codes were derived directly from the WBS; this allowed for tracking of the process using the POA&M for performance and financial analysis.

Internal Elements and Boundaries

Process Beginning   The process started with the receipt of an approved material request form from the operating division.

Process Work Activities   The process work activities included the receipt and logging in of the request by the procurement section, forwarding the request for approval to Mr. Leander (if over 10K), forwarding to the controller for review and approval, and return of the approved request to the procurement section.

Process Ending   The process ended when the procurement section received the required materials.

Process Function Outputs and Customers

Process Products and Services   The process produced the procurement of the required materials for the LWCI 1600 production process.

Process Customers   The internal customers of this process were Mr. Leander and the controller, who receive a properly completed request for materials, and the procurement section, which receives a fully approved request that is ready to go into the next phase of the process. The external customer is the production division, which receives the appropriate raw materials and parts needed for production.

Process Function Input and Suppliers

Process Inputs   The process input was a properly completed request form.

Process Suppliers   The suppliers to this process function was the division manager, who provides the original form.

Process Work Activities, Sub-Processes, and Flows

The team then defined the work activities that were to be accomplished with each of the five process functional areas:

- ► 4.1.1 Requirements
    - 4.1.1.1 Research the basic requirements for the material; quantity, possible resources, requirement dates (JIT).

4.1.1.2 Determine the actual delivery requirements based upon the research.

4.1.1.3 Document the requirements and provide the standard LWCI procurement form.

▶ 4.1.2 Specifications

4.1.2.1 Requirements; determine the technical requirements for the materials or components.

4.1.2.2 Write specifications to accompany the procurement request.

▶ 4.1.3 Sources

4.1.3.1 Research the sources available for procurement of the specified material.

4.1.3.2 Based upon the research, select a minimum of three potential bidders or determine to advertise for the material needed.

▶ 4.1.4 Bids

4.1.4.1 Advertise for bidders or

4.1.4.2 Request quotes from the selected potential resources

4.1.4.3 Receive the sealed bids

▶ 4.1.5 Procure

4.1.5.1 Select the best bid based upon quality, cost, and schedule.

4.1.5.2 Buy the material and receive it.

4.1.5.3 Test the material to ensure that it meets specification, unless the material is received from a certified supplier (ISO 9000).

4.1.5.4 Accept the material and transfer to WIP.

LWCI's Procurement Improvement Team completed the process definition phase and developed the detailed flow chart for the process (see Example Figure 7-2).

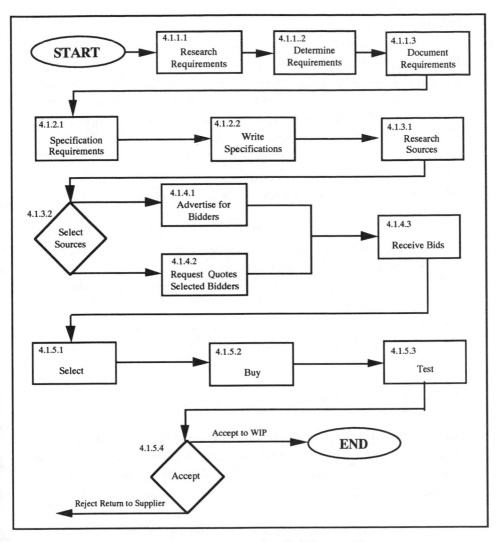

EXAMPLE FIGURE 7-2 Detailed Process Flow

Process Measures

The third phase for the team was to determine the metrics for the processes. These were the process measures for managing the process. This phase builds on the information the team gathered during the process definition phase. The team reviewed the Team Planning Summary Sheet for the Procurement Improvement Team and confirmed that the goals of accomplishing a process analysis, reducing the cost of the process, and improving the responsiveness of the process were still viable. The measures of success for the process are, therefore:

- ► Overall cost of the procurement process and the costs of the sub-processes and process elements
- ► Cycle times for the procurement process, the sub-processes, and process elements
- ► Quality of the material produced by the process
- ► Time to meet the required delivery date

Review All Process Elements

Here is where numbering the process elements will be of great assistance to the team. The Procurement Improvement Team determined how to effectively measure each critical process work activity or function in terms of:

- ► Time required to accomplish the element
- ► Resulting cost in labor time
- ► Rejection rate of the request form during the process
- ► Rejection of requested material
- ► Timeliness of the material receipt

At this point, the team was prepared to develop the pilot procurement process so as to provide data to continue performing process analysis.

CHAPTER 8

Analysis of Quantitative Data

> STATISTICAL ANALYSIS BRINGS ORDER TO DATA
> AND PROVIDES FOR FACT-BASED DECISIONS.

Over the years, statistical methods have become prevalent throughout business, industry, and science. With the availability of advanced, automated systems that collect, tabulate, and analyze data, the practical application of these quantitative methods continues to grow. Statistics today play a major role in all phases of modern business and are indispensable in the Management 2000 environment. These tools are essential in evaluating and improving your processes for new products and services.

More important than the quantitative methods themselves is their impact on the basic philosophy of business. The statistical point of view takes decision making out of the subjective, autocratic decision making arena by providing the basis for objective decisions based upon quantifiable facts. This change provides some very specific benefits:

- ► Improved process information
- ► Better communication
- ► Process discussion based upon facts

- ▸ Consensus for process action
- ▸ Uniform decision making information for process changes

The analysis of quantitative data takes advantage of the natural characteristics of any process. All business activities can be described as specific processes with known tolerances and measurable variation. The measurement of this variation, and the resulting information, provide the basis for continuous process improvement. The tools presented here provide both a graphical and also a measured representation of the process data. The systematic application of these tools, through the Management 2000 model, empowers business people to develop, control, and improve products and processes to become world class competitors.

The basic tools of statistical process control are data tables, Pareto analysis, cause-and-effect analysis, trend analysis, histograms, scatter diagrams, and control charts. These basic tools provide for the efficient collection of information and data, the measurement of the data, identification of patterns, and analysis for improvement or corrective action. Figure 8-1 shows the relationships among these seven tools and their use for the identification and analysis of improvement opportunities. We will review these tools briefly and discuss their implementation and applications.

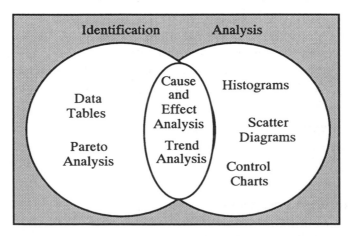

FIGURE 8-1   The Seven Quality Control Tools

DATA TABLES

Data Tables, or data arrays, provide a systematic method for collecting and displaying data. In most cases, data tables are forms designed for the purpose of collecting specific data. These tables are used most frequently where data is available from automated media. They provide a consistent, effective, and economical approach to gathering data, organizing it for analysis, and displaying it for preliminary review. Data tables sometimes take the form of manual check sheets where automated data is not necessary or available. Data tables and check sheets should be designed to minimize the need for complicated entries. Simple to understand, straightforward tables are a key to successful data gathering.

The effective use of data tables requires that certain decisions must be made concerning the data to be collected, compiled, and analyzed. The following are some of these considerations:

- ▶ **Purpose:** Determine why you are collecting the data and what specific analysis and analytical methods you will use.
- ▶ **Requirement:** Identify what type of data is needed to perform the analysis.
- ▶ **Source:** Determine if the data is currently available, and from what source, and on what media.
- ▶ **Collection:** Identify where, when, and how the data will be collected and by whom. Clearly define the data categories as you design your data table.
- ▶ **Data Reduction:** Identify what data reduction tools you will use (automated, manual, programs) and how you will organize the data.
- ▶ **Conclusions and Recommendations:** What actions are contemplated? Will the data collected support the planned conclusions and recommendations?

Figure 8-2 is an example of an attribute (pass/fail) data table for the Material Inspection function process element 5.1.5.3 in Figure 7-7. (See how this numbering system simplifies references to process elements.) From this simple check sheet, several data points become

Defect	Supplier				
	A	**B**	**C**	**D**	**Total**
Incorrect Invoice	////	/		//	7
Incorrect Inventory	~~////~~	//	/	/	9
Damaged Material	///		//	///	8
Incorrect Test Documentation	/	///	////	//	10
Totals	13	6	7	8	34

FIGURE 8-2　Data Table for Material Receipt and Inspection

important decision information. The total number of defects is 34. The highest number of defects is from Supplier A, and the most frequent defect is incorrect test documentation. We can subject these data to further analysis by using Pareto analysis, cause-and-effect analysis, and other statistical tools.

Defect	Shift 30 Day Period			
	1	**2**	**3**	**Total**
Run-up Test	15	10	30	55
System Integration	25	20	30	75
Motor Static Test	45	20	0	65
Motor Integration	5	50	60	115
Totals	90	100	120	310

FIGURE 8-3　Data Table of Failure During the Manufacturing Process by Work Shift

Figure 8-3 shows a data table developed for the process element 5.1.5.4 of Figure 7-7. This table provides the data for failures of the several in-process inspections by work shift. An analysis of these data also reveals specific problem areas.

This data table provides a basis for further analysis using Pareto or cause-and-effect analysis. It is evident from the data table that motor integration and the third shift are potential problem areas. You should exercise caution in performing a direct analysis of this data, as will be explained in the following sections.

CAUSE-AND-EFFECT ANALYSIS

After identifying a problem, it is necessary to determine its cause. The cause-and-effect relationship is at times obscure. A considerable amount of analysis often is required to determine the specific cause or causes affecting the problem.

Cause-and-effect analysis uses diagramming techniques to identify the relationship between an effect and its causes. Cause-and-effect diagrams are also known as fishbone diagrams. Figure 8-4 demon-

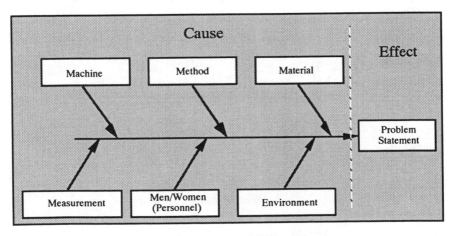

FIGURE 8-4   Cause-and-Effect Diagram

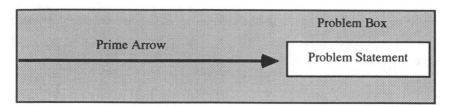

FIGURE 8-5   Establish Prime Arrow and Problem Box

strates the basic fishbone diagram. The problem box contains the problem statement being evaluated for cause and effect. The prime arrow functions as the foundation for the major categories. Establish the problem box and prime arrow, as indicated in Figure 8-5.

The six basic categories for the primary causes of the problems are, most frequently, personnel, method, materials, machinery, measurements, and environment, as shown in Figure 8-6. Other categories may be specified, based upon the needs of the analysis.

When you have identified the major causes contributing to the problem, then you can determine the causes related to each of the major categories. Using your cross-functional team in a brainstorming session, identify the possible causes related to each of the categories, as shown on Figure 8-7.

Based upon the cause-and-effect analysis of the problem and the determination of causes contributing to each major category, identify corrective action. The corrective action analysis is performed in the

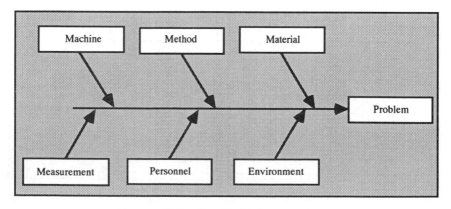

FIGURE 8-6   Specify Major Categories

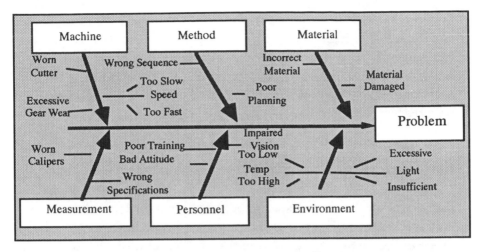

FIGURE 8-7   Completed Cause-and-Effect Diagram

same manner as the cause-and-effect analysis. The cause-and-effect diagram is simply reversed so that the problem box becomes the corrective action box. Figure 8-8 displays the method for identifying corrective action.

Bar Charts

A bar chart is a graphical representation of data as a frequency distribution. This tool is valuable in evaluating both attribute (pass/

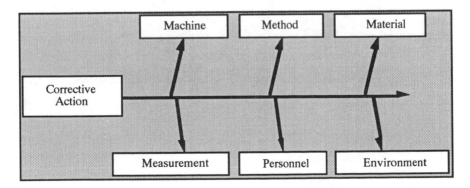

FIGURE 8-8   Identify Corrective Action

fail) and variable (measurement) data. Bar charts offer a quick look at the data at a single point in time; they do not display variation or trends over time. A bar chart displays how the cumulative data looks *today*. It is useful in understanding the relative frequencies (percentages) or frequency (numbers) of the data and how that data is distributed.

Bar Charts for Attribute Data

Bar charts for attribute data are easy to construct from data tables and check sheets. The bar chart in Figure 8-9 is based on the data figure in Figure 8-3. A bar chart of this data graphically demonstrates the relationships and frequencies of defects found in the manufacturing process.

The frequency of occurrence appears on the vertical (Y) axis and the attribute elements are on the horizontal (X) axis. This same data can be evaluated as a relative frequency distribution by converting the data to percentages (relative frequencies, as shown in Figure 8-10).

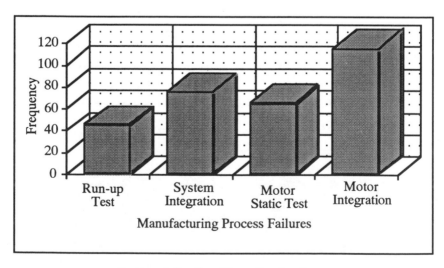

FIGURE 8-9   Bar Chart for Attributes

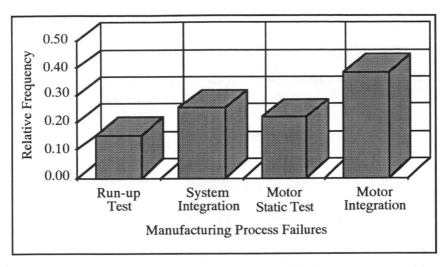

FIGURE 8-10   Relative Frequency Distribution

Bar Charts for Variable Data

Bar charts for variable data are similar to those for attributes, in that they provide a graphic demonstration of the data and its frequency distribution. The frequencies or relative frequencies are listed on the vertical (Y) axis, and the measurements (variables) are listed on the horizontal (X) axis. We will use the variable data in Figure 8-12 to construct a variable bar chart. This data was derived from the soldering certification test scores of 50 employees (Figure 8-11). We are interested in the distribution of scores with respect to experience, stated in months.

The number of columns in the variable bar chart is dependent on the total number of data points to be evaluated. Generally, a variable bar chart should have a minimum of five columns and a maximum of 20. Figure 8-12 is derived from several sources and is generally accepted as a standard.

The class boundaries are the highest and lowest measurements that are under evaluation. This measurement variable is placed on the horizontal axis of the bar chart. In the data set, we are looking at the

Employee No.	Experience (Months)	Score	Employee No.	Experience (Months)	Score
1	120	0.88	26	69	0.72
2	119	0.92	27	66	0.77
3	118	0.90	28	64	0.86
4	118	0.86	29	58	0.76
5	114	0.76	30	52	0.69
6	114	0.99	31	51	0.78
7	113	0.72	32	48	0.81
8	112	0.76	33	48	0.82
9	97	0.87	34	48	0.86
10	96	0.82	35	46	0.79
11	96	0.92	36	46	0.75
12	96	0.88	37	44	0.74
13	94	0.76	38	43	0.73
14	88	0.83	39	40	0.80
15	86	0.85	40	36	0.77
16	77	0.66	41	36	0.76
17	76	0.72	42	32	0.70
18	74	0.73	43	28	0.88
19	73	0.75	44	28	0.90
20	73	0.88	45	22	0.86
21	73	0.77	46	22	0.94
22	73	0.80	47	21	0.97
23	70	0.72	48	12	0.86
24	69	0.88	49	12	0.87
25	69	0.62	50	6	0.88

FIGURE 8-11   Solder Qualification Test Scores

Data Points	Columns
< 50	5-7
51 - 100	8-10
101 - 250	10-12
>250	12-20

FIGURE 8-12   Criteria for Determining the Number of Columns in a Variable Bar Chart

class boundaries of 0.99 for Employee 6 and 0.62 for Employee 25. Therefore, the upper class boundary is 0.99 and the lower class boundary is 0.62. To determine the class intervals or group size, use the difference between the class boundaries, divided by the number of columns.

$$\text{Interval} = \frac{\text{Upper Class Boundary} - \text{Lower Class Boundary}}{\text{Columns}}$$

$$\text{Interval} = \frac{(0.99) - (0.62)}{5} = \frac{(0.37)}{5} = 0.07$$

We have determined that there are five classes, each of 0.07 width. It would be difficult to identify each of these five columns by using the lower and upper boundaries for each class interval (i.e. 0.62 to 0.68, 0.69 to 0.75, and so on). It is easier and more effective to identify the column by its class mark or midpoint. The class intervals and the class marks also form the first two elements of the frequency distribution. The frequency distribution is the number of occurrences in each class. The class intervals, class marks, and frequencies are shown in Figure 8-13.

We are now prepared to draw the bar chart. Figure 8-14 is the completed bar chart, which demonstrates the relationship of test scores to their frequency of occurrence. This same data can also be used to construct a relative frequency bar chart. First, transform the

Class Intervals	Class Marks	Frequency (f)	Relative Frequency
0.62 - 0.69	0.66	2	0.04
0.70 - 0.77	0.74	11	0.22
0.78 - 0.85	0.82	15	0.30
0.85 - 0.92	0.89	15	0.30
0.93 - 0.99	0.96	7	0.14
		50	1.00

FIGURE 8-13   Relative Frequency Table

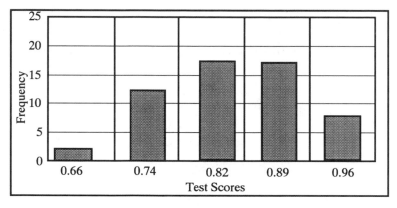

FIGURE 8-14   Solder Qualification Bar Chart

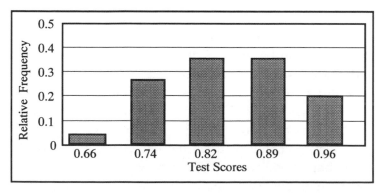

FIGURE 8-15   Solder Qualification Relative Frequency Bar Chart

numbers to relative frequencies in Figure 8-13. Then, construct the bar chart as demonstrated in Figure 8-15.

Many candidates for improvement can be identified using this one elementary tool. The frequency and shape of the data distribution provide insights that would not be apparent from the data tables alone. Bar charts also form the basis for two other tools that we frequently use: Pareto analysis and process capability.

PARETO ANALYSIS

A Pareto diagram is a special type of bar chart that helps us to identify and prioritize problem areas. The construction of a Pareto diagram may involve data collected from data tables, maintenance data, repair data, parts scrap rates, or other sources. By identifying types of nonconformity from any of these data sources, the Pareto diagram directs attention to the most frequently occurring element.

There are three uses and types of Pareto analysis. The basic Pareto analysis identifies the "vital few" contributors that account for most quality problems in any system. The comparative Pareto analysis focuses on any number of program options or actions. The weighted Pareto analysis gives a measure of significance to factors that may not appear significant at first, e.g., such additional factors as cost, time, and criticality. Pareto analysis can be used to evaluate:

Quality	Cost	Schedule
Failures	Repair	Cycle Times
Warranty Returns	Warranty	Throughput
Conformance	Labor	Delivery Times
Frequency of Repairs	Facilities	Milestones
Rejects	Disability	Deadlines
Reliability	Compensation	Shipping Schedules
Mean Time to Failure	Rates of Returns	Receipt Schedules
Frequency of Failures	Unit Costs	Process Times

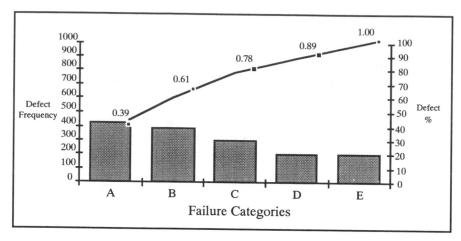

FIGURE 8-16   Basic Pareto Analysis for Frequency of Failures

Basic Pareto Analysis

Basic Pareto analysis is performed to determine the significant (vital) few and the insignificant many. This Pareto analysis arranges the bar chart data by frequency of occurrence and provides the cumulative percentages of occurrence as indicated in Figure 8-16. The discrete frequency is given on the left side of the chart and the percentage is given on the right side of the chart.

In the basic Pareto analysis for frequency of failure, in Figure 8-16, Failure Category A is the most frequently occurring, accounting for 39% of all failures, Failure Category B is the next most frequently failing, and the cumulative percentage of failures for Category A and B is 61%. Using this information, it becomes easy to understand where to concentrate corrective action efforts.

Comparative Pareto Analysis

Pareto analysis diagrams are also used to determine the effect of corrective action or to analyze the difference between two or more processes and methods. Figure 8-17 displays the use of this Pareto

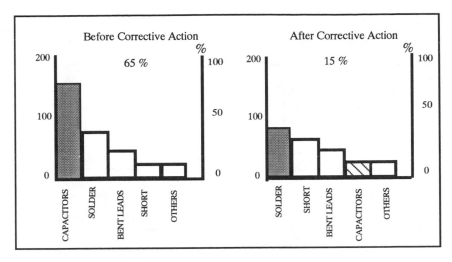

FIGURE 8-17   Comparative Pareto Analysis

method to assess the difference in defects after corrective action. As indicated in the figure, the capacitor failure rate was 65% before corrective action; after corrective action, the failure rate for capacitors was 15%.

Weighted Pareto Analysis

Weighted Pareto analysis provides the opportunity to consider other factors, such as cost and time. The weighted Pareto analysis uses a statistically weighted average to modify the frequency of occurrences. Using the same data from the Basic Pareto Analysis for Frequency of Failures, in Figure 8-16, we have weighted the failure data based upon cost and modified the Pareto graphs to account for the cost of repairing the failures, as shown in Figures 8-18 and 8-19.

A review of Pareto analysis, weighted for cost, indicates that shorts (D) are the most expensive failing component, despite the fact that they are not the most frequently occurring. The expense results from the intensive labor required to fault isolate a short.

Pareto Analysis Weighted by Cost

Failure	Failing Frequency	% Failing	Unit Cost	Total Cost	Weighted Index	Weighted % Failing	Cum. Weighted % Failing
A. Capacitor	700	0.39	1.39	973.00	379.47	39	39
B. Solder	400	0.22	0.13	52.00	11.44	1	40
C. Bad Leads	300	0.17	0.76	228.00	38.76	4	44
D. Short	200	0.11	24.80	4960.00	545.60	55	99
E. All Others	200	0.11	Various	76.00	8.36	1	100
Totals	1800	1.00		6289.00	983.63	100	

Pareto Analysis Weighted by Cost in Descending Order

Failure	Failing Frequency	% Failing	Unit Cost	Total Cost	Weighted Index	Weighted % Failing	Cum. Weighted % Failing
D. Short	200	0.11	24.80	4960.00	545.60	55	55
A. Capacitor	700	0.39	1.39	973.00	379.47	39	94
C. Bad Leads	300	0.17	0.76	228.00	38.76	4	98
B. Solder	400	0.22	0.13	52.00	11.44	1	99
E. All Others	200	0.11	Various	76.00	8.36	1	100
Totals	1800	1.00		6289.00	983.63	100	

FIGURE 8-18   Weighted Pareto Analysis

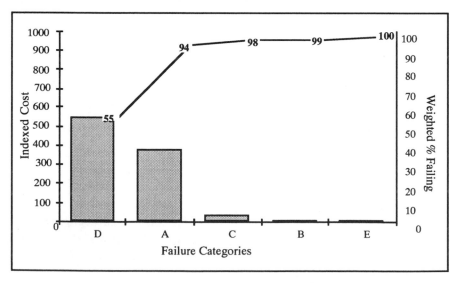

FIGURE 8-19   Weighted Pareto Analysis for Frequency

SCATTER DIAGRAMS

Another pictorial representation of process control data is the scatter plot, or scatter diagram. A scatter diagram organizes data using two variables: an independent variable and a dependent variable. This data is then recorded on a simple graph with X and Y coordinates showing the relationship between the variables. Figure 8-20 displays the relationship between two of the data elements from the solder qualification test scores in Figure 8-11. The independent variable, experience in months, is listed on the X-axis. The dependent variable is the score, which is recorded on the Y-axis.

Evaluating Scatter Plots

Scatter plots can be used to demonstrate the relationship between dependent and independent variables, to determine the dependence of variables, and to predict the response of a dependent variable based upon a specific setting of an independent variable.

These relationships fall into several categories, as shown in Figure 8-21. In the first scatter plot, there is no correlation; the data points are widely scattered with no apparent pattern. The second scatter plot shows a curvilinear correlation demonstrated by the U shape of the graph. The third scatter plot has a negative correlation, as indi-

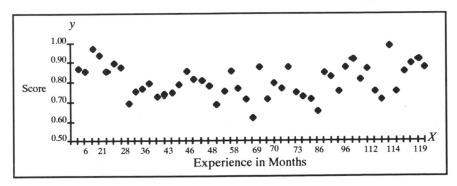

FIGURE 8-20   Solder Certification Test Scores—Data Relationship

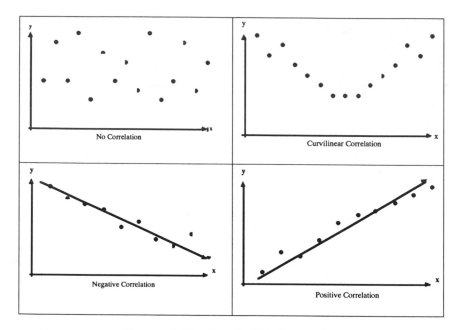

FIGURE 8-21   Scatter Plot Correlation

cated by the downward slope. The final scatter plot has a positive correlation with an upward slope.

From Figure 8-20, we can see that the scatter plot for solder certification testing is somewhat curvilinear. The least and the most experienced employees scored highest, whereas those with an intermediate level of experience did relatively poorly. The next tool, trend analysis, will help clarify and quantify these relationships.

Trend Analysis

Trend analysis is a method for determining the equation that best fits the data in a scatter plot. Trend analysis quantifies the relationships of the data, determines the equation, and measures the fit of the equation to the data. This method is also known as curve fitting, or least squares regression analysis.

Trend analysis can determine optimal operating conditions by providing an equation that describes the relationship between the dependent (output) and independent (input) variables. An example is the data set concerning experience and scores on the solder certification test.

The equation of the regression line, or trend line, provides a clear and understandable measure of the change caused in the output variable by every incremental change of the input or independent variable. Using this principle, we can predict the effects of changes in the process.

Trend analysis is a natural outgrowth of process analysis and the other product and process control tools. Much of the work required for trend analysis is already accomplished during process analysis and in utilizing the other product and process control tools. Figure 8-22 is the data table we will use to demonstrate trend analysis. In Figure 8-23, the trend analysis scatter plot for solder quality and certification score is demonstrated.

Calculate and Evaluate the Equation of the Trend

The equation of the trend is also known as the regression equation, or regression line. Here, we will study the linear regression line as it is represented by the equation:

$$Y = aX + b$$

where:

a = The slope of the regression line
b = The constant value of Y when X = 0
X = The value of the independent variable
y = The value of the dependent variable

To determine the equation of the line, we must first accomplish a few intermediate steps. We can calculate the slope of the regression line using the following equation:

SAMPLE	SCORE X	QUALITY Y	$(X - \overline{X})$	$(Y - \overline{Y})$	$(Y - \overline{Y})^2$	$(X - \overline{X})(Y - \overline{Y})$	$(X - \overline{X})^2$
1	0.62	0.86	-0.1970	-0.0820	0.0067	0.0162	0.0388
2	0.69	0.83	-0.1270	-0.1120	0.0125	0.0142	0.0161
3	0.72	0.86	-0.0970	-0.0820	0.0067	0.0080	0.0094
4	0.74	0.89	-0.0770	-0.0520	0.0027	0.0040	0.0059
5	0.75	0.90	-0.0670	-0.0420	0.0018	0.0028	0.0045
6	0.76	0.92	-0.0570	-0.0220	0.0005	0.0013	0.0032
7	0.76	0.93	-0.0570	-0.0120	0.0001	0.0007	0.0032
8	0.77	0.94	-0.0470	-0.0020	0.0000	0.0001	0.0022
9	0.79	0.93	-0.0270	-0.0120	0.0001	0.0003	0.0007
10	0.80	0.96	-0.0170	0.0180	0.0003	-0.0003	0.0003
11	0.82	0.97	0.0030	0.0280	0.0008	0.0001	0.0000
12	0.83	0.97	0.0130	0.0280	0.0008	0.0004	0.0002
13	0.86	0.96	0.0430	0.0180	0.0003	0.0008	0.0018
14	0.87	0.98	0.0530	0.0380	0.0014	0.0020	0.0028
15	0.88	0.98	0.0630	0.0380	0.0014	0.0024	0.0040
16	0.88	0.99	0.0630	0.0480	0.0023	0.0030	0.0040
17	0.90	0.99	0.0830	0.0480	0.0023	0.0040	0.0069
18	0.94	0.99	0.1230	0.0480	0.0023	0.0059	0.0151
19	0.97	0.98	0.1530	0.0380	0.0014	0.0058	0.0234
20	0.99	1.00	0.1730	0.0580	0.0034	0.0100	0.0299
SUM	16.34	18.83			0.0481	0.0816	0.1726
AVG	0.817	0.942					

FIGURE 8-22   Trend Analysis Data Table

$$a = \frac{\Sigma (X_i - \overline{X})(Y_i - \overline{Y})}{\Sigma (X_i - \overline{X})^2}$$

where:

X_i = The value of the ith observation of the independent variable

$\overline{X}$ = The average value of the independent variable

Y_i = The value of the ith observation of the dependent variable

$\overline{Y}$ = The average value of the dependent variable

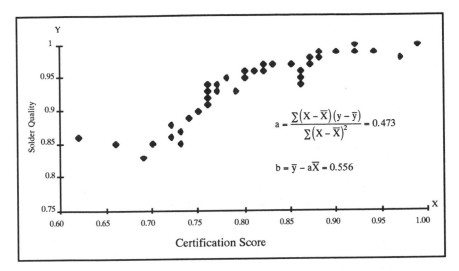

FIGURE 8-23 Scatter Plot: Solder Quality and Certification Score

The next intermediate step is to determine the value of b, the constant value of y when x is equal to zero:

$$b = \overline{Y} - a\overline{X}$$

Using the data from Figure 8-22, we can now calculate the values for a and b in the trend equation. The slope (a) of the regression line is calculated using the equation shown earlier and the data from the table.

$$a = \frac{\Sigma (X_i - \overline{X})(Y_i - \overline{Y})}{\Sigma (X_i - \overline{X})^2} = \frac{0.0816}{0.1726} = 0.473$$

We calculated the value of Y when X is equal to zero (b) using the equation for that factor and the information derived from the spreadsheet. The average values ($\overline{Y}$ and $\overline{X}$) are taken directly from the spreadsheet. The value for (a) was calculated, and the average value for X is shown in Figure 8-22.

$$b = \overline{Y} - a\overline{X} = .942 - (.473)(.817) = 0.556$$

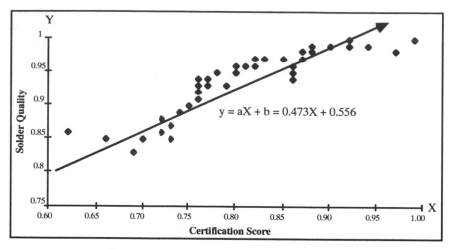

FIGURE 8-24   Scatter Plot: Solder Quality and Certification Score

Therefore, the equation of the trend (or regression) line is:

$$Y = aX + b = .473(X) + .556$$

In Figure 8-24, we have drawn the line of the equation through the scatter plot of the data to clarify the relationship of the trend equation to the data. The numbers for the (a) and (b) factors have been rounded to two places for clarity.

Evaluate the Equation of the Trend

Now that we have developed the trend equation and understand how it relates to the data on the scatter plot, we can use the equation to make projections. The (a) element of the equation is the slope of the trend line. For every unit of movement of the independent variable, the dependent variable moves a unit. In this example, the value for (a) is 0.47. The units for both the independent (Y) and dependent (X) variables are percentages. Therefore, for every percentage point that is gained in the solder qualification score, 0.47 percent (on average) is gained in quality. We can use the equation in this way to make projections. If we could improve the minimum standard for the solder qualification score from 0.75 to 0.85, what effect would this improvement have on the quality of the solder process?

Qualification score of 0.75:
$$Y = aX + b = (0.47)(0.75) + .56 = 0.91$$

Qualification score of 0.85:
$$Y = aX + b = (0.47)(0.85) + .56 = 0.96$$

We can project that requiring a minimum solder certification score of .85 for our employees will improve the quality of soldering from 0.91 to 0.96.

LOSS FUNCTION

The traditional view in industry of a loss function has been binomial; does the product dimension meet the specification or not. If the product was within specification, there was "apparently" no loss in value. All products that met specification were shipped, and all products that failed specification were repaired, reworked, or scrapped. This goalpost approach to the cost of quality is represented in Figure 8-25.

Dr. Genichi Taguchi recognized that there was a cost associated with the variability of products even if they were within the specification limits. He used the loss function to describe and quantify that cost. The loss function measures the dollar value of inconsistent products and services to the customer and to the manufacturer. There is a direct relationship between the cost of quality and the variation of the products and processes from the ideal value. Any amount of variation from this ideal or nominal value is a loss of quality, an additional cost to the manufacturer and the customer, and a reduction in the efficiency of the process. Dr. Taguchi popularized the loss function as a parabolic approximation of the actual loss to the customer and the manufacturer in specific dollar values associated with product variation. This expresses quality in terms of dollars, which

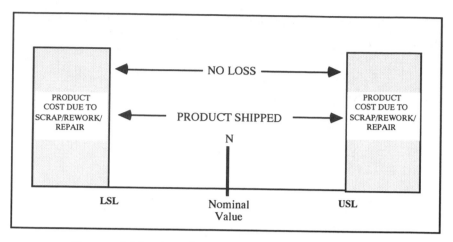

FIGURE 8-25   Specification Approach to Quality Loss

makes business sense to managers and executives who are making business decisions. Figure 8-26 is a graphic presentation of the Taguchi Loss Function.

This loss function indicates that any variation from nominal, even variation within the specified parameters displaying a process capability of 1.0 or better, represents a loss. Variation in your products is

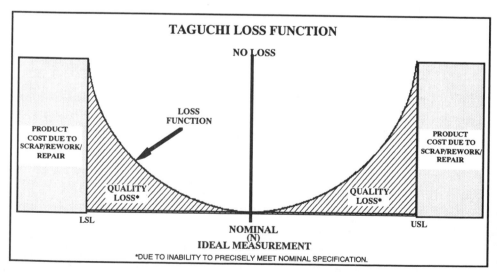

FIGURE 8-26   The Taguchi Loss Function

what causes difficulty in assembly, integration, automatic feeding, and application of robotics manufacturing methods. Variation also represents a loss of process efficiency and product effectiveness. Variation can also cause losses due to customer dissatisfaction, warranty costs, and broader market opportunities. Process variability always translates to dollars in some way.

To develop the loss function, we will use data previously presented in the process control section for a drive shaft diameter. This data is presented using the $\overline{X} \notin R$ control chart in Figure 8-27.

The effectiveness of the loss function can best be understood when we develop its relationship to specific data. Figure 8-28 superimposes the data from the previous tables on the loss function. Generally speaking, the process looks good, especially from a traditional point of view. Since $\pm 3\sigma$ are within the specification limits, the process capability is better than one (Cp of 1.2), and the process is in statistical control. However, overlaying the Taguchi Loss Function to

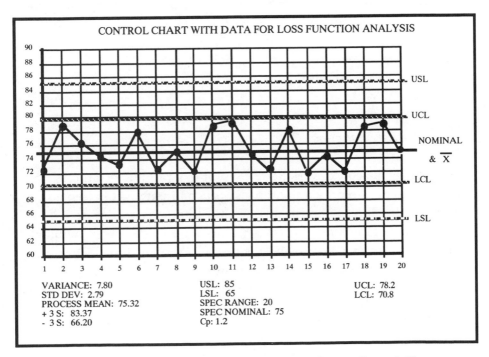

FIGURE 8-27 Basic Loss Function Statistics from a Control Chart

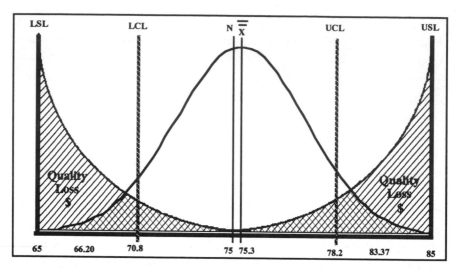

FIGURE 8-28   Relationship of the Loss Function to the Normal Distribution

this distribution clearly shows that there is an opportunity to gain quality value by reducing the variability. The area beneath both the loss function curve and the normal distribution curve (the double-shaded area) represents the existing dollar loss per unit based on the current process variability.

Loss Function Equation

To quantify the cost of variability present in a product or process, we use an equation representing the loss function parabola presented in Figure 8-28. To accomplish this, we must know two or more points on the trace of the function. These points are provided as the nominal or ideal measurement (N), and the points where the total loss occurs at the upper or lower specification limits (USL, LSL). Using cost as the value of quality variation from the nominal, the equation for the loss function is:

$$L = K(\overline{Y} - N)^2$$

where:

> L = The loss in dollars per unit
>
> K = Constant used to convert the process or product variance into dollars
>
> $\overline{Y}$ = The measured value of the quality characteristic (Process Mean)
>
> N = The nominal value or target value set by the specification

For multiple products or processes the equation becomes:

$$L = K\sigma^2$$

The constant K factor is derived from the product or process scrap cost at the specification limits. The constant is the scrap cost over distance squared from the specification nominal value to the specification limit.

$$K = \frac{\text{Total Loss Cost}}{(N - LSL)^2}$$

Loss Function Analysis

The loss function is used to measure critical process elements and as a decision making tool in three distinct ways: first, in its most traditional role as a measure of the impact of the cost of quality variability; secondly, to compare the effects of different or new products, processes, and procedures; and finally, as a tool to determine the feasibility of variability-reduction projects.

Selecting a Product or Process for Loss Function Analysis

For developing products and processes, the loss function is used to determine what the cost of variability in the product will be and to compare competing processes, procedures, equipment, or materials.

Data can be made available for this analysis from pilot runs or analysis of the process capabilities from specifications.

In processes that are currently on-line, the loss function quantifies the loss in value caused by product variability. This provides a basis to improve these processes and aids in the decision as to what variability reduction tools or techniques are cost-effective. Data to perform this loss function analysis is inherent in any process under statistical process control. The existing process must be under process control (C_p of 1.0 or better) before the loss function becomes a meaningful tool.

For both types of process, specific data elements are required to perform loss function analysis. The following are the minimum data elements required to perform loss function analysis; the values provided are from the example above and will be used in developing the loss function.

Data Element	Value
The Specified Nominal Value (N)	75
The Upper and Lower Specification Limits (LSL/USL)	65–75
The Specification Range (R)	±10
The Process Quality Characteristic (Y)	75.32
The Process Variance (σ^2)	7.80
The Process Standard Deviation (σ)	2.79
The Process $\pm 3\sigma$	66.20–83.37
Total Product Value Loss at Specification Limits	$135.00

Determine the K Factor

Determine the cost of the total loss of the product due to failure to conform to the process specification, LSL or USL. This cost can at times include such additional costs as warranty costs, customer dissatisfaction, and loss of market opportunity, all due to product variability. From the product specification, determine the specification range, using the specification range of ±10 from the data above and the total cost of scrapping a drive shaft of $135.

$$K = \frac{135}{10^2} = 1.35$$

Calculate the Loss Function

Using the data elements above, we can now calculate the loss function for the drive shaft diameter. The constant factor is 1.35 and the process variance is 7.80. The multiple products form of the loss function equation is used because the data are derived from multiple processes.

$$L = K\sigma^2$$

$$L = (1.35)(7.80) = \$10.53 \text{ per unit}$$

EXAMPLE

The manufacturing equipment division of LWCI maintains a service department to service the customers of the division. The department provides technical assistance, equipment set-up service, and on-site repair for the manufacturing equipment produced by the division. In keeping with the LWCI goal of becoming a world class competitor and to achieve implementation of continuous measurable improvement, the service department performs a process analysis of its key processes. For example, the customer service and support department formed an operating team to accomplish the process analysis. Here we will review how the team applied the product and process control tools to the field service of the LWCI 1587 coating machine.

The LWCI 1587 coating machine applies liquid preservative coatings to metal services using a closely controlled spray. The machine applies the spray through a high-pressure application system that uses a flow rate controller to measure the application of the product. The machine applies the coating to surfaces by moving a jointed arm around the item being preserved. An electronic motion controller controls the arm movements. The system operates on a low pressure hydraulic system that is run by electric motors. The system uses separate power supplies for the electronic controllers and drive motors. The application arm is driven by a central drive shaft.

As a part of the process analysis, the service department needed to determine what controls were in place within that department and how they were being employed to provide world class service for this equipment, both at the time of the analysis and in the future. This assessment was keyed to providing better service to the customers and feedback to those responsible for the design and development of the coating machines.

- ► Analysis of the service requirements of the LWCI 1587 system
- ► Analysis to determine the out year requirements for the LWCI 1587 system

For the first analysis, the team members selected to perform data collection determined that they could accomplish the evaluation using service call data already on hand for the system. There were 725 LWCI 1587 systems in use. To provide data that represented recent requirements and to smooth out any fluctuations in the data, the team decided to use the most recent 12 months of service reports. They placed these manual reports into a data table, in Example Figure 8-1. The data table provided a structured view of the data and provided the basis for further analysis.

From the data table, the team determined that 102 service calls were made for the LWCI 1587 during the previous 12-month period.

Item	Name	Months												Total
		1	2	3	4	5	6	7	8	9	10	11	12	
A	Central Drive Shaft	5	7	2	5	3	5	5	6	2	6	6	4	56
B	Controller Board	1	0	1	1	0	0	1	2	0	0	4	0	10
C	Drive Motor	1	2	1	0	2	1	2	0	0	1	3	2	15
D	Hydrolic System	2	1	0	0	2	2	0	2	0	2	1	2	14
E	Power Supply	0	0	1	2	1	0	0	1	1	0	0	1	7
	LWCI 1587 (Total)	9	10	5	8	8	8	8	11	3	9	14	9	102

EXAMPLE FIGURE 8-1   LWCI 1587 System Service Calls

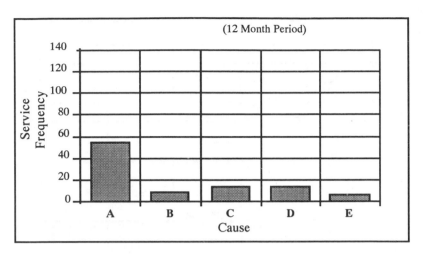

EXAMPLE FIGURE 8-2   LWCI 1587 Service Calls

The data table also provided totals for each assembly that required service and the number of service calls during each of the 12 months.

The next tool the team used to evaluate the data was a histogram. They produced the histogram using a standard spreadsheet program on a personal computer. The resulting histogram is demonstrated in Example Figure 8-2. The letter code for each column of the histogram represents the associated name of the failing assembly from the data table in Example Figure 8-1.

The histogram further clarified the data. Since this was attribute data, no frequency distribution could be derived from the histogram. Instead, the team decided to employ the basic Pareto analysis tool for frequency of occurrence to analyze this data further. They used the same simple spreadsheet program to create the Pareto diagram in Example Figure 8-3.

From this Pareto analysis, the team determined several important facts concerning the service calls for the 725 LWCI 1587 systems currently being used by customers. The central drive shaft (A) accounted for the highest number of service calls with 51 failures, or 55% of all service calls, during the previous 12 months. Drive motor (C) failures were the next most frequent, with 15 failures, or 15% of the service calls. The cumulative failure rate for central drive shafts and drive motors together is 70%. The hydraulic system (D) ac-

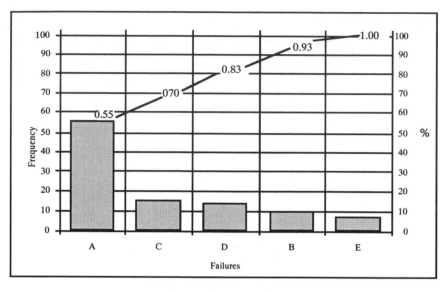

EXAMPLE FIGURE 8-3   LWCI 1587 System Pareto Analysis

counted for 14 service calls, or 13% of the total calls. The cumulative total of service calls for items A, C, and D is 83%. Compared to these, the failure rates for the controller board (B) and power supply (E) were of little consequence. The controller board required ten service calls during the year and the power supplies only seven.

The Pareto analysis provided the team with a clear picture of the most frequently occurring service calls. The service department could use this information to be better prepared to respond to calls and to plan on what tools, training, and personnel would provide the best service for the LWCI 1587 customers.

- ▶ Central Drive Shafts: Failures 52; Cumulative 0.55
- ▶ Drive Motors: Failures 15; Cumulative 0.70
- ▶ Hydraulic System: Failures 14; Cumulative 0.83
- ▶ Controller Boards: Failures 10; Cumulative 0.93
- ▶ Power Supplies: Failures 7; Cumulative 1.00

The picture concerning the service requirements for the LWCI 1587 was becoming much clearer, and the department was better able to plan and organize the actions needed to control the service process. One element that highlighted itself very clearly was the proportion of service calls associated with the central drive shaft (significant few, insignificant many). The team wanted to analyze the failures causing these service calls for corrective action. The team, with the concurrence of the management steering committee, reformed itself to perform cause-and-effect analysis.

This team included personnel from the production and design departments of the manufacturing equipment division, as well as engineers and production personnel from the machine tool division, where the drive shafts were produced. The cause-and-effect analysis team, after some initial training and team building, decided to use the random method of cause-and-effect analysis. Shaft failures were caused by physical damage to the shafts; they were worn on the ends connecting them to the drive motor and in some cases were actually warped. The team brainstormed the possible causes of failure of the drive shaft and constructed the cause-and-effect analysis shown in Example Figure 8-4.

The analysis clearly indicated that the cause of the failures was the "quality" of the shafts coming from the machine tool division. This problem affected the service department directly, since the shafts

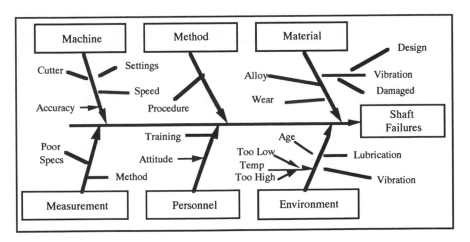

EXAMPLE FIGURE 8-4   LWCI 1587 System Drive Shaft Cause-and-Effect Analysis

are the primary cause of failure for this system. Further action was required by the machine tool division as a product and process improvement.

The service department also wanted to control its responsiveness to the customers by better forecasting of customer needs. The team decided to look at the service data relative to the age of the systems fielded and determine if any service requirements were influenced by age-related degradation of the systems. Data were available from the service records and from the date associated with LWCI 1587 serial numbers. The data for the 725 systems produced in the last four years and currently in use are available in existing records. The machines were produced at the rate of about 180 per year during that period, and the service calls for that period are listed in Example Figure 8-5. The figure also shows the number of maintenance calls based upon the age of the systems, stated in months. The team used data in this figure to create the scatter plot in Example Figure 8-6.

From the scatter plot, the team was able to determine that there was a positive correlation between the dependent (Y) and independent (X) variables. The number of service calls is related to system age in months: as age increases, the number of service calls increases.

Age (Months)	Service Calls	Age (Months)	Service Calls	Age (Months)	Service Calls	Age (Months)	Service Calls
1	3	13	5	25	6	37	5
2	0	14	6	26	4	38	6
3	0	15	5	27	6	39	9
4	2	15	7	28	7	40	6
5	1	17	5	29	7	41	7
6	0	18	6	30	6	42	8
7	2	19	6	31	7	43	9
8	4	20	6	32	6	44	8
9	3	21	4	33	7	45	9
10	2	22	5	34	7	46	8
11	3	23	6	35	8	47	10
12	4	24	5	36	7	48	10

EXAMPLE FIGURE 8-5   LWCI 1587 Data

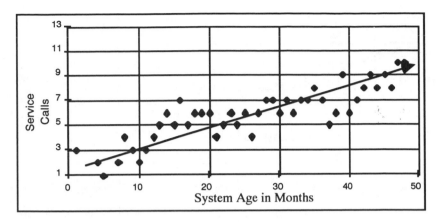

EXAMPLE FIGURE 8-6   LWCI 1587 System Service Calls

The team therefore predicted that as the systems aged, there would be more service calls from the customers. This was not a surprise, but the analysis enabled them to understand those relationships much better and to understand how to control the service requirements to a much better degree.

The team decided to perform a trend analysis on the scatter plot data, to forecast the requirements for the next year. They made a trend analysis data chart and evaluated it using the linear trend equation. The data chart is presented in Example Figure 8-7. The team then proceeded to use the information from the data figure to determine the equation of the trend line:

$$Y = aX + b$$

To evaluate the slope of the line (a):

$$a = \frac{\Sigma (X_i - \overline{X})(Y_i - \overline{Y})}{\Sigma (X_i - X)^2} = \frac{1453.98}{9229.98} = 0.16$$

To evaluate the constant value of (b):

$$b = \overline{Y} - a\overline{X} = 5.48 - (0.16)(24.48) = 1.56$$

	Age X	Service Y	$(X-\overline{X})$	$(Y-\overline{Y})$	$(Y-\overline{Y})^2$	$(Y-\overline{Y})(X-\overline{X})$	$(X-\overline{X})^2$
	1	3	-23.48	-2.48	6.15	58.23	551.31
	2	0	-22.48	-5.48	30.03	123.19	505.35
	3	0	-21.48	-5.48	30.03	117.71	461.39
	4	2	-20.48	-3.48	12.11	71.27	419.43
	5	1	-19.48	-4.48	20.07	87.27	379.47
	6	0	-18.48	-5.48	30.03	101.27	341.51
	7	2	-17.48	-3.48	12.11	60.83	305.55
	8	4	-16.48	-1.48	2.19	24.39	271.59
	9	3	-15.48	-2.48	6.15	38.39	239.63
	10	2	-14.48	-3.48	12.11	50.39	209.67
	11	3	-13.48	-2.48	6.15	33.43	181.71
	12	4	-12.48	-1.48	2.19	18.47	155.75
	13	5	-11.48	-0.48	0.23	5.51	131.79
	14	6	-10.48	0.52	0.27	-5.45	109.83
	15	5	-9.48	-0.48	0.23	4.55	89.87
	15	7	-9.48	1.52	2.31	-14.41	89.87
	17	5	-7.48	-0.48	0.23	3.59	55.95
	18	6	-6.48	0.52	0.27	-3.37	41.99
	19	6	-5.48	0.52	0.27	-2.85	30.03
	20	6	-4.48	0.52	0.27	-2.33	20.07
	21	4	-3.48	-1.48	2.19	5.15	12.11
	22	5	-2.48	-0.48	0.23	1.19	6.15
	23	6	-1.48	0.52	0.27	-0.77	2.19
	24	5	-0.48	-0.48	0.23	0.23	0.23
	25	6	0.52	0.52	0.27	0.27	0.27
	26	4	1.52	-1.48	2.19	-2.25	2.31
	27	6	2.52	0.52	0.27	1.31	6.35
	28	7	3.52	1.52	2.31	5.35	12.39
	29	7	4.52	1.52	2.31	6.87	20.43
	30	6	5.52	0.52	0.27	2.87	30.47
	31	7	6.52	1.52	2.31	9.91	42.51
	32	6	7.52	0.52	0.27	3.91	56.55
	33	7	8.52	1.52	2.31	12.95	72.59
	34	7	9.52	1.52	2.31	14.47	90.63
	35	8	10.52	2.52	6.35	26.51	110.67
	36	7	11.52	1.52	2.31	17.51	132.71
	37	5	12.52	-0.48	0.23	-6.01	156.75
	38	6	13.52	0.52	0.27	7.03	182.79
	39	9	14.52	3.52	12.39	51.11	210.83
	40	6	15.52	0.52	0.27	8.07	240.87
	41	7	16.52	1.52	2.31	25.11	272.91
	42	8	17.52	2.52	6.35	44.15	306.95
	43	9	18.52	3.52	12.39	65.19	342.99
	44	8	19.52	2.52	6.35	49.19	381.03
	45	9	20.52	3.52	12.39	72.23	421.07
	46	8	21.52	2.52	6.35	54.23	463.11
	47	10	22.52	4.52	20.43	101.79	507.15
	48	10	23.52	4.52	20.43	106.31	553.19
Sum	1175	263			299.98	1453.98	9229.98
Avg	24.48	5.48					

EXAMPLE FIGURE 8-7   Trend Analysis Spreadsheet

Therefore, the equation of the trend line is:

$$Y = aX + b$$

$$Y = (0.16)(X) + 1.56$$

The equation could be used to forecast service calls for a system of any age (in months). In the equation below, the team evaluated the maintenance requirements based upon the 49th month with the current population of 725 systems.

$$Y = aX + b$$

$$Y = (.16)(49) + 1.57$$

$$Y = 9.41$$

The result was 9.41, or between nine or ten service calls. But how accurate is this estimate? Does the team want to use this equation to forecast maintenance requirements? To determine the answer, the team performed a correlation analysis using the data from Example Figure 8-7. They evaluated the coefficient of determination (r^2) using the equation:

$$r^2 = \frac{a(\Sigma\ xy)}{\Sigma\ (\bar{y} - y)^2}$$

$$r^2 = \frac{(.16)(1453.98)}{299.98} = \frac{232.63}{299.98}$$

$$r^2 = .78$$

The r^2 value of .78 indicated a strong correlation between the age of systems and the service calls received. It showed that the equation was sufficiently representative of this relationship to be used for forecasting. Using this data, the team forecasted the total service requirements for the next 12-month period. The division production schedule would remain the same as in previous years; therefore, the forecast needed to account for maintenance calls for the existing systems for

	Next 12 Month Period		
Month	Existing System Calls	New System Calls	Total System Calls
1	9.41	1.73	11
2	9.57	1.89	11
3	9.73	1.57	11
4	9.89	2.21	12
5	10.05	2.37	12
6	10.21	1.57	12
7	10.37	2.69	13
8	10.53	2.85	13
9	10.69	3.01	14
10	10.85	1.57	11
11	11.01	3.33	14
12	11.17	3.49	15
Total	123.48	26.71	150

EXAMPLE FIGURE 8-8   LWCI 1587 System Service Call Forecast

months 49 to 60 and new systems with ages of 1 to 12 months. This information is presented in Example Figure 8-8.

The forecast provided fact-based information for the service division to control its service call process. This information, and the data from the previous evaluations, provided a projection of the number of service calls that would be needed and the approximate proportion of the calls for each specific assembly (for example, 55% drive shafts). In addition to the frequency and types of calls, this analysis also provided geographic information regarding the service calls. At this point, the department was ready to consider using control charts.

9

Design of Experiments

> TO COMPETE IN TODAY'S GLOBAL MARKETPLACE,
> YOUR PRODUCTS AND SERVICES MUST BE ON
> TARGET THE FIRST TIME, EVERY TIME.

The design and development of new products and services has been made more difficult by the advent of three factors in the global marketplace. These factors are: the rapid growth and innovation of technology, the shortened product life cycle brought about by that technological growth, and the diversification of customer needs. In this environment, the complete life cycle of a product or service may be very short. The life cycle of medical lasers is now only two years from concept to obsolescence!

In many industries, this is also compounded by the necessity to diversify the depth and breadth of product lines. You can no longer offer a Ford Model T in any color, as long as it is black. Put all together, the bottom line is that you must produce more types of products, bring them to market faster, and do so competitively, controlling Quality, Cost, and Schedule (Q$S). How can you do that? Thus far in this book, we have covered many of the tools needed to accomplish this feat, and now we will put the frosting on the cake with design of experiments. The most direct route to optimizing the Quality, Cost, and Schedule factors is Design of Experiments and the associated variability reduction that results from employing the various Design of Experiments and Analysis of Variance methods.

THE DESIGN AND
IMPROVEMENT PROCESS

The final decision for change is always a business decision. The business leader must, therefore, have confidence in the information used to make product and process development and improvement decisions. The quality of the information used to make these decisions is dependent on the structure of the process, the validity of experimental design, and the analytical methods. Business people also must be able to address questions of experimental design and analysis in making the decisions to allocate resources.

Here we will integrate the tools of process and product design with the new tools of Analysis of Variance (ANOVA) and Design of Experiments (DOE). These new tools will allow us to structure our design, development, and improvement efforts for new and existing products and processes. Figure 9-1 provides the structured approach to these vital processes.

All programs to achieve world class competition must start with an in-depth understanding of the voice of the customer, as we explained in the very beginning of this book. It is crucial to understand what is expected in the marketplace and to establish the product and process design, parameters, and tolerances accordingly. We have employed the seven management tools to translate the voice of the customer to a quality function deployment, putting the marketplace language into technical terms so that engineers, analysts, and managers can design a process. By evaluating the resulting process, you can find the optimum parameters for the services or products and their associated processes.

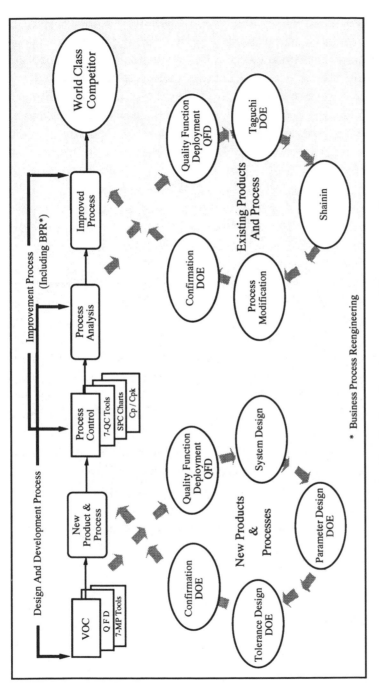

FIGURE 9-1   The Design, Development, and Improvement Processes

The process is stabilized using the process control tools and further improved with process analysis. For these existing processes, we recommend Analysis of Variance (ANOVA) to evaluate the existing data to find candidates for further improvement and QFD and DOE to improve the process. The loss function enables you to determine if the improvement to the process will result in a cost-effective change. Here, we will explore the application and implementation of the improvement tools and how they fit into the design and improvement processes.

In this chapter, we will present new tools for the planning, management, and evaluation of your new product and process. First, we will examine ANOVA. ANOVA is an advanced statistical technique that partitions variation and enables us to make decisions based upon experimental and process data.

We will then focus on Design of Experiments (DOE). This section will include a review of the classical methods as the foundation of the Taguchi and Shainin Methods. We recommend the use of Taguchi Quality Engineering as our primary DOE tool for the design and development of new products and processes. Therefore, we will examine the Taguchi methods of System Design, Parameter Design, Tolerance Design, and Taguchi ANOVA in some detail. During the improvement process, we recommend the application of the Statistical Engineering Approach developed by Dorian Shainin.

Each of the methods of ANOVA and DOE have their primary applications; however, they are cross-functional and overlay as indicated in Figure 9-1. This figure provides us a graphic view of the design, development, and improvement methods, their cross-functionality, and how they are structured into a process. We will follow this process flow as we develop the design and development process for new products and services.

- ► Analysis Of Variance (ANOVA)
- ► Classical Design of Experiments
- ► Taguchi Quality Engineering
- ► Shainin Statistical Engineering

> The purpose of analysis of variance, as its name implies, is to determine how much of the variation among observations is due to variation in each input factor influencing the output characteristic being studied.

ANALYSIS OF VARIANCE

Analysis of Variance (ANOVA) is an important tool for making business and technical decisions. It tells us whether several different treatments (for example, different manufacturing processes) all have the same effect on the quality characteristic of interest. These treatments are specific values of an input (independent) variable. The variable(s) whose values are affected by these treatments are often called response variables, outcome variables, or dependent variables. The best common-sense explanation of ANOVA that we have seen is from a 1939 book by a renowned scientist, Dr. George Gaylord Simpson.

The computation for ANOVA can be complex and tedious. In most cases, ANOVA is accomplished using an automated computer program such as MINITAB. We strongly recommend this approach. We have also simplified the manual approach to ANOVA by developing a generic computation and decision table, which shows all the intermediate steps in ANOVA (Figure 9-2).

There are several aspects of ANOVA that we should understand when using this ANOVA for the evaluation of existing processes data or data from designed experiments. These factors are discussed in the following paragraphs. Here, we will concentrate on understanding and implementing ANOVA for the continuous measurable improvement process.

- ► Hypothesis testing
- ► Concept of variation
- ► Sum of the squares
- ► Degrees of freedom

SOURCE OF VARIATION		SUM OF SQUARES	DEGREES OF FREEDOM	MEAN SQUARES	F RATIO	F' CRITICAL	STRENGTH
TREATMENTS — **MAIN EFFECTS**	A	SS_A	df_A	MS_A	F_A	F'_A	ω^2_A
	B	SS_B	df_B	MS_B	F_B	F'_B	ω^2_B
	C	SS_C	df_C	MS_C	F_C	F'_C	ω^2_C
INTERACTIONS	AB	SS_{AB}	df_{AB}	MS_{AB}	F_{AB}	F'_{AB}	ω^2_{AB}
	AC	SS_{AC}	df_{AC}	MS_{AC}	F_{AC}	F'_{AC}	ω^2_{AC}
	BC	SS_{BC}	df_{BC}	MS_{BC}	F_{BC}	F'_{BC}	ω^2_{BC}
	ABC	SS_{ABC}	df_{ABC}	MS_{ABC}	F_{ABC}	F'_{ABC}	ω^2_{ABC}
WITHIN		SS_{Within}	df_{Within}	MS_{Within}			
TOTAL		SS_{Total}	df_{Total}				

FIGURE 9-2   Analysis of Variance

- ► Mean squares
- ► Fisher's F statistic
- ► Level of significance
- ► Strength of statistical relationship
- ► Evaluating the results of ANOVA

Hypothesis Testing

When performing ANOVA, the assumption is always made that the population is homogeneous. Therefore, the null hypothesis is that the means of the data for all treatment groups are equal. Symbolically, the null hypothesis is stated as:

$$H_O : \mu_1 = \mu_2 = \mu_3$$

The alternate hypothesis, therefore, is that at least one of the population means is not equal. Symbolically, the alternate hypothesis is:

$$H_A = \begin{cases} \mu_1 \neq \mu_2 \neq \mu_2 \\ \mu_1 = \mu_2 \neq \mu_2 \end{cases}$$

To apply hypothesis testing to process and experimental data, we must first establish some basic facts about the data. We will use the data demonstrated in Figure 9-3 for this purpose. There are four treatments. Each treatment is measured by six samples, repeats, or replicates. Therefore, there are 24 sample measurements. The assumption of homogeneity indicates that the null hypothesis for this data is that the means of the data produced by treatments A, B, C, and D are the same.

When stating the null hypothesis for the sample data in the above example, we use the symbol $(\overline{X})$ to represent the mean of the sample data and the symbol (μ) to represent the mean of the population, or the true mean. The null hypothesis (H_O) for this ANOVA is therefore that the means $(\overline{X})$ of the treatments are equal:

$$H_O : \overline{X}_A = \overline{X}_B = \overline{X}_C = \overline{X}_D$$

And the alternate hypothesis (H_A) is that the means $(\overline{X})$ of at least one or more of the population means are not equal:

SAMPLE	TREATMENTS			
n	A	B	C	D
1	69	83	79	76
2	71	77	85	73
3	73	79	77	77
4	76	77	70	71
5	76	74	79	78
6	70	84	69	71

FIGURE 9-3   Basic ANOVA Data Table

$$H_A = \begin{cases} \overline{X}_A \neq \overline{X}_B \neq \overline{X}_C \neq \overline{X}_D \\ \overline{X}_A = \overline{X}_B \neq \overline{X}_C = \overline{X}_D \end{cases}$$

The Concept of Variation

Figure 9-4 illustrates the concept of variability between and within treatments. Variation between treatments A and B occurs when there is a significant difference between the means of the data for those treatments. The significance of these differences is measured using the F statistic, as discussed in a following section.

Sum of the Squares

The sum of the squares is the first calculation on the ANOVA table. For main effects and interactions (SS_a, SS_{ab}), we summarize the squared values of the grand mean, subtracted from the mean value of

No Variance Between Or Within Treatments

A	B
75	75
75	75
75	75

Variance Only Between Treatments

A	B
75	77
75	77
75	77

Variance Both Between and Within Treatments

A	B
75	77
73	77
76	72

FIGURE 9-4   Concept of Variance

each treatment level, and multiply that quantity by the sample size for each treatment combination. The generalized equations for main effects and interactions are:

For Main Effects (A, B, C, . . . , K)

$$SS_k = \Sigma[n_k \Sigma(\overline{X}_k - \overline{\overline{X}})^2]$$

For Interactions (A × B, A × C, B × C, . . . , J × K)

$$SS_{kj} = \Sigma[n_k \Sigma(\overline{X}_k - \overline{\overline{X}})^2] + \Sigma[n_j \Sigma(\overline{X}_j - \overline{\overline{X}})^2] - SS_k - SS_j$$

The sum of the squares for the total variation SS_{Total} is calculated by subtracting the grand mean from the individual values of all samples, as indicated in the following equation.

$$SS_{Total} = \Sigma(X - \overline{\overline{X}})^2$$

The sum of the squares for treatments and within are additive to the total sum of the squares, therefore, the sum of the squares for within can be derived by subtracting the SS_{Total} from $SS_{MainEffects}$ and $SS_{Interactions}$.

$$SS_{Within} = SS_{Total} - SS_{Treatments}$$

Remember that these calculations are most frequently accomplished using a computer program. Before using such a program, however, it is important to understand the purpose and methods of the procedure.

Degrees of Freedom

Degrees of freedom (*df*) are the number of independent comparisons available to estimate a specific treatment or level of a treatment. This is also an element of the critical value of F. Degrees of freedom are used for both the numerator and denominator of the F statistic. The number of degrees of freedom for treatment main effects is $T_a - 1$ or the number of applicable treatment levels minus one. The degrees

		Treatment A			
		A1	A2		
Treatment B	B1	76, 81, 74	78, 76, 77	C1	Treatment C
		75, 71, 75	76, 81, 74	C2	
	B2	76, 71, 74	76, 83, 77	C1	
		78, 81, 76	81, 79, 74	C2	

FIGURE 9-5   Sample Data to Illustrate Degrees of Freedom

of freedom for treatment interactions is $(T_a - 1)(T_b - 1)$ or the degrees of freedom for each of the effects in the interaction. The total degrees of freedom are the total number of independent comparisons for all treatments, treatment levels, and replicates, $N - 1$ or the total number of data elements in the sample minus one. The degrees of freedom applicable to variation within treatments (error) is the total degrees of freedom minus the degrees of freedom for treatments and treatment interactions. This can be demonstrated using the data in Figure 9-5.

Treatment Main Effects

The degrees of freedom derived from this data, for the treatment main effects, are the number of treatment levels for each treatment minus one. In this example, there are two treatment levels for each treatment; $df_{\text{MainEffects}}$ are:

$$df \text{ Treatment A} = T_a - 1 = 2 - 1 = 1$$
$$df \text{ Treatment B} = T_b - 1 = 2 - 1 = 1$$
$$df \text{ Treatment C} = T_c - 1 = 2 - 1 = 1$$

Treatment Interactions

The degrees of freedom derived from this data, for treatment interactions, are the multiplied degrees of freedom for the associated treatments. In this example, there are four possible treatment interactions: AB, AC, BC, and ABC; therefore, $df_{\text{Interactions}}$ are:

$$df \text{ Interaction A} \times \text{B} = (T_a - 1)(T_b - 1) = 1 \times 1 = 1$$

$$df \text{ Interaction A} \times \text{C} = (T_a - 1)(T_c - 1) = 1 \times 1 = 1$$

$$df \text{ Interaction B} \times \text{C} = (T_b - 1)(T_c - 1) = 1 \times 1 = 1$$

$$df \text{ Interaction A} \times \text{B} \times \text{C} = (T_a - 1)(T_b - 1)(T_c - 1)$$
$$= 1 \times 1 \times 1 = 1$$

The degrees of freedom for within treatments (or error) is derived by subtraction of the $df_{\text{MainEffects}}$ and $df_{\text{Interactions}}$ from the df_{Total}:

$$df_{\text{Total}} - df_{\text{Treatments}} - df_{\text{Interactions}} = 23 - 3 - 4 = 16$$

The total degrees of freedom for this figure is the total number of samples (24) minus one.

$$df_{\text{Total}} = N - 1 = 24 - 1 = 23$$

Mean Squares

The mean squares (MS) element of the ANOVA table is the quotient of the sum of the squares divided by the degrees of freedom (df):

$$MS_{\text{MainEffects}} = \frac{SS_{\text{MainEffects}}}{df_{\text{MainEffects}}} \qquad MS_{\text{Interactions}} = \frac{SS_{\text{Interactions}}}{df_{\text{Interactions}}}$$

$$MS_{\text{Within}} = \frac{SS_{\text{Within}}}{df_{\text{Within}}}$$

F Ratio

There are in this example two F_{Ratio}s. The $F_{\text{RatioMainEffects}}$ is the quotient of the $MS_{\text{MainEffects}}$ divided by the MS_{Within}, and the $F_{\text{RatioInteractions}}$ is the quotient of the $MS_{\text{Interactions}}$ divided by the MS_{Within}:

$$F_{\text{RatioMainEffects}} = \frac{MS_{\text{MainEffects}}}{MS_{\text{Within}}} \qquad F_{\text{RatioInteractions}} = \frac{MS_{\text{Interactions}}}{MS_{\text{Within}}}$$

Fisher's F Statistic

ANOVA determines if the means for several treatments are equal by examining population variances using Fisher's F Statistic. The F statistic is based upon the evaluation of the variance (s^2) of the data. ANOVA compares two estimates of this variance, one estimate attributable to the variance within treatments (s^2_{Within}) and one estimate from between treatment means ($s^2_{\text{Treatments}}$).

We calculate the first estimate from the variance within all the data from a single treatment (univariant) or several distinct treatments or different levels of a treatment (multivariant). This within-treatment estimate is the unbiased estimate of variance that remains the same, whether the means of the treatments are the same or different. It is the average, or mean, of the variances found within the data.

The second estimate of the population variance is calculated from the variance between the treatment means ($s^2_{\text{Treatments}}$). This estimate is a true representation of the mean variance only if there is no significant difference between it and the variance within sample means (s^2_{Within}). Fisher's F statistic measures the difference in means based upon the ratio of the variance between and the variance within treatments, and we compare that ratio to the critical value of F (F_{Critical}). The statistics that apply to our ANOVA application are therefore:

$$F_{\text{Treatments}} = \frac{MS_{\text{Treatments}}}{MS_{\text{Within}}} \qquad F_{\text{MainEffects}} = \frac{MS_{\text{MainEffects}}}{MS_{\text{Within}}}$$

$$F_{\text{Interactions}} = \frac{MS_{\text{Interactions}}}{MS_{\text{Within}}}$$

We then compare this F ratio to the critical value of F (F_{critical}) to determine if the F ratio is significant. The critical value of F is determined by referring to the F Table (Table A-2 in Appendix A) for the applicable degrees of freedom and significance level selected for this evaluation. The degrees of freedom for the numerator are the degrees of freedom for Treatments, Main Effects, or Interactions. The degrees of freedom for the denominator are the degrees of freedom for within or error.

$$F'_{df_{Numerator} \, df_{Denominator} \, \alpha}$$

The variance is significant, if means are significantly different, when the F_{Ratio} is equal to or exceeds the $F_{Critical}$ value:

$$F_{Ratio} \geqslant F_{Critical} = \text{SIGNIFICANT}$$

$$F_{Ratio} < F_{Critical} = \text{NOT SIGNIFICANT}$$

Strength of Statistical Relationship

To evaluate the level of significance, we will use the omega squared (ω^2) method for fixed effects. This method provides an estimate of the percentage of variation contributed by the treatment compared to the total variation of the process. From the computation and decision table, we will use the equation:

$$\omega^2 = \frac{SS_{Treatments} - (T - 1)(MS_{Within})}{SS_{Total} + MS_{Within}}$$

Level of Significance

The determination of the critical value of F ($F_{Critical}$) is dependent upon the selection of a level of significance (α) for the ANOVA. The level of significance applied to the analysis can be a very subjective choice where no specific standards exist. It is important that some standard for selection of the significance level be implemented and applied to analysis uniformly throughout the business. The selection of the level of significance often reflects the consequences of the decision that will result from the analysis. A typical decision table for level of significance is provided in Figure 9-6.

DECISION	α LEVEL
CRITICAL SYSTEMS PARAMETERS System reliability System safety requirements System performance Systems competitive capability	0.01
PROCESS EFFICIENCY OR EFFECTIVENESS Process improvement options Process selection Process differentiation Equipment selection	0.05
ADMINISTRATIVE/BUSINESS DECISIONS Payment of bonuses Return on investment Marketing decisions	0.10

FIGURE 9-6   Significance Decision Table

For example, if we are determining whether there is any significance between auto air bag manufacturers, we will tolerate only a very low probability of decision error. Therefore, we would select a significance level of 0.01. In decisions regarding the effectiveness or efficiency of equipment or processes for improvement purposes, a significance level of 0.05 may apply. For routine business decisions, a significance level of 0.10 could be used.

Evaluating the Results of ANOVA

Now that we understand the basic principles of ANOVA, we can apply them to the evaluation of a Multivariant Analysis of Variance (MANOVA). This type of ANOVA enables the manager, engineer,

SOURCE OF VARIATION		SUM OF SQUARES	DEGREES OF FREEDOM	MEAN SQUARES	F RATIO	F CRITICAL	ω^2
Main Effects	A	SSa=2.55	$dfa = 1$	MSa = 2.55	Fa=2.71	F'a=4.08	.01
	B	SSb= 30.08	$dfb = 1$	MSb = 30.08	Fb=32.00	F'b=4.08	.22
	C	SSc=18.75	$dfc = 1$	MSc=18.75	Fc=19.96	F'c=4.08	.14
INTERACTIONS	AB	SSab=1.78	$dfab = 1$	MSab = 1.78	Fab=1.89	F'ab=4.08	.005
	AC	SSac=8.78	$dfac = 1$	MSac = 8.78	Fac=9.34	F'ac=4.08	.06
	BC	SSbc=2.07	$dfbc = 1$	MSbc = 2.07	Fbc=2.20	F'bc=4.08	.007
	ABC	SSabc=24.20	$dfabc = 1$	MSabc = 24.20	Fabc=25.74	F'abc=4.08	.18
WITHIN		SSwithin = 37.71	$dfwithin = 40$	MSwithin= .94			
TOTAL		SStotal= 125.92	$dftotal = 47$				

TREATMENTS

FIGURE 9-7 Completed Analysis and Decision Table

and entrepreneur to evaluate multiple treatments of a product or process simultaneously. This capability is important to the ability to perform designed experiments with optimum effectiveness and efficiency. Multivariant ANOVA is a potent decision making tool for improvement of existing processes, as well as for the analysis of experiments for new and developing programs. We can now apply this last element to the example of a completed MANOVA Computation and Decision Table, as demonstrated in Figure 9-7.

We can now use the completed table as a fact-based decision making tool. A few of the important facts that we can extract from the table are listed below. These facts form the basis for business decisions concerning such things as material procurement, training, variability reduction programs, and management of further designed experiments.

- ► The variability of the process is significant for treatments B and C and for the interaction of treatments AC.
- ► The Main Effect of Treatment B is contributing 22% to the total process variability.
- ► The Main Effect of Treatment C is contributing 14% to the total process variability.
- ► The Interaction of Treatments AC is contributing 6% to the total process variability.

CLASSICAL METHODS OF DOE

Basic Concepts of DOE

Design of Experiments (DOE) is one of the most powerful tools for the design, characterization, and improvement of products and services. DOE is a group of techniques used to organize and evaluate experimentation to obtain the maximum data using the minimum assets. The language of DOE is colored by its genesis in the scientific, statistical, and engineering communities. Do not be intimidated by the verbiage; DOE is directly applicable to many types of businesses and can be effectively applied by the average business person with a little training. A "designed experiment" is no more than a test or trial program that has been well structured to measure the results (response variable) accurately in comparison to the inputs (treatments or input variables). Let's start with a brief survey of the basic concepts of DOE.

Experimental Matrix

Figure 9-8 displays a typical DOE experimental matrix or test matrix. The matrix indicates the number of treatments, levels of the treatments, and the treatment combinations for each experimental run (trial or test).

Orthogonal Array

The DOE experimental matrix translates directly to an orthogonal array. This matrix lays out the DOE in runs, indicating the levels for each run applied to the main effects and interactions of the treatments. In Figure 9-9, the treatment combination A2B2C2 is represented as experimental run 1, with main effects for A set as low (−),

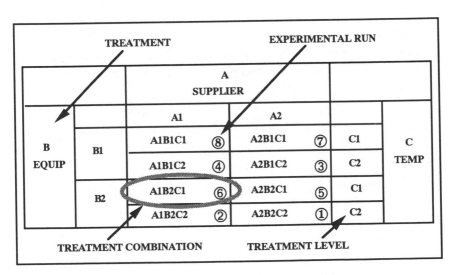

FIGURE 9-8   DOE Experimental Matrix

		A				
		A1	A2			
B	B1	A1B1C1	A2B1C1	C1		
		A1B1C2	A2B1C2	C2	C	
	B2	A1B2C1	A2B2C1	C1		
		A1B2C2	A2B2C2	C2		

	Main Effects			Interactions				Sample	
RUN	A	B	C	AB	AC	BC	ABC	Y_1	Y_2
1	-	-	-	+	+	+	-		
2	+	-	-	-	-	+	+		
3	-	+	-	-	+	-	+		
4	+	+	-	+	-	-	-		
5	-	-	+	+	-	-	+		
6	+	-	+	-	+	-	-		
7	-	+	+	-	-	+	-		
8	+	+	+	+	+	+	+		

FIGURE 9-9   DOE Analytical Matrix

B set as low ($-$), and C set as low ($-$). The interactions for this experimental run are AB set as high ($+$), AC set as high ($+$), BC set as high ($+$), and the three-way interaction ABC set as Low ($-$).

Analyzing the results of a designed experiment includes calculating the mean effect of the levels of each treatment. To accomplish this result, it is necessary for the experiment to be balanced. A balanced set of experiments contains an equal number of experiments for each level of each treatment. The example in Figure 9-10 demonstrates this principle of a balanced experiment.

There are three criteria that can be applied to determine if a test array is orthogonal:

► **First:** Sum all the levels in each column. If there is an equal number of levels in each column, then we have passed the first test for an orthogonal array. In each column of Figure 9-10, the

RUN	A	B	C	AB	AC	BC	ABC
1	-	-	-	+	+	+	-
2	+	-	-	-	-	+	+
3	-	+	-	-	+	-	+
4	+	+	-	+	-	-	-
5	-	-	+	+	-	-	+
6	+	-	+	-	+	-	-
7	-	+	+	-	-	+	-
8	+	+	+	+	+	+	+
+ -	4 4	4 4	4 4	4 4	4 4	4 4	4 4

FIGURE 9-10 Orthogonal Array

treatment has 4 plus level (+) and 4 minus level (−) values. The orthogonal array forms the basis for many designed experiments, so it is important to recognize when a proposed test array is or is not orthogonal.

► **Second:** All rows having identical patterns in a given column must have an equal number of occurrences of settings in the other columns.

► **Third:** The selected matrix must have the least number of rows that satisfy the first two criteria for the selected number of treatments.

Main Effect

The main effect of a treatment is the measured change in the response as a result of changing that specific treatment. In Figures 9-10 and 9-11, the main effects are for treatments A, B, and C.

Interaction

Interaction is the measured change in the response as a result of the combined effect of two or more treatments. In Figures 9-10 and 9-11, the interactions are for treatment combinations AB, AC, BC, and ABC.

RUN	RAND	A	B	C	AB	AC	BC	ABC
1	3	-	-	-	+	+	+	-
2	5	+	-	-	-	-	+	+
3	4	-	+	-	-	+	-	+
4	7	+	+	-	+	-	-	-
5	2	-	-	+	+	-	-	+
6	8	+	-	+	-	+	-	-
7	6	-	+	+	-	-	+	-
8	1	+	+	+	+	+	+	+

FIGURE 9-11   Randomized Experimental Runs

Treatment

Treatments are the controllable factors used as inputs to the products and processes under evaluation. These are the input variables (also called the independent variables) that can be varied to change the effect on the output, or dependent variable. In Figures 9-9 and 9-10 above, the treatments are: (A) the supplier, (B) the equipment used in the process, and (C) the temperature.

Level

Levels are the value of the treatments being studied. In most instances of designed experiments, we can use two levels of the treatments: a high level, symbolized by a (+) sign or the number 1, and a low-level, symbolized by a (−) sign or the number 2. In the figure above, there are two levels for each treatment: Supplier A1 (+) and A2 (−), Equipment B1 (+) and B2 (−), and Temperature C1 (+) and C2 (−). There can be more levels than two; however, this makes the experiment progressively more complex and difficult to manage.

Treatment Combination

A treatment combination is the set of treatments and the associated levels used for an individual experimental run. In Figure 9-8, the treatment combinations are displayed for each experimental run. For instance, A1B2C1 indicates that experimental run will be accomplished using material from Treatment A (Supplier) at Level 1 ($+$), Treatment B (Equipment) at Level 2 ($-$), and Treatment C (Temperature) at Level 1 ($+$). These treatment combinations also describe the treatments and levels of an experiment and determine the number of experimental runs required.

Experimental Run

An experimental run is the accomplishment of a single trial (test or experiment) at a specific treatment combination. In the above example, there are three treatments at two levels (2^3) or eight experimental runs in this designed experiment. The number of experimental runs needed in a designed experiment can be determined by the number of treatments and the levels of each treatment. These are stated as an exponential expression (2^t), with the levels being the base number and the treatments being the exponent. We therefore can calculate the number of experimental runs required for any combination of treatments and levels as indicated below:

$$2^2 = 4 \qquad 3^2 = 9$$
$$2^3 = 8 \qquad 3^3 = 27$$
$$2^4 = 16 \qquad 3^4 = 81$$
$$2^5 = 32 \qquad 3^5 = 243$$
$$2^6 = 64 \qquad 3^6 = 729$$
$$2^7 = 128 \qquad 3^7 = 2187$$

These factorial combinations can have as few as four experimental runs (2^2) or as many as 2187 (three levels with seven treatments 3^7). This clearly demonstrates that DOE can cover a wide range of experimental combinations and levels of data. As we progress through this chapter, we will describe DOE methods for dealing with large experiments.

Sample

The sample size is the number of times each experimental run is accomplished as a repeat or replicate. A repeat sample is used when the experiment is simply duplicated for each experimental run.

A replicate sample is used when the experimental run is a measure-ment that is sensitive to set-up, environment, or some other factor outside the sample treatments. The minimum sample size for a de-signed experiment is two. This minimum is required to establish a variance about the mean of the response variable. The sample size then becomes dependent upon the levels of confidence needed in the experiment, as indicated during our discussion on ANOVA. The sample size for each experimental run is indicated by a lower case n, and the total sample size for the complete experiment is indicated by an upper case N. The samples for a designed experiment then can be described by $N = nL^t$.

It is apparent that we can use the sample size and number of experimental runs to plan our data management needs. If we run the simplest experiment, with the minimum number of samples, there will be only eight resulting data points. In a (3^7) full-factorial experi-ment with the minimum number of samples, there would be 4,374 data points.

$$(2)(2^2) = 8 \qquad (2)(3^2) = 18$$
$$(2)(2^3) = 16 \qquad (2)(3^3) = 54$$
$$(2)(2^4) = 32 \qquad (2)(3^4) = 162$$
$$(2)(2^5) = 64 \qquad (2)(3^5) = 486$$
$$(2)(2^6) = 128 \qquad (2)(3^6) = 1,458$$
$$(2)(2^7) = 256 \qquad (2)(3^7) = 4,374$$

Response

A response is a result of an experimental run. It is the dependent variable (also called the response variable). It is the measured effect, on the product or process, of using the specific combination of treatments and levels. In a 2^7 full-factorial experiment with 2 repeti-tions, there are 256 responses.

Randomization

We assign a treatment combination to an experimental run by ran-dom chance, using a randomization program or randomization table.

Randomization prevents the influence of data due to any uncontrolled environmental variables in any test run. Randomization must always be used when the experimenter does not have total control over the environment or when there are input variables outside the experiment that may affect the process. Figure 9-11 has randomized the experimental runs first demonstrated in Figure 9-10. The random order of the experimental runs is presented in the second column of the figure.

DOE Process

The DOE process in Figure 9-12 applies to designed experiments for new product and process development as well as for existing processes. This process integrates many of the tools we have reviewed in previous chapters and introduces the use of ANOVA and the design of experiments. As with all of our technical tools, we first need to define the process to gain a clear understanding of what we desire to improve. The process and product must be understood at a detailed level to determine all the treatments (input variables) that affect the product's quality characteristics (output variables). We need to know what these parameters are, how they were set, what relevance they have to the customer needs, and how we can affect the end product. This understanding of the process provides us with the information to identify improvement opportunities.

If this improvement opportunity relates to existing process, we can use available data. This data must be of sufficient quality and quantity to evaluate and determine which response variables and treatments can be subjected to ANOVA evaluation to further our improvement process. The availability of this data can significantly reduce the number of experimental runs that will be required by providing a priori information to reduce the number of screening runs required.

If no data is available concerning the process or product, we must use: the 7-M tools and 7-QC tools to develop the required information. This data is subjected to a brainstorming session by an integrated team of subject matter experts (SMEs), to select treatments, levels,

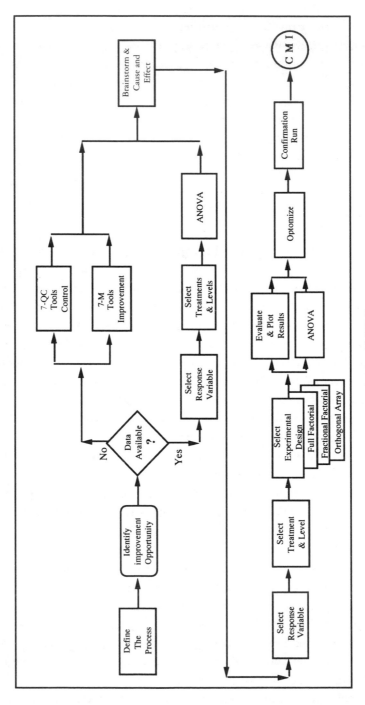

FIGURE 9-12   DOE Process

and response variables. The next step in the DOE process is to select the appropriate experimental design.

The selection of an experimental design is dependent upon the number of treatments that are to be evaluated, the level of data that is required, and the cost associated with accomplishing the experimental runs. Since full-factorial experiments are the most comprehensive, they are also the most costly and time consuming to run. Fractional factorials provide information only on a limited scope of data and are less costly. Orthogonal arrays (including Taguchi Designs) also provide a limited scope of data, but can provide some information concerning interactions. When many treatments are under consideration, we recommend that you first perform screening experiments using orthogonal arrays to identify the significant contributors to variance, and then use fractional factorials or full-factorials as refining experiments.

We evaluate the results of these experiments using two distinct methods. First, the data are evaluated for level effects and graphed for visual analysis. Second, we subject the data to ANOVA to determine if the effects are significant, which treatments are the most significant, and (using ω^2) the percent contribution to overall variance from the treatments and their levels. We will review these methods as we develop full-factorial designed experiments. A complete discussion and step-by-step procedure for accomplishing these analyses are contained in the workbook associated with the text.

Several DOE methods have been developed by some statisticians and engineers, each proposing his particular model as the best or only solution. It is not our purpose to support or detract from the any of these approaches. That conflict is academic; we will focus upon applications. The following approaches to design of experiments apply most directly to management, industrial, and administrative processes of concern to business.

- ► Full-Factorial Designs
- ► Fractional Factorial Designs
- ► Taguchi Quality Engineering
- ► Shainin Statistical Engineering

We will discuss each one of these approaches to designed experiments in capsule form.

Full-Factorial DOE

Full-factorial experimental designs provide a comprehensive analysis of all treatments, levels, and interactions related to a selected quality characteristic. The full-factorial designs we will discuss are commonly called the 2^t designs, where 2 is the number of levels and t represents the number of treatments. The orthogonal arrays for other designs such as 3^t are provided in Appendix B. These designs will be discussed only briefly due to their complexity. The analytical principles for all orthogonal arrays are essentially the same and can be applied to all factorial experiments.

Selecting a Full-Factorial Design

To select the appropriate full-factorial design for your experiment, use the table of 2^t factorial designs demonstrated in Figure 9-13 below. The complete table is provided in Appendix A. The selected design is based upon the number of treatments and levels selected for the experiment. The figure demonstrates the full-factorial designs for two-treatment (2^2), three-treatment (2^3), and four-treatment (2^4) experimental designs at two levels. If we were to select a design for three treatments (ABC) at two levels from this table, the resulting designed-experiment orthogonal array would take the form of Figure 9-14, a full-factorial for three treatments at two levels (2^3).

Evaluation of Full-Factorial Experimental Designs

Evaluating full-factorial experiments includes: (1) the analysis of the effects of the treatments and treatment levels, (2) graphing these effects, (3) performing an ANOVA to determine the significance of

Treatment Combinations

Run	Design	A	B	AB	C	AC	BC	ABC	D	AD	BD	ABD	CD	ACD	BCD	ABCD
1	2^t	−	−	+	−	+	+	−	−	+	+	−	+	−	−	+
2	2^2	+	−	−	−	−	+	+	−	−	+	+	+	+	−	−
3		−	+	−	−	+	−	+	−	+	−	+	+	−	+	−
4		+	+	+	−	−	−	−	−	−	−	−	+	+	+	+
5	2^3	−	−	+	+	−	−	+	−	+	+	−	−	+	+	−
6		+	−	−	+	+	−	−	−	−	+	+	−	−	+	+
7		−	+	−	+	−	+	−	−	+	−	+	−	+	−	+
8		+	+	+	+	+	+	+	−	−	−	−	−	−	−	−
9	2^4	−	−	+	−	+	+	−	+	−	−	+	−	+	+	−
10		+	−	−	−	−	+	+	+	+	−	−	−	−	+	+
11		−	+	−	−	+	−	+	+	−	+	−	−	+	−	+
12		+	+	+	−	−	−	−	+	+	+	+	−	−	−	−
13		−	−	+	+	−	−	+	+	−	−	+	+	−	−	+
14		+	−	−	+	+	−	−	+	+	−	−	+	+	−	−
15		−	+	−	+	−	+	−	+	−	+	−	+	−	+	−
16		+	+	+	+	+	+	+	+	+	+	+	+	+	+	+

FIGURE 9-13 2^t Factorial Designs

RUN	RAND	A	B	AB	C	AC	BC	ABC
1	3	-	-	+	-	+	+	-
2	5	+	-	-	-	-	+	+
3	4	-	+	-	-	+	-	+
4	7	+	+	+	-	-	-	-
5	2	-	-	+	+	-	-	+
6	8	+	-	-	+	+	-	-
7	6	-	+	-	+	-	+	-
8	1	+	+	+	+	+	+	+

FIGURE 9-14 2^3 Orthogonal Array

the treatment and treatment levels, and (4) determining the percentage to contribution of the variance at each level. To better visualize exactly how the effects are calculated and how they relate to the test matrix and orthogonal array, we will apply the data directly to the orthogonal array as indicated in Figure 9-15.

		TREATMENT A			
		A1	A2		
TREATMENT B	B1	74, 77, 78	75, 76, 77	C1	TREATMENT C
		75, 71, 75	76, 71, 74	C2	
	B2	76, 71, 74	79, 80, 76	C1	
		78, 72, 76	81, 79, 74	C2	

Run	Rand	A	B	AB	C	AC	BC	ABC	y_1	y_2	y_3	$\bar{y}$	Range
1	3	-	-	+	-	+	+	-	81	79	74	78.00	7
2	5	+	-	-	-	-	+	+	78	72	76	75.33	6
3	4	-	+	-	-	+	-	+	76	71	74	73.67	5
4	7	+	+	+	-	-	-	-	75	71	75	73.67	4
5	2	-	-	+	+	-	-	+	79	80	76	78.33	4
6	8	+	-	-	+	+	-	-	76	71	74	73.67	5
7	6	-	+	-	+	-	+	-	75	76	77	76.00	2
8	1	+	+	+	+	+	+	+	74	77	78	76.33	4

FIGURE 9-15   Orthogonal Array With Data Applied

Effects

To calculate the effects of the treatment and treatment levels on our quality characteristic, we must determine the difference that each of these is making. We previously applied the data to the orthogonal array in the above figure. Now we will apply the first calculation for effects to the same matrix. First, we summarize the experimental data for each treatment and its associated level (Σ_k+, Σ_k-) at the bottom of the matrix, as indicated in Figure 9-16. The data summarized in the previous figure can now be applied directly to the equation to evaluate effects. The equation is:

$$\text{Effect}_K = \Sigma \frac{k+}{(+)} - \Sigma \frac{k-}{(-)}$$

Applying the data from Figure 9-16, we can calculate the effects for each main effect and interaction.

$$\text{Effect}_A = \Sigma \frac{A+}{+} - \Sigma \frac{A-}{-} = \frac{299}{4} - \frac{306}{4} = -1.75$$

$$\text{Effect}_B = \frac{300}{4} - \frac{305}{4} = -1.25$$

$$\text{Effect}_C = \frac{304}{4} - \frac{301}{4} = 0.75$$

$$\text{Effect}_{AB} = \frac{306}{4} - \frac{299}{4} = 1.75$$

$$\text{Effect}_{AC} = \frac{302}{4} - \frac{303}{4} = -0.25$$

$$\text{Effect}_{BC} = \frac{306}{4} - \frac{299}{4} = 1.75$$

$$\text{Effect}_{ABC} = \frac{304}{4} - \frac{301}{4} = 0.75$$

Run	Rand	A	B	AB	C	AC	BC	ABC	y_1	y_2	y_3	$\bar{y}$	Range
1	3	-	-	+	-	+	+	-	81	79	74	78.00	7
2	5	+	-	-	-	-	+	+	78	72	76	75.33	6
3	4	-	+	-	-	+	-	+	76	71	74	73.67	5
4	7	+	+	+	-	+	-	-	75	71	75	73.67	4
5	2	-	-	+	+	-	-	-	79	80	76	78.33	4
6	8	+	-	-	+	+	-	+	76	71	74	73.67	5
7	6	-	+	-	+	-	+	-	75	76	77	76.00	2
8	1	+	+	+	+	+	+	+	74	77	78	76.33	4
	Σ+	299.00	299.67	306.33	304.33	301.67	305.67	303.67					
	Σ-	306.00	305.33	298.67	300.67	303.33	299.33	301.33					

FIGURE 9-16   Summary of Experimental Data

We can now graph the main effects and interactions to evaluate what effect the treatments and treatment levels are having on the quality characteristic. Figure 9-17 displays the graphs associated with the above effects.

Optimizing the quality characteristic depends upon the metric selected and the nature of the process. If we are measuring a process yield, maximum is best; for failure rates, minimum is best; for the deviation from a variable standard, nominal is best. The slope of the line for main effects indicates the significance of the effect. The steeper the slope, the more significant the effect is. The graph also indicates which treatment level is producing the desired effect of optimizing the process. If the lines of the graph are intersecting or converging, there is an interaction. If the lines run parallel, there is no interaction.

This graph of the main effects and interactions indicates that the yield for this process can be maximized by selecting Treatment A at the low setting, treatment B at the low setting, and treatment C at the high setting. There are apparent interactions between AB and BC but no interaction between AC.

Analysis of Variance

Analysis of Variance, applied as part of a designed experiment, is used to measure the significance of the main effects and interactions, and level of contribution as measured by ω^2, that we previously discussed in the Analysis of Variance section of this chapter. Figure 9-18 is an example of an ANOVA table used for that purpose.

This ANOVA Decision Table indicated that Treatment B is significant and contributed 22% to the overall process variation. This clearly indicates to us which treatment is to be the target of improvement processes such as CMI and Variability Reduction Programs. It also indicates which of the treatments in our experimental design has the most effect on our outcome.

Fractional Factorial DOE

Factorial designs are the best designed experiments to use when evaluating all main effects and interactions. However, there may be

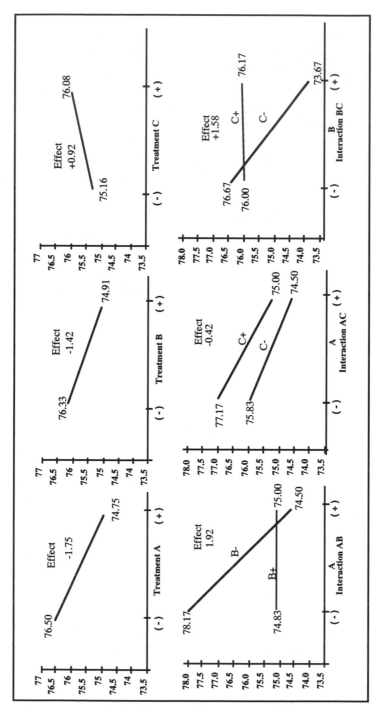

FIGURE 9-17   Effects Graphs

Source of Variation	Sum of the Squares	Degrees of Freedom	Mean Squares MS	F Ratio	F' Critical	ω^2
A	18.375	1	18.375	11.163	3.050	7%
B	12.042	1	12.042	7.316	3.050	3%
C	5.042	1	5.042	3.063	3.050	0%
AB	22.042	1	22.042	13.391	3.050	9%
AC	1.042	1	1.042	0.633	3.050	0%
BC	15.042	1	15.042	9.138	3.050	5%
ABC	2.042	1	2.042	1.240	3.050	0%
Within	100.000	16	6.250			
Total	175.625	23				

FIGURE 9-18   ANOVA Analysis and Decision Table

too many factors for this type of experiment to be practicable. Conducting the full-factorial experiments might be too costly, or take too long, or the facilities and personnel might not be available.

In such cases (which constitute the majority), fractional factorial designed experiments provide a reasonable alternative that still allows for the evaluation of main effects and key interactions, but requires fewer trial runs. To achieve this result, we confound the higher-order interactions (three or greater) with the main effect and two-way interactions. Three-way interactions often are insignificant, and to affect three-way interactions, we would alter the treatment main effects, in any case. The fractional-factorial technique enables the experimenter to reduce the number of runs needed by confounding these interactions with other design runs.

This method is easier to visualize if we use the already familiar 2^3 factorial. The treatment combinations (main effects and interactions) for this orthogonal array are given in Figure 9-19. The higher-order interaction (ABC) here is the defining factor for confounding. The eight-run experiment can be separated into two four-run designs that separate the treatment combinations according to the sign ($+$ or $-$) conversion of interaction ABC.

We will separate the full-factorial into two fractional factorials, each with four runs. Four runs designated by ABC are equal to

RUN	A	B	AB	C	AC	BC	ABC
1	-	-	+	-	+	+	-
2	+	-	-	-	-	+	+
3	-	+	-	-	+	-	+
4	+	+	+	-	-	-	-
5	-	-	+	+	-	-	+
6	+	-	-	+	+	-	-
7	-	+	-	+	-	+	-
8	+	+	+	+	+	+	+

FIGURE 9-19   Fractional-Factorial Design

Full Factorial							
RUN	A	B	AB	C	AC	BC	ABC
1	-	-	+	-	+	+	-
2	+	-	-	-	-	+	+
3	-	+	-	-	+	-	+
4	+	+	+	-	-	-	-
5	-	-	+	+	-	-	+
6	+	-	-	+	+	-	-
7	-	+	-	+	-	+	-
8	+	+	+	+	+	+	+

1/2 Fractional Factorial							
RUN	A	B	AB	C	AC	BC	ABC
2	+	-	-	-	-	+	+
3	-	+	-	-	+	-	+
5	-	-	+	+	-	-	+
8	+	+	+	+	+	+	+

1/2 Fractional Factorial			
RUN	A	B	C
1	+	-	-
2	-	+	-
3	-	-	+
4	+	+	+

FIGURE 9-20   Fractional Factorial for 2^3

minus, and four runs designated by ABC are equal to plus. The resulting two fractional factorial arrays are demonstrated in Figure 9-20. This method creates aliases; that is, more than one factor with the same treatment combination. The aliases result when more than one factor has the same treatment levels in the same run. In the upper portion of Figure 9-20 the aliases are:

$$B = AC$$

$$A = BC$$

$$C = AB$$

By using the orthogonal array defined in the lower portion of Figure 9-20, we can accomplish the experiment in four runs instead of eight. The main effects are confounded with the interactions. This can be accomplished due to the assumption that interactions are unimportant. The main effects can still be estimated. This reduces the experimental burden (time, cost, facilities) by half. The effect of this becomes obvious when considering the following:

Full Factorial Runs	1/2 Factorial Runs	1/4 Factorial Runs
$2^3 = 8$	4	
$2^4 = 16$	8	4
$2^5 = 32$	16	8
$2^6 = 64$	32	16

We evaluate fractional-factorial designs in the same way as full-factorials, using ANOVA and effects.

TAGUCHI QUALITY ENGINEERING

Quality Engineering is a design, development, and improvement strategy to optimize the design of a product, service, or process. Basically, it deals with activities that reduce the variability of products and processes through a series of optimization analyses, using design of experiments as a basic tool. There are two phases of Quality Engineering: On-Line and Off-Line Quality Engineering.

Noise and Robustness

Variability in products and processes is the enemy of quality and the cause of unnecessary cost and scheduling problems. The primary cause of variability is the uncontrolled or uncontrollable environment that a system is subjected to in production and use. Dr. Taguchi calls variation coming from these sources "noise." Just as the factors that the design team uses to optimize a system are called control factors, these uncontrolled factors are called noise factors.

Noise and factors can be classified by their source. Outer noises are factors that affect product and process performance from an external source. Outer noise factors are such things as ambient temperature, training, operating conditions, or anything that affects the system that is external to the product or process. Inner noises are the system conditions that cause variation from within the product or process. Inner noise factors are such things as tool wear, process procedures, component capability, different materials, and any other factor that is part of the system, product, or process that causes variability. Between-Product Noises are the factors that cause variability between products when produced by exactly the same process. This variability is related very closely to the common-cause variation of process control. It is caused by such factors as machine capability, process capability, operator competency, and others. The effect of these noise factors is demonstrated in Figure 9-21.

It is not critical to identify and categorize each source of noise. It is imperative, however, that the design team designs products and processes to be insensitive to all types of noise. A system that is designed

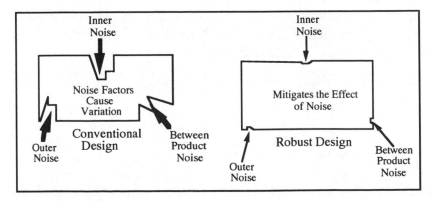

FIGURE 9-21   Noise Effects Upon Products and Processes

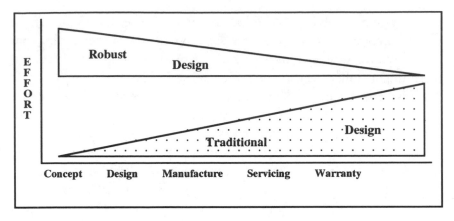

FIGURE 9-22   Comparative Effort (Cost and Time)

to perform at a high level of quality, despite being subjected to uncontrollable environmental conditions in manufacture and use, is said to be robust.

Robustness is synonymous with high-quality, low-cost, and on schedule processes. High-quality, low-cost, and on schedule is the optimum state for any system. Therefore, it is the goal of the design team to search for and find robust designs for products and processes. The best method for achieving this goal is through Taguchi Off-Line Quality Engineering during the design and development process. If robustness is achieved for systems, products, and processes early in the life cycle of the product, fewer problems will occur during the manufacturing process and when the product is in the hands of the customer for use. The relationship of these efforts is demonstrated in Figure 9-22.

Quality Characteristics

One of the first steps in performing quality engineering is to identify the Quality Characteristics that we are going to measure. These are the output or dependent variables of our designed experiment. The basic types of Quality Characteristics are listed below.

A Nominal-is-Best characteristic is one that has a specific target value with a tolerance limit around the nominal value. A Smaller-is-Better characteristic always has an ideal value of zero. A Larger-is-Better characteristic has infinity as its ideal value. Classified attributes are characteristics that are not amenable to measurement on a continuous scale. These characteristics are graded on a qualitative scale. The dynamic characteristic measures the direct relationship between a systems' input and output: more fuel equals more speed.

- Nominal-is-Best (NIB)
  - Dimensions
  - Clearances
  - RPM

- Smaller-is-Better (SIB)
  - Scrap
  - Warranty Returns
  - MTBF

- Larger-is-Better (LIB)
  - Expected Life
  - Process Yield
  - Miles Per Gallon

- Classified Attribute
  - On/Off
  - Grade I/II/III
  - Pass/Fail

Understanding what type of characteristic to measure is an important first step in measuring your response variable. The characteristic you select must be relevant to the product or process you are measuring. There must be a functional link between your selected characteristic and the Quality, Cost, or Schedule of the product or process under analysis. Do not select a measure simply because it is available and easy to obtain and understand. Selecting the proper quality characteristic to measure is not always an easy task. The characteristic you select should relate the functional inputs directly to the output. Remember what your goal is and that you are designing and developing a robust system. Some measures of yield, for instance, do not relate directly to customer satisfaction; therefore, they are poor measures. To quote Dr. Taguchi from the 1990 Taguchi Symposium, "To get quality, don't measure quality." This means that to optimize the goal, do not measure the goal itself; measure the characteristics that make up the goal.

On-Line Quality Engineering

On-Line Quality Engineering activities are utilized as process and product improvement strategies. The purpose of On-Line Quality Engineering is to control the process and products to ensure that they meet the robust design standards established during the design and development process and to improve those products and processes. Figure 9-1 demonstrated the elements of this process. It is the aim of this process to balance design, control, and improvement with Quality, Cost, and Schedule. As described in Chapters 7 and 8, many of the 7-QC tools are used in this effort, as well as the tools of DOE and QFD. Further information can be obtained concerning the improvement process from *Management 2000, A Practical Guide to World Class Competition*. The focus of this text is the design and development cycle; therefore, we will concentrate upon Off-Line Quality Engineering.

Off-Line Quality Engineering

Off-line Quality Engineering is performed early in the design and development process of a product. The intent of Off-Line Quality Engineering is to optimize the functionality of a system through a design strategy that will render a robust system. The product, or process, is designed to be robust against the environments of use, production, materials, and other pertinent factors selected by the design team.

This method of design focuses on how to design a product that can withstand the environment rather than one that is designed to meet every specific related problem. This guides the engineer in developing efficient processes and effective products that enhance capabili-

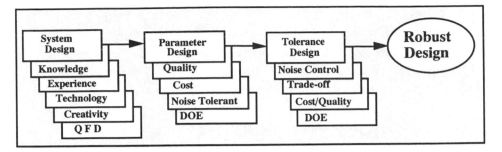

FIGURE 9-23   Off-Line Quality Engineering

ties, rather than just meet needs. The process is efficient because the materials, methods. and processes are optimized to enhance the controllable factors of Quality, Cost, and Schedule during the design and production process. The product is effective because the design engineer has made the design to be robust to operate in the user's environment. As we first indicated in Figure 9-1, these activities take place during the design-and-development phase of a product life cycle. Off-Line Quality Engineering is performed using the three phases demonstrated in Figure 9-23.

Dr. Taguchi describes the engineering design and improvement cycle in three phases: System Design, Parameter Design, and Tolerance Design. The system design phase occurs when the fundamental design and concept for a product or service are established. This phase is centric to the engineering and subject expert technologies.

System Design

The system design phase requires the design engineer and the design team to use their knowledge and experience to build a system that is technically able to meet the customers needs, requirements, and wants. The best tool to use in establishing this system, its requirements, and the associated assemblies is the QFD process used to build the House of Quality described in Chapter 5, "Answering the Voice of the Customer."

In this phase, the basic concept of the system is formed and the system technologies are selected. Based upon the VOC, the desired output parameters of the system are defined and the assemblies, components, and parts are selected that will meet these requirements. The intent of this effort is to develop the best technical approach to producing the desired function. The What/How method of QFD is the best approach to structuring this effort successfully.

Parameter Design

In the parameter design phase, we design the specifications of the system. That is, we improve quality without controlling or eliminating the sources of variance that occur in the customer or production environment. These sources influence target dimensions, material properties, voltages, and other parameters. We set these parameters to make the product less sensitive to the causes of variation. Parameter design makes the product more robust to the causes of variation.

Parameter design is the most important step in Off-Line Quality Engineering. In this phase, the system's capability to best perform its function is developed and the system is made to be robust against the production and user's environments. This phase is where the design team will select the specific levels for the system factors that will lead to a high-quality, low-cost, robust product that satisfies the voice of the customer. The goal of parameter design is to combine levels for the product or process parameters that achieve robustness at the least cost. Taguchi Design of Experiments is the best tool for performing parameter design and selecting the optimized system.

Parameter-design studies typically involve two basic types of factors: *control factors* and *noise factors*. Control factors are the treatments that can be controlled by the engineer and are typically referred to as treatments. These can be set, specified, and maintained during the test runs and throughout the life cycle of the system, production, and use. Noise factors are the factors that cannot be controlled from a technical, practical, or economical standpoint; these are the factors that appear as the error factors in ANOVA. As you can see from the ANOVA tables previously used in this chapter, noise (error) can constitute a significant proportion of the variability of a system. Parameter design allows you to design your factors/treatments so that they can overcome the effects of the environment.

Control and noise factors must be included in any DOE for parameter design. The inclusion of these two types of factors is required to assess their relationship. This relationship between the levels of the control factors and the associated Signal-to-Noise (S/N) ratio is the primary selection factor for designing robust systems. We will utilize a parameter design to demonstrate the Taguchi method of performing a design of experiments later in this section.

Tolerance Design

Tolerance design is used when a further optimization of a system is required. If you have accomplished all you can by performing parameter design, and the system still does not meet the requirements of the customer, you must now attempt to control the noise (environment). This phase focuses on the tradeoff between the cost of controlling the environment and the quality obtained. This is measured using the loss function we previously introduced. Tolerance design is the judicious manipulation of the levels of tolerances, materials, and components. The design team judiciously considers upgrading materials and components, using higher grade processes, and tightening tolerances only for those factors having a significant effect on quality. The strategy for tolerance design is to reduce noise by increasing cost. Tolerance design should be considered only after a complete parameter design has been completed. The Taguchi method for performing Design of Experiments is the best method for performing tolerance design.

Taguchi Design of Experiments

The Taguchi method of Design of Experiments uses orthogonal arrays that are balanced forms of the fractional factorial arrays previously presented in this chapter. Dr. Taguchi indicates that there are no order interactions (three interactions or more) that are critical. Key two-way interactions can be considered, based upon engineering and technical assessment, but they are assumed to be less significant than main effects. The focus of the Taguchi DOE methods is clearly main effects, with interactions as a secondary consideration for the experimenter. We will review the Taguchi methods of Design of Experiments that are the most widely applicable: the design and development of new products and services. We will use a parameter design DOE to demonstrate the Taguchi Method of DOE. Parameter values for each product or process element of the system should be designed to provide consistent performance with little or no variability due to process or use noise. We will develop the Taguchi method of DOE in eight steps:

1. Identify an element of the system design for analysis.
2. Perform a cause-and-effect analysis.
3. Select treatments, levels, and values.
4. Determine how experimental results will be expressed.
5. Select a designed experiment.
6. Conduct the experiment.
7. Perform data analysis.
8. Graph the results.

Step 1. *Identify an Element of the System Design for Analysis*

The first step in parameter design is to identify the process or product element of the system design that we need to evaluate. The most effective way to accomplish this is the use of the Process Analysis, 7 M&P Tools, and the 7-QC Tools. These opportunities can be derived from many sources in existing and new processes, products, and services. Examples include:

► Opportunities for variability reduction to improve the efficiency and effectiveness of existing processes
► Opportunities to improve products and services based upon customer requirements

► Opportunities to reduce reject and scrap rates
► Opportunities to improve the development of new products and services

Step 2. Perform a Cause-and-Effect Analysis

Figure 9-24 below is an example of a fishbone diagram for cause-and-effect analysis. This is an example based upon the production of a composite material to be used in signs. We will follow this example through our development of parameter design. To identify the opportunities for improvement, four subject experts spent approximately one hour of their time to brainstorm the problem and create the cause-and-effect analysis.

Step 3. Select Treatments, Levels, and Values

Based upon the cause-and-effect analysis, the team selected which factors will be tested and determined the levels of the factors and assigned a test value for each level. From our previous example, the factors and levels are indicated in Figure 9-25.

The team determined that the composite must be designed to be robust against three noise factors. Those factors and their levels are indicated in Figure 9-26.

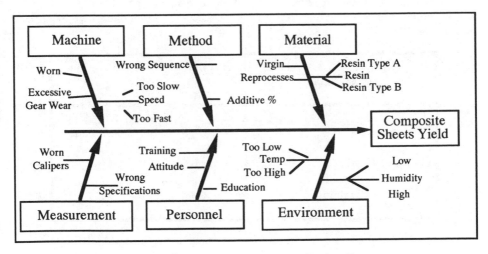

FIGURE 9-24   Potential Parameter Design Factors

Control Factors	Levels	
	1	2
A. Plastic Material	Virgin	Reprocessed
B. Fiberglass Additive	40%	20%
C. Binder Resin	A	B

FIGURE 9-25   Selected Parameter Design Factors, Levels, and Values

Step 4. Determine How Experimental Results
Will Be Expressed

Determine how the experimental results will be expressed. What quality characteristic will we try to measure? This is the output variable for the designed experiment. From the cause-and-effect analysis, we have completed the quality characteristic which will be quantified as follows:

Yield as Acceptable   4 × 8 Sheets Per Hour

Noise Factors	Levels	
	1	2
D. Humidity	High Amb.	Low Amb.
E. Temperature	High	Low
F. Operator Training	Company	OJT

FIGURE 9-26   Selected Noise Factors, Levels, and Values

Step 5. Select a Designed Experiment

Based upon the number of factors and factor levels required to evaluate the output variable, select the appropriate Taguchi designed experiment from the statistical appendix. Remember the basic rules for selecting an experimental design: the design must be orthogonal and must contain the minimum number of runs to satisfy the requirements.

In our continuing example, we have three factors at two levels each, 2^3. In the list of Taguchi orthogonal arrays in the appendix, our experiment, with three levels and two factors, is most closely represented by the L_4 orthogonal array. The array is presented in Figure 9-27. The L_4 orthogonal array indicates that we will require four test runs to evaluate the three factors at two levels. The letters across the top of the table represent column headings and corresponds to the factors we selected in Figure 9-25. This array is called the inner array because it represents the control factors of our designed experiment.

We must now select an array for the evaluation of the noise factors (outer array). The same rules apply to the selection of an orthogonal array to evaluate noise factors. Therefore, a Taguchi L_4 array will be selected to evaluate the effects of noise on the process of producing composite sheets. The L_4 orthogonal array in Figure 9-28 represents the noise factors from Figure 9-26.

	INNER ARRAY		
	CONTROL FACTORS		
RUN	A	B	C
1	1	1	1
2	1	2	2
3	2	1	2
4	2	2	1

FIGURE 9-27   Taguchi L_4 Orthogonal Array for Control Factors

OUTER ARRAY			
	NOISE FACTOR		
RUN	D	E	F
1	1	1	1
2	1	2	2
3	2	1	2
4	2	2	1

FIGURE 9-28   Taguchi L_4 Orthogonal
Array for Noise Factors

The inner and outer arrays must now be arranged to provide for the distribution of the noise factors over the range of response data from the control factors. This is accomplished by rearranging the standard L_4 array as indicated in Figure 9-29. Note that to accomplish this, it is necessary to test the number of replicates or repeats equal to the number of runs in the outer noise array. In this example,

					OUTER ARRAY			
				Noise	RUN			
				Factor	1	2	3	4
				D	1	1	2	2
INNER ARRAY				E	1	2	1	2
	Control Factor			F	1	2	2	1
RUN	A	B	C					
1	1	1	1		y_1	y_2	y_3	y_4
2	1	2	2		y_5	y_6	y_7	y_8
3	2	1	2		y_9	y_{10}	y_{11}	y_{12}
4	2	2	1		y_{13}	y_{14}	y_{15}	y_{16}

FIGURE 9-29   Test Layout for Taguchi L_4 Array with Noise Factors

it will be necessary to accomplish 16 test runs (y_1 through y_{16}) to satisfy all the test requirements of the control and noise factors.

In this example, the number of factors for control and noise were equal to the factors and levels for the L_4 array. It is not necessary to model your experiment to fit any specific Taguchi orthogonal arrays. The array can be customized to fit any experimental requirement. Due to limited space in this text, the methods for customizing orthogonal arrays will be fully explained in the accompanying workbook.

Step 6. Conduct the Experiment

Using the experimental design formulated in Step 5, conduct the required series of tests. Measure the quality characterisitic, using the measure determined in Step 4. Record the results on your work sheet, along with any notes on related circumstances that might provide information concerning the test results. The resulting data can be recorded as indicated in Figure 9-30 or on a separate spreadsheet if the experiment is large and there are many data points. In any case, use automated data acquisition whenever possible and always use software or a spreadsheet program to perform your analysis.

					OUTER ARRAY			
				Noise	RUN			
				Factor	1	2	3	4
				D	1	1	2	2
	INNER ARRAY			E	1	2	1	2
		Control Factor		F	1	2	2	1
RUN	A	B	C					
1	1	1	1		28	27	28	29
2	1	2	2		22	24	23	21
3	2	1	2		23	24	21	22
4	2	2	1		26	25	25	24

FIGURE 9-30   Record the Results of the Designed Experiment

Step 7. Perform Data Analysis

To perform data analysis of your designed experiment, it will be necessary to calculate several factors. Using the data from the experimental results, calculate the:

- ► S/N Ratio
- ► Level Averages
- ► Grand Average
- ► Level Effects

Using the experimental results, calculate the Signal-to-Noise Ratio (S/N). The Signal to Noise Ratio calculation is dependent upon the characteristic of the response (Smaller-is-Better—SIB, Nominal-is-Better—NIB, and Larger-is-Better—LIB) using the appropriate equations as indicated below:

$$\text{SIB: S/N ratio } \eta = -10 \log \frac{1}{n} (y_1^2 + y_2^2 + \cdots + y_n^2)$$

$$\text{NIB: S/N ratio } \eta = -10 \log \frac{1}{n} [(y_1 - y)^2 + (y_2 - y)^2$$
$$+ \cdots + (y_n - y)^2]$$

$$\text{LIB: S/N ratio } \eta = -10 \log \frac{1}{n} \left(\frac{1}{y_1^2} + \frac{1}{y_2^2} + \cdots + \frac{1}{y_n^2} \right)$$

Since the quality characteristic we are measuring (yield) is a Larger-is-Better characteristic, the LIB equation is used to calculate the Signal-to-Noise Ratio for each of the four test runs in our example:

$$\text{Run 1: } \eta = -10 \log \frac{1}{4} \left(\frac{1}{28^2} + \frac{1}{27^2} + \frac{1}{28^2} + \frac{1}{29^2} \right)$$
$$= -10 \log \frac{1}{4} (.0013 + .0014 + .0013 + .0012)$$
$$= 28.93$$

Run 2: $\eta = 27.01$

Run 3: $\eta = 27.01$

Run 4: $\eta = 27.95$

This data can now be entered into the DOE data table and spreadsheet as indicated in Figure 9-31. All the other calculations required to complete the analysis of your designed experiment can be accomplished directly on the spreadsheet.

Level Average Obtain the level means by adding all the observations at that level for each main effect and interaction and dividing by the total number of observations for that level. In our example, the level averages are calculated as follows:

					OUTER ARRAY					
				Noise		RUN				
				Factor	1	2	3	4		
				D	1	1	2	2		
	INNER ARRAY			E	1	2	1	2		
	Control Factor			F	1	2	2	1		
RUN	A	B	C						$\bar{y}$	S/N
1	1	1	1		28	27	28	29	28.00	28.93
2	1	2	2		22	24	23	21	22.50	27.01
3	2	1	2		23	24	21	22	22.50	27.01
4	2	2	1		26	25	25	24	25.00	27.95
LA1	27.97	27.97	28.44	NOTES						
LA2	27.48	27.48	27.01		LA=Level Average					
GA	27.73	27.73	27.73		GA=Grand Average					
LE1	0.24	0.24	0.71		LE=Level Effects					
LE2	-0.24	-0.24	-0.71		TE=Total Effects					
TE	0.49	0.49	1.43							

FIGURE 9-31   Calculate and Record the Results of the Data Analysis

$$\text{Level Average} = \text{LA} = \frac{\text{Observations Level}_x}{n_x}$$

$$\text{LA}_{A1} = \frac{28.93 + 27.01}{2} = 27.97$$

$$\text{LA}_{A2} = \frac{27.01 + 27.95}{2} = 27.48$$

$$\text{LA}_{B1} = 27.97 \qquad \text{LA}_{C1} = 28.44$$

$$\text{LA}_{B2} = 27.48 \qquad \text{LA}_{C2} = 27.01$$

Grand Average   Obtain the grand average by adding the S/N from each control factor run and dividing by the total of control factor runs. In our example, the Grand Average is calculated as follows:

Grand Average =

$$\frac{\text{S/N Ratio Run} + \text{S/N Ratio Run 2} + \cdots + \text{S/N Ratio Run } i}{\text{Control Factor Runs}}$$

$$\text{Grand Average} = \frac{28.93 + 27.01 + 27.01 + 27.95}{4} = 27.73$$

Level Effects   The level effect is calculated by subtracting the grand average (27.73) from each level mean.

$$\text{Level Effects (LE)} = \text{Level Average} - \text{Grand Average}$$

$$\text{LE}_{A1} = 27.97 - 27.73 = 0.24$$

$$\text{LE}_{A2} = 27.48 - 27.73 \approx -0.24$$

$$\text{LE}_{B1} = 0.24 \qquad \text{LE}_{C1} = 0.71$$

$$\text{LE}_{B2} = -0.24 \qquad \text{LE}_{C2} = -0.71$$

Total Effect   The total effect is calculated by subtracting the least level effect from the greatest level effect (the range).

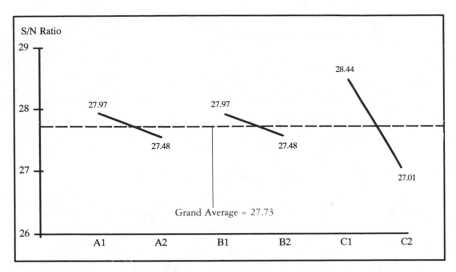

FIGURE 9-32   Graphing the Results

Total Effect (TE) = Greatest Level Effect − Least Level Effect

$$TE_A = 27.97 - 27.48 = 0.49 \qquad TE_B = 0.49 \qquad TE_C = 1.43$$

Step 8. Graph the Results

To confirm the information provided by the calculations and to provide a graphical understanding of the effects upon the product and process, graph the results as shown in Figure 9-32.

Based upon the Larger-is-Better criterion, the optimized process inputs for the manufacture of plastic sheets are A1, B1, and C1, with the C1 factor clearly being the most significant.

Predicting Optimum Results

To predict the optimum results based upon our evaluation in Step 8, insert the optimum treatment and level input variables into the equation to estimate the value of the optimized quality characteristic:

$$\hat{Y} = \frac{T}{n} + \left(A_x - \frac{T}{n}\right) + \left(B_x - \frac{T}{n}\right) + \cdots + \left(F_x - \frac{T}{n}\right)$$

where:

$\hat{Y}$ = Predicted Value of Quality Characteristic

T = Total of All Experimental Results

n = Number of Samples

$\frac{T}{n}$ = Grand Average

$A_x, B_x, \ldots, F_x$ = Performance values at optimum level for each factor

Applying the data from our example to the optimization equation, we obtain:

$$\hat{Y} = \frac{T}{n} + \left(A_1 - \frac{T}{n}\right) + \left(B_1 - \frac{T}{n}\right) + \left(C_1 - \frac{T}{n}\right)$$

$$\hat{Y} = \frac{392}{16} + \left(25.25 - \frac{392}{16}\right) + \left(25.25 - \frac{392}{16}\right)$$

$$+ \left(26.5 - \frac{392}{16}\right)$$

$$\hat{Y} = 24.5 + .75 + .75 + 2 = 28$$

The predicted yield of the optimized production process is 28 acceptable sheets per hour. Please note that we used the actual data to perform this prediction. We must now verify this prediction. The confirmation experiment is run using the optimum factor levels, based upon the Larger-is-Better (LIB) criteria.

Taguchi-Style ANOVA

Taguchi-style analysis of variance uses several methods developed to facilitate the calculation and understanding of ANOVA. The basic rules of ANOVA apply here also, with regard to hypothesis testing, partitioning of variance, and measures of significance. One of the important elements of Taguchi-Style ANOVA is the integration of the percent contribution directly into the ANOVA calculations. The clear advantages of this method are the ease in performing the calculations and the integration of the percent contribution. We will use the data from our DOE example to construct the ANOVA. This may be accomplished using the transformed S/N data or the raw data. For the purposes of clarity, we will calculate the ANOVA using the raw data, from Figure 9-31.

1. Calculate the grand average.
2. Calculate the level mean and level effects.
3. Compute the sum of the squares.
4. Compute the mean squares.
5. Calculate the F_{ratio}.
6. Determine the critical value of F (F_{crit}).
7. Calculate the pure sum of the squares.
8. Determine the percent contribution.

Step 1. Calculate the Grand Average

The grand average is calculated by adding the S/N from each control factor run and dividing by the total number of runs.

$$\text{Grand Average} = \frac{\text{Sum of Individual Observations}}{\text{Total Number of Observations}}$$

Using the three levels of data from the parameter design DOE as an example, we obtain the following:

Grand Average

$$= \frac{28 + 27 + 28 + \cdots + 24 + 21 + 22 + \cdots + 24}{16}$$

$$= 24.50$$

Step 2. Calculate the Level Mean, Level Effects, and Total Effects

The level mean is calculated by summarizing the observations at each level or treatment and dividing by the number of observations in that level.

$$\text{Level Mean} = \frac{\Sigma \ (\text{All Observations at Level i})}{\text{Number of Observations at Level i}}$$

Using the two levels of data from the parameter design DOE with the Plastic Material at level 1, we obtain:

Level A1

$$= \frac{28 + 27 + 28 + 29 + 22 + 24 + 23 + 21}{8} = 25.25$$

The level effect is calculated by subtracting the grand average from the level mean. The total effect is calculated by subtracting the least level mean from the greatest level mean:

$$\text{Level Effects} = \text{Level Mean} - \text{Grand Average}$$

$$\text{Total Effect} = \text{Greatest Level Mean} - \text{Least Level Mean}$$

This data is consolidated in tabular form below for ease of application to the ANOVA.

Factor	Level	Level Mean	Level Effect	Total Effect
A Plastic Material	1	25.25	0.75	
	2	23.75	−0.75	1.50
B Fiberglass Additive	1	25.25	0.75	
	2	23.75	−0.75	1.50
C Binder Resin	1	26.5	2.00	
	2	22.5	−2.00	4.00

Step 3. Compute the Sum of the Squares

The next step is to calculate the sum of the squares for each of the following elements:

Sum of the Squares Total: $SS_{Total} = $ [Distance of individual observations from the grand average]^2

Sum of the Squares for Factors/Interactions: $SS_{Factor} = $ [Level Effects at each level]$^2 \times $ [Number of Observations at each level]

Sum of the Squares for Replications: $SS_{Rep} = $ Sum of [Grand Average − Average of each replication column]$^2 \times $ Number of test runs

Sum of the Squares for Error: $SS_{Error} = SS_{Total} - $ [$SS_{Factors} + SS_{Interactions} + SS_{Replications}$]

Using the three levels of data from the parameter design DOE with the main effects, we obtain:

$$SS_A \text{ Plastic Material} = 9$$
$$SS_B \text{ Fiberglass Additive} = 9$$
$$SS_C \text{ Binder Resin} = 64$$
$$SS_{Total} = 96$$
$$SS_{Error} = 14$$

Step 4. Compute the Mean Squares

Next, we calculate the mean squares (MS) for each factor, interaction, replication, and error. The mean squares are the sum of the squares divided by the degrees of freedom:

$$MS = \frac{\text{Sum of the Squares}}{\text{Degrees of Freedom}}$$

Using the data from the our parameter design DOE for material, additive, and resin, calculate the mean squares:

$$MS_{Material} = \frac{9}{1} = 9$$

$$MS_{Additive} = \frac{9}{1} = 9$$

$$MS_{Resin} = \frac{64}{1} = 64$$

$$MS_{Error} = \frac{14}{12} = 1.16$$

Step 5. Calculate the F_{Ratio}

Calculate the F_{Ratio} for each treatment and interaction by dividing the mean square for the factor or interaction by the mean square for error.

$$F_{Ratio} = \frac{\text{Mean Squares for Factors/Interactions}}{\text{Mean Square for Error}}$$

$$F_{Material} = \frac{9}{1.16} = 7.71$$

$$F_{Additive} = \frac{9}{1.16} = 7.71$$

$$F_{Resin} = \frac{64}{1.16} = 54.86$$

Step 6. Determine the critical value of F (F_{Crit})

Determine F_{Crit} using the F Table in Appendix A for each factor and interaction at the 0.05 or 0.01 level of significance (95% or 99% confidence level), respectively. The F Table column headers represent the degrees of freedom in the numerator, and the row headers represent the degrees of freedom in the denominator:

$$F_{Crit} = f(F_\alpha, df)$$

Using the data from the parameter design DOE, for the main effects and interactions for diameter and location, we get the following:

Factor	F_{Ratio}	$F_{Critical}$ .95	.99	Significance
Material	7.71	4.75	9.33	Significant
Additive	7.75	4.75	9.33	Significant
Resin	55.17	4.75	9.33	Highly Significant

Step 7. Calculate the Pure Sum of the Squares

Calculate the pure sum of the squares (SS′) as indicated in the following equation:

$$SS' = SS_{Factor} - [MS_{Error} \times df_{Factor}]$$

Using the data from the parameter design DOE, for the main effects and interactions for diameter and location, we obtain these results:

$$SS'_{Material} = 9 - [1.16 \times 1] = 9 - 1.16 = 7.84$$

$$SS'_{Additive} = 9 - [1.16 \times 1] = 9 - 1.16 = 7.84$$

$$SS'_{Resin} = 64 - [1.16 \times 1] = 64 - 1.16 = 62.84$$

Step 8. Determine the Percent Contribution

Calculate the percentage of the contribution to variability for each factor, interaction, and replication using the following equation:

$$\% \text{ Contribution} = \frac{\text{Pure Sum of the Squares}}{\text{Total Sum of the Squares}} \times 100$$

To calculate the percent contribution for error ($\%$ CONT$_{\text{Error}}$), use the following equation:

$\%$ CONT$_{\text{Error}} = 100 -$

$$\Sigma \, [\% \text{ Contribution of all Factors/Interactions/Replicates}]$$

Using the data from the parameter design DOE, for the main effects and interactions for diameter and location, we obtain:

$$\% \text{ CONT}_{\text{Material}} = \frac{7.84}{96} \times 100 = 8.16$$

$$\% \text{ CONT}_{\text{Additive}} = \frac{7.84}{96} \times 100 = 8.16$$

$$\% \text{ CONT}_{\text{Resin}} = \frac{62.84}{96} \times 100 = 65.46$$

$$\% \text{ CONT}_{\text{Error}} = 100 - [8.16 + 8.16 + 65.46]$$

$$= 100 - 81.78 = 18.22\%$$

With the Taguchi ANOVA, complete fact-based decision making becomes almost effortless. It is clear that all factors are making contributions to variation but the degree of that contribution is clearly greater for resin. The resin factor is contributing 65.46% of the total variation in plastic sheet yield.

SHAININ STATISTICAL ENGINEERING

Shainin Statistical Engineering is a group of diagnostic tools designed to be simple enough to be implemented by engineers and line workers alike. These tools are intended by Shainin to be logical, intuitive methods that are universal in scope and application. A few of the DOE tools that Shainin has innovated are:

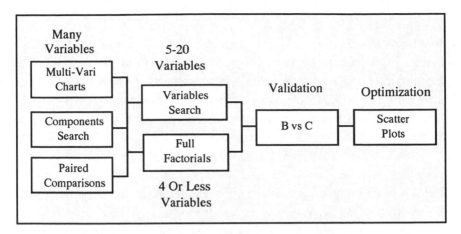

FIGURE 9-33   Shainin Design of Experiments

- ► Components Search
- ► Paired Comparisons
- ► Variables Search
- ► B vs. C
- ► Realistic Tolerance Parallelogram

The application of these tools also follows the same logical sequence. Figure 9-33 demonstrates this logical sequence and its applications.

Multi-Vari Charts

Multi-Vari charts reduce a large number of factors that may be contributing to variability to a manageable number. This smaller number of factors (input variables) narrows the possible causes of variation and focuses on the prime suspects containing the Red X and Pink X variables. The Red X, in Shainin lexicon, is the number one culprit contributing to product or process variation. The second most important cause is called the Pink X, and the third most important is referred to as the Pale Pink X.

Multi-Vari Charts are stratified experiments used to determine whether the variation that is occurring is attributable to positional, cyclic, or temporal factors. When this determination is made, the factors that are not contributing significantly to variation can be eliminated from the experiment. This will narrow the focus of your analysis and reduce the number of experiments that are required to achieve product or process optimization.

The chart is constructed using runs of three to five units produced consecutively. The runs are repeated periodically until 80% of the out-of-control variation under investigation is captured. The results are plotted in Multi-Vari Charts, as demonstrated in Figure 9-34, to determine if the largest variation is positional, cyclical, or temporal.

▶ **Positional** Variation is variation that occurs within a single unit, batch, or run. This may be variation measured from machine-to-machine, operator-to-operator, or plant-to-plant.

▶ **Cyclical** Variation is variation between consecutive units drawn from a single process. These are differences in the quality characteristics measured among groups of units, batch-to-batch or lot-to-lot.

▶ **Temporal** Variation is time related, such as hour-to-hour, day-to-day, or week-to-week.

Components Search

Components Search is another method by which many possible causes of variation can be reduced to a smaller group of related possible causes. Components Search is used to discover and isolate the controlling causes of variation for main effects and interactions. Components search is accomplished in four stages.

▶ **Ballpark Stage:** This stage is used to determine if the factors, processes, assemblies or components selected contain the Red X and Pink X.

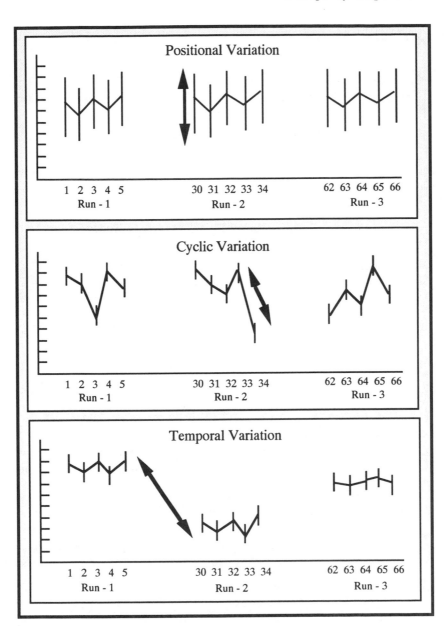

FIGURE 9-34   Multi-Vari Chart

- ► **Elimination Stage:** The purpose of this stage is to eliminate all the unimportant factors.
- ► **Capping Run Stage:** This stage verifies or validates that the important factors selected in Stage 2 are important and that the unimportant factors have been sorted out.
- ► **Factorial Analysis Stage:** This stage is an analysis drawn from the data generated in Stages 1 and 2. A full-factorial matrix is used to quantify the importance of the main effects and interactions.

There are four prerequisites to a components search:

- ► The technique is applicable in manufacturing processes.
- ► The quality characteristic must be measurable and repeatable.
- ► The units must be capable of disassembly and reassembly.
- ► There must be at least two assemblies or systems with clearly different levels of output (Quality Characteristic).

Components Search can then be accomplished in ten steps:

1. Select the best and the worst performing unit from a run, lot, or shift.
2. Determine the quality characteristic by which good and bad units are to be measured. Measure both units and record the readings.
3. Disassemble the good unit twice. Reassemble and remeasure it each time. Disassemble the bad unit twice. Reassemble and remeasure it. The three good unit readings must all rank better than all three bad units and the difference between the median values of the good and bad units must exceed the average range by a minimum ratio of 1.25:1. Only then can a significant and repeatable difference between the good and bad units be established.
4. Based upon engineering knowledge of the design of the system, rank the component names in descending order of perceived importance.

5. Switch the top-ranked component from the good unit or assembly with the corresponding component in the bad assembly. Measure the two assemblies.

6. If there is no change (i.e., if the good assembly stays good and the bad assembly stays bad within calculated control limits) the top component, A, is unimportant. Go to component B.

   If there is a partial change out of the control limits for one or both of the two assembly outputs, A is not the only important variable. A is important but not alone. Further, A's interaction effects with other components cannot be ruled out. Go to component B.

   If there is a complete reversal in the outputs of the two assemblies, A would be the part having a Red X quality characteristic. There is no further need for components search.

7. In each of the three alternatives in Step 6, restore component A to the original good and bad units (before Step 5) to ensure that the original condition is repeated. Repeat Steps 5 and 6 with the next most important component B, then C, then D, etc. if the results in each component swap are 6(a) or 6(b).

8. Ultimately, the Red X family involving two or more components will be indicated. If there are two or more significant changes, a Red X interaction could be found in the Step 10 analysis.

9. With the important components identified, a capping run of these important components banded together in the good and bad assemblies must be conducted to verify their importance.

10. Finally, a factorial matrix, using the data generated in Steps 2, 6, and 7, is drawn to determine, quantitatively, main effects and interaction effects. Steps 9 and 10 are best explained using a real-life case study.

Paired Comparisons

The paired components method is similar to the components search method, with the same objective of finding the Red X. This technique is effective when the components or subassemblies cannot be disassembled or reassembled, there are several good and very few bad units that can be paired, and a suitable parameter can be used to distinguish the good from the bad. Paired comparisons are accomplished in five steps.

1. Select one good unit and one bad unit (drawn, where possible, close to the same production time).
2. Call this pair one. Observe in detail to note differences between these two units. The differences can be visual, dimensional, electrical, mechanical, chemical, etc. The observation techniques could involve the eye, X-rays, scanning electron microscopes, test to destruction, etc.

WHAT → HOW	Classical Design of Experiments		Taguchi Robust Design	Shainin Statistical Engineering
	Full Factorial	Fractional Factorial		
New Design		○	●	
Many Factors		○	●	△
Few Factors	●		○	●
Known Interactions	●	○	○	●
Few Interactions	○		●	○
Costly Test Run		△	●	
Inexpensive Test Run	●		●	●
Costly Test Item	△	○	* ●	
Inexpensive Test Item	●		○	
VRP		○	●	●
Process Centric			○	●
Improvement	○		●	●
High Reliability Required	●	△	○	●
Failure Analysis		△	○	●

Best ●   VRP = Variability Reduction Process
Good ○   * Taguchi usually followed by Confirmation Run
Fair △

FIGURE 9-35   Design of Experiments

3. Select a second pair of good and bad units. Observe and note the differences, as in Step 2.
4. Repeat this search process with a third, fourth, fifth, and sixth pair, until the observed differences show a pattern of repeatability.
5. Disregard differences that show contrary directions among the pairs. Usually by the fifth or sixth pair, the consistent differences will be narrowed down to a few factors, providing a strong clue for the major cause of variation.

In addition to these initial methods for refining the focus of experimental design, Shainin's Statistical engineering utilizes Variables Search, B vs. C, and Scatter Plots to optimize the design of products and processes.

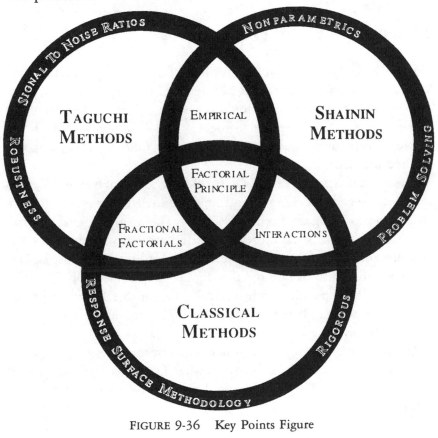

FIGURE 9-36   Key Points Figure

KEY POINTS

Analysis of Variance (ANOVA) is an important tool for making business and technical decisions. It tells us whether several different treatments (for example, different manufacturing processes) all have the same effect on the quality characteristics of interest. Analysis of Variance can be applied to existing process data and DOE data.

Design of Experiments is the most valuable single set of tools for the optimization and improvement of products and processes. The table in Figure 9-35 indicates the recommended applications of the three types of DOE discussed in this chapter. Figure 9-36 presents a graphical comparison of these three types of DOE.

EXAMPLE

The QFD for the LWCI 1600 series manufacturing equipment stated MTBF as a critical engineering design element of the new system. The benchmark requirement for this system MTBF is 3000 hours as stated in the QFD. The Electronic Control Division of LWCI was tasked to provide a digital control assembly that met this basic system requirement.

A team consisting of the LWCI 1600 program management, design engineers, service personnel, and analysts met to determine the approach to providing the needed assembly. The team first evaluated all the available process data for the existing assembly. From this data, they determined that the controller A12 board was the most significant contributor to MTBF for the digital control assembly. The customer service department's historical data on this board indicated that it currently exhibited an MTBF of 2750 operating hours in the customer's environment.

The team then performed a cause-and-effect analysis, using additional subject experts, to determine what factors contributed to the A12 board MTBF. The resulting analysis is demonstrated in Example Figure 9-1.

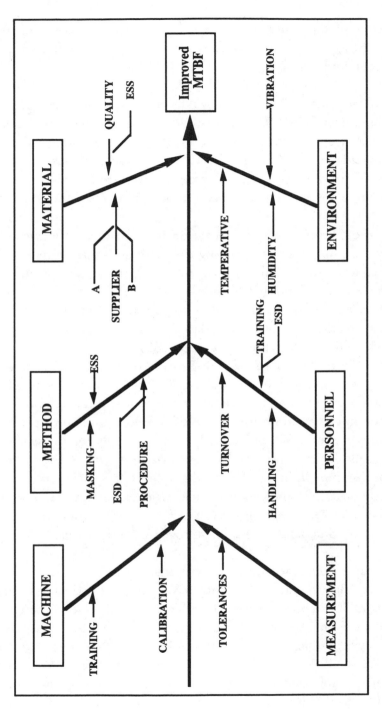

EXAMPLE FIGURE 9-1   Cause-and-Effect Analysis

Based upon this cause-and-effect analysis and the knowledge of the subject specialists, the team selected three factors or treatments that could contribute most significantly to MTBF:

Board Supplier: LWCI is using two board suppliers for existing digital controllers. The boards had the same performance characteristics, but the suppliers produced them using different methods and technologies. Both boards had previously met all LWCI supplier quality requirements and were one-to-one interchangeable. These treatments will be Supplier A1 and Supplier A2.

Vibration Protection: The vibration induced upon the assembly by the equipment itself and by the customer's environment was a concern to the subject specialists and the system engineers. The existing controller assembly and its associated boards are assembled to the system without any special vibration damping. The treatments will be called Vibration Protection (Damper) (B1) and No Vibration Protection (B2).

Electro-Static Discharge (ESD): Sensitivity to ESD had not been very well defined in the past. LWCI is currently using ESD standards that are acceptable in the industry. There was very little information on the effects of ESD and no known correlation between ESD and customer service calls for the existing systems. The engineers and subject matter experts (SMEs) wanted to determine if, in fact, ESD had any effect on system service life. Improved ESD protection standards, devices, and training are available. The treatments selected for this evaluation are Existing ESD Standards (C1) and Improved ESD Standards (C2).

The team determined that the experimental results would be expressed (quality characteristic, output variable, dependent variable) as hours MTBF. The experimental process would be incorporated at the end of the Environmental Stress Screening (ESS) cycle as an accelerated life cycle test, and the systems would be tested to failure or to the equivalent of 3,750 hours (125% of that requirement). There was a consensus among the team members no interactions would be significant. Therefore, the designed experiment considered the following factors:

		A SUPPLIER			
		A1	A2		
B DAMPING	B1	A1B1C1	A2B1C1	C1	ESD PROTECTION C
		A1B1C2	A2B1C2	C2	
	B2	A1B2C1	A2B2C1	C1	
		A1B2C2	A2B2C2	C2	

EXAMPLE FIGURE 9-2   Test Matrix

► Treatment A: Supplier
► Treatment B: Vibration Protection
► Treatment C: ESD Protection
► Experimental Results: Hours MTBF

The resulting design matrix is demonstrated in Example Figure 9-2. To evaluate this experiment completely for main effects and interactions would require a 2^3 full-factorial experiment or eight test runs. The expense and time requirements for accelerated life cycle testing are significant and are of concern to the team and management. Therefore, a Taguchi L_4 orthogonal array was selected as meeting these needs and the requirements for orthogonality.

The team next prepared a worksheet for the experiment to manage the data more effectively and to estimate the data management requirements. The experiment was then run, using the data from four samples after initial ESS was completed. The resulting data table is shown in Example Figure 9-3.

The next step in evaluating the Taguchi DOE for improving MTBF is to determine the level effects and total effects. To accomplish this, the team used the spreadsheet in Example Figure 9-4.

Example Figure 9-5 provides a graphical representation of the level effects and total effects calculated from the Taguchi DOE. To determine the level of significance of the effects and the percent contribution, the team then performed a Taguchi-Style ANOVA.

The team then placed all this data into the Taguchi ANOVA Table in Example Figure 9-6 to evaluate the results. The team evaluated the

COLUMN	A	B	C	RESULTS				$\overline{y}$
RUN				1	2	3	4	
1	+	+	+	5365	5791	4902	5523	5395.25
2	+	-	-	4615	5110	4790	4988	4875.75
3	-	+	-	5112	4976	5378	5500	5241.50
4	-	-	+	5045	4798	5110	4811	4941.00
LEVEL 1	5135.5	5318.38	5168.13					
LEVEL 2	5091.25	4908.38	5058.63	GRAND AVERAGE = 5113				

EXAMPLE FIGURE 9-3   MTBF Data Table

results of the analysis and was able to make the following "fact-based decisions":

► Treatment B is making a significant contribution to the MTBF of the A12 Board in this experiment.
► Treatments A and C are not significant.
► Treatment B is contributing 43.49% of the total variation in MTBF.
► Due to the relatively large SS, MS, and percent contribution for error, there may be significant contributors to MTBF that were not considered in this DOE or that are attributable to common cause variation.

TREATMENT	NAME	LEVEL	LEVEL MEAN	LEVEL EFFECT	TOTAL EFFECT
A	SUPP	+	5135.5	22	44
		-	5091.25	-22	
B	VIB	+	5318.38	205	410
		-	4908.38	-205	
C	ESD	+	5168.13	55	110
		-	5058.63	-55	

EXAMPLE FIGURE 9-4   MTBF Level and Total Effect

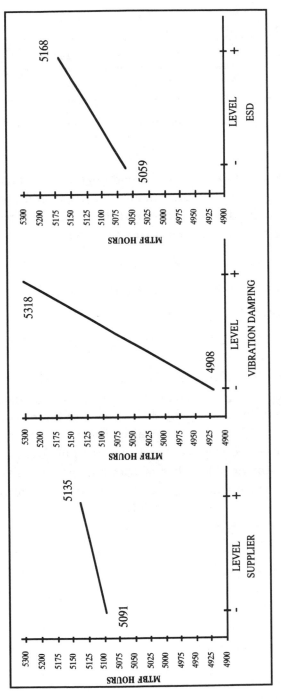

EXAMPLE FIGURE 9-5   DOE Graph

SOURCE OF VARIATION	df	SS	MS	F	F'	SS'	% CONT
A	1	7832	7832	0.117	4.75	2241.33	0.15
B	1	672400	672400	10.022	4.75	666809.10	43.49
C	1	47961	47961	0.715	4.75	42370.08	2.76
ERROR	12	805092	67091				53.60
TOTAL	15	1533285					

EXAMPLE FIGURE 9-6   MTBF DOE Taguchi ANOVA Table

Based upon this information, the team determined that optimization of the MTBF would occur with all treatments set at the high level (+), based upon the Larger-is-Better (LIB) principle. Therefore, the estimate of the results of the optimized function is:

$$\hat{Y} = 5113.4 + (5135.5 - 5113.4) + (5318.4 - 5113.4)$$
$$+ (5168.1 - 5113.4)$$
$$= 5113.4 + 22.1 + 205.0 + 54.75 = 5395.3$$

Based upon the results of this designed experiment, the team determined that the QFD design and manufacturing matrix goal of 5000 hours could be met by the A12 controller board with an optimized MTBF of 5395. The team also determined that there were other opportunities to improve MTBF based upon Treatments, Interactions, Environment, and other factors not included in this study. The team recommended damping as a vibration protection as the most significant contribution to MTBF.

10

Business Process Reengineering

> TO BE COMPETITIVE IN TODAY'S MARKETPLACE, CHALLENGE EXISTING ASSUMPTIONS, PAVING THE WAY FOR RADICAL REENGINEERING OF YOUR BUSINESS PROCESSES.

Over the past 90 years, the industrialized world has been perfecting the industrial model: "Make a product, and a customer will buy it." The paradigm that companies built their entire asset base upon was the make and sell concept. Large companies focused on efficiencies, economies of scale, functional specialization, organizational span of control, and management hierarchies to manage the complexities of big business. Consumer demand seemed limitless, and companies responded by mass producing enormous quantities of goods, from radios to refrigerators, from automobiles to ashtrays. New industrial powers rose from the ashes of World War II to further flood the world with new and ever improved products.

By the 1970s, a new phenomenon broke upon the world stage and began to shape competitive forces for the next two decades. The phenomenon was called "Quality," and it sent a wake-up call shivering up the spine of the American industrial complex. New industrial powerhouses, such as Japan and Germany, gained huge market share by building high-quality, competitively priced products for the world's consumers. Markets were no longer national; they were international.

As companies and countries raced to be market leaders and innovators, a new product came to the market in the late 1970s that would not only change the competitive landscape for decades to come, but would also usher in a new era: one that would require a new paradigm for management, workers, competitors, and customers. The product was the *microchip*; the new era was the *Information Age*.

Today, companies are buffeted by a sea of change unrivaled in depth and pace. Time to market is critical. Customer satisfaction is paramount. Quality is a given. Service is waning as a differentiator. The rules have changed. New management precepts espouse mass customization, cross-functional integration of business processes, employee empowerment, self-managed work teams, the networked organization, and above all, a zealous customer focus. This book has been about how you can be successful in winning the competition. But it is not enough to win the competition—you must earn a profit and grow wealth.

To remain competitive in this ever-changing environment, and earn a profit and grow wealth, organizations need to aggressively mount a campaign to transform their businesses to the new paradigm. The focus will be on end results: significant cost reduction, improved quality, reduced cycle time, and enhanced customer service. They will need to challenge existing assumptions, paving the way for radical reengineering of business processes.

Mike Hammer, who coined the term business process reengineering (BPR), tells us to use the power of Information Technology (IT) to radically redesign our business processes to achieve dramatic improvements in their performance. In this context, reengineering is the fundamental rethinking and radical redesign of everything associated with business. The key terms in this definition are:

▶ **Fundamental:** This is the "why we do what we do" and the "why we do it the way we do it" rationale as applied to the company. We begin the process with no assumptions and no givens. BPR determines <u>what</u> a company must do, then <u>how</u> to do it.

► **Radical:** BPR is about process reinvention, not process improvement, enhancement, or modification. Disregard all existing structures and procedures to invent new ways of accomplishing work.

► **Dramatic:** Business process reengineering is necessary when a need exists for "heavy blasting." Dramatic improvement demands blowing up the old ways and replacing them with something new. Marginal or continuous improvement requires fine tuning.

► **Process:** the most important word in the definition of BPR. This is a collection of activities, taking one or more kinds of input, and creating an output of value to the customer.

Three kinds of companies typically undertake BPR. The first kind is a business that is already in trouble and has no other choice but to initiate the change. They have become desperate, have "hit the wall," and are lying on the ground still breathing.

The second kind is not yet in trouble, but management has the foresight and sees trouble on the horizon. They have been cruising along at high speed but see something rushing toward them in their headlights. The third kind of company is in peak condition, with no discernable difficulties, but management is ambitious and aggressive. They see opportunities to further their lead over competition and take every advantage.

BPR is not the introduction of automation, software reengineering, restructuring, downsizing, or rightsizing. It is not reorganizing, relayering, or flattening. BPR is not continuous improvement (Kaizen) or Total Quality Management (TQM). BPR is a new beginning. The process requires starting over with a clean sheet of paper, rejecting the conventional wisdom, and inventing new approaches to process structure. It requires reversing the industrial revolution and searching for new models for organizing work.

Recurring themes and characteristics in BPR are the combining of several jobs into one, workers empowered to make decisions, process steps being performed in a more natural order (not linearized), multiple versions of the process being performed, and the work being performed where it makes the most sense. Checks and controls have been reduced, with reconciliation being minimized. Case managers provide for single points of contact, and hybrid centralized and decentralized operations are prevalent.

BUSINESS PROCESS REENGINEERING (OR IS IT REDESIGN)?

Business Process Reengineering (BPR) is a common yet often misunderstood term used to describe a wide range of activities being conducted within public and private sector organizations. These activities have varying objectives, from incremental improvements in functional areas of the business to the wholesale rethinking of the entire business entity. It is clear that such divergent objectives should not be approached with a single, inflexible, non-modular reengineering methodology. Therefore, three types of BPR have been identified to describe the breadth of activity that is typically encountered:

- ▶ **Type I—Process Redesign for Functional Improvement:** reducing costs and/or improving cost-effectiveness through incremental change and streamlining within a business function or department
- ▶ **Type II—Process Redesign for Cross-Functional Improvement:** seeking higher levels of performance improvement through the redesign of today's business processes, breaking down organizational boundaries by taking a cross-functional view
- ▶ **Type III—Business Reinvention:** developing radical change in the nature of the business by redefining the mission and vision, products/services, distribution channels, markets, and organizational structures

These designations are intended to help in communicating and defining the degree of change and the corresponding level of effort associated with various types of BPR initiatives. None of these types is inherently superior to any other, despite the implication in the literature that radical change is better than incremental change. Indeed, much of the challenge in structuring a BPR program is to select the type of BPR approach that is best suited to a specific situation, taking into account the organization's objectives, capabilities, and competitive or economic environment.

It is entirely possible that some business areas within an organization may benefit most from a Type I redesign that results in rapid implementation of improvements. Other business areas in the same organization may need more dramatic restructuring of existing processes (Type II) or radical rethinking of their mission and vision (Type III). Accordingly, it may be possible and desirable to mix the types of BPR initiatives within a single organization's overall BPR program. Experience has also shown that individual BPR projects may evolve over time from one type to another, as participants in the design process gain experience and as the problems, issues, and opportunities are more clearly defined.

These designations are not intended to produce artificial boundaries or barriers by declaring that there are only three possible types of BPR. In practice, they are more like points on a continuum, with many variations existing between each of the three types. Figure 10-1 illustrates some typical characteristics of each type of BPR initiative.

For BPR to be most effective, it should include fundamental redesign and coordination on five fronts (Figure 10-2):

- ► **Cross-functional work flow:** The flow of physical objects and information into, through, and out of the organization must be redesigned without regard for the constraints of traditional functions or boundaries.
- ► **Information technology:** It is a crucial enabling factor, allowing compression of time and distance, providing broader access to information and knowledge assets, and eliminating barriers between customers and suppliers.

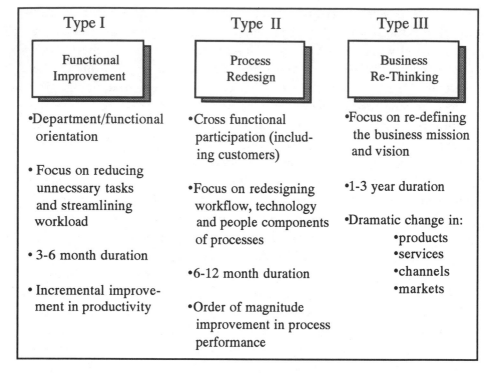

FIGURE 10-1   Types of Business Process Reengineering

▶ **Human resources:** The key element for the future viability and growth of the organization is the human resource asset in a continuous learning environment. As business processes are redesigned, the focus is on the "knowledge worker," who must be enabled with appropriate skills, experiences, and tools, empowered to learn and act, and rewarded based on the organization's values and measures.

▶ **Physical infrastructure:** The physical facilities, equipment, and tools used by workers should be designed to support and take advantage of changes in workflow, information technology, and human resources.

▶ **Policies, legislation, and regulations:** Changes to existing policies, regulations, and legislation may be required to allow the conduct of the new business processes.

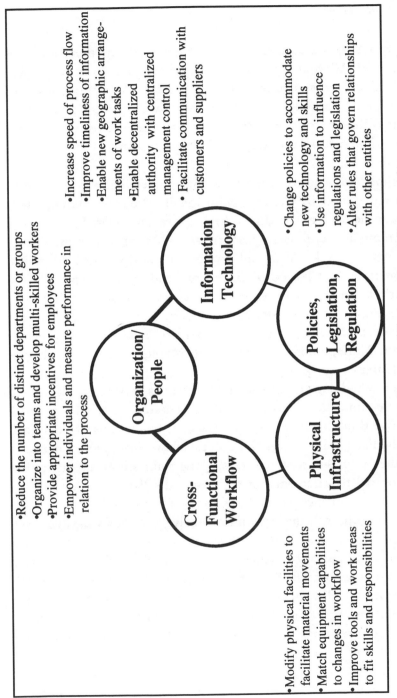

*Reduce the number of distinct departments or groups
*Organize into teams and develop multi-skilled workers
*Provide appropriate incentives for employees
*Empower individuals and measure performance in relation to the process

*Increase speed of process flow
*Improve timeliness of information
*Enable new geographic arrangements of work tasks
*Enable decentralized authority with centralized management control
* Facilitate communication with customers and suppliers

Information Technology

Organization/People

Policies, Legislation, Regulation

* Change policies to accommodate new technology and skills
*Use information to influence regulations and legislation
*Alter rules that govern relationships with other entities

Cross-Functional Workflow

Physical Infrastructure

*Modify physical facilities to facilitate material movements
* Match equipment capabilities to changes in workflow
* Improve tools and work areas to fit skills and responsibilities

FIGURE 10-2 The Five Fronts of Business Process Reengineering

BPR Methodology

There probably are as many approaches to BPR as there are BPR practitioners. We found that to be the case. As a result, we have spent considerable time and resources in defining and gaining consensus on one overall philosophy, approach, and methodology for conducting our BPR efforts. The methodology has been designed so that it can be tailored to fit the needs and objectives of each type of BPR initiative.

Our methodology consists of six core phases that are required to define and execute BPR efforts. Additionally, **Program Management** addresses the need to coordinate BPR efforts and related activities in a programmatic approach. **Performance Management** provides a framework to track the overall impact of multiple BPR efforts on the organization. **Change Management** concepts are applied continuously to ensure that the BPR efforts result in real and effective change. Figure 10-3 illustrates the relationship between the core phases of the methodology and the three related dimensions of **Program Management, Performance Management,** and **Change Management.**

This methodology represents a comprehensive framework to help companies link their vision with their redesign objectives, provoke innovative thinking, and develop realistic expectations of the effort. The modular nature of this framework allows BPR project teams to direct their efforts to targeted areas, while maintaining a holistic view of the overall requirements for success of the BPR program.

One of the challenges in developing a BPR methodology is to present an approach that is comprehensive, yet allows flexible levels of effort to meet specific needs. The phases of our methodology are designed to be executed sequentially and to move the organization from "thinking about BPR" to redesigning and implementing one or more processes. Based on the organizations's previous experience and objectives, it may not be necessary to formally execute all of the phases. However, BPR practitioners should be aware of the conceptual content of each of the six phases.

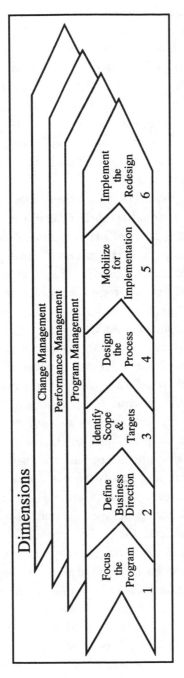

FIGURE 10-3   Business Process Reengineering Phases and Related Dimensions

Phase 1—Focus the Program: Assess and test the appropriateness of BPR as an approach to help the organization achieve its performance goals and determine the organizations's readiness to undertake various types of BPR. This phase includes (1) identifying the underlying issues that are driving the need for BPR, and (2) setting appropriate expectations of the potential results and effort required. At the end of this phase, there should be some agreement on the type (I, II, and /or III) of effort that should be pursued and the scope and objectives for one or more subsequent phases of work.

Phase 2—Define Business Direction: Develop a clear understanding of the actionable and measurable business strategies that will direct the BPR effort to achieve significant improvements in business performance. During this phase, the business strategy is used to select processes that have significant potential to impact the business strategy. This phase may include strategy development in cases where the current business strategy has significant shortcomings. At the end of this phase, key executives should arrive at a common understanding of the organization's strategies and the processes that are likely candidates for BPR, based on their relationship to the strategies.

Phase 3—Identify Scope and Targets: Identify the business processes selected in the previous phase, where BPR will have the greatest potential benefits, and where the risk factors are manageable. During this phase, the current process performance is measured and compared to customer requirements and benchmarked organizations. Organizational and technical risk factors are assessed and processes that should be redesigned are selected and sequenced. Objectives are set for individual process redesign efforts and the anticipated type of effort (I, II, or III) is determined. At the end of this phase, the organization should have a clearly defined plan for one or more process design efforts.

Phase 4—Design the Process: Analyze the current process and design new ways of doing business to achieve the desired levels of performance. During this phase, individual process design teams are formed and information is collected to gain an in-depth understanding of strengths, weaknesses, and opportunities for improvement. One or more new process designs are conceived and tested and estimates are developed for process performance, implementation costs, and benefits. At the end of this phase, the design team should be able to describe the future process in terms of workflow, organization, human resources, information technology, physical infrastructure, and the impact on policies, legislation, and regulations. The design team and the executive sponsor should have a shared understanding of the predicted performance of the new process, as well as high-level estimates of implementations costs and tangible benefits.

Phase 5—Mobilize for Implementation: Document the detailed activities and resources required to implement the new design, as well as the sequence of anticipated implementation phases. Risks associated with the implementation are identified, and tactics to minimize risk are developed. Alternative migration options may be considered, based on time-phased costs/benefits and risk. Commitment to the change involved is developed, and plans to communicate the change and coordinate the implementation with other organizational initiatives are prepared. At the end of this phase, the organization should have a clearly articulated plan for implementing the redesigned process.

Phase 6—Implement the Redesign: Roll out the new ways of doing business across the organization to realize the full benefits of reengineering. This includes implementation project planning; development of new policies and procedures; development and implementation of new technology; and implementation of changes in organization, human resources, and physical infrastructure. In some cases, implementation will also require effecting changes in regulations and legislation.

This phased approach is designed to support an efficient, high-value BPR effort by starting with a potentially broad scope and continually narrowing the breadth of study, while simultaneously increasing the depth and intensity of information gathering and analysis. This is intended to avoid "boiling the ocean" and gathering or performing analyses that are not ultimately used to add value to the organization. The concept is most evident in the beginning phases of the methodology.

Phase 1, "Focus the Program," is used to quickly evaluate the overall position of the organization and the objectives of the sponsoring executives, and then determine whether some type of BPR is appropriate as a possible approach to achieve these objectives. This is done largely by experience, along with information and analysis regarding industry comparisons of company performance. At the point that BPR is determined to be an appropriate solution, the methodology begins to evaluate and selectively filter the processes in the business to arrive at the few critical processes that can and should be redesigned. This filtering process is illustrated in Figure 10-4.

In Phase 2, "Define Business Direction," the selection of processes is based on relationships of processes to business strategies and intuitive judgement about process characteristics. These criteria can then be quickly applied to a large number of processes, without collecting and analyzing large amounts of information.

In Phase 3, "Identify Scope and Targets," the process selection criteria are based on actual data about process performance and on analysis of technical and organizational risk factors. These criteria require some investment in data collection and analysis to be performed on a smaller set of candidate processes.

Detailed data collection and analysis of the internal workings of processes is delayed until Phase 4, "Design the Process," to avoid spending significant time documenting and analyzing processes that are not slated to be redesigned. This approach also minimizes information collected early in the BPR program on processes that are sequenced for redesign later in the overall BPR program. This helps eliminate the possibility that information will become outdated or irrelevant before it can be used.

Each phase of the methodology is designed to yield information to guide subsequent phases, while gradually building knowledge and leading the organization to more specific actions. Figure 10-5 illus-

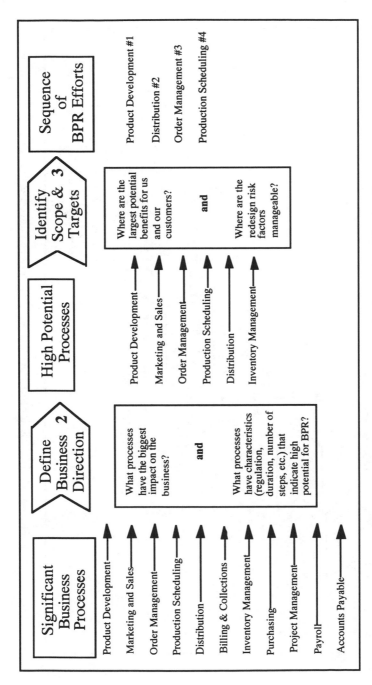

FIGURE 10-4   The Business Process Reengineering Filtering Process

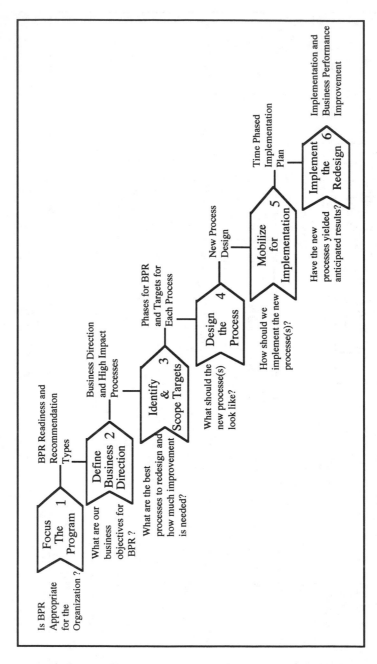

FIGURE 10-5   Relationships of Business Process Reengineering Phases

trates the major questions addressed by each phase, as well as the relationship of the outcomes of each phase to the next phase.

This view of the methodology illustrates some of the various "entry and exit points" that may be appropriate for individual organizations, based on their objectives, experience, and internal capabilities. For example, an organization may have defined its business direction and selected appropriate processes for BPR and therefore should enter the methodology at Phase 4, "Design the Process." In this case, the BPR team should validate that the objectives and the deliverables of the previous phases have occurred (e.g.: Is there a shared understanding of the business direction and agreement on the objectives and expectations for each design effort?) before beginning Phase 4, "Design the Process."

A Structured View of the BPR Methodology

The methodology provides a flexible structure to support different situations and is adaptable to project scopes as broad as the entire enterprise or as focused as a specific business unit or process within the organization. The structure of the methodology includes *Phases, Activities, and Tasks*. These are defined, as follows:

- ▶ **Phases** produce a major deliverable, end in a key management decision or milestone, and are potentially stand-alone projects.
- ▶ **Activities** produce a complete, self-contained deliverable, work product, or result and are focused on a single set of closely related issues.
- ▶ **Tasks** are primarily procedural and describe the suggested organization of work within an activity.

The structure of phases and activities in the methodology through Phase 5, "Mobilize for Implementation," is illustrated in Figure 10-6. Phase 6, "Implement the Redesign," is a transition point to other methodologies to facilitate organizational change, manage system development, and to implement changes to policies, procedures,

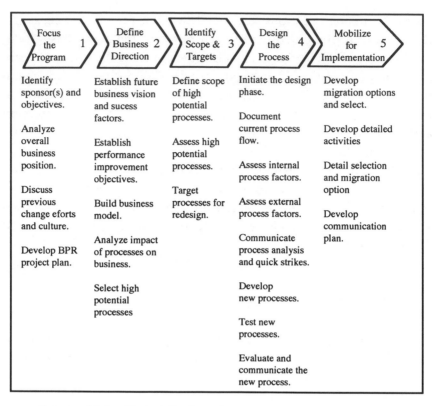

Focus the Program 1	Define Business 2 Direction	Identify Scope & 3 Targets	Design the 4 Process	Mobilize for 5 Implementation
Identify sponsor(s) and objectives.	Establish future business vision and sucess factors.	Define scope of high potential processes.	Initiate the design phase.	Develop migration options and select.
Analyze overall business position.	Establish performance improvement objectives.	Assess high potential processes.	Document current process flow.	Develop detailed activities
Discuss previous change eforts and culture.	Build business model.	Target processes for redesign.	Assess internal process factors.	Detail selection and migration option
Develop BPR project plan.	Analyze impact of processes on business.		Assess external process factors.	Develop communication plan.
	Select high potential processes		Communicate process analysis and quick strikes.	
			Develop new processes.	
			Test new processes.	
			Evaluate and communicate the new process.	

FIGURE 10-6   Typical Business Process Reengineering Activities Within Phases

organization, physical infrastructure, and regulations. As a result, the BPR methodology does not specify activities and tasks for Phase 6.

The structure of the methodology is intended to allow customization for different levels (Types I, II, and III) of BPR efforts. Phases 4 and 5, "Design the Process" and "Mobilize for Implementation," should provide more than enough tools, techniques, and structure to execute Type I efforts. This type of BPR effort may not require formal activities to define the business direction and may only require execution of scoping and targeting activities to define the scope and objectives of the redesign effort.

Type II BPR requires the use of most of the phases and activities. If a scope of only one or two Type II efforts has been previously identi-

	Focus the Program 1	Define Business Direction 2	Identify Scope & Targets 3	Design the Process 4	Mobilize for Implementation 5
Type I Functional Improvement	Required	Not Required	Only required to identify project objectives.	Required, but may not execute all activities & tasks.	Required, but may be limited in scale.
Type II Process Redesign	Required	Strongly Suggested	Required	Required	Required
Type III Business Re-thinking	Required	Required with development of NEW business strategies.	Required, may include processes that do not currently exist	Required for multiple purposes	Required, with coordination across several processes and programs.

FIGURE 10-7   Business Process Phase Selection Guidelines

fied by the organization, Phases 2 and 3, "Define Business Direction" and "Identify Scope and Targets," may pertain to these processes only.

Type III efforts will typically require the complete execution of all phases and activities, possibly with additional activities to develop new product, market, and business strategies. Type III efforts will also require a significant investment in program management and coordination of multiple process redesigns. Phase selection guidelines for each type of BPR effort are summarized in Figure 10-7.

Context of the Methodology

BPR may be thought of as a new way of combining and executing a mix of old and new approaches. It combines established practices, such as systems analysis, flowcharting, and other traditional industrial engineering techniques, with newer practices, including business visioning and user-driven, cross-functional design teams. These approaches have been enhanced and extended by adding emerging approaches, such as the design of human factors (people skills, training, performance measures, and incentives), organizational change management, and rapid prototyping of technology, as illustrated in Figure 10-8. In BPR, all of these approaches are applied to the business process (the basic unit of business design).

There are a number of different types of efforts that could or should be going on simultaneously with BPR initiatives. It is important that they be considered in the design of the BPR program and integrated with it, where possible. These programs may include Change Management, Performance Management, Program Management, Continuous Improvement, Systems Development, and Downsizing.

BPR and Change Management

Management of organizational change is a key component of BPR. Four areas to address are:

- ► **Sponsorship**—At the onset, identify all stakeholders for the business processes being redesigned. Then determine the level of involvement and support required from each potential sponsor, and work with those individuals to gain commitment and define the actions they need to take.
- ► **Resistance to Change**—Everyone personally affected by a changed business process will resist to some degree. By anticipating the nature, sources, and strength of resistance, an implementation plan can be built that assists people in overcoming their resistance and accepting the change. To the extent possible, this includes involvement in designing the new processes and procedures.
- ► **Change Agent Skills**—In preparing for implementation, ensure that change agent roles are understood, and assess agent skills to determine areas of risk that should be addressed.
- ► **Culture**—The success of many breakthrough design efforts relies on cultural change. Corporate cultures are notoriously tenacious and act as an inertial force that slowly regresses from the new business process back to its historical form. It is important to determine the extent to which a BPR implementa-

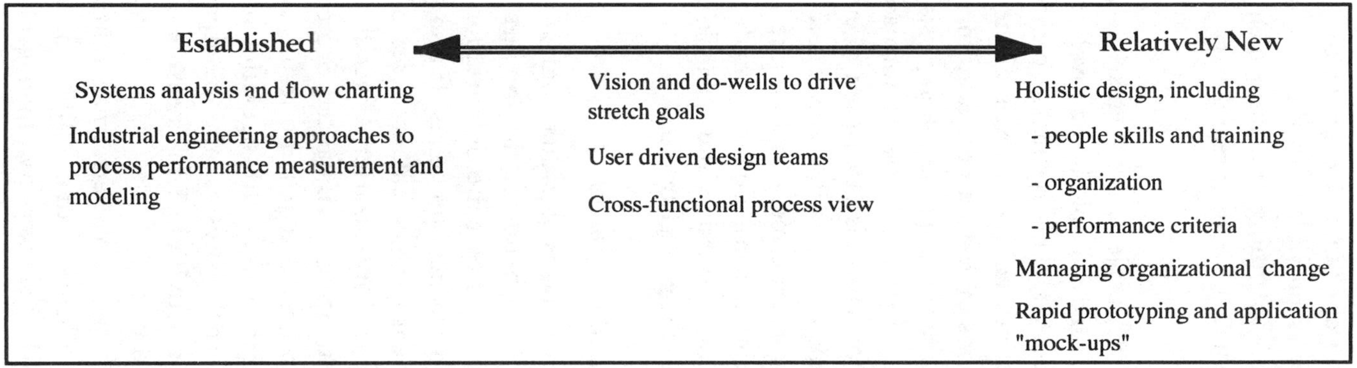

Established

Systems analysis and flow charting

Industrial engineering approaches to process performance measurement and modeling

Vision and do-wells to drive stretch goals

User driven design teams

Cross-functional process view

Relatively New

Holistic design, including

- people skills and training

- organization

- performance criteria

Managing organizational change

Rapid prototyping and application "mock-ups"

FIGURE 10-8   Business Process Reengineering Combines Approaches

tion requires cultural change. Generally, the designs should be aligned as closely as possible with the existing culture. Where this is not possible, planning and implementing the necessary cultural change should be an integral part of the coordinated campaign.

Some elements of BPR projects are themselves tactics to manage organizational change. One example is the involvement of executives in setting stretch objectives. This results in ownership and understanding of the project at the highest levels of the organization and ensures that design teams understand the need to effect fundamental structural change. Another example is the analysis and collection of information about the current process performance and customer requirements. This information is often used to emphasize the need for dramatic improvement in organizations where change resistance is high. Specific change management tools and techniques should be used at various points in the methodology to analyze previous experience with change, assess sponsorship and agent skills, and predict the impact of change and change resistance.

BPR *and Performance Management*

Performance Management takes on a dual context in BPR initiatives. As a part of the BPR methodology, it provides a framework for developing stretch objectives that the organization needs to encourage dramatic change in business processes. It also provides a powerful mechanism for identifying a balanced set of measures to be utilized in measuring the organization's overall performance. Performance Management, using a "Balanced Scorecard" framework, includes financial measures that tell the results of actions already taken. These are complemented with operational measures of customer satisfaction, internal processes, and the organization's innovation and improvement activities. This measurement framework is illustrated in Figure 10-9.

As a project management tool, Performance Management can be used to track the accomplishment of the BPR program's overall objectives and determine whether executive management's expectations

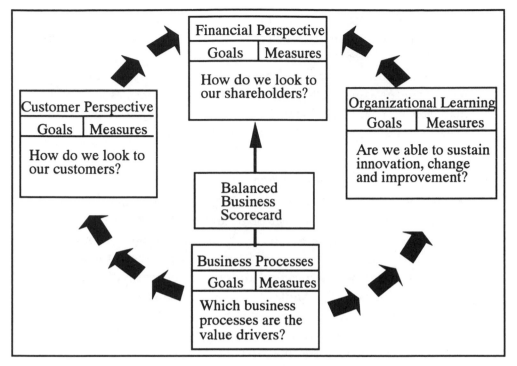

FIGURE 10-9   Balanced Scorecard Framework For Performance Measurement

are being met. Establishing quantifiable goals for improvement and making sure that the BPR effort is geared to achieving those results is an important piece of Performance Management.

BPR and Program Management

BPR needs to be managed as a program within the enterprise because it will touch on many other initiatives being undertaken. These initiatives may include information technology activities (e.g., strategic planning or IT architecture development), business and facilities planning, human resource programs, and continuous improvement efforts. Program Management provides the umbrella to coordinate all of these related initiatives in a programmatic approach, which is particularly important when multiple BPR initiatives are being launched simultaneously. Coordination between these multiple initiatives is paramount for successful management of the overall program, as well as to prevent confusion and frustration.

Independent projects to address quick strike opportunities may result from on-going BPR programs. These quick strikes need to be managed as part of the overall program to track performance improvements and coordinate overall efforts of BPR work teams.

BPR and Continuous Improvement (CI)

It has been said that "Continuous Improvement is like lighting a thousand candles under a steel plate and gradually warming it up, while BPR is like using a blowtorch to burn a hole through the plate." This analogy and the mental images it produces are accurate portrayals of the similarities and differences between BPR and CI. The blowtorch and the candle both use the same technique (combustion) and produce some of the same results (the metal gets hotter). However, the objective of the blowtorch is to fundamentally alter the shape of the plate in a fairly short period of time. Likewise, BPR attempts to produce a dramatic change in a portion of the organization over a relatively short period of time, while Continuous Improvement programs aim to produce incremental improvement throughout the organization over a long time. This is illustrated in Figure 10-10.

Despite the difference in focus and results, BPR and CI programs should be compatible and complementary, as illustrated in Figure 10-11. Indeed, a common result of a BPR project is that a project team continuously improves the redesigned process, even while it is being implemented. It is logical to expect to see organizations conduct multiple BPR efforts within or alongside a CI program. This occurs because the two approaches share many of the same tools and techniques, but differ in how these tools are used. Part of the purpose of Program Management may be to coordinate the scope of CI and BPR efforts, as well as to communicate the results of these efforts to individuals and groups that are working in separate, but related parts of the overall program.

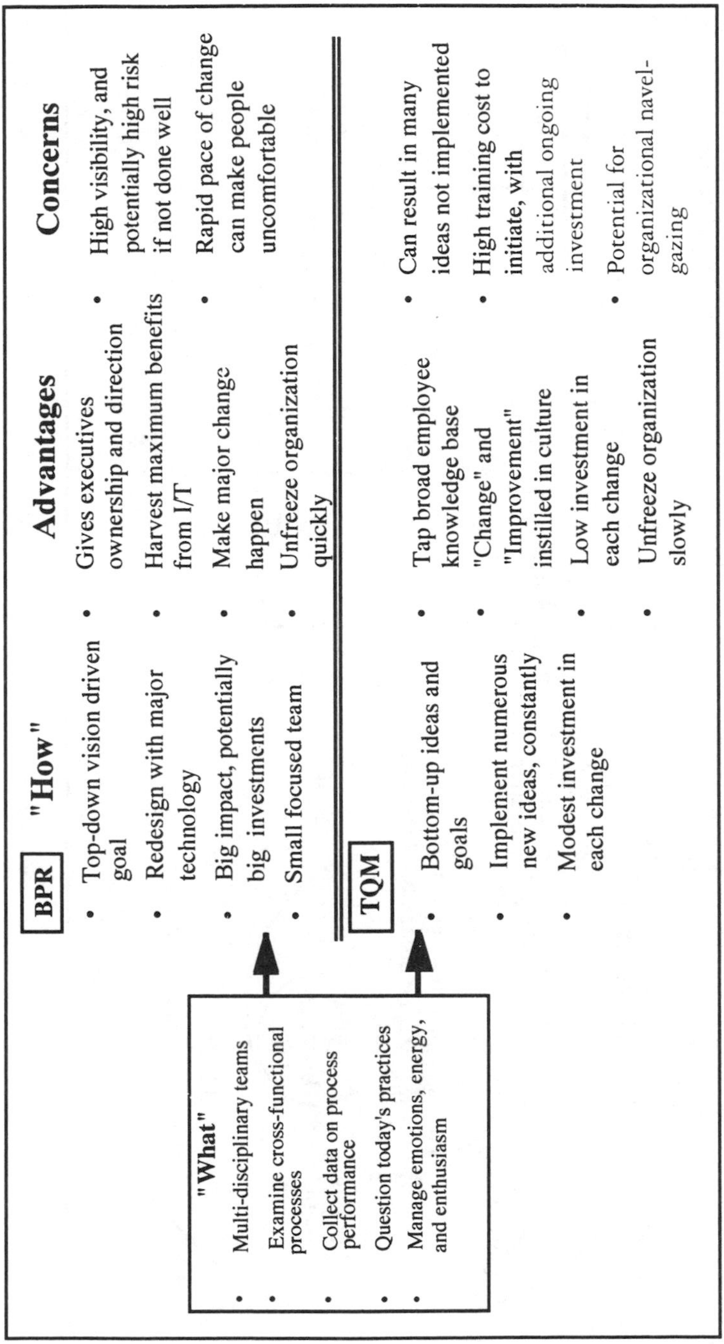

BPR

"How"
- Top-down vision driven goal
- Redesign with major technology
- Big impact, potentially big investments
- Small focused team

Advantages
- Gives executives ownership and direction
- Harvest maximum benefits from I/T
- Make major change happen
- Unfreeze organization quickly

Concerns
- High visibility, and potentially high risk if not done well
- Rapid pace of change can make people uncomfortable

TQM

"How"
- Bottom-up ideas and goals
- Implement numerous new ideas, constantly
- Modest investment in each change

Advantages
- Tap broad employee knowledge base
- "Change" and "Improvement" instilled in culture
- Low investment in each change
- Unfreeze organization slowly

Concerns
- Can result in many ideas not implemented
- High training cost to initiate, with additional ongoing investment
- Potential for organizational navel-gazing

"What"
- Multi-disciplinary teams
- Examine cross-functional processes
- Collect data on process performance
- Question today's practices
- Manage emotions, energy, and enthusiasm

FIGURE 10-10   Relationship Between Business Process Reengineering and Continuous Improvement

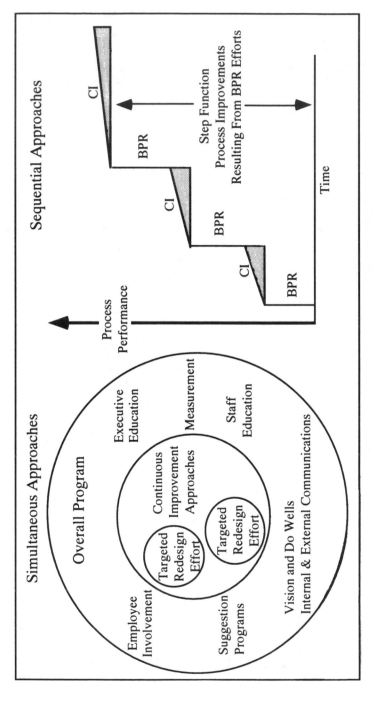

FIGURE 10-11   Simultaneous and Sequential Approach to BPR and CI

Two years after winning the Malcolm Baldrige National Quality Award (MBNQA), American Express undertook a reengineering project to reduce costs. This sparked a heated, internal debate regarding the relationship between BPR and CI. American Express' Senior Vice President of Quality and Reengineering, Randy Christofferson, resolved their conflict by redefining BPR with MBNQA terminology. Specifically, he replaced Category Five of the MBNQA Criteria, "Management of Process Quality," with BPR—in essence describing BPR as a subset of Total Quality Management.

BPR and System Development

BPR programs and projects are often confused with computer system design and development efforts. Typical system development methodologies using information engineering and other approaches seek to carefully document how business is conducted today and what pieces of information are required. These development methodologies then proceed to follow a structured, step-wise approach that results in automation of the business with current processes as a basic assumption. However, experienced systems professionals will effectively utilize their system development life cycle (SDLC) methodology to challenge current requirements and, therefore, alter existing business processes. Although in many instances these initiatives appear to be BPR-like in their activities, they are fundamentally a systems design and implementation project. This usually means that the organization conducting such an initiative is not perceiving it as a BPR undertaking. But often the greatest point of opportunity for companies to embrace BPR concepts is when they are contemplating large system replacement or development efforts.

Since BPR seeks to define new and dramatically different ways of doing business, BPR efforts can and usually do lead to new technology requirements. The technology requirements resulting from BPR efforts should provide the initial stages of a system development methodology using the newly designed process as the assumed target of automation. In these situations, the system development methodology may need to be modified to use the future process design as the "as is" business process.

BPR and Downsizing

Downsizing is typically a reaction to economic difficulties that result in across the board reductions in staff. While BPR efforts may result in staff reductions, they are targeted reductions to eliminate excess capacity produced by making work simpler and eliminating non-value-added activities. More often, BPR efforts result in changes in skill mix requirements that may necessitate retraining or recruiting of individuals with specific capabilities to perform adequately in the new process design.

BPR and IPPD

Integrated Product and Process Development (IPPD) is primarily responsive to external voices (e.g., customers, users, society, government, etc.) while BPR is responsive to internal voices (e.g., management, engineering, technology, manufacturing, quality, material, etc.). IPPD focuses on original design and development efforts, while BPR focuses on redesign and replacement.

Principles of Business Process Reengineering

As a direct result of the many successes and failures of BPR, seven basic principles have evolved; they are:

1. Organize around outcomes, <u>not</u> tasks. (Have one person perform all the tasks in a process.)
2. Have those who use the output of a process (i.e., the customers) actually do it themselves. (Have persons who need the result of a process do it for themselves.)
3. Integrate information-processing work into the real work that produces the information. (Have persons who perform the process and generate data act on it.)
4. Treat geographically-dispersed resources as though they were centralized. (Have persons who perform decentralized but similar processes use centralized data bases, telecommunica-

tions networks, and standardized processing systems to obtain the benefits of scale and coordination, while maintaining the benefits of flexibility and service.)

5. Link parallel activities instead of integrating their results. (Forge links between parallel processes to coordinate them while they operate, rather than after they are completed.)

6. Put the decision point where the work is performed, and build control into the process. (Have persons who perform the process make the related decisions using built-in control systems.)

7. Capture information once at the source. (Collect data as soon as it becomes available and store it in an on-line data base for all who need it.)

KEY POINTS

To remain competitive in this ever-changing environment, and earn a profit and grow wealth, organizations need to aggressively mount a campaign to transform their business to the new paradigm. The focus will be on end results: significant cost reduction, improved quality, reduced cycle time, enhanced customer service.

Reengineering is the fundamental rethinking and radical redesign of everything associated with business. The key terms in this definition are:

- ► **Fundamental:** BPR determines <u>what</u> a company must do, then <u>how</u> to do it.
- ► **Radical:** BPR is about process reinvention, not process improvement, enhancement, or modification.
- ► **Dramatic:** Dramatic improvement demands blowing up the old ways and replacing them with something new.
- ► **Process:** This is a collection of activities, taking one or more kinds of input, and creating an output of value to the customer.

Three kinds of companies typically undertake BPR:

► A business that is already in trouble and has no other choice
► A business not yet in trouble, but management has the foresight and sees trouble on the horizon
► A business that is in peak condition with no discernable difficulties, but management sees opportunities to further their lead over competition and take every advantage

Three types of BPR have been identified to describe the breadth of activity that is typically encountered:

► Type I—Process Redesign for Functional Improvement
► Type II—Process Redesign for Cross-Functional Improvement
► Type III—Business Reinvention: developing radical change in the nature of the business

For BPR to be most effective, it should include fundamental redesign and coordination on five fronts:

► **Cross-functional work flow:** The flow of physical objects and information into, through, and out of the organization must be redesigned without regard for the constraints of traditional functions or boundaries.
► **Information technology:** It is a crucial enabling factor, allowing compression of time and distance, providing broader access to information and knowledge assets, and eliminating barriers between customers and suppliers.
► **Human resources:** The key element for the future viability and growth of the organization is the human resource asset in a continuous learning environment.
► **Physical infrastructure:** The physical facilities, equipment, and tools used by workers should be designed to support and take advantage of changes in workflow, information technology, and human resources.

▶ **Policies, legislation, and regulations:** Changes to existing policies, regulations, and legislation may be required to allow the conduct of the new business processes.

BPR Methodology

There probably are as many approaches to BPR as there are BPR practitioners. We found that to be the case. As a result, we have spent considerable time and resources in defining and gaining consensus on one overall philosophy, approach, and methodology for conducting our BPR efforts. The methodology has been designed so that it can be tailored to fit the needs and objectives of each type of BPR initiative.

There are six core phases required to define and execute BPR efforts:

Phase 1—Focus the Program: Assess and test the appropriateness of BPR as an approach to help the organization achieve its performance goals and determine the organizations's readiness to undertake various types of BPR.

Phase 2—Define Business Direction: Develop a clear understanding of the actionable and measurable business strategies that will direct the BPR effort to achieve significant improvements in business performance.

Phase 3—Identify Scope and Targets: Identify the business processes selected in the previous phase, where BPR will have the greatest potential benefits, and where the risk factors are manageable.

Phase 4—Design the Process: Analyze the current process and design new ways of doing business to achieve the desired levels of performance.

Phase 5—Mobilize for Implementation: Document the detailed activities and resources required to implement the new design, as well as the sequence of anticipated implementation phases.

Phase 6—Implement the Redesign: Roll out the new ways of doing business across the organization to realize the full benefits of reengineering.

There are a number of different types of efforts that could or should be going on simultaneously with BPR initiatives. These programs may include Change Management, Performance Management, Program Management, Continuous Improvement, Systems Development, and Downsizing.

EXAMPLE

LWCI, as part of its ongoing process of implementing the Management 2000 approach to Integrated Product and Process Development, is performing a Business Process Reengineering Analysis of all company-level critical processes. The Executive Steering Council determined that a critical process within LWCI is one that is necessary for achieving the company vision.

Phase 1: Focus the Program

The Department Staff Steering Committee selected the administrative process of material procurement as a critical process. As you recall from Chapter 7, this process was consolidated at the company level, reporting directly to Mr. Leander. The cost of procurement has been a significant cost element within the company, and there has been dissatisfaction, by the operating divisions, with the process. Presently, there is a section within the company staff that performs the procurement of all raw material, equipment, and supplies.

LWCI established the team indicated in Example Figure 10-1 to perform the analysis of the procurement process. The team consisted of one member from each of the operating divisions, a member from the company controller's staff, and the head of the company procurement section. The team used the six phase Business Process Reengineering (BPR) approach to accomplish the evaluation.

Team Planning Summary Sheet		
Team Name: Procurement Business Process Reengineering		Date: 9/22/94
Organization: Company		Revision: ___ORIG.___

1. Team Members:

Ms. Goodwill
Mr. Freeman
Mr. Dyer
Mr. Everett
Ms. Clausen
Mr. Beauchamp
Mr. Leander (Sr. Advisor)

2. Mission Statement:

Evaluate the LWCI centralized procurement process and implement business process reengineering to achieve improvements in quality, cost and schedule.

3. Goal(s):

• Perform a business process reengineering evaluation

• Reduce the cost of this function

• Improve the responsivness of this process

4. Method(s) of Measuring Success:

• Schedule to plan

• Cost of procurement

• Procurement cycle time

• Quality

5. Completion Criteria:

• Business process reengineering recommendation

• Transition plan

• Transition implemented

7. Achievements:

• Determined mission, goals and objectives for the team

• Selected process for evaluation

• Trained team on business process reengineering

* Attach continuation sheets if necessary.

EXAMPLE FIGURE 10-1   Team Planning Summary Sheet

Phase 2: Define the Business Direction

The Procurement BPR team members had a common understanding of the business strategy; the optimization of Quality, Cost, and Schedule. The relationship between this BPR and the process under consideration is evident by the review of the three key quality characteristics for this process. The measures of Quality, Cost, and Schedule are represented in Example Figures 10-2 (Cycle Times), 10-3 (Process Costs) and 10-4 (Quality Measures).

Cycle Times

As indicated below, the highest overall contributor to procurement cycle time was the equipment procurement process. The column

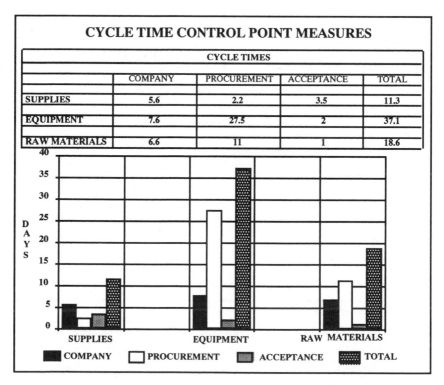

	COMPANY	PROCUREMENT	ACCEPTANCE	TOTAL
SUPPLIES	5.6	2.2	3.5	11.3
EQUIPMENT	7.6	27.5	2	37.1
RAW MATERIALS	6.6	11	1	18.6

EXAMPLE FIGURE 10-2   Cycle Times

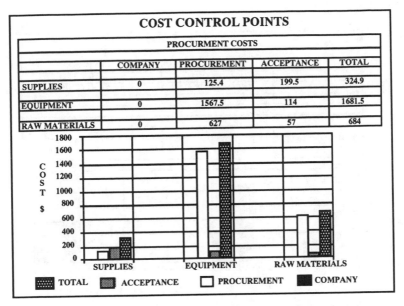

COST CONTROL POINTS

PROCURMENT COSTS

	COMPANY	PROCUREMENT	ACCEPTANCE	TOTAL
SUPPLIES	0	125.4	199.5	324.9
EQUIPMENT	0	1567.5	114	1681.5
RAW MATERIALS	0	627	57	684

EXAMPLE FIGURE 10-3   Process Costs

titled "Company" is the average time from when an item is ordered until it is received at LWCI. This process also has the longest cycle time for the sub-process of processing in the procurement section.

Process Costs

There are no costs associated with the supplier (company) processing an order. The highest overall contributor to procurement cost was the equipment procurement process, which also had the longest cycle time. Also of interest is the relatively high cost of processing the acceptance of supplies. The team attributed this cost to the tedious inventory process and repackaging of supplies for forwarding to the operating divisions.

Quality Measures

A very low percentage of supplies, raw materials, and equipment was rejected during the receipt phase of the procurement process.

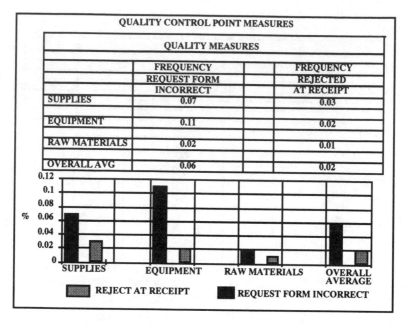

QUALITY CONTROL POINT MEASURES				
QUALITY MEASURES				
	FREQUENCY REQUEST FORM INCORRECT			FREQUENCY REJECTED AT RECEIPT
SUPPLIES	0.07			0.03
EQUIPMENT	0.11			0.02
RAW MATERIALS	0.02			0.01
OVERALL AVG	0.06			0.02

EXAMPLE FIGURE 10-4   Quality Measures

These basic process measures provided a clear understanding of the business strategies that were to direct the actions of the team. All the company key executives arrived at a common understanding of the plan for the Procurement BPR Team.

Phase 3: Identify the Scope and Targets

The third phase for the LWCI Procurement BPR Team is to identify the scope and targets for BPR. This phase will build on the information the team gathered during Phase 2. The team reviewed the Team Planning Summary Sheet for the Procurement BPR Team and confirmed that the goals of accomplishing a process analysis, reducing the cost of the process, and improving the responsiveness of the process still were viable. The targets for improvement are therefore:

► The overall cost of the procurement process and the cost of the sub-processes and process elements
► The cycle times for the procurement process, the sub-processes, and process elements
► The quality of the material produced by the process

The team reviewed the process output requirements for the LWCI procurement process. The output requirements for the process are basically the requested supplies, equipment, and raw materials. These outputs can be best measured by:

► **Accuracy:** Are the supplies, equipment, and raw materials received correct?
► **Cost** of the supplies, equipment, and raw materials
► **Timeliness** of the delivery of the supplies, equipment, and raw materials
► **Internal cost** to process the procurement requests

Review Process Input Requirements

There is but a single process input requirement: the form requesting procurement for supplies, equipment, and raw materials. The best measures of these forms are:

► **Accuracy:** Are the supplies, equipment, and raw materials correctly specified on the form? Is the justification sufficient to process the request?
► **Timeliness:** Is the form submitted with sufficient lead time to meet the required delivery date?

Phase 4: Design the Process

The next phase for the LWCI Procurement Business Process Reengineering Team is new process definition. They first looked at the current upper level flow from a functional point of view. At this point in the Business Process Reengineering, the team could identify the

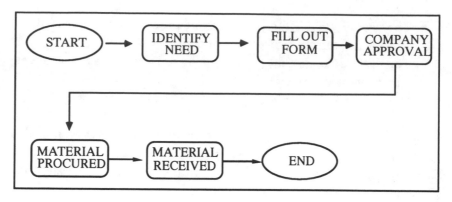

EXAMPLE FIGURE 10-5   Selected Process Functional Flowchart

process only at the functional level, as indicated previously. (See Example Figure 10-5.) They could not perform any useful evaluation of the process because there was insufficient process detail, and there was no way to measure the work activities of the process.

The team then used the process analysis techniques discussed in Chapter 7 to identify and define the details of the current process for this phase of Business Process Reengineering. (See Example Figure 10-6.)

The Procurement BPR Team reviewed their data and decided that this process was indeed an opportunity to enhance LWCI's competitiveness. They decided that the implementation of Statistical Process Control at each of the measurement points would enable them to manage the procurement process.

The Procurement BPR Team identified the following improvements as immediate needs:

- ► Automation of the procurement process
- ► Streamlining the company approval process
- ► Decentralizing the supplies procurement process
- ► Implementing competitive bidding for raw materials

The Procurement BPR Team concluded that the metrics they established were appropriate for the goals they set for their activity. They

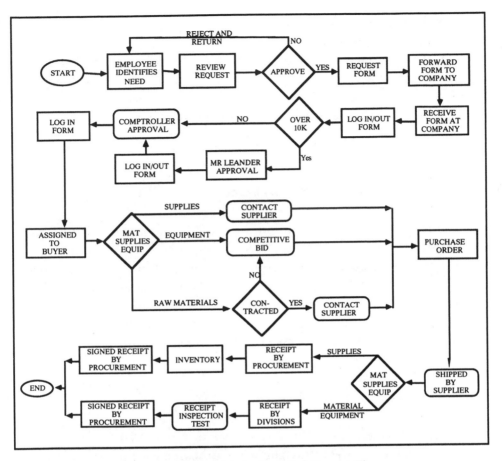

EXAMPLE FIGURE 10-6   Detailed Process Flow

also decided that they should continue and implement Statistical Process Control throughout the process.

The team also concluded that:

► The company approval process is unnecessarily complex and caused unnecessary delays in the process.
► The centralization of the supplies procurement introduced unnecessary opportunities for delays and errors.

- ► The manual nature of the procurement process provided unnecessary opportunities for errors.
- ► The contracts for raw materials were not managed and had not been reviewed in many years.

This evaluation resulted in a streamlined process, as indicated in Example Figure 10-7:

Phase 5: Mobilize for Implementation

The team developed a clear estimate of the resources required to implement their recommendations. A return on investment analysis was also performed to demonstrate the benefits from following their recommendations. A plan of action and milestone chart was developed for the execution of their recommendations. When this package was presented to the executives, they included an analysis of the risks associated with implementing their recommendations.

Phase 6: Implement the Redesign

The Procurement BPR Team recommended that LWCI implement the redesigned process throughout the procurement cycle—and that this effort be the responsibility of the cognizant work groups.
    The team also recommended that:

- ► The company approval element caused unnecessary delays in the process
- ► The company contract with a distributor for supplies, but the individual divisions order their own materials and have them shipped directly to them
- ► The ordering system be automated and that information copies be directed to the company controller and Mr. Leander (for purchases over $10,000.00)

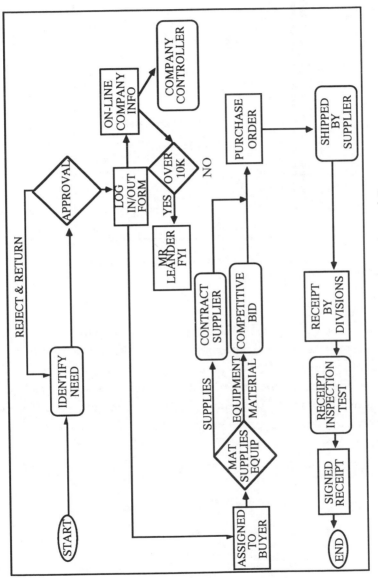

EXAMPLE FIGURE 10-7   Reengineered Process

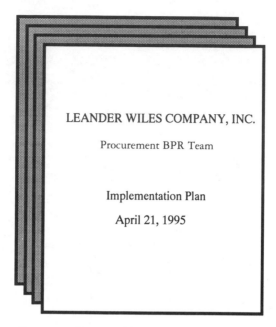

EXAMPLE FIGURE 10-8   BPR Team Implementation Plan

► The Procurement BPR Team developed a plan of action and
milestone chart for implementing their recommendations (Example Figure 10-8). This plan required execution at the division
level, as well as the company level. The team's plan called for
statusing, scoring, and reporting to the Procurement BPR Team,
which, in turn, reported progress to the LWCI Executive Steering Council.

Statistical Tables

TABLE A-1   FACTORS FOR CONTROL CHART AND STANDARD DEVIATION FORMULAS

SUBGROUP SIZE	FACTORS STANDARD DEVIATION d_2	X & R CHARTS FACTORS FOR			X & S CHARTS FACTORS FOR			X - Rm CHARTS FACTORS FOR		
		X-CHART CONTROL LIMITS A_2	R-CHART CONTROL LIMITS LCL D_3	UCL D_4	X-CHART CONTROL LIMITS A_3	S-CHART CONTROL LIMITS LCL B_3	UCL B_4	X-CHART CONTROL LIMITS E_2	Rm-CHART CONTROL LIMITS LCL D_3	UCL D_4
2	1.128	1.880	-	3.267	2.659	-	3.267	2.260	-	3.267
3	1.693	1.023	-	2.574	1.954	-	2.568	1.772	-	2.574
4	2.059	0.729	-	2.282	1.628	-	2.266	1.457	-	2.282
5	2.326	0.577	-	2.114	1.427	-	2.089	1.290	-	2.114
6	2.534	0.483	-	2.004	1.287	0.030	1.970	1.184	-	2.004
7	2.704	0.419	0.076	1.924	1.182	0.118	1.882	1.011	0.076	1.924
8	2.847	0.373	0.136	1.864	1.099	0.185	1.815	1.054	0.136	1.864
9	2.970	0.337	0.184	1.816	1.032	0.239	1.761	1.010	0.184	1.816
10	3.078	0.308	0.223	1.777	0.975	0.284	1.716	0.975	0.223	1.777
11	3.173	0.285	0.256	1.744	0.927	0.321	1.679	0.946	0.256	1.744
12	3.258	0.266	0.283	1.717	0.886	0.354	1.646	0.921	0.283	1.717
13	3.336	0.249	0.307	1.693	0.850	0.382	1.618	0.899	0.307	1.693
14	3.407	0.235	0.328	1.672	0.817	0.406	1.594	0.881	0.328	1.672
15	3.472	0.223	0.347	1.653	0.789	0.428	1.572	0.864	0.347	1.653
16	3.532	0.212	0.363	1.637	0.763	0.448	1.552	0.849	0.363	1.637
17	3.588	0.203	0.378	1.622	0.739	0.466	1.534	0.836	0.378	1.622
18	3.640	0.194	0.391	1.608	0.718	0.482	1.518	0.824	0.391	1.608
19	3.689	0.187	0.403	1.597	0.698	0.497	1.503	0.813	0.403	1.597
20	3.735	0.180	0.415	1.585	0.680	0.510	1.490	0.803	0.415	1.585
21	3.778	0.173	0.425	1.575	0.663	0.523	1.477	0.794	0.425	1.575
22	3.819	0.167	0.434	1.566	0.647	0.534	1.466	0.785	0.434	1.566
23	3.858	0.162	0.443	1.577	0.633	0.545	1.455	0.778	0.443	1.557
24	3.895	0.157	0.451	1.548	0.619	0.555	1.445	0.770	0.451	1.548
25	3.931	0.153	0.459	1.541	0.606	0.565	1.435	0.763	0.459	1.541

TABLE A-2 F TEST

DF DENOM	1−α	DF NUMERATOR 1	2	3	4	5	6	7	8	9	10
1	0.90	39.90	49.50	53.60	55.80	57.20	58.20	58.90	59.40	59.90	60.20
	0.95	161.00	200.00	216.00	225.00	230.00	234.00	237.00	239.00	241.00	242.00
2	0.90	8.53	9.00	9.16	9.24	9.29	9.33	9.35	9.37	9.38	9.39
	0.95	18.50	19.00	19.20	19.20	19.30	19.30	19.40	19.40	19.40	19.40
	0.99	98.50	99.00	99.20	99.20	99.30	99.30	99.40	99.40	99.40	99.40
3	0.90	5.54	5.46	5.39	5.34	5.31	5.28	5.27	5.25	5.24	5.23
	0.95	10.10	9.55	9.28	9.12	9.10	8.94	8.89	8.85	8.81	8.79
	0.99	34.10	30.80	29.50	28.70	28.20	27.90	27.70	27.50	27.30	27.20
4	0.90	4.54	4.32	4.19	4.11	4.05	4.01	3.98	3.95	3.94	3.92
	0.95	7.71	6.94	6.59	6.39	6.26	6.16	6.09	6.04	6.00	5.96
	0.99	21.20	18.00	16.70	16.00	15.50	15.20	15.00	14.80	14.70	14.50
5	0.90	4.06	3.78	3.62	3.52	3.45	3.40	3.37	3.34	3.32	3.30
	0.95	6.61	5.79	5.41	5.19	5.05	4.95	4.88	4.82	4.77	4.74
	0.99	16.30	13.30	12.10	11.40	11.00	10.70	10.50	10.30	10.20	10.10
6	0.90	3.78	3.46	3.29	3.18	3.11	3.05	3.01	2.98	2.96	2.94
	0.95	5.99	5.14	4.76	4.53	4.39	4.28	4.21	4.15	4.10	4.06
	0.99	13.70	10.90	9.78	9.15	8.75	8.47	8.26	8.10	7.98	7.87
7	0.90	3.59	3.26	3.07	2.96	2.88	2.83	2.78	2.75	2.72	2.70
	0.95	5.59	4.74	4.35	4.12	3.97	3.87	3.79	3.73	3.68	3.64
	0.99	12.20	9.55	8.45	7.85	7.46	7.19	6.99	6.84	6.72	6.62
8	0.90	3.46	3.11	2.92	2.81	2.73	2.67	2.62	2.59	2.56	2.54
	0.95	5.32	4.46	4.07	3.84	3.69	3.58	3.50	3.44	3.39	3.35
	0.99	11.30	8.65	7.59	8.01	6.63	6.37	6.18	6.03	5.91	5.81
9	0.90	3.36	3.01	2.81	2.69	2.61	2.55	2.51	2.47	2.44	2.42
	0.95	5.12	4.26	3.86	3.63	3.48	3.37	3.29	3.23	3.18	3.14
	0.99	10.60	8.02	6.99	6.42	6.06	5.80	5.61	5.47	5.35	5.26
10	0.90	3.28	2.92	2.73	2.61	2.52	2.46	2.41	2.38	2.35	2.32
	0.95	4.96	4.10	3.71	3.48	3.33	3.22	3.14	3.07	3.02	2.98
	0.99	10.00	7.56	6.55	5.99	5.64	5.39	5.20	5.06	4.94	4.85
15	0.90	3.07	2.70	2.49	2.36	2.27	2.21	2.16	2.12	2.09	2.06
	0.95	4.54	3.68	3.29	3.06	2.90	2.79	2.71	2.64	2.59	2.54
	0.99	8.68	6.36	5.42	4.89	4.56	4.32	4.14	4.00	3.89	3.80
20	0.90	2.97	2.59	2.38	2.25	2.16	2.09	2.04	2.00	1.96	1.94
	0.95	4.35	3.49	3.10	2.87	2.71	2.60	2.51	2.45	2.39	2.35
	0.99	8.10	5.85	4.94	4.43	4.10	3.87	3.70	3.56	3.46	3.37
30	0.90	2.88	2.49	2.28	2.14	2.05	1.98	1.93	1.88	1.85	1.82
	0.95	4.17	3.32	2.92	2.69	2.53	2.42	2.33	2.27	2.21	2.16
	0.99	7.56	5.39	4.51	4.02	3.70	3.47	3.30	3.17	3.07	2.98
40	0.90	2.84	2.44	2.23	2.09	2.00	1.93	1.87	1.83	1.79	1.76
	0.95	4.08	3.23	2.84	2.61	2.45	2.34	2.35	2.18	2.12	2.08
	0.99	7.31	5.18	4.31	3.83	3.51	3.29	3.12	2.99	2.89	2.80
60	0.90	2.79	2.39	2.18	2.04	1.95	1.87	1.82	1.77	1.74	1.71
	0.95	4.00	3.15	2.76	2.53	2.37	2.25	2.17	2.10	2.04	1.99
	0.99	7.08	4.98	4.13	3.65	3.34	3.12	2.95	2.82	2.72	2.63
120	0.90	2.75	2.35	2.13	1.99	1.90	1.82	1.77	1.72	1.68	1.65
	0.95	3.92	3.07	2.68	2.45	2.29	2.17	2.09	2.02	1.96	1.91
	0.99	6.85	4.79	3.95	3.48	3.17	2.96	2.79	2.66	2.56	2.47

TABLE A-2   F TEST (Continued)

DF DENOM	1−α	DF NUMERATOR								
		12	15	20	30	40	50	60	100	120
1	0.90	60.70	61.20	61.70	62.30	62.50	62.70	62.80	63.00	63.10
	0.95	244.00	246.00	248.00	250.00	251.00	252.00	252.00	253.00	253.00
2	0.90	9.41	9.42	9.44	9.46	9.47	9.47	9.47	9.48	9.48
	0.95	19.40	19.40	19.40	19.50	19.50	19.50	19.50	9.48	19.50
	0.99	99.40	99.40	99.40	99.50	99.50	99.50	99.50	99.50	99.50
3	0.90	5.22	5.20	5.18	5.17	5.16	5.15	5.15	5.14	5.14
	0.95	8.74	8.70	8.66	8.62	8.59	8.58	8.57	8.55	8.55
	0.99	27.10	26.90	26.70	26.50	26.40	26.40	26.30	26.20	26.20
4	0.90	3.90	3.87	3.84	3.82	3.80	3.80	3.79	3.78	3.78
	0.95	5.91	5.86	5.80	5.75	5.72	5.70	5.69	5.56	5.66
	0.99	14.40	14.20	14.00	13.80	13.70	13.70	13.70	13.60	13.60
5	0.90	3.27	3.24	3.21	3.17	3.16	3.15	3.14	3.13	3.12
	0.95	4.68	4.62	4.56	4.50	4.46	4.44	4.43	4.41	4.40
	0.99	9.89	9.72	9.55	9.38	9.29	9.24	9.20	9.13	9.11
6	0.90	2.90	2.87	2.84	2.80	2.78	2.77	2.76	2.75	2.74
	0.95	4.00	3.94	3.87	3.81	3.77	3.75	3.74	3.71	3.70
	0.99	7.72	7.56	7.40	7.23	7.14	7.09	7.06	6.99	6.97
7	0.90	2.67	2.63	2.59	2.56	2.54	2.52	2.51	2.50	2.49
	0.95	3.57	3.51	3.44	3.38	3.34	3.32	3.30	3.27	3.27
	0.99	6.47	6.31	6.16	5.99	5.91	5.86	5.82	5.75	5.74
8	0.90	2.50	2.46	2.42	2.38	2.36	2.35	2.34	2.32	2.32
	0.95	3.28	3.22	3.15	3.08	3.04	3.02	3.01	2.97	2.97
	0.99	5.67	5.52	5.36	5.20	5.12	5.07	5.03	4.96	4.95
9	0.90	2.38	2.34	2.30	2.25	2.23	2.22	2.21	2.19	2.18
	0.95	3.07	3.01	2.94	2.86	2.83	2.80	2.79	2.76	2.75
	0.99	5.11	4.96	4.81	4.65	4.57	5.52	4.48	4.42	4.40
10	0.90	2.28	2.24	2.20	2.16	2.13	2.12	2.11	2.09	2.08
	0.95	2.91	2.85	2.77	2.70	2.66	2.64	2.62	2.59	2.58
	0.99	4.71	4.56	4.41	4.25	4.17	4.12	4.08	4.01	4.00
15	0.90	2.02	1.97	1.92	1.87	1.85	1.83	1.82	1.79	1.79
	0.95	2.48	2.40	2.33	2.25	2.20	2.18	2.16	2.12	2.11
	0.99	3.67	3.52	3.37	3.21	3.13	3.08	3.05	2.98	2.96
20	0.90	1.89	1.84	1.79	1.74	1.71	1.69	1.68	1.65	1.64
	0.95	2.28	2.20	2.12	2.04	1.99	1.97	1.95	1.91	1.90
	0.99	3.23	3.09	2.94	2.78	2.69	2.64	2.61	2.54	2.52
30	0.90	1.77	1.72	1.67	1.61	1.57	1.55	1.54	1.51	1.50
	0.95	2.09	2.01	1.93	1.84	1.79	1.76	1.74	1.70	1.68
	0.99	2.84	2.70	2.55	2.39	2.30	2.25	2.21	2.13	2.11
40	0.90	1.71	1.66	1.61	1.54	1.51	1.48	1.47	1.43	1.42
	0.95	2.00	1.92	1.84	1.74	1.69	1.66	1.64	1.59	1.58
	0.99	2.66	2.52	2.37	2.20	2.11	2.06	2.02	1.94	1.92
60	0.90	1.66	1.60	1.54	1.48	1.44	1.41	1.40	1.36	1.35
	0.95	1.92	1.84	1.75	1.65	1.59	1.56	1.53	1.48	1.47
	0.99	2.50	2.35	2.20	2.03	1.94	1.88	1.84	1.75	1.73
120	0.90	1.60	1.55	1.48	1.41	1.37	1.34	1.32	1.27	1.26
	0.95	1.83	1.75	1.66	1.55	1.50	1.46	1.43	1.37	1.35
	0.99	2.34	2.19	2.03	1.86	1.76	1.70	1.66	1.56	1.53

TABLE A-3   STUDENTS t TABLE

Degrees of Freedom	α				
	0.010 $t_{0.01}$	0.050 $t_{0.05}$	0.250 $t_{0.025}$	0.010 $t_{0.01}$	0.005 $t_{0.005}$
1	3.078	6.314	12.706	31.821	63.657
2	1.886	2.353	1.303	6.965	9.925
3	1.638	2.132	3.182	4.541	5.841
4	1.533	2.015	2.776	3.747	4.604
5	1.476	1.943	2.571	3.365	4.032
6	1.440	1.895	2.447	3.143	3.707
7	1.415	1.860	2.365	2.998	3.499
8	1.397	1.833	2.306	2.896	3.355
9	1.383	1.812	2.262	2.821	3.250
10	1.372	1.796	2.228	2.764	3.169
11	1.363	1.782	2.201	2.718	3.106
12	1.356	1.771	2.179	2.681	3.055
13	1.350	1.761	2.160	2.650	3.012
14	1.345	1.753	2.145	2.624	2.977
15	1.341	1.746	2.131	2.602	2.947
16	1.337	1.740	2.120	2.583	2.921
17	1.333	1.734	2.110	2.567	2.898
18	1.330	1.729	2.101	2.552	2.878
19	1.328	1.725	2.093	2.539	2.861
20	1.325	1.697	2.086	2.528	2.845
30	1.310	1.684	2.042	2.457	2.750
40	1.303	1.671	2.021	2.423	2.704
60	1.296	1.661	2.000	2.390	2.660
120	1.290	1.645	1.984	2.358	2.626

TABLE A-4   FULL FACTORIAL DESIGNS

RUN	DESIGN	A	B	AB	C	AC	BC	ABC	D	AD	BD	ABD	CD	ACD	BCD	ABCD	E
1	2^1	-	-	+	-	+	+	-	-	+	+	-	+	-	-	+	-
2		+	-	-	-	-	+	+	-	-	+	+	+	+	-	-	-
3	2^2	-	+	-	-	+	-	+	-	+	-	+	+	-	+	-	-
4		+	+	+	-	-	-	-	-	-	-	-	+	+	+	+	-
5		-	-	+	+	-	-	+	-	+	+	-	-	+	+	-	-
6	2^3	+	-	-	+	+	-	-	-	-	+	+	-	-	+	+	-
7		-	+	-	+	-	+	-	-	+	-	+	-	+	-	+	-
8		+	+	+	+	+	+	+	-	-	-	-	-	-	-	-	-
9		-	-	+	-	+	+	-	+	-	-	+	-	+	+	-	-
10		+	-	-	-	-	+	+	+	+	-	-	-	-	+	+	-
11		-	+	-	-	+	-	+	+	-	+	-	-	+	-	+	-
12	2^4	+	+	+	-	-	-	-	+	+	+	+	-	-	-	-	-
13		-	-	+	+	-	-	+	+	-	-	+	+	-	-	+	-
14		+	-	-	+	+	-	-	+	+	-	-	+	+	-	-	-
15		-	+	-	+	-	+	-	+	-	+	-	+	-	+	-	-
16		+	+	+	+	+	+	+	+	+	+	+	+	+	+	+	-
17		-	-	+	-	+	+	-	-	+	+	-	+	-	-	+	+
18		+	-	-	-	-	+	+	-	-	+	+	+	+	-	-	+
19		-	+	-	-	+	-	+	-	+	-	+	+	-	+	-	+
20		+	+	+	-	-	-	-	-	-	-	-	+	+	+	+	+
21		-	-	+	+	-	-	+	-	+	+	-	-	+	+	-	+
22		+	-	-	+	+	-	-	-	-	+	+	-	-	+	+	+
23		-	+	-	+	-	+	-	-	+	-	+	-	+	-	+	+
24	2^5	+	+	+	+	+	+	+	-	-	-	-	-	-	-	-	+
25		-	-	+	-	+	+	-	+	-	-	+	-	+	+	-	+
26		+	-	-	-	-	+	+	+	+	-	-	-	-	+	+	+
27		-	+	-	-	+	-	+	+	-	+	-	-	+	-	+	+
28		+	+	+	-	-	-	-	+	+	+	+	-	-	-	-	+
29		-	-	+	+	-	-	+	+	-	-	+	+	-	-	+	+
30		+	-	-	+	+	-	-	+	+	-	-	+	+	-	-	+
31		-	+	-	+	-	+	-	+	-	+	-	+	-	+	-	+
32		+	+	+	+	+	+	+	+	+	+	+	+	+	+	+	+

TREATMENT COMBINATIONS

TABLE A-4   FULL FACTORIAL DESIGNS (Continued)

	DESIGN	TREATMENT COMBINATIONS														
RUN		AE	BE	ABE	CE	ACE	BCE	ABCE	DE	ADE	BDE	ABDE	CDE	ACDE	BCDE	ABCDE
1		+	+	-	+	-	-	+	+	-	-	+	-	+	+	-
2		-	+	+	+	+	-	-	+	+	-	-	-	-	+	+
3		+	-	+	+	-	+	-	+	-	+	-	-	+	-	+
4		-	-	-	+	+	+	+	+	+	+	+	-	-	-	-
5		+	+	-	-	+	+	-	+	-	-	+	+	-	-	+
6		-	+	+	-	-	+	+	+	+	-	-	+	+	-	-
7		+	-	+	-	+	-	+	+	-	+	-	+	-	+	-
8		-	-	-	-	-	-	-	+	+	+	+	+	+	+	+
9		+	+	-	+	-	-	+	-	+	+	-	+	-	-	+
10		-	+	+	+	+	-	-	-	-	+	+	+	+	-	-
11		+	-	+	+	-	+	-	-	+	-	+	+	-	+	-
12		-	-	-	+	+	+	+	-	-	-	-	+	+	+	+
13		+	+	-	-	+	+	-	-	+	+	-	-	+	+	-
14		-	+	+	-	-	+	+	-	-	+	+	-	-	+	+
15		+	-	+	-	+	-	+	-	+	-	+	-	+	-	+
16		-	-	-	-	-	-	-	-	-	-	-	-	-	-	-
17		-	-	+	-	+	+	-	-	+	+	-	+	-	-	+
18		+	-	-	-	-	+	+	-	-	+	+	+	+	-	-
19		-	+	-	-	+	-	+	-	+	-	+	+	-	+	-
20		+	+	+	-	-	-	-	-	-	-	-	+	+	+	+
21		-	-	+	+	-	-	+	-	+	+	-	-	+	+	-
22		+	-	-	+	+	-	-	-	-	+	+	-	-	+	+
23		-	+	-	+	-	+	-	-	+	-	+	-	+	-	+
24		+	+	+	+	+	+	+	-	-	-	-	-	-	-	-
25	2^5	-	-	+	-	+	+	-	+	-	-	+	-	+	+	-
26		+	-	-	-	-	+	+	+	+	-	-	-	-	+	+
27		-	+	-	-	+	-	+	+	-	+	-	-	+	-	+
28		+	+	+	-	-	-	-	+	+	+	+	-	-	-	-
29		-	-	+	+	-	-	+	+	-	-	+	+	-	-	+
30		+	-	-	+	+	-	-	+	+	-	-	+	+	-	-
31		-	+	-	+	-	+	-	+	-	+	-	+	-	+	-
32		+	+	+	+	+	+	+	+	+	+	+	+	+	+	+

TABLE A-5   8 RUN SCREENING DESIGN

RUN	MEAN	A	B	C	D	E	F	G
1	+	+	+	+	-	+	-	-
2	+	-	+	+	+	-	+	-
3	+	-	-	+	+	+	-	+
4	+	+	-	-	+	+	+	-
5	+	-	+	-	-	+	+	+
6	+	+	-	+	-	-	+	+
7	+	+	+	-	+	-	-	+
8	+	-	-	-	-	-	-	-

REFLECTED AND REPLICATED

RUN	MEAN	A	B	C	D	E	F	G
1	+	+	+	+	-	+	-	-
2	+	-	+	+	+	-	+	-
3	+	-	-	+	+	+	-	+
4	+	+	-	-	+	+	+	-
5	+	-	+	-	-	+	+	+
6	+	+	-	+	-	-	+	+
7	+	+	+	-	+	-	-	+
8	+	-	-	-	-	-	-	-
9	+	-	-	-	+	-	+	+
10	+	+	-	-	-	+	-	+
11	+	+	+	-	-	-	+	-
12	+	-	+	+	-	-	-	+
13	+	+	-	+	+	-	-	-
14	+	-	+	-	+	+	-	-
15	+	-	-	+	-	+	+	-
16	+	+	+	+	+	+	+	+
R1	+	+	+	+	-	+	-	-
R2	+	-	+	+	+	-	+	-
R3	+	-	-	+	+	+	-	+
R4	+	+	-	-	+	+	+	-
R5	+	-	+	-	-	+	+	+
R6	+	+	-	+	-	-	+	+
R7	+	+	+	-	+	-	-	+
R8	+	-	-	-	-	-	-	-
R9	+	-	-	-	+	-	+	+
R10	+	+	-	-	-	+	-	+
R11	+	+	+	-	-	-	+	-
R12	+	-	+	+	-	-	-	+
R13	+	+	-	+	+	-	-	-
R14	+	-	+	-	+	+	-	-
R15	+	-	-	+	-	+	+	-
R16	+	+	+	+	+	+	+	+

TABLE A-6   8 RUN SCREENING DESIGN

RUN	MEAN	A	B	C	D	E	F	G	H	I	J	K
1	+	+	+	-	+	+	+	-	-	-	+	-
2	+	+	-	+	+	+	-	-	-	+	-	+
3	+	-	+	+	+	-	-	-	+	-	+	+
4	+	+	+	+	-	-	-	+	-	+	+	-
5	+	+	+	-	-	-	+	-	+	+	-	+
6	+	+	-	-	-	+	-	+	+	-	+	+
7	+	-	-	-	+	-	+	+	-	+	+	+
8	+	-	-	+	-	+	+	-	+	+	+	-
9	+	-	+	-	+	+	-	+	+	+	-	-
10	+	+	-	+	+	-	+	+	+	-	-	-
11	+	-	+	+	-	+	+	+	-	-	-	+
12	+	-	-	-	-	-	-	-	-	-	-	-

TABLE A-7   16 RUN SCREENING DESIGN

RUN	MEAN	A	B	C	D	E	F	G	H	I	J	K	L	M	N	O
1	+	+	-	-	-	+	-	-	+	+	-	+	-	+	+	+
2	+	+	+	-	-	-	+	-	-	+	+	-	+	-	+	+
3	+	+	+	+	-	-	-	+	-	-	+	+	-	+	-	+
4	+	+	+	+	+	-	-	-	+	-	-	+	+	-	+	-
5	+	-	+	+	+	+	-	-	-	+	-	-	+	+	-	+
6	+	+	-	+	+	+	+	-	-	-	+	-	-	+	+	-
7	+	-	+	-	+	+	+	+	-	-	-	+	-	-	+	+
8	+	+	-	+	-	+	+	+	+	-	-	-	+	-	-	+
9	+	+	+	-	+	-	+	+	+	+	-	-	-	+	-	-
10	+	-	+	+	-	+	-	+	+	+	+	-	-	-	+	-
11	+	-	-	+	+	-	+	-	+	+	+	+	-	-	-	+
12	+	+	-	-	+	+	-	+	-	+	+	+	+	-	-	-
13	+	-	+	-	-	+	+	-	+	-	+	+	+	+	-	-
14	+	-	-	+	-	-	+	+	-	+	-	+	+	+	+	-
15	+	-	-	-	+	+	-	-	+	+	-	+	-	+	+	+
16	+	-	-	-	-	-	-	-	-	-	-	-	-	-	-	-

TABLE A-8   20 RUN SCREENING DESIGN

RUN	MEAN	A	B	C	D	E	F	G	H	I	J	K	L	M	N	O	P	Q	R	S
1	+	+	+	-	-	+	+	+	+	-	+	-	+	-	-	-	-	+	+	-
2	+	+	-	-	+	+	+	+	-	+	-	+	-	-	-	-	+	+	-	+
3	+	-	-	+	+	+	+	-	+	-	-	-	-	-	-	+	+	-	+	+
4	+	-	+	+	+	+	-	+	-	+	-	-	-	-	+	+	-	+	+	-
5	+	+	+	+	+	-	+	-	+	-	-	-	-	+	+	-	+	+	-	-
6	+	+	+	+	-	+	-	+	-	-	+	-	+	+	-	+	+	-	-	+
7	+	+	+	-	+	-	+	-	-	-	+	+	+	-	+	+	-	-	+	+
8	+	+	-	+	-	+	-	-	-	-	-	+	-	+	+	-	-	+	+	+
9	+	-	+	-	+	-	-	-	-	+	+	-	+	+	-	+	+	+	+	+
10	+	+	-	+	-	-	-	-	-	+	+	+	+	+	-	-	+	+	+	-
11	+	-	+	-	-	-	-	-	+	+	-	-	+	-	-	+	+	+	+	+
12	+	+	-	-	-	+	+	-	+	-	-	-	+	+	+	+	-	-	+	-
13	+	-	-	-	-	+	+	-	+	+	+	-	+	+	+	+	-	+	-	+
14	+	-	-	-	+	+	-	+	+	-	+	+	+	+	+	-	+	-	+	-
15	+	-	-	+	+	-	+	+	-	-	+	+	+	+	-	+	-	+	-	-
16	+	-	+	+	-	+	+	-	-	+	+	+	+	-	+	-	+	-	-	-
17	+	+	+	-	+	+	-	-	+	+	-	+	-	+	-	+	-	-	-	-
18	+	+	-	+	+	-	-	+	+	+	+	-	+	-	+	-	-	-	-	+
19	+	-	+	+	+	-	-	+	+	+	+	-	+	-	+	-	-	-	+	+
20	+	-	-	-	-	-	-	-	-	-	-	-	-	-	-	-	-	-	-	-

TABLE A-9   L-4 TAGUCHI DESIGN

RUN	FACTOR		
	1	2	3
1	1	1	1
2	1	2	2
3	2	1	2
4	2	2	1

TABLE A-10   L-8 TAGUCHI DESIGN

RUN	FACTOR						
	1	2	3	4	5	6	7
1	1	1	1	1	1	1	1
2	1	1	1	2	2	2	2
3	1	2	2	1	1	1	2
4	1	2	2	2	2	2	1
5	2	1	2	1	2	2	2
6	2	1	2	2	1	1	1
7	2	2	1	1	2	2	1
8	2	2	1	2	1	1	2

TABLE A-11   L-12 TAGUCHI DESIGN

RUN	FACTOR										
	1	2	3	4	5	6	7	8	9	10	11
1	1	1	1	1	1	1	1	1	1	1	1
2	1	1	1	1	1	2	2	2	2	2	2
3	1	1	1	2	2	1	1	1	2	2	2
4	1	2	2	2	2	1	2	2	1	1	2
5	1	2	2	1	2	2	1	2	1	2	1
6	1	2	2	2	1	2	2	1	2	1	1
7	2	1	1	2	1	1	2	2	1	2	1
8	2	1	1	1	2	2	2	1	1	1	2
9	2	1	1	2	2	2	1	2	2	1	1
10	2	2	2	1	1	1	1	2	2	1	2
11	2	2	2	2	1	2	1	1	1	2	2
12	2	2	2	1	2	1	2	1	2	2	1

TABLE A-12   L-16 TAGUCHI DESIGN

RUN	FACTOR														
	1	2	3	4	5	6	7	8	9	10	11	12	13	14	15
1	1	1	1	1	1	1	1	1	1	1	1	1	1	1	1
2	1	1	1	1	1	1	1	2	2	2	2	2	2	2	2
3	1	1	1	2	2	2	2	1	1	1	1	2	2	2	2
4	1	1	1	2	2	2	2	2	2	2	2	1	1	1	1
5	1	2	2	1	1	2	2	1	1	2	2	1	2	2	2
6	1	2	2	1	1	2	2	2	2	1	1	2	1	1	1
7	1	2	2	2	2	1	1	1	1	2	2	2	1	1	1
8	1	2	2	2	2	1	1	2	2	1	1	1	2	2	2
9	2	1	2	1	2	1	2	1	2	1	2	2	1	1	2
10	2	1	2	1	2	1	2	2	1	2	1	1	2	2	1
11	2	1	2	2	1	2	1	1	2	1	2	1	2	2	1
12	2	1	2	2	1	2	1	2	1	2	1	2	1	1	2
13	2	2	1	1	2	2	1	1	2	2	1	2	2	2	1
14	2	2	1	1	2	2	1	2	1	1	2	1	1	1	2
15	2	2	1	2	1	1	2	1	2	1	1	1	1	1	2
16	2	2	1	2	1	1	2	2	1	2	2	2	2	2	1

TABLE A-13   2 LEVEL INTERACTION TABLE

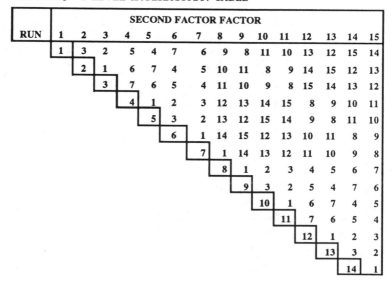

RUN	SECOND FACTOR FACTOR														
	1	2	3	4	5	6	7	8	9	10	11	12	13	14	15
	1	3	2	5	4	7	6	9	8	11	10	13	12	15	14
		2	1	6	7	4	5	10	11	8	9	14	15	12	13
			3	7	6	5	4	11	10	9	8	15	14	13	12
				4	1	2	3	12	13	14	15	8	9	10	11
					5	3	2	13	12	15	14	9	8	11	10
						6	1	14	15	12	13	10	11	8	9
							7	1	14	13	12	11	10	9	8
								8	1	2	3	4	5	6	7
									9	3	2	5	4	7	6
										10	1	6	7	4	5
											11	7	6	5	4
												12	1	2	3
													13	3	2
														14	1

TABLE A-14   L-9 TAGUCHI DESIGN
(3 LEVEL)

RUN	FACTOR			
	1	2	3	4
1	1	1	1	1
2	1	2	2	2
3	1	3	3	3
4	2	1	2	3
5	2	2	3	1
6	2	3	1	2
7	3	1	3	2
8	3	2	1	3
9	3	3	2	1

TABLE A-15   L-27 TAGUCHI DESIGN (3 LEVEL)

RUN	FACTOR												
	1	2	3	4	5	6	7	8	9	10	11	12	13
1	1	1	1	1	1	1	1	1	1	1	1	1	1
2	1	1	1	1	2	2	2	2	2	2	2	2	2
3	1	1	1	1	3	3	3	3	3	3	3	3	3
4	1	2	2	2	1	1	1	2	2	2	3	3	3
5	1	2	2	2	2	2	2	3	3	3	1	1	1
6	1	2	2	2	3	3	3	1	1	1	2	2	2
7	1	3	3	3	1	1	1	3	3	3	2	2	2
8	1	3	3	3	2	2	2	1	1	1	3	3	3
9	1	3	3	3	3	3	3	2	2	2	1	1	1
10	2	1	3	3	1	2	3	1	1	3	1	2	3
11	2	1	3	3	2	3	1	2	2	1	2	3	1
12	2	1	3	3	3	1	2	3	3	2	3	1	2
13	2	2	1	1	1	2	3	2	2	1	3	1	2
14	2	2	1	1	2	3	1	3	3	2	1	2	3
15	2	2	1	1	3	1	2	1	1	3	2	3	1
16	2	3	2	2	1	2	3	3	3	2	2	3	1
17	2	3	2	2	2	3	1	1	1	3	3	1	2
18	2	3	2	2	3	1	2	2	2	1	1	2	3
19	3	1	2	2	1	3	2	1	1	2	1	3	2
20	3	1	2	2	2	1	3	2	2	3	2	1	3
21	3	1	2	2	3	2	1	3	3	1	3	2	1
22	3	2	3	3	1	3	2	2	2	3	3	2	1
23	3	2	3	3	2	1	3	3	3	1	1	3	2
24	3	2	3	3	3	2	1	1	1	2	2	1	3
25	3	3	1	1	1	3	2	3	3	1	2	1	3
26	3	3	1	1	2	1	3	1	1	2	3	2	1
27	3	3	1	1	3	2	1	2	2	3	1	3	2

TABLE A-15   3-LEVEL INTERACTION TABLE

RUN	FACTOR												
	1	2	3	4	5	6	7	8	9	10	11	12	13
	1	3	2	2	6	5	5	9	8	8	12	11	11
		4	4	3	7	7	6	10	10	9	13	13	12
		2	1	1	8	9	10	5	6	7	5	6	7
			4	3	11	12	13	11	12	13	8	9	10
			3	1	9	10	8	7	5	6	6	7	5
				2	13	11	12	12	13	11	10	8	9
				4	10	8	9	6	7	5	7	5	6
					12	13	11	13	11	12	9	10	8
					5	1	1	2	3	4	2	4	3
						7	6	11	13	12	8	10	9
						6	1	4	2	3	3	2	4
							5	13	12	11	10	9	8
							7	3	4	2	4	3	2
								12	11	13	9	8	10
								8	1	1	2	3	4
									10	9	5	7	6
									9	1	4	2	3
										8	7	6	5
										10	3	4	2
											6	5	7
											11	1	1
												13	12
												12	1
													11

APPENDIX *B*

Bibliography

1. Abegglen, James C., and Stalk Jr., George, *Kaisha, The Japanese Corporation*. New York: Basic Books, Inc., 1985.
2. Bernstein, Albert J. & Rozen, Sydney Craft, *Dinosaur Brains*. New York: John Wiley & Sons, Inc., 1989.
3. Beyer, William H., *Handbook Of Tables For Probability And Statistics*. 2nd Edition: CRC Press, 1991.
4. Bonoma, Thomas V., *(The) Marketing Edge, Making Strategies Work*. New York: The Free Press, 1985.
5. Bossert, James L., *Quality Function Deployment, A Practitioner's Approach*. Milwaukee: Quality Press, 1991.
6. Brassard, Michael, *The Memory Jogger Plus +* ™. Methuen: Goal/ QPC, 1989.
7. Brownlee, K. A., *Statistical Theory And Methodology In Science And Engineering*, 2nd Edition. New York: John Wiley & Sons, Inc., 1967.
8. Byham, Dr. William C. with Cox, Jeff, *Zapp! The Lightning of EMPOWERMENT*. Pittsburgh: Development Dimension International Press, 1989.
9. Data Myte Corporation, *Data Myte Handbook*. Minnetonka MN: Data Myte Corporation, 1993.

10. Deming, W. Edwards, *Out Of The Crises*. Boston: Massachusetts Institute of Technology, 1986.
11. Deming, W. Edwards, *Quality, Productivity, and Competitive Position*. Boston: Massachusetts Institute of Technology, 1986.
12. Eureka, William E. and Ryan, Nancy E. *The Customer Driven Company, Managerial Perspectives on QFD*. Dearborne: ASI Press, 1988.
13. Feigenbaum, Armand V., *Total Quality Control*. New York: McGraw-Hill, 1983.
14. Goldratt, Eliyahu M. and Cox, Jeff, *(The) Goal*. Croton-On-Hudson: North River Press, 1984.
15. Goldratt, Eliyahu M., *Theory Of Constraints*. Croton-on-Hudson: North River Press Inc., 1990.
16. Grant, Eugene L. and Leavenworth, Richard S., *Statistical Quality Control*, 6th Edition. New York: McGraw-Hill, 1988.
17. Hall, Robert W., *Zero Inventories*. Homewood: Dow Jones-Irwin.
18. Hall, Robert W., *Attaining Manufacturing Excellence*. Homewood: Dow Jones-Irwin, 1987.
19. Harrington, James, *(The) Improvement Process—How America's Leading Companies Improve Quality*. Milwaukee: Quality Press, 1987.
20. Hazlewood, Robert H. and Wheelwright, Steven C., *Restoring Our Competitive Edge, Competing Through Manufacturing*. New York: John Wiley and Sons, Inc., 1984.
21. Fox, Ronald J. with Field, James L., *The Defense Management Challenge*. Boston: Harvard Business School Press, 1988.
22. Hudiberg, John J., *Winning With Quality, The FPL Story*. White Plains: Quality Resources, 1991.
23. Hogg, Robert V. and Craig, Allen T., *Introduction To Mathematical Statistics*, 3rd Edition. New York: The MacMillan Company, 1970.
24. Imai, Maska, *Kaizen*. New York: Random House, 1986.
25. Ishikawa, Kaoru, Translator, Loftus, John H. *Introduction To Quality Control*. Tokyo: Juse Press Ltd.
26. Ishikawa, Kaoru, Translator, Lu, D. J., *What is Total Quality Control*. Englewood Cliffs: Prentice-Hall, Inc., 1985.

27. Jablonski, Joseph R., *Implementing Total Quality Management, Competing In The 1990's*. Albuquerque: Technical Management Consultants Inc., 1991.

28. Juran, J. M., *Juran On Planning For Quality*. New York: The Free Press, 1988.

29. Juran, J. M., *Managerial Breakthrough*. New York: McGraw-Hill, 1964.

30. Juran, J. M. and Gryna, F. M. Jr., *Quality Planning & Analysis*. New York: McGraw-Hill, 1980.

31. Ishikawa, Kaoru, *Guide To Quality Control*. White Plains: Quality Resources, 1982.

32. Karastu, Hajime, *TQC Wisdom of Japan, Managing for Total Quality Control*. Cambridge: Productivity Press, 1988.

33. Kececioglu, Dimitri, *Reliability Engineering Handbook*, Volume 1 and Volume 2. Englewood Cliffs: Prentice-Hall, Inc., 1991.

34. Kepner, Charles H. and Trego, Benjamin B., *The New Rational Manager*. Princeton: Kepner Trego Inc., 1981.

35. Khazanie, Ramakant, *Elementary Statistics In A World Of Applications*. Santa Monica: Goodyear Publishing Co. Inc., 1979.

36. King, Bob, *Better Designs In Half The Time—Implementing GFD In America*. Methuen: Goal/QPC, 1987.

37. King, Bob, *Hoshin Planning, The Developmental Approach*. Methuen: Goal/QPC, 1989.

38. Kerzuer, Harold, *Project Management, A Systems Approach to Planning, Scheduling and Controlling*. New York: Van Nostrand Reinhold, 1992.

39. Levin, Richard I., *Statistics For Management*, 2nd Edition. Englewood Cliffs: Prentice-Hall, Inc., 1981.

40. Li, Jerome C. R., *Statistical Inference*. Ann Arbor: Edwards Brothers, Inc., 1964.

41. Lubben, Richard T., *Just-in-Time Manufacturing, An Aggressive Manufacturing Strategy*. New York: McGraw-Hill, 1988.

42. Marsh, S., Moran, J. W., Nakui, S., and Hoffherr, G., *Facilitating And Training In Quality Function Deployment*. Methuen: Goal/QPC, 1991.

43. Mizuno, Shigeru, *Management for Quality Improvement—the 7 New Quality Tools.* Cambridge: Productivity Press, 1988.
44. Ohmae, Kenichic, *The Mind of the Strategist, The Art of Japanese Business.* New York: McGraw-Hill, 1982.
45. Orsburn, John D., Musselwhite, Ed, Zegler, John H., with Perrin, Craig, *Self-Directed Work Teams; The New American Challenge.* Homewood: 1990.
46. Ouchi, William, *(The) M-Form Society.* Reading: Addison-Wesley Publishing Co., 1984.
47. Ouchi, William G., *Theory Z.* New York: Avon Books, 1981.
48. Peters, Tom, *Thriving On Chaos.* New York: Alfred A. Knopf, Inc., 1988.
49. Re Velle, Jack B. Ph.D, *The New Quality Technology (An Introduction To Quality Function Deployment (QFD) And The Taguchi Methods).* Los Angeles: Hughes Aircraft Company, 1990.
50. Rosander, A.C., *The Quest For Quality In Services.* Milwaukee: Quality Press, 1989.
51. Ross, Phillip J., *Taguchi Techniques For Quality Engineering.* New York: McGraw-Hill, 1988.
52. Robson, George D., *Continuous Process Improvement, Simplifying Work Flow Systems.* Westport: The Free Press, 1991.
53. Rosander, A.C., *The Quest for Quality in Services.* Milwaukee: Quality Press, 1989.
54. Rubinstein, Moshe F. and Pfeiffer, Kenneth, *Concepts In Problem Solving.* Englewood Cliffs: Prentice-Hall, Inc., 1975.
55. Rubinstein, Moshe F., *Tools for Thinking and Problem Solving.* Englewood Cliffs: Prentice-Hall, Inc., 1986.
56. Ryan, Thomas P., *Statistical Methods For Quality Improvement.* New York: John Wiley & Sons, Inc., 1989.
57. Sanage, Charles M., *Fifth Generation Management.* Bedford: Digital Press, 1990.
58. Sandras, William A. Jr., *Just-In-Time: Making It Happen, Unleashing The Power Of Continuous Improvement.* Essex Junction: Oliver Wight Limited Publications, Inc., 1989.

59. Sanders, Donald H., Murphy, A. F., and Eng, Robert J., *Statistics, A Fresh Approach*, 2nd Edition. New York: McGraw-Hill, 1980.

60. Satty, Thomas L., *Decision Making For Leaders, The Analytical Process For Decisions In A Complex World*. Pittsburgh: University Of Pittsburgh, 1988.

61. Scherkenbach, William W., *Deming's Road To Continual Improvement*. Knoxville: SPC Press, Inc., 1991.

62. Schonberger, Richard J., *Building A Chain Of Customers*. Westport: The Free Press, 1990.

63. Schonberger, Richard J., *World Class Manufacturing & Casebook— Implementing JIT And TQC*. New York: The Free Press, 1986.

64. Shetty, Y. K. & Buehler V. M., *Productivity & Quality Through People*. Westport: The Free Press, 1985.

65. Smith, Preston G., and Reinertsen, Donald G., *Developing Products In Half The Time*. New York: Van Nostrand Reinhold, 1991.

66. Stephanson, S. E. and Spiegl, F., *The Manufacturing Challenge From Concept to Production*. New York: Van Nostrand Reinhold, 1992.

67. Steudel, Harold J., and Desruelle, Paul, *Manufacturing In The Nineties*. New York: Van Nostrand Reinhold, 1992.

68. Sundararajan, C., *Guide To Reliability Engineering*. New York: Van Nostrand Reinhold, 1991.

69. Tenner, Arthur R. and De Toro, Irving J., *Total Quality Management, Three Steps to Continuous Improvement*. Reading, Massachusetts: Addison-Wesley Publishing Co. Inc., 1992.

70. Thurow, Lester, *Head To Head*. New York: William Morrow and Co., Inc., 1992.

71. Tregoe, Benjamin B., Zimmerman, John W., Smith, Ronald A., and Tobia, Peter M., *Vision In Action, Putting A Winning Strategy to Work*. New York: Simon & Schuster, Inc., 1990.

72. Turban, Efraim, and Meredith, Jack R., *Fundamentals Of Management Science*. Plano: Business Publications, Inc., 1981.

73. Turino, Jon, *Managing Concurrent Engineering, Buying Time to Market*. New York: Van Nostrand Reinhold, 1992.

74. Weinberg, Gerald M., *Becoming A Technical Leader—An Organic Problem-Solving Approach.* New York: Dorset House Publishing, 1986.
75. Walton, Mary, *The Deming Management Method.* New York: The Putnam Publishing Group, 1986.
76. Wriston, Walter B., *Risk & Other Four-Letter Words.* New York: 1987.

Glossary

Accuracy: The deviation of measures or observed values from the true value.

Advanced Statistical Methods: A term used by statisticians, members of secret handshake societies, and consultants to convince business people that they cannot survive without them.

Alias: The alternative factor(s) which could cause an observed effect due to confounding.

Analysis of Variance (ANOVA/AOV): In design of experiments, a method of investigation which determines how much each factor contributes to the overall variation from the mean. Also determines the amount of variation produced by a change in levels and the amount due to random error.

Analytical Approach (to management improvement): an approach based on learning from the evaluation of past experience.

Attribute Data: Pass/fail, qualitative data that can be counted binomially. These include the presence or absence of specific characteristics, such as conformance to a specification. Pass or fail on a go/no-go gauge.

Automation (Jidohka): A word coined to describe a feature of the Toyota production system whereby a machine is designed to stop automatically whenever a defective part is produced.

Average: The sum of a group of values divided by the number of values (n). The average is designated by the symbol ($\overline{X}$); the grand average of several groups of data is designated by the symbol ($\overline{\overline{X}}$).

Awareness: Understanding the interrelationship of quality and productivity. Knowing the management and technical tools needed to achieve continuous measurable improvement.

Balanced Design: An experimental design which has an equal distribution of levels within each factor.

Basic Statistical Methods: The applied theory of variation used for statistical process control, design of experiments, loss function, analysis of variance, and many other useful evaluation tools.

Bigger is Better Characteristic: Performance characteristic that gives improved performance as the value of the characteristic increases; e.g., tensile strength.

Binomial Distribution: A discrete Probability Distribution for attribute data that is applied to pass/fail and go/no-go attribute data.

Block: A block is a strata of data that is homogeneous.

Blocking: A technique to eliminate nuisance factors by setting them as extra factors in the experiment, often using up the higher order interaction columns to save resources.

Capability: Process Capability

Cause and Effect Diagram: A comprehensive tool used to focus problem solving. This is also called a fishbowl diagram or Ishikawa diagram.

Central Line: The line on a control chart that represents the average or median value of the items being plotted.

Characteristic: A distinguishing feature of a process or its output on which variables or attributes data can be collected.

Check Points and Control Points: Both check points and control points are used in measuring the progress of improvement-related activities between different managerial levels. Check points represent process-oriented criteria. Control points represent result-oriented criteria. What is the check point to the manager becomes a control point to the next-level manager. For this reason, check points and control points are also used in policy deployment.

Column Modification: Modifying an O. A. to allow for fewer (Column Degrading) or greater (Column Upgrading) number of levels to be evaluated.

Common Cause: A source of variation that affects all the individual values of the process output being studied. In control chart analysis, it appears as part of the random process variation.

Comparative Experiments: An experiment whose objective is to compare the treatments, rather than to determine absolute values.

Confirmation Experiment: A designed experiment which defines improved conditions of produce/process design. An experimental run at these conditions is intended to verify the experimental predictions.

Confounding: Confusing. Where two factors (or interactions) are inseparable in regard to their effect on the response. Used to advantage by confounding high order interactions which have no practical value.

Consecutive: Units of output produced in succession; a basis for selecting subgroup samples.

Control: See Statistical Control.

Control Chart: A graphic representation of a characteristic of a process, showing plotted values of some statistic gathered from that characteristic, a central line, and one or two control limits. It minimizes the net economic loss from Type I and Type II errors. It has two basic uses: as a judgment to determine if a process has been operating in statistical control and as an operation to aid in maintaining statistical control.

Control: A line (or lines) on a control chart used as a basis for judging the significance of the variation from subgroup to subgroup. Variation beyond a control limit is evidence that special causes are affecting the process. Control limits are calculated from process data and are not to be confused with engineering specifications.

Cross-Functional Management: The inter-departmental coordination required to realize the policy goals of a KAIZEN and a Total Quality Control program. After corporate strategy and planning are determined, top management sets objectives for cross-functional efforts that cut laterally throughout the organization.

Cross-functional management is the major organizational tool for realizing TQC improvement goals. (While cross-functional management may resemble certain Western managerial techniques, it is distinguished from them by an intensive focus on the follow-through to achieve the success of goals and measures.)

Degrees of Freedom (DF): The number of independent values associated with a given factor (usually the number of a factor level minus 1).

Deming Cycle: The concept of a continuously rotating wheel used by W. E. Deming to emphasize the necessity of constant interaction among research, design, production, and sales so as to arrive at an improved quality that satisfies customers. (See PDCA Cycle.)

Design Approach (to management improvement): tries to build a better approach through predetermined goals. The design approach should receive greater attention in future applications of the management process.

Design of Experiments: The planned, structured, and organized observation of two or more input/independent variables (factors) and their affect on the output/dependent variable(s) under study.

Detection: A past-oriented strategy that attempts to identify unacceptable output after it has been produced and then separate it from the good output. (See also Prevention.)

Distribution: A way of describing the output of a common-cause system of variation, in which individual values are not predictable but in which the outcomes, as a group, form a pattern that can be described in terms of its location, spread, and shape. Location is commonly expressed by the mean or average or by the median; spread is expressed in terms of the standard deviation or the range of a sample; shape involves many characteristics, such as symmetry and peakedness, but these are often summarized by using the name of a common distribution, such as the normal, binomial, or Poisson.

Effect: The change in level of the response variable due to the change in a factor; the average response at the high level of a factor minus the average response at the low level of a factor. There are both main effects (due to single factors) and interaction effects.

Effect of a Factor: The effect of a factor is the change in response produced by a change in the level of the factor. (Applicable only for factors at two levels each.)

Experiment: A planned set of operations which leads to a corresponding set of observations.

Experimental Condition: A specific combination of factors and levels to be evaluated in a designed experiment.

Experimental Error: Failure of two identical treatments to yield the same response; process standard deviation present during the experiment; sigma of the experiment.

Experimental Run: A combination of experimental conditions which is required to produce experimental results; a treatment combination; a cell in the design.

Experimental Unit: One item to which a single treatment is applied in one replication of the basic experiment.

F Test: A means for determining statistical significance of a factor by comparing calculated F values to those contained in an F Table.

F Value: A ratio of the factor effect to the random error effect, within a designed experiment.

Factor: A processing variable whose level may change the response variable; a method, material, machine, person, environment, or measurement variable changed during the experiment in an attempt to cause change in a response variable; independent variable.

Factorial Experiment: An experiment in which at least one experimental observation is made for each distinct treatment combination.

Factor–Independent Variable: A feature of the experimental conditions which may be varied from one observation to another. May be qualitative or quantitative, fixed or random.

Fractional Factorial: An abbreviated version of a full-factorial designed experiment which reduces the minimum number of experimental runs but which introduces confounding.

Full Factorial: A balanced, designed experiment which tests each possible combination of levels that can be formed from the input/independent factors.

Homoscedasticity: Constant common cause variation across all levels of all factors.

Individual: A single unit or a single measurement of characteristic.

Improvement: Improvement as a part of a successful KAIZEN strategy goes beyond the dictionary definition of the word. Improvement is a mind-set inextricably linked to maintaining and improving standards. In a still broader sense, improvement can be defined as leadership and innovation, where a leadership strategy maintains and improves the working standard through small, gradual improvements, and innovation calls forth radical improvements as a result of large investments in technology and/or equipment.

A successful leadership strategy clearly delineates responsibility for maintaining standards to the worker, with management's role being the improvement of standards. The Japanese perception of management boils down to one precept: maintain and improve standards.

Inner Array: Used in parameter design, it is that portion of a designed experiment which contains the O. A. for the controllable factors.

Interaction: If the effect of one factor is different at different levels of another factor, the two factors are said to interact or to have interaction.

Interaction Effect: The effects on the output/dependent response variable caused by the combination of two or more factors, independent of their individual effects. An interaction exists between two or more factors if the response curve of one or more factors is dependent upon the level of other factor(s).

Just-in-Time: A production and inventory control technique that is part of the Toyota production system. It was designed and perfected at Toyota by Taiichi Ohno specifically to cut waste in production.

KAIZEN: means improvement. Moreover, it means continuing improvement in personal life, home life, social life, and working life. When applied to the workplace, it means continuing improvement involving everyone—managers and workers alike.

Levels of a Factor: The various values of a factor considered in the experiment are called levels.

Linear Graph: A series of numbered lines and dots with one-to-one correspondence to the columns of a related O. A. Each linear graph is associated with one O. A.; however, an O.A. can have several linear graphs. Linear graphs facilitate assignment of factors to specific columns of an O. A. (See Triangular Tables, which perform the same function.)

Location: A general concept for the typical values or central tendency of a distribution.

Loss Function: See Quality Loss Function.

Main Effect: The average effect of a factor is called the main effect of the factor.

Maintenance: Refers to activities that are directed to maintaining current technological, managerial, and operating standards.

Mean: The average of values in a group of measurements.

Mean Square (V): The average deviation from the target value or nominal specification.

Nested Design: An experimental design used to estimate the components of variation at various stages of a sampling plan or analytical test method.

Noise Factor: Any uncontrollable factor that causes a product's quality characteristic to vary is called noise. There are three types of noise:

1. Noise due to external causes, such as temperature, humidity, etc.
2. Noise due to internal causes, such as wear and deterioration.
3. Noise due to part-to-part variation.

Nominal is Best Characteristic: Performance characteristic that has an attainable target or nominal value; e.g., length, voltage, etc.

Non-Comparative Experiment: An experiment whose objective is the determination of the characteristics of a population.

Non-Conforming Unit: A unit or units that do not conform to a specification or standard. These can also be called discrepant or defective units. p and np control charts are used to measure and analyze processes producing non-conforming units.

Non-Conformities: Specific occurrences of a condition which does not conform to specifications or other inspection standards; sometimes called discrepancies or defects. An individual non-conforming unit can have the potential for more than one non-conformity (a door could have several dents and dings; a functional check of a carburetor could reveal any of a number of potential discrepancies). c and u control charts are used to analyze systems producing non-conformities.

Normal Distribution: A continuous, symmetrical, bell-shaped frequency distribution for variables data that underlies the control charts for variables. When measurements have a normal distribution, about 68.26% of all individuals lie within plus or minus one standard deviation unit of the mean, about 95.44% lie within plus and minus two standard deviation units of the mean, and about 99.73% lie within plus and minus three standard deviation units of the mean. These percentages are the basis for control limits and control chart analysis (since subgroup averages are normally distributed even if the output as a whole is not) and for many capability decisions (since the output of many industrial processes follows the normal distribution).

Nuisance: A nuisance factor affects the process but is not of interest in this experiment; e.g., a difference in raw materials which we are already managing.

Off-Line Quality Control: Methods which focus on product and process design and experimentation.

On-Line Quality Control: Methods which focus on production, corrective actions, and process control. Includes the use of the Seven QC Tools (statistical Process Control).

Operational Definition: A means of clearly communicating quality expectations and performance. It consists of: (1) a criterion to be applied to an object or to a group, (2) a test of the object or of the group, and (3) a decision—yes or no; the object or the group did or did not meet the criterion.

Optimal Condition: That combination of factors and levels that produces the most desirable results.

Orthogonal Array (O.A.): A matrix of numbers arranged in rows and columns. Each row represents the state of the factors in a given experiment. Each column represents a specific factor, variable, or condition that can be changed between experimental runs. The array is called orthogonal because the effects of the various factors resulting from an experiment can be separated, one from the other.

Outcome (Response) Dependent Variable: The result of a trial with a given treatment is called a response.

Outer Array: Used in parameter design, it is that portion of a designed experiment which contains the O.A. for the uncontrollable, environmental, or noise factors.

Parameter Design: The design stage where parameter (factor) levels of performance characteristic are determined so that a product functions at an optimal performance level (least variability/cost).

Pareto Diagram: An important tool for problem solving that involves ranking all potential problem areas or sources of variation according to their contribution to cost or to total variation. Typically, a few causes account for most of the cost (or variation), so problem-solving efforts are best prioritized to concentrate on the "vital few" causes, temporarily ignoring the "trivial many."

PDCA Cycle: Means plan, do, check, action—an adaptation of the Deming Wheel. Where the Deming Wheel stresses the need for constant interaction among research, design, production, and sales, the PDCA Cycle asserts that every managerial action can be improved by careful application of the sequence: plan, do, check, action.

Percent Contribution: The amount of influence each factor contributes to the variation in the experimental results.

Performance Characteristic: The resultant of a designed experiment to be evaluated. Taguchi uses three criteria to evaluate performance characteristics: bigger is better, smaller is better, and nominal is best.

Poisson Distribution: A discrete probability distribution for attributes data; applies to non-conformities and underlies the c and u control charts.

Policy Deployment: The process of implementing the policies of a leadership program, directly through line managers and indirectly through cross-functional organization.

Policy Prioritization: A technique to ensure maximum utilization of resources at all levels of management in the process of policy deployment. Top management's policy statement must be restated at all management levels in increasingly specific and action-oriented goals, eventually becoming precise quantitative values.

Pooling: Following an ANOVA/AOV, the combining of factors which have minimal percent contribution.

Precision: A measurement's precision is related to its repeatability in terms of the deviation of a group of observations from a mean value. While the terms accuracy and precision are often used interchangeably, they could be distinguished as accuracy being the measure of the approach to a true value, while precision is a measure of consistency or repeatability.

Prevention: A future-oriented strategy that improves quality and productivity by direction analysis and action toward correcting the process itself. Prevention is consistent with a philosophy of never-ending improvement. (See also Detection.)

Problem-Solving: The process of moving from symptoms to causes (special or common) to actions that improve performance. Among the techniques that can be used are Pareto charts, cause-and-effect diagrams, and statistical process control techniques.

Process: The combination of people, equipment, materials, methods, and environment that produce output—a given product or service. A process can involve any aspect of our business. A key tool for managing processes is statistical process control.

Process Average: The location of the distribution of measured values of a particular process characteristic, usually designated as an overall average, X.

Process Control: See Statistical Process Control.

Process-Oriented Management: A style of management that is also people-oriented, in contrast to one that is oriented solely toward results.

Process Spread: The extent to which the distribution of individual values of the process characteristic varies. Often shown as the process average plus or minus some number of standard deviations (such as $X + 3$).

Pure Sum of Squares (S): A value not used in classical/traditional ANOVA/AOV but used in Taguchi-style ANOVA/AOV to account for the degrees of freedom and the mean square error when determining the percent contribution.

QC (Quality Control): A system of means to economically produce goods or services that satisfy customer requirements.

Qualitative: Levels of the variable may be changed only to discrete levels; e.g., off/on, machine A vs. B.

Quality: Taguchi's definition is "the minimum loss imparted by the product to society from the time the product is shipped."

Quality Assurance: Quality assurance means assuring that the quality of the product is satisfactory, reliable, and yet economical for the customer.

Quality Characteristic: See Performance Characteristic.

Quality Deployment: A technique to deploy customer requirements (known as "true quality characteristics") into designing characteristics (known as "counterpart characteristics") and deploy them into such subsystems as components, parts, and production processes.

Quality Loss Function: Parabolic approximation of the financial loss which results when performance characteristic deviates from its best (or target) value.

Quantitative: Levels of the variable may be changed on some underlying continuous scale; e.g., pressure.

Quasi-Interaction Effect: A crude estimate of an interaction from a screening design.

Randomization: Chance assignment of experimental units to treatment combinations so that any systematic trends do not bias the results.

Randomness: A condition in which individual values are not predictable, although they may come from a definable distribution.

Range: The difference between the highest and lowest values in a subgroup. The expected range increases both with sample size and with the standard deviation.

Reflection: A copy of the original design with " + " and " − " signs transposed. Retains attractive features when combined with the original design. Allows main effect estimates clear of two factor interactions.

Repeat: An additional experimental run which can be used to estimate part of the experimental error from the range between repeats but which does not include all sources of experimental error.

Repeatability: Describes the measurement variation obtained when one person measures the same dimension or characteristic several times with the same gauge or test equipment (sometimes referred to as "equipment variation").

Replicate: An additional experimental run which can be used to estimate experimental error from the range between replicates; includes all sources of experimental error.

Reproducibility: A term popularized in the automotive industry as representing the variation in measurement averages when more than one person measures the same dimension or characteristic using the same measuring instrument.

Response Variable: A characteristic whose distribution you wish to change (i.e., its mean, variance, or shape); dependent variable; quality output characteristic; usually one of the key variables identified in Step 2 of the Eight-Step Procedure.

Response: The numerical result of a trial based on a given treatment combination.

Results-Oriented Management: This style of management is well established in the West and emphasizes controls, performance, results, rewards (usually financial), or the denial of rewards and even penalties. Criteria, or R Criteria, are easily quantifiable and short-term. Western-style management emphasizes R Criteria almost exclusively.

Robust: Products/process designs that function with reduced variability in spite of diverse and changing conditions of environment, wear, or component-to-component variations; i.e., insensitivity of product/process performance to the presence of noise.

Run: A consecutive number of points consistently increasing or decreasing or above or below the central line. Can be evidence of the existence of special causes of variation.

Run Chart: A simple graphic representation of a characteristic of a process, showing plotted values of some statistic gathered from the process (often individual values) and a central line (often the median of the values), which can be analyzed for runs. (See also Control Chart.)

Sample: In process control applications, a synonym with subgroup. This use is totally different from the purpose of providing an estimate of a larger group of people or items.

Shape: A general concept for the overall pattern formed by a distribution of values.

Sigma (σ): The Greek letter used to designate a standard deviation.

Signal Factor: With dynamic characteristics, a factor which controls responses in a specified or designed manner. In measurement studies, a factor used to generate different measurement results.

Signal-to-Noise Ratio (S/N): S/N is a metric used to project (from experimental results) field performance. S/N is calculated in decibels and depends on the type of characteristic being considered. (See Performance Characteristic.)

Smaller is Better Characteristic: Performance characteristics belonging to the category of characteristics having zero as a best value; e.g., wear, deterioration.

Special Cause: A source of variation that is intermittent, unpredictable, unstable; sometimes called an assignable cause. It is signaled by a point beyond the control limits or a run or other non-random patterns of points within the control limits.

Specification: The engineering requirement for judging acceptability of a particular characteristic. A specification is never to be confused with a control limit.

Spread: A general concept for the extent by which values in a distribution differ from one another: dispersion.

Stability (for Gauge Studies): The variation in the measurement averages when the measuring instrument values are recorded over a specified time interval.

Stability (for control charts): The absence of special causes of variation; the property of being in statistical control.

Stable Process: A process that is in statistical control.

Standard Deviation: A measure of the spread of the process output or the spread of a sampling statistic from the process (of subgroup averages); denoted by the Greek letter sigma (σ).

Statistic: A value calculated from or based upon sample data (a subgroup average or range), used to make inferences about the process that produced the output from which the sample came.

Statistical Control: The condition describing a process from which all special causes of variation have been eliminated and only common causes remain. Evidenced on a control chart by the absence of points beyond the control limits and by the absence of non-random patterns or trends within the control limits.

Statistical Process Control: The use of statistical techniques such as control charts to analyze a process or its outputs so as to take appropriate actions to achieve and maintain a state of statistical control and to improve the process capability.

Subgroup: One or more events or measurements used to analyze the performance of a process. Rational subgroups are usually chosen so that the variation represented within each subgroup is as small as feasible for the process (representing the variation from common causes) and so that any changes in the process performance (special causes) will appear as differences between subgroups. Rational subgroups are typically made up of consecutive pieces, although random samples are sometimes used.

Suggestion System: The Japanese system emphasizes morale-boosting benefits and positive employee participation over the economic and financial incentives that are stressed in the American-style systems.

System Design: The first stage in product design, where engineering knowledge is applied to select materials, parts, components, and assembly systems so that a product/process functions at a desired target value.

Tolerance Design: The final stage in product design, where allowable component tolerances are tightened if it is expected to result in greater loss avoidance than the cost of tightening.

TQC (Total Quality Control): Organized leadership activities involving everyone in a company—managers and workers—in a totally integrated effort toward improving performance at every level. Feigenbaum describes TQC as an effective system for integrating the quality development, quality maintenance, and quality improvement efforts of the various groups in an organization, so as to enable marketing, engineering, production, and service at the most economical levels which allow for full customer satisfaction.

Treatment Combination: The set of levels of all factors included in a trial in an experiment is called a treatment or treatment combination.

Triangular Table: A table designed to identify sets of interacting columns in an O. A. (See Linear Graph, which performs the same function.)

Type I Error: Rejecting an assumption that is true; taking action appropriate for a special cause when, in fact, the process has not changed: overcontrol.

Type II Error: Failing to reject an assumption that is false; not taking appropriate action when, in fact, the process is affected by special causes: undercontrol.

Uncontrollable Factor: A factor that is difficult, undesirable, or impossible to alter. (See Noise Factor.)

Variables Data: Quantitative data, where measurements are used for analysis. Examples include the diameter of a bearing journal in millimeters, the closing effort of a door in kilograms, the concentration of electrolyte in percent, or the torque of a fastener in Newton-meters. $\overline{X}$ (X-Bar) and R as well as individual control charts are used for variables data. (See also Attributes Data.)

Variation: The inevitable differences among individual outputs of a process. The sources of variation can be grouped into two major classes: common causes and special causes.

INDEX